The Last Midnight

The Last Midnight

Essays on Apocalyptic Narratives in Millennial Media

Edited by LEISA A. CLARK,
AMANDA FIRESTONE *and* MARY F. PHARR

CRITICAL EXPLORATIONS IN
SCIENCE FICTION AND FANTASY, 53

Series Editors Donald E. Palumbo *and* C.W. Sullivan III

McFarland & Company, Inc., Publishers
Jefferson, North Carolina

LIBRARY OF CONGRESS CATALOGUING-IN-PUBLICATION DATA

Names: Clark, Leisa A., 1968– editor. | Firestone,
Amanda, 1982– editor. | Pharr, Mary editor.
Title: The last midnight : essays on apocalyptic narratives in millennial
media / edited by Leisa A. Clark, Amanda Firestone and Mary F. Pharr.
Description: Jefferson, North Carolina : McFarland & Company, Inc.,
Publishers, 2016 | Series: Critical explorations in science fiction
and fantasy ; 53 | Includes index.
Identifiers: LCCN 2016038346 | ISBN 9781476663234
(softcover : acid free paper) ∞
Subjects: LCSH: Apocalypse in mass media. |
Mass media—Religious aspects—Christianity.
Classification: LCC P96.A66 L37 2016 | DDC 070.4/492023—dc23
LC record available at https://lccn.loc.gov/2016038346

BRITISH LIBRARY CATALOGUING DATA ARE AVAILABLE

ISBN (print) 978-1-4766-6323-4
ISBN (ebook) 978-1-4766-2526-3

Front cover image of Apocalypse © 2016 cyano66/iStock

Printed in the United States of America

McFarland & Company, Inc., Publishers
Box 611, Jefferson, North Carolina 28640
www.mcfarlandpub.com

Table of Contents

Acknowledgments

This collection could not have existed without the support of numerous people. We begin by thanking the contributors who have generously presented their analyses and insights within their essays.

Leisa would particularly like to thank the friends, family, and anonymous benefactors who helped her through a particularly rough patch during the spring and summer of 2015. Her plight is not unique, as many adjuncts struggle to earn a living wage while doing jobs for which they are more than qualified and passionate about, but the outpouring of support she received from so many people worldwide is definitely unusual, renewing her faith that maybe we'll survive the apocalypse after all!

Leisa would also like to acknowledge her nieces and nephews: Brittany Robb, Michael James Albohn, Emily Brennan, Austin Dunlavey, Belle Albohn, Brooklyn Albohn, Allisa Dunlavey, Alexis Dunlavey, and Jack Brennan—some of you live nearby, but the rest of you are far away, though always in her heart. Some of you are already readers, and it is her hope that you will all grow to discover the magic words can bring to your world. And finally, Leisa would like to thank the Proud Werepup Parents community, for being an amazing group of people, and the Portkey to Magic Group for giving her an excuse to get out of the house sometimes!

Amanda wishes to acknowledge the mentors who took a particular interest in her and dramatically shaped her character and love for learning. In chronological order: Sharon Sipe, John Marrs, Rebecca Drenchko, Edward Kowalczyck, Margaret Moul Carli, Alana Haag, Frank Schwartz, Brenda Johnson, Wayne McMullen, Lisa Hogan, Rod Bingaman, Jennifer Mittelstadt, Aaron Matthews, Elizabeth Bell, A. David Payne, Loyd Pettegrew, Kim Golombisky, and Katherine Rogers. This is by no means an exhaustive list as there are lessons to be learned and growth to be gained from many interactions and relationships with other people. Amanda recognizes that were it not for the care, support, tough love, and encouragement of many individuals, she would not be the person she is today.

Mary would like to thank the administration and staff of Florida Southern College for their assistance. She is also grateful to her family (especially Pat Dechert and Jenny Brouillet) and her fellow editors for their forbearance during the months spent working on the book project. Nothing is ever easy, but family and friends make the effort worthwhile.

And all the editors of this volume gratefully acknowledge the invaluable assistance of Donald Pharr in the preparation of our final manuscript.

Preface

Amanda Firestone

In a promotional interview for the film version of *Into the Woods* (2014), director Rob Marshall shares an anecdote about watching President Barack Obama's speech addressing the tenth anniversary of 9/11. Marshall recalls that as the President spoke to the victims' families who were present for the occasion, he reminded them that "you are not alone," that "no one is alone." Marshall then reflects, "I remember hearing that and I thought it's such an important message for today and it's obviously sort of the main, to me, the main song in the piece in *Into the Woods,* and I felt this might be the time for kids of today, families of today, to hear that there is some hope in the world" ("Into the Woods Interviews"). The fairy tale characters of Stephen Sondheim and James Lapine's musical live first in a world where they constantly repeat the refrain, "I wish." Eventually, their wishes are fulfilled, only to discover that by indulging those wishes, they have unwittingly brought potential apocalypse to the kingdom in the form of a lady giant. In the wake of the destruction, the characters unsurprisingly begin to point fingers at one another in an effort to place blame *and* be absolved. At this pivotal moment, The Witch sings "The Last Midnight," a song about the unwillingness of people to take responsibility and do the very thing that will end the giantess's rampage—even if that "thing" may make them *bad* people.

I brought this anecdote up to both Mary and Leisa at one of our meetings, and Mary immediately said, "Well, 'The Last Midnight' is as apocalyptic a song as you could possibly get." Originally, we had come together to cook up this project after Leisa's partner told her to get a hobby. As it turns out, her hobby is the apocalypse. We've shared a lot of banter about how amusingly morbid we are in our unusual fascination with the destruction of Earth. We've also recognized that we are three women from three different generations. Each of us has seen and experienced life, including national and global tragedies and triumphs. We have watched wars on our TV screens and felt

1

the cultural pride and anxiety of committing soldiers to fight them. We have marveled at the incredible pace of technological advances. Mary recalls crafting her dissertation by electric typewriter while Leisa and I have never used anything but computers. But all three of us have heard about the vast destruction of rain forests and the extinction of species barely studied. Then again, we've also heard of a species or two once thought extinct but rediscovered alive but rare, like the coelacanth—hope out of seeming hopelessness.

Through our lengthy conversations, including the one focused on *Into the Woods*, it has occurred to me that the essays selected for this book speak both to Marshall's desire to see hope emerge in the world and to the reluctance of people to examine the consequences of their wishes turned into actions. As the millennium turned, there was an undeniable shift in the mediated social consciousness that the three of us were aware of. And we weren't the only ones. From our general call, we received numerous queries and abstracts, each analyzing one or more of the ever increasing texts produced since 2000 that speak to cultural fears, social concerns, and psychological anxieties stemming from the idea of apocalypse.

Apocalyptic narratives aren't anything new, yet those old fears of the end of days have been compounded by a simultaneously smaller and larger globalized world, our fears heightened by the rapid growth of technology. Critical scholars remain invested in analyzing and better understanding our long-term involvement in the end of the world. Many of the essays in this volume speak to a kind of indomitable human spirit in the face of the worst tragedies, while others rhetorically ask questions about the repercussions of pursuing advanced futures that appear *inevitably* to end with apocalypse. Early on, we recognized a gap in published literature focusing on apocalyptic media in the new millennium. Our desire was to produce a book both accessible in content and thematically sound, offering thorough, well-researched essays that understand the undeniable changes in millennial media and apocalyptic themes.

H. G. Wells, one of the most enduring authors of the apocalyptic literature genre, has a line in *The War of the Worlds* that resonates with me: "I did not dare to go back towards the pit, but I felt a passionate longing to peer into it" (23). In so many ways, this sentence encapsulates our shared interest in the awful and awe-filled idea of apocalypse. Our contributors come from diverse disciplines and span the globe as critical scholars, yet we all share a driving desire to peer into the "pit" and discover what may be hidden there. While we fear what could be lurking in the abyss, we know that nothing can be avoided unless it is perceived and understood. This book may not prevent apocalypse, but we believe that by engaging in discourse about its presence in both media and reality, we are at least doing more than just saying "I wish."

WORKS CITED

Into the Woods. Dir. Rob Marshall. Walt Disney Pictures, 2014. Film.

"Into the Woods Interviews—Anna Kendrick, Chris Pine, James Corden, Emily Blunt, Meryl Streep." Flicks and the City. Online Video Clip. *YouTube*. YouTube, 25 Nov. 2014. Web. 14 Dec. 2014.

Wells, H. G. *The War of the Worlds.* 1897. New York: Berkley Highland Books, 1970. Print.

Introduction

MARY F. PHARR, LEISA A. CLARK
and AMANDA FIRESTONE

In January 2015, members of the Science and Security Board of the *Bulletin of the Atomic Scientists* moved the hands of the Doomsday Clock ahead to 11:57 p.m., the closest it has been to midnight since 1983, arguably the height of the Cold War. Kennette Benedict, the *Bulletin's* executive director, noted the reasons for this action: "Today, unchecked climate change and a nuclear arms race resulting from modernization of huge arsenals pose extraordinary and undeniable threats to the continued existence of humanity. And world leaders have failed to act with the speed or on the scale required to protect citizens from potential catastrophe. These failures of leadership endanger every person on Earth" (qtd. in "It Is Now 3 Minutes to Midnight"). Could humankind really be approaching the last midnight?

It seems as if we have been waiting for the end of the world ever since it began. Once *Homo sapiens* became aware of our mortality, death and destruction have been themes in song, art, and literature. The oldest extant piece of fiction known to archaeologists is *The Epic of Gilgamesh*, which dates back to approximately 2100 BCE Mesopotamia and includes the story of Utnapishtim, the only man to survive a world-destroying flood after the god Enki (Ea) ordered him to build a boat to save himself, his wife, and various flora and fauna. The familiarity of this story rings through similar legends around the world. The "Great Flood" story that is most familiar today and that is one of the oldest Judeo-Christian and Islamic narratives is that of Noah (Nuh) and the apocalyptic flood brought about by God to punish evil humans. Predictive Biblical texts, such as those found in the Old Testament books of Isaiah, Jeremiah, Amos, and Micah, as well as in large parts of Daniel and throughout the Christian New Testament, suggest the ways in which our world will end in apocalyptic scenarios. Some scholars have suggested that

4

many of these works come from even older Babylonian and Egyptian texts (Massey), lending credence to the idea that we have been looking towards the end almost from the beginning.

As for the word *apocalypse,* Elizabeth K. Rosen (citing the work of John J. Collins) has noted that the etymology of the word is *apokalypsis,* the Greek word for "unveiling," but that *apocalypse,* "as it denotes cosmic events, is not used before it appears specifically attached to the Book of Revelation in the New Testament" (xiii). The word remained attached to this religious, revelatory context as one millennium turned into another. When Christianity dominated Medieval Europe, the realities and hardships of life amid repeated outbreaks of famine, plague, war, and despair had artists and writers frequently thinking about End Days. Apocalypse and the Judgment of God seemed closer than ever. The Bubonic Plague of the late fourteenth and early fifteenth centuries killed anywhere from a third to over half of the population of Europe, leaving many survivors convinced they were living in End Times as predicted by the Book of Revelation. Artwork reflecting the idea of *memento mori* both celebrated physical mortality and embraced its inevitability. Inevitable, too, was reflection that leapt from one's own Earthly demise to that of all humankind in the time of the Last Judgment. Albrecht Dürer's fourteenth-century engraved Apocalypse series of fifteen woodcuttings based on the Book of Revelation and Hieronymus Bosch's *The Garden of Earthly Delights* (1490–1510) both suggest the Medieval European preoccupation with the terrible fate awaiting much of humanity. Terrible though death, judgment, and damnation were, they also were the stuff of morbid fascination, as generations born long after the Middle Ages still worried they would be among the innumerable sinners caught in the grip of what the eighteenth-century preacher Jonathan Edwards (among others) described as "an angry God."

Yet the eighteenth century also saw the beginning of the Age of Revolutions and of Industrialization, and as time rolled on, each new uprising and new invention disrupted the old Chain of Being, moving humanity up the links in knowledge and self-esteem but not—ironically—making humans more comfortable with their own mortality. In this context, Mary Shelley's *Frankenstein* (1818) is, perhaps, not only the first science fiction novel but also the first creative work to express a modern perspective toward the attempt of man to use technology to raise himself to godlike status. That Victor Frankenstein fails so badly is not as significant as is his dying declaration that "I have myself been blasted in these hopes, yet another may succeed" (217–18). Victor has already admitted that his real purpose was to create a "new species" (54)—and he does. After unleashing the terrible power of his creation upon the Earth, the creator first abandons it, then finds he cannot control it, and then dies—having learned nothing. Within this framework, one can more easily argue that the first apocalyptic novel also comes from

Mary Shelley, who in 1826 published *The Last Man*, which focuses on a world ravaged by plague and which clearly draws imagery from medieval artists. That this lesser known novel, which ends with but one confirmed survivor still struggling for life, has been the inspiration for at least three apocalyptic films seems another verification of Shelley's unique place in the modern and postmodern perspective. Toward the end of the nineteenth century, H. G. Wells's *The Time Machine* (1895) resonates with an eerie prescience when its author describes what sounds like a nuclear holocaust but is the aftermath of a (fictional at the time) world war that devastates Earth. In his 1898 novel, *War of the Worlds,* Wells invents the "alien invasion narrative" that will become one of the most popular apocalyptic themes of the modern and postmodern eras. By the mid-twentieth century, the increasing popularity of paperback novels and comic books (which offered platforms for exploring science fiction in new ways), combined with ever more dangerous technologies and an increasing fear of "Others," led to a wave of interest in the apocalyptic—first in film, then television, and later video and web games. As the new millennium began, the wave became a tsunami that still flows over us today.

With the exception of a few radio programs, the media wave began at the movies.

Narrative film has existed as an art form for over a hundred years, but apocalyptic narrative film was a rarity until the last half of the twentieth century. The few early films with a true apocalyptic focus are remembered today primarily as curiosities. The Danish film *The End of the World* (1916) suggests the chaos of the ongoing Great War and the stir over the 1910 "visit" of Halley's Comet in its "comet collides with Earth" plot, but the suggestions tend to dissolve in the movie's unconvincing melodrama. Some years later, Abel Gance directed a different *End of the World* movie (1931), in which he also uses a comet to create an impending apocalypse, but this time as a demonstration of political folly and the need for a unified world government. Unfortunately, Gance lost control of the movie during production, and the badly abridged, studio-controlled version that eventually reached French theatres was a failure. In America, RKO had a minor success with the apocalyptic melodrama *Deluge* (1933), but its awkward script (focusing on the difference between true love and passion as the Earth is overwhelmed by natural disasters) limited its emotional impact.

Even the earlier Hollywood films adapted from apocalyptic episodes in the Bible (e.g., Michael Curtiz's 1928 *Noah's Ark*) often used Scriptural tales as a loose counterpoint to modern stories of secular sin and divine retribution—both point and counterpoint made as sensational as possible by pre–Production Code standards. Then when the Production Code ruled American cinema, the grim reality of warfare and hunger on a worldwide scale left audiences looking for escape, and the studio system responded with romantic comedies, musicals, Westerns, monster movies, literary adaptations, biopics, suspense films, gangster melodramas, and historical adventure films. Moviegoers were willing to escape into almost any kind of studio story—except the speculative story of the way human civilization might end.

Time and history redirected moviegoers. The second half of the twentieth century was bound to include increasing reflections on the end of the old millennium and the start of something new. In August 1945, however, the world was given a brutal, real-time preview of one possible future. The atomic age exploded into the public consciousness when America dropped A-bombs on Japan. By 1949, the Soviet Union had its own bomb, and with the development of thermonuclear weapons in the 1950s, the prospect of a total, manmade apocalypse moved from the mythical to the possible. The über force of such weapons was not even the worst part; the invisible radiation produced by nuclear energy quickly unleashed a new fear of unseen forces with the potential to wipe out humanity. World War II also stimulated rocket research, but, paradoxically, as the public accepted the idea of space as a new frontier, both the government and the people also dwelt on the danger to their home (country and planet) from whoever—or whatever—might come at them from across this frontier. Fear of the Other flowed like radiation. More than a half century later, Wheeler Winston Dixon worried that the American government's "policy of perpetual alarmism" would create "a self-fulfilling prophecy" (129), but the import of Wheeler's words goes all the way back to the Cold War era. As early as 1947, the *Bulletin of Atomic Scientists* began to use an illustration of a Doomsday Clock to suggest just how close the Earth was to annihilation.

Of course, no introduction can consider more than a fraction of the apocalyptic films that have made their mark on modern and postmodern culture, but among the essentials are Robert Wise's *The Day the Earth Stood Still* (1951), perhaps the first major Hollywood film to reflect the new perspective toward apocalypse. According to Carl Macek, "The anxieties felt at the dawning of the atomic age, combined with the rise of UFO sightings in the late 1940s, set the stage for this literate science-fiction thriller concerning a flying saucer which lands in Washington, D.C." (589). Shot and edited in a black and white style that suggests both documentary and film noir, *The Day the Earth Stood Still* quietly contemplates an Earth that evinces little understanding of the dark potential in its new weapons technology—and of the grim threat a more advanced (and more unified) alien civilization makes in response. George Pal's 1953 adaptation of H. G. Wells's *The War of the Worlds* is a more conventional movie than Wise's film—but hardly more optimistic since (as in the novel) mankind is saved only by the invading aliens' susceptibility to common viruses.

In Japan, Ishiro Honda's *Gojira* (1954) presented in its *kaiju* a metaphor for the monstrous atomic mutations Nippon had come to imagine through its own too recent brush with a potential apocalypse unleashed by powerful "aliens." Back in America, Don Siegel's adaptation of Jack Finney's *Invasion of the Body Snatchers* (1956) suggested another kind of apocalypse, one precipitated by emotionless, predatory beings from space, pod creatures who do not want to destroy Earth but rather to absorb the life of all its human inhabitants. Siegel's movie can be interpreted as deeply conservative or wildly liberal; either way, the film signals the growing tension beneath America's postwar prosperity. Appropriately enough, the 1950s ended with the release of Stanley Kramer's adaptation of Nevil Shute's *On the Beach* (1959), which attempts to move apocalyptic speculation from the metaphorical to the realistic by showing the inevitable death by radiation of ordinary people in the aftermath of a nuclear war. Although the film received significant attention, it was not a commercial success. Twenty-five years later, Lynn Littman's *Testament* (1984) would face similar reluctance as its quiet depiction of a small town's post-nuclear death garnered critical praise but minimal theatrical distribution.

Inevitably, familiarity with the idea of the nuclear lessened the immediate fear of its apocalyptic potential and forced filmmakers to reach either into the bizarre or back into the fantastic. In 1964, Stanley Kubrick's *Dr. Strangelove* became "the first significant film of the absurd" (Nash and Ross 680), a film that mocked Cold War politics but ended in worldwide obliteration. In 1968 Franklin J. Schaffner directed *Planet of the Apes*, a very loose adaptation of Pierre Boule's novel and the progenitor of many sequels, prequels, and remakes. The 1968 film, an uneven mix of adventure and satire, uses an Earthly apocalypse as its twist ending, and the film's cinematic descendants have continued to layer that idea for almost fifty years. By the 1970s, apocalyptic metaphor no longer needed even to mention bombs or aliens—just the certainty of doom in ever more fantastic circumstances. George Romero's original re-envisioning of the zombie trope in *Night of the Living Dead* (1968) had morphed into his far more apocalyptic *Dawn of the Dead* (1978), which uses a mall as a metaphor for the modern venality that both defines and damns the human species. In *Blade Runner* (first release, 1982), Ridley Scott covered the narrative bones of Philip K. Dick's *Do Androids Dream of Electric Sheep?* with his own very different postapocalyptic muscle. Scott tinkered with his replicant film for some twenty-five years before producing a "Final Cut" in 2007, but every version begins on a dreary, dying Earth, where the line between organic and artificial life proves as murky as the weather.

The Terminator films (1984–2015) destroyed whatever remained in the popular imagination about the unique nature of human sentience. In his original

Terminator film, James Cameron starts with the idea of Skynet, a megalithic computer system designed to control weaponry and strategy without the possibility of human error. But Skynet soon grows self-aware and wages an apocalyptic war of machines against humans. The premise is reminiscent of the much earlier *Colossus: The Forbin Project* (1970), both narratives presuming that any artificial intelligence with extraordinary power will not serve man like a dumb machine. Colossus determines to be a benevolent dictator; Skynet decides to nuke humanity out of existence. But humanity always fights back, as signified by *T1* survivor Sarah Connor's stark carving of "No Fate" into a table (*Terminator 2: Judgment Day,* 1991). The later films in the series, however, reflect more of what Kirsten Moana Thompson calls *"apocalyptic dread,"* which she defines as "social anxieties, fears, and ambivalence about global catastrophe" (1)—cinematic reminders of that ever present Doomsday Clock.

During the 1990s, Hollywood loaded the world's screens with highly topical depictions of "us against apocalypse," some reflecting dread and others showing an optimism that whistles in the dark of the theatres. A few of these films proved to be challenging puzzles, foremost among them Terry Gilliam's *12 Monkeys* (1995), with its enigmatic revelations of the grim truth a hapless time traveler seeks while attempting to stop a virus from destroying most of the world's population. The scattered but repeated outbreaks of Ebola in Africa had already raised virulent disease as a possible source of apocalypse, but Gilliam's film is more a study of madness as a Möbius strip than an investigation into what caused a pandemic. Roland Emmerich's *Independence Day* (1996) is a much different film that achieved tremendous popularity based on its ostentatious special effects and its simplistic but crowd-pleasing plot. The jingoistic narrative involves a small cross-section of Americans first defying and then quickly destroying the highly advanced alien spaceships that are raining fiery destruction on Earth's cities. Two years later, Michael Bay's *Armageddon* (1998) found widespread box office success (despite negative reviews) by reminding its audience that if NASA cannot handle the job of exploding an asteroid on a collision course with Earth, a group of roughneck deep-sea oil drillers most certainly can—and do. Nothing about the film is remotely psychologically or scientifically convincing, but it does make us feel good about humanity's chance to survive dangers that we choose to ignore until effectively too late. After all, a movie theater is a dream palace.

As Y2K theories speculated on possible computer chaos at the dawn of the new millennium, the Wachowskis released *The Matrix* (1999) to commercial and critical acclaim. *The Matrix* is a postmodern amalgamation of ideas regarding the struggle to discern reality from simulacra, ideas earlier explored by (among others) Philip K. Dick, William Gibson, Masamune Shirow, and Jean Baudrillard. Focusing on the postapocalyptic struggle between a few authentic humans and the machines that keep most of mankind bound to a grid that provides a "dream life" for the humans and energy for the machines, the narrative follows the awakening of Neo, the One whose destiny is to free humanity. Referencing the original meaning of *apokalypsis*, Rosen has remarked, "With its epistemological theme, *The Matrix* is fundamentally built around notions of seeing and revealing" (101)—in Neo's case, coming to see the reality beyond "reality." The first movie gives a satisfying hint of an epic conflict to come, but the two sequels are far less satisfactory. Still, the postapocalyptic era had come to Hollywood.

Y2K problems proved to be minimal in the year 2000. In 2001, however, the horror of the 9/11 terrorist attacks rocked America, creating a sense of vulnerability beyond either the government's or the media's control. America's diminishing prestige across the globe, the embittered arguments over climate change and species extinction, the real estate market's collapse, sweeping corporate greed, the endless political impasse—all were part of a culture that seemed to expect apocalypse. By focusing on its aftermath, however, the Hollywood myth of a happy ending could still find credibility. Thus, Pixar's *WALL•E* (2008) begins with the premise of a ruined Earth, its natural resources trashed and abandoned by greedy consumers and corporations. The remnants of humanity are now, in the distant future, well on their way to trashing themselves through a meaningless life on a cruise ship in space. By the end of this animated film, however, a garbagebot has defeated the automated system responsible for keeping humans inert in space and has helped the ship's captain bring his people back to Earth to begin the planet's resurrection. *WALL•E* is a lovely work of art. Other, more recent cautionary tales, like *X-Men: Days of Future Past* (2014) and *Edge of Tomorrow* (2014), use the increasingly familiar devices of time travel and state-of-the-art special effects to fix apocalyptic errors in films that can be read as our postmodern culture's determination to change the world in imagination rather than reality.

The millennial need to speculate on what might happen to and after our civilization is signified as well by the presence of numerous best-selling young adult postapocalyptic novels—many of which have now been filmed (e.g., the ongoing *Divergent* and *Maze Runner* series). Lionsgate's adaptations of Suzanne Collins's *The Hunger Games* trilogy (2012–2015) have been the most successful of these YA movies. Although *The Hunger Games* films are limited by their studio's determination to keep them firmly within a PG-13 rating, they are surprisingly serious as cautionary tales, honorable depictions of the ambiguity inherent in the human response to crisis. Other millennial films, like *Zombieland* (2009) and *Warm Bodies* (2013), also demonstrate the YA influence but this time by using postmodern twists on comedy and romance to assure moviegoers that family and love can still exist in a postapocalyptic world. *The SpongeBob Movie: Sponge Out of Water* (2015) actually makes apocalypse fun for all ages. As a general rule, of course, genres tend to demonstrate a level of burnout when they begin to parody themselves (e.g., *Cabin in the Woods* [2012] and *This Is the End* [2013]). More often, however, postmodern postapocalyptic films seem determined to rewrite the point of the genre rather than disparage it.

Christopher Nolan's *Interstellar* (2014), for example, suggests at least the possibility of hope past apocalypse. With a worldwide crop blight dooming life on Earth, an aged professor and his NASA team decide, in the words of Dylan Thomas, to "not go gentle into that good night." Through human determination, abetted by the transcendental application of theoretical physics, the central astronaut hero saves the human species (though surely not all of humanity). Effort still matters in this High Romantic film, as it does in Disney's *Tomorrowland* (2015), a less appealing film that uses a mélange of SF tropes (e.g., a jet pack, humanoid androids, and a "tachyon machine") to help the middle-aged hero and the YA heroine avert apocalypse. At its core, however, *Tomorrowland* can too easily be read as an extended commercial for Disney World. Something more somber can be found in the small "arthouse" movie *Z for Zachariah* (2015), loosely adapted from Robert C. O'Brien's novel. Set in a strangely blooming valley that has somehow survived the nuclear apocalypse that depopulated Earth, the film deliberately eschews a clear conclusion in its depiction of an "accidental" couple trying to come to terms with their differences of belief and behavior both before and after an unexpected stranger appears in the valley. The Garden of Eden metaphor is apparent, but *Z for Zachariah* is mostly a lingering look at the complexity of relationships. As movies go, this one is more a thought-provoking vision than a waking dream. Aiming, perhaps, both to rewrite *and* revere the genre, George Miller rebooted his own apocalyptic tale in *Mad Max: Fury Road* (2015), which manages to be a contemporary feminist statement and a violent confirmation of postapocalyptic volatility—both themes convincingly merged into a sweeping visual adventure. Clearly, the cinematic big parade goes on.

In the fullness of time, the apocalypse reached inside our homes.

In 1989, Andrew Tudor argued that "cultural phenomena only exist in as far as people 'read' them, ascribe them meaning; they are constituted as *cultural* in the act of reading" (1, emphasis in original). Following Tudor, we can argue that the marked increase in apocalyptic texts in the twenty-first century suggests a national need to deal collectively with the trauma of terrorism. Although art and literature have included apocalyptic themes for as long as there have been art and literature, the arrival of the millennium precipitated the flood of apocalyptic materials and the events of 9/11 exacerbated this cultural trend. As Marleen S. Barr observed, "September 11, 2001, caused Americans to fear apocalypse occurring—right here and right now" (x). The unthinkable terrorist attack seemed to imply that even America might finally be running out of time. This heightened social anxiety, as well as a lingering belief in Biblical texts, offers at least a partial explanation for the current American fixation on Doomsday. In the millennium, the crisp, pretty, highly-technical world of flying cars, transporters, and drive-thru restaurants in space, the future as imagined in 1950s and 1960s science fiction, seems darkened and blurred by the realities of twenty-first-century life. Looking backwards, science fiction television series of the past, such as *Lost in Space* (1965–1968), while sometimes thematically sincere, now seem naïve or even comical in retrospect. In spite of their "Warning! Warning!" scenarios, such shows were more about ray guns, special effects, and robots than gritty realism. In other words, these works were pre-millennial in spirit as well as in time.

Living in a new millennium allows us to imagine "what if" on a completely new level: we will not live to see 3000, but most of our twentieth-century narratives placed the twenty-first century squarely in the realm of "the future" even when it was right around the corner. Those of us who were born in the mid to late 1900s still have a tendency to look at this year's date on our computer and think "But 2015 is science fiction!" Science fiction and fantasy television programs of the past fifty years have reflected our hopes, fears, and concerns, as well as our predictions for new technologies and ideologies. Although programs were produced for a consumer audience right after World War II, only in the 1950s did television became a household norm, as the economic rise of the middle class, combined with post-war nationalism, enabled TV's egalitarian technology to unite families from coast to coast. Given the concept of the "least objectionable programming," which "court[ed] the largest possible audience, people in the TV business did not wish to offend or anger" (Ashby 298). Television producers and script writers of the 1950s and 1960s were limited in how much they could challenge the status quo. Even when some science fiction shows addressed cultural concerns about race, class, and gender issues, these shows still focused heavily on "family values" in the future. In 1950s science fiction television, almost everyone was white, middle class, and happy. Ironically, these same "happy" families were living with the reality of the Cold War, making most people fear the atomic bomb and the Soviet Union. So when the apocalypse reared its ugly head on TV, it was generally in the form of a post-bomb world, such as those depicted in episodes of *The Twilight Zone* (1959–1964): "Time Enough at Last" (1959), "Two" (1961), and "The Old Man in the Cave" (1963). In its "Atomic Attack" episode (1954), an even earlier show, *The Motorola Television Hour*, also posited a world in which few survivors remained—and just barely at that.

During the 1950s and 1960s, alien invasion was also a popular concern for people. Television picked up this concern by centering a few of its shows on alien apocalypses, such as those seen in *Doctor Who* (1963 to present) and *The Invaders* (1967–1968), though this trend was shown earlier and more often in movies than on television. The most popular science fiction TV shows of the 1950s and 1960s were action adventure shows like *Buck Rogers* (1950–1951), *Flash Gordon* (1954–1955), *The Jetsons* (1962–1963), *Lost in Space* (1968–1968), and *Star Trek* (1966–1969), which all suggested a future of space stations and space exploration that would increase American presence and power throughout the universe: Manifest Destiny for the Milky Way. Most of these shows were marketed as family entertainment—a justification for the well-defined (sometimes to the point of absurdity) optimism that flowed off the pages of the scripts and out of the *mise-en-scène* elements of the productions. *Star Trek* was far more creative, more original, and more challenging—but it also posited a limitless future for mankind as explorer and (no matter the Federation's directives) civilizer of the galaxy.

In the 1970s, science fiction was one of the least produced genres on television, as the Vietnam War and Watergate scandal began to replace the space program as areas of interest to viewers, who were starting to worry about America's leadership. Even worse, America in the 1970s and 1980s seemed stuck on the precipice of the Cold War, and the nuclear terrors of previous decades had increased with the advent of new technologies that made world destruction possible with the push of a button. When the unexpected popularity of 1977's *Star Wars* led to an influx of SF television shows, most of them had a postapocalyptic setting. The 1979 reboot of *Buck Rogers* was set on an Earth that had been destroyed by global nuclear war, and 1978's *Battlestar Galactica* started with the complete destruction of several planets by the Cylons. Unfortunately, both series were poorly written—just not very good drama. The 1977–1978 TV version of the movie *Logan's Run*, *Ark II* (1976–1979), *Survivors* (1975–1977), and *Red Dwarf* (off and on, 1988 to present) all took place in varying postapocalyptic worlds or habitats that were usually explained by the disastrous impact of nuclear war/accident, pollution, or disease—genuine trepidations for audiences of the time. But the most influential apocalypse genre television series of the 1980s was *V* (1983–1985), aired first as a miniseries and later as a failed weekly program. *V* dealt with the invasion of Earth by aliens and spawned a fascination with "alien apocalypse" tales that drove television's science fiction narratives for the next decade, when shows like *The X-Files* (1993–2002), *Babylon 5* (1993–1998), *Roswell* (1999–2002), *Farscape* (1999–2003), and the *Stargate* franchise (1997–2009) suggested worlds other than our own filled with non-humans *and* the possibility of a postapocalyptic survival beyond Earth.

Since the turn of the millennium, television programs dealing with the apocalypse or postapocalypse have flooded the airways with various degrees of success. Sci-Fi (SyFy) channel's successful reboot of *Battlestar Galactica*

(2004–2009), as well as the success of Suzanne Collins's *The Hunger Games* book series (2008–2010), along with reboots of past TV successes such as *Survivors* (2008) and *V* (2009)—all helped to spur interest in a cluster of programs aimed at both young adult and mature audiences. The plethora of apocalypse-themed shows from the early 2000s illustrates the genre's spectacular increase in popularity: *The Tribe* (1999–2003), *Dark Angel* (2000–2002), *Jeremiah* (2002–2004), *Firefly* (2002–2003), *Fringe* (2008–2013), *Jericho* (2006–2008), *New Tomorrow* (2006), *Terminator: The Sarah Connor Chronicles* (2008–2009), *Terra Nova* (2011), *Torchwood: Miracle Day* (2011), *The Last Man on Earth* (2015 to present), *Falling Skies* (2011 to present), *Outcasts* (2011), *Dominion* (2014 to present), *Continuum* (2012–2015), *Defiance* (2013 to present), *Revolution* (2012–2014), *The Strain* (2014 to present), and *The 100* (2014 to present). *The Last Ship* (2014 to present) on TNT started off slow and disconnected in its first season, but has since picked up steam with a more intense and complex narrative that now encompasses world politics and apocalyptic cults. Subscription channels are also getting into the action, with offerings such as the Netflix original series *Between* (2015 to present), an arguably mediocre show aimed at a young adult audience and capitalizing on the success of teen genre novels. Arguably the most popular apocalyptic television program of all time is AMC's *The Walking Dead* (2010 to present), which successfully combines the terror of an ongoing zombie apocalypse with the awareness that human beings are more of a threat in this new millennium than the monsters we are supposed to fear. The semi-prequel series *Fear the Walking Dead* premiered in August 2015, and the publicity devoted to this show (as well as the ready-made audience of fans who will watch anything related to *The Walking Dead*) guaranteed its instant popularity, although not necessarily its critical success. While the cultural significance of these newer series is still being determined, that so many of these shows still remain on the air at the time of this writing demonstrates the continuing preoccupation with apocalypse and postapocalypse for American and, arguably, worldwide TV audiences.

And now we can all participate in the apocalypse!

Once scientists realized that computers could be used for more than just calculating complicated algorithms, programming gameplay into a computer became inevitable. But it was not until the late 1950s that civilians were brought into the game. In 1958, William Higinbotham (of the Brookhaven National Laboratory) developed a simple table tennis game to impress visitors to his lab, who had been previously unimpressed with the lab's boring "static exhibits" (Bakie 4). Then, in 1961, an MIT student, Steve Russell, created *Spacewar*, the precursor of many first-person shooters still flooding the market today (Bakie 5). However, the technology needed to produce more complex games with complicated storylines did not exist until the late 1970s. The advent of game consoles, such as Atari and Activision, soon brought the arcade experience into the home. This platform allowed developers to create games that were not dependent on storylines or computer programming knowledge (as was needed for their precursors, the text-based games of the 1960s and 1970s). Indeed, the *Ludoscience* website has noted that "in popular culture, *Pong* (Atari, 1972) is usually considered as the first video game" designed for purely entertainment purposes, rather than as a training module for professionals (Djaouti et al. 4–5). One of the earliest of such entertainment games, *Space Invaders* (1978), was originally developed as an arcade game and later formatted for the Atari 2600 and 5200 systems. Arguably, *Space Invaders* was a pre-apocalyptic game, in that the goal was to prevent alien aggressors from landing on Terran soil. But seeing as how the game abruptly ended when the ships touched ground, it does not really qualify as the first apocalyptic game. That honor more plausibly belongs to 1988's *Wasteland*. *Wasteland* is a PC game that ran on Commodore 64, Apple II, and DOS, and was set centuries after a nuclear holocaust had destroyed America. It was unique in that it was mostly text-based, but it allowed gamers to play up to four different characters, all with unique stats, over the course of gameplay.

As video games have grown exponentially in popularity since the 1980s, apocalyptic narratives have led the way. From a generational perspective, the postmodern audience is usually familiar with challenging extant technologies, yet Millennials often also feel as if they have less control over their lives than they would like. Games offer players a temporary sense of control. The popularity of apocalyptic and postapocalyptic settings for many video games may stem in part from the way these games allow players to exist in a game-world where one of the primary challenges is to control an ever-shifting environment. MS-DOS / SCUMM engine games, such as 1988's *Zak McKracken and the Alien Mindbenders*, gave players the power to *prevent* the apocalypse, something most people could never do in real life. One thing that separates video games from television and movies is that they are, by their very nature, interactive and immersive. Even first-person shooters, such as *Rage* (2011), *Borderlands 2* (2012–2014), *Fallout: New Vegas* (2010–2012), *S.T.A.L.K.E.R. 2* (2012), and *Ravaged* (2012) allow gamers to control the outcome, creating a sense of power. The players "read" the game, and the readers "write" different endings by entering the text. What often frightens us in real-life crises is the way they make us feel helpless when faced with something beyond the scope of our ordinary life. The fact that pre- and postapocalyptic settings prevail in so many video games speaks to the sense of futility so many of us feel when we look at the shape of the world today. How wonderful it would be to push a few buttons, make some quick choices, and save the entire planet or even the galaxy! Video games allow players to do exactly that, and if we fail at our designated mission, then the reset button is a very useful tool for starting over. Reliance on a reset may, of course, be dangerous fantasy, but it can also be seen as positive therapy, a temporary release from stress.

Sometimes a release is necessary. The video games of the 1990s reflected lingering Cold War fears, nuclear war, in particular. *Fallout* (1997) and its sequels immersed the player in a postapocalyptic world where radiation has created mutants, as well as hostile human survivors who feel hopeless. The premise is simple: the avatar must find water in a barren wasteland, but the interactive features and world building have allowed the series to remain popular. Before the *Fallout 4* release at the end of 2015, its trailers promised an even darker scenario, allowing players to delve into the reasons why "War.... War never changes." Many pre-millennial RPGs (role-playing games) allowed the player to exist in a world that had been destroyed by human stupidity, though the common theme of alien invasion and wars with sentient robots also prevailed in games such as *Duke Nukem* (1991–1992), *Steel Harbinger* (1996), *Rayman 2* (1999), and *Rampage 2: Universal Tour* (1999). However, the current trend in video games within this genre leans more towards survival in a zombie apocalypse than anything else. This is due in part to the increased popularity of television shows like *The Walking Dead.* Games such as *All Zombies Must Die!* (2011), *The Walking Dead: The Game* (2012), *7 Days to Die* (2013), *The Last of Us* (2013), and *H1Z1* (2014) submerge players in multiple scenarios from first-person shooters to role-playing games, all designed to allow one to navigate and survive the zombie hordes. Perhaps playing a Rick Grimes figure allows the player not only to assert control and save if not humanity then at least a few humans, but also to triumph over entropy—that most inevitable force within the universe.

The new millennium has birthed so many new technologies and gaming systems that it seems impossible to analyze them all, but one thing is certain: the games are more graphically exciting and richly detailed than ever before, allowing for immersive game play in seemingly realistic environments. Players who used to sit at a console and mash buttons now can control gameplay with a movement of the head or a flick of the wrist—making the players even more organically involved in the game worlds. Multiplayer console games like *Halo* (2001) and *Left 4 Dead* (2008–2009), as well as massively multiplayer online role-playing games (MMORPGS) like *Fallen Earth* (2009) and *Urban Dead* (2005), require teams of players to navigate the game world successfully. The newest trend of social network games allows players to use their laptops, tablets, and smartphones to download apps from Google Plus and Facebook with both multiplayer and asynchronous gameplay options, further blurring the demarcation between real life and gameplay in new and inventive ways. *The Hunger Games Adventures* (2012) and *The Last Stand* (2013) permit players to navigate apocalyptic scenarios on Facebook while interacting with strangers and friends who can help provide assistance on missions. Collaborative gameplay forces group interaction, so that the image of the lonely guy playing video games in his mom's basement is becoming passé. In many ways, this trend mirrors the cooperative nature of any apocalyptic scenario in which working together—if it can be done—will ensure a better chance for survival in the long run.

It's everywhere!

Perhaps the thing that most particularly sets apocalyptic media in the millennium apart from its predecessors is the unprecedented fluidity with which producers distribute and fans access texts. The process, sometimes noted as convergence culture, grew with the rise of the internet in the 1990s, when media producers seized opportunities to connect with audiences in new ways. Today, nearly all mass-marketed films, TV shows, video games, and big-release books are "tied in" to other media formats. For audience members, this means multiple platforms that can be used to enrich the original textual experience. For creators, producers, and companies, it means an increase in profits as fans go out of their way to get more of their favorite texts. Convergence culture can be thought of in terms of the interconnectivity that happens with media as it is created, consumed, manipulated, repurposed, and extinguished. It is a flexible negotiation between what happens as producers distribute media texts and what happens to these texts in the hands of consumers. What was once considered a single-sided interaction or relationship, from the fan to the inert text, is today recognized as a participatory process. And there is a huge potential for community building among consumers: "Convergence occurs within the brains of individual consumers and through their social interactions with others" (Jenkins 3). Individual fans then become a collective resource for creators to tap into.

For example, *The Walking Dead* originated as a graphic novel, written by Robert Kirkman. But in 2010 it was adapted into a TV series by the AMC network, a series that has since become wildly popular, arguably King of the Zombie Fictions. With the growing visibility presented by the TV medium, *The Walking Dead* reached millions globally, and the franchise exploded. Both official and unofficial merchandise is widely available for purchase. For fans who want a much more personal experience, there are conventions to attend where the show's actors are regular guests and tours of the filming sites outside Atlanta, Georgia. Newly aired episodes instruct viewers to synch their tablets or laptops with websites during the broadcasts, offering more detailed information about the plots and behind-the-scenes photos and footage of the cast. Fans express their connections to the show by dressing in costumes (cosplay), writing fan fiction, and making fan art. The web allows a large number of fans to connect in real, consequential ways when Facebook pages, Twitter feeds, and Tumblr threads act as spaces where fans can meet and share interests and ideas.

Convergence culture also becomes apparent in other media, particularly in advertising. Ahead of the July 2015 release of the film *Terminator Genisys,* a marketing campaign aimed at audience saturation meant offerings like the Genisys burger (complete with jalapeños galore) from franchise Red Robin and TG_ONe energy power drink, made in Germany and available for order online. Additionally, the summer of 2015 produced a tongue-in-cheek commercial for Progressive Insurance featuring "spokescharacter" Flo and a friend playing video games on the couch while "Apocalypse Andy" becomes increasingly agitated by floods, fire, and vandalism—all of which are covered by Progressive, of course, leading Apocalypse Andy to declare: "Worst apocalypse ever." The self-reflexivity inherent in the ability to poke fun at the end of the world is something new, perhaps suggesting a need to laugh in the face of fear, or to embrace the idea of survival at all costs.

Each of the apocalyptic texts analyzed by the authors in this volume aims for the same flow and commingling between creators and consumers. As Henry Jenkins puts it, "Rather than talking about media producers and consumers as occupying separate roles, we might now see them as participants who interact with each other according to a new set of rules that none of us fully understands" (3). While some apocalyptic narratives appear more limited as one-time, stand-alone texts within a specific mass medium, others have tremendous, ongoing fan followings that ensure new and innovative uses for available formats and technologies. The sheer number of these end-of-days narratives keeps them at the forefront of our minds. Every possible conduit is jammed with stories of the apocalypse, and in our daily lives we debate which of us would successfully survive the zombie horde and which life skills are necessary for rebuilding society and the social contract. These chapters are a snapshot of the cultural saturation we have experienced since the turn of the millennium, and each essayist interrogates different ways the apocalypse transforms our lives. To that end, we have divided the essays into a prelude and five parts, each focusing on significant cultural, psychological, and technological challenges addressed within the millennial media that have so often focused on apocalyptic narrative.

The Prelude, by Andrew McAlister, explores some of the technologies used to produce media in the last decades. Technological innovations in film, television, gaming, and computer power generally both feed, and feed on, the need within millennial Western culture to define itself (in part at least) through apocalyptic narratives. In film, digital and sensory tools have granted new levels of immediacy and investment in a traditional medium; these new levels heighten the medium's ability to deliver amplified experiences for the audience—including experiences of crisis, chaos, and doom. Meanwhile, television continues to expand temporally, with increasing channels of endless flow, and physically, with greater presence in social spaces. Television's enhanced cultural significance also enhances its ability to portray millennial obsessions like apocalypse. More recently, especially after moving out of public arcades and into the home, gaming enjoys both a more varied and a more natural relationship with technological progress than does either film or television. McAlister also interrogates the ways that advances in technology and in accessible equipment have destabilized the barriers between industry and consumer, allowing both "feedback between producer and audience and muddying the waters between supply and demand." Ultimately, this Prelude challenges both the saturation of media technologies and the growing ease with which users can sidestep responsibility for the effects of particular devices such as smartphones and drones.

Turning to specific apocalyptic narratives, Part I, "Culture, Values and Anxiety," opens with Angela Tenga's examination of the representation and significance of the South in the postapocalyptic America of AMC's *The Walking Dead*. The presentation of an America so drastically reduced as to make the North almost irrelevant implies that one outcome of the "civil war" between humans and zombies may be a new ascendance of the South. Yet the very name of the series also hints at lingering Southern issues: e.g., the region's continued adherence to capital punishment suggests a double meaning for the idea of "dead men walking" in the show's infected South. Tiffany A. Christian then looks at the cultural representation of women on the National Geographic Channel's *Doomsday Preppers*. Most women on the show are the wives of male preppers. And while the show may intend to display diversity by presenting a few female preppers, these female preppers base their preparations on patriarchal ideas about apocalypse and endurance. Since the show frames the performances of survivalism by many of these women as gendered and stereotypical, it implies that females carrying out masculine ideas seldom perform well enough to satisfy the demands of hegemonic masculinity. Next, Stephen Joyce analyzes the Sci-Fi channel's remake of *Battlestar Galactica*. *BSG* focuses on the aftermath of a nuclear attack by the robotic Cylons. Unlike the original 1970s series, however, the millennial *BSG* is concerned not so much with human goodness versus Cylon evil as with the way the surviving human community threatens to tear itself apart through fear, feuds, and disunity. Joyce argues that the show parallels events after 9/11, when the U.S. government's attempt to divide the world into good and evil foundered in the wake of the Iraq War, returning America once more to postmodern instability. Closing out Part I, Mark McCarthy's essay begins with the premise that in the millennium, threat has moved from the exception to the norm, resulting in relentless anxiety. The new catastrophe trope is the "lost apocalypse," which recognizes the inevitability of the end. The fear in films like *28 Days Later,* the remake of *Dawn of the Dead,* and *Snowpiercer* is never resolved. Even characters who fight for survival remain under sustained threat as they attempt to eke out a meaningful existence—leading to outcomes so bleak as to make one wonder if survival would even be worthwhile.

Part II, "Globalization, Corporate Power and Class Struggles," picks up on the theme of anxiety in contemporary apocalyptic texts. Dahlia Schweitzer considers the emergence of disease outbreak narratives that connect the apparent collapse of the human immune system with the breaching of global, political, and personal borders. Focusing on the film *Contagion,* Schweitzer notes that more traditional films like *The Andromeda Strain,* with their projections of localized infection, now seem dated to viewers anxious about the permutations of global politics, world economics, and infectious diseases. Thus, outbreak narrative film now often reflects new understandings of disease, humanity, and the world itself. Tim Bryant also looks at globalization, but this time within the context of the *Left Behind* series, originally based on pre-millennial dispensationalist interpretations of the Biblical Apocalypse. Having gone from popular novels into a proliferation of multimedia formats, *Left Behind* has always eschewed narrative ambiguity in favor of moral assurance. The narrative's return to the big screen in a 2014 remake signifies the current preoccupation with global catastrophe, but the remake compartmentalizes spiritual debates within the external trappings of a disaster movie— and by fumbling both debates and trappings, the movie leaves its conversion narrative still without a sustainable cinematic platform. Bill Clemente then examines the remake of *RoboCop* and the Canadian film *Fido* to discern the way these millennial narratives present their title characters as "Others" who are misused by corporate forces amid potential or actual apocalyptic situations. Within both films, corporations with global interests use media propaganda, economic and political clout, and brutal physical control to dupe their respective societies into thinking that corporations are protectors of the people. While entertainment clearly dominates both films, the roles assigned both Robo and Fido underscore disturbing elements within millennial society. Like the outbreak films, these movies act to raise their audience's awareness. Lennart Soberon concludes this section with an inquiry into the multitude of postapocalyptic totalitarian regimes in millennial film. Deconstructing cinematic narratives like *The Hunger Games* and *Snowpiercer,* Soberon finds that these narratives depict both the survival of the human species and the structures present that attempt to preserve the new order. Such films also portray the stages of societal restructuring, presenting issues of class struggle and the reshaping of ethical standards. Symbolically, these cinematic narratives often allude to contemporary states of inequality, present-day structural divides, and the struggles that accompany them. Thus, the films reveal real-world totalitarianism.

In Part III, "Memory and Identity," Max Despain examines the postapocalyptic narratives in the television series *Dark Angel* and the films *Divergent* and *Insurgent*. In both narratives, the apocalypse has created a social fissure that requires two forms of memory to bridge the gap. The pre-apocalyptic past is largely available to characters through media sources that serve as "memory" added onto everyone's direct experience and that emphasize community obligations. But the central characters struggle with a private sense of identity that sometimes conflicts with the public behavior they have learned to demonstrate—struggles that suggest America's concern about remaining connected to its past while negotiating an uncertain future. Equally concerned with negotiating the future, Ryan Lizardi's essay investigates mental time travel, a variation on traditional time travel fantasy in which bodies do not travel through time, but minds do—allowing the traveler to retain knowledge and memory of the future while reliving and changing the past. Films such as *Edge of Tomorrow* and *X-Men: Days of Future Past* use this conceit to redo history and avoid apocalypse. The "if only I would have" rumination implied in such films is an understandable response to contemporary apocalyptic fear. Next, Frances Auld looks at zombies in the BBC's *In the Flesh* as figures of empathetic horror who do not carry a mindless virus. Reclaimed by government-sponsored medical therapy, these zombies (the Risen) are formally classified as victims of Partially Deceased Syndrome. Medical treatments allow many PDS survivors to go home, but like real-world soldiers returning from war with Post-Traumatic Stress Syndrome, the Risen live in a liminal state, forever separated from those who have not shared their experiences. Memory—corrosive and inescapable—of what the Risen and the fully human did to survive the Rising is itself apocalyptic. Ceren Mert and Amanda Firestone then analyze the CW's postapocalyptic series *The 100* in terms of Otherness. Ninety-seven years after a nuclear war devastated the Earth, the Ark, a space station where survivors live amid failing resources, sends one hundred young delinquents back to Earth to see if it is once again habitable. The 100 soon encounter the "Grounders," descendants of those originally left behind. Although both groups are human, they each see the "not us" group as the Other. Thus, the relationship between representation and identity formation within the context of the new spatial relations blurs the boundaries between Earth as a utopia and Earth as a dystopia, even as it also distorts the construction of the Other.

Part IV, "Simulation, Psychology and Inevitability," begins with Sharon Diane King's essay on simulation as the hallmark of the postmodern era. Following Baudrillard and using millennial supermonster movies as texts, King finds that the apocalyptic threat is decentered in these films, undermined by the media-generated narratives that describe it. *Cloverfield's* hand-held camera and found-footage format make the monster's destruction of New York

City a mere backdrop to a doomed love story. In *Pacific Rim,* a commander speaks of "cancelling the apocalypse," as if it were a low-rated TV series. And *Godzilla* shows the destruction of the simulacrum-cities embedded in Las Vegas, after which the title hero saves mankind from the monsters only for his own reasons—"real" human civilization being irrelevant in the postmodern universe. From a different perspective, Patrick L. Smith uses classic Freudian theory to analyze psychological responses and defense mechanisms at work in films depicting unthinkable catastrophe. In *Children of Men,* people respond to humanity's collective infertility in grimly realistic ways (e.g., sacrifice, violence, betrayal, escape) even after an unexpected glimpse of hope appears. In contrast, *Fido* uses satire to demonstrate the psychological mechanisms by which the inhabitants of a stereotypical town respond to the totalitarian aftermath of the "Zombie Wars." Though drawn with broadly different strokes, both films confirm that inner turmoil can guide human behaviors in the ongoing struggle to maintain psychological equilibrium. Mary F. Pharr closes out this section by analyzing *The World's End* (2013) as it moves from a postmodern pastiche parodying "bad behavior" buddy films to a clever apocalyptic satire, mining classic 1950s science fiction films to warn against social conformity for the sake of order. Thus, even before its postapocalyptic conclusion, Simon Pegg and Edgar Wright's narrative implies that free will is the central identifying (if not always heroic or even sensible) marker for the human species. Ultimately, with its mix of genres, *World's End* also amply demonstrates the human tendency toward anarchy—making apocalypse inevitable but also giving whatever is left of humanity the energy to go on amid the ruins.

Part V, "Being Human in a Techno-Universe," begins with Leisa A. Clark's analysis of the blurring of the organic and the inorganic in what Donna Haraway calls the "post-gender world." In the millennial television series *Battlestar Galactica* and *Terminator: The Sarah Connor Chronicles,* Cylons and Terminators were clearly constructed under the lens of the male gaze—but something more subversive is also apparent. It may be that what separates humans from other life forms is our belief in our own existence and purpose. In *BSG* and *Sarah Connor,* however, the boundaries that separate self-awareness and programmed identity are consistently blurred—leaving machines that are still not human but that may be a new species superior to their human creators. Eddie Brennan then looks at *H+,* a web series with a premise of affluent adults using the "H+" implant to overlay their senses with a computer interface—instant internet. But a computer virus infects the H+ network, immediately killing millions of H+ users—instant apocalypse. Openly representing the anxiety and religiosity associated with digital technology, *H+* is often perceived as an exploration of the intersections between technology and faith. But Brennan notes that the series is itself grounded in the rhetoric of the technological sublime while its characters lack dimension. Neglecting the conflict between the perceptions of human life as unique and human life as reducible to information patterns, *H+* may have its real faith in technology corporations. Bjarke Liboriussen's essay also examines the influence of technology on humanity, this time within the context of the alien invasion at the center of the computer game *XCOM: Enemy Within*. As humanity's last defense, players must reverse engineer weapons technology captured from the invaders; the twist comes when, hoping to benefit from the result, the aliens prove to be manipulating humanity toward our next evolutionary step. Postapocalyptic humanity could thus be construed as transhumanity. At its conclusion, the game does stabilize the human-inhuman binary, but Liboriussen believes it might have been an even better game had it offered players a final choice between humanity as it is and as what comes after. In the final essay in this collection, Amanda Firestone challenges the often heard disparagement of cellular telephone technologies as a sinister means of intellectual apocalypse and physical isolation by arguing that some applications do promote connectivity. *Zombies, Run!* is one such app, enticing people to exercise through convergence culture, transmedia storytelling, and community building. Through personal narrative and critical analysis, Firestone details her own fitness journey using this app, while also interrogating the allure of the zombie trope. Users of the app become immersed in the postapocalyptic zombie space while also interacting with their physical surroundings—connectivity created through multimedia channels and real-world experience.

Apocalyptic narratives within millennial media have become so numerous that it is easy to see them as a fictional genre rather than an evocative catalogue of the ways in which our planet is tottering on the brink of disaster. But even when apocalyptic narratives become reflexive parody or therapeutic exercises, they still signify humankind's failure as stewards of the Earth. They still warn that hamartias, those fatal human errors in judgment and action, may finally be the ultimate cause of global tragedy. It seems too much to bear—but as warnings, apocalyptic narratives also signify our species' growing awareness of danger, of the need both to recognize and react to what does not have to be inevitable. Humans still have the choice to work for the world's survival. It's not quite midnight yet.

WORKS CITED

Ashby, LeRoy. *With Amusement for All: A History of American Popular Culture Since 1830.* Lexington: University Press of Kentucky, 2006. Print.

Bakie, Robert T. "A Brief History of Video Games." *Introduction to Game Development.* Ed. Steve Rabin. 2nd ed. Independence: Cengage Learning, 2009. 3–42. Print.

Barr, Marleen S. Preface. *Envisioning the Future: Science Fiction and the Next Millennium.* Ed. Barr. Middletown: Wesleyan University Press, 2003. ix-xxi. Print.

Dixon, Wheeler Winston. *Visions of the Apocalypse: Spectacles of Destruction in American Cinema.* London: Wallflower Press, 2003. Print.

Djaouti, Damien, Julian Alvarez, Jean-Pierre Jessel, and Olivier Rampnoux. "Origins of Serious Games." *Ludoscience: Studying Video Games.* Ludoscience, Nov. 2013. Web. 12 Feb. 2015.

"It Is Now 3 Minutes to Midnight." Press Release. *Bulletin of the Atomic Scientists* 22 Jan. 2015. Web. 13 Feb. 2015.

Jenkins, Henry. *Convergence Culture: Where Old and New Media Collide.* New York: New York University Press, 2006. Print.

Macek, Carl. "*The Day the Earth Stood Still.*" *Magill's Survey of Cinema.* Ed. Frank N. Magill. Englewood Cliffs: Salem Press, 1981. Print. English Language Films Ser. 2.

Massey, Gerald. *Ancient Egypt: The Light of the World.* Vols. 1 and 2 Complete with Biography and Poems. 1907. Provo: ZuuBooks, 2011. Ebook.

Nash, Jay Robert, and Stanley Ralph Ross. *The Motion Picture Guide: C-D, 1927–1983.* Chicago: Cinebooks, 1985. Print.

Rosen, Elizabeth K. *Apocalyptic Transformation: Apocalypse and the Postmodern Imagination.* Lanham: Lexington-Rowman & Littlefield, 2008. Print.

Shelley, Mary W. *Frankenstein or, The Modern Prometheus* (1818 text). 1969. London: Oxford University Press, 1971. Print.

Thompson, Kirsten Moana. *Apocalyptic Dread: American Film at the Turn of the Millennium.* Albany: State University of New York Press, 2007. Print.

Tudor, Andrew. *Monsters and Mad Scientists: A Cultural History of the Horror Movie.* Oxford: Basil Blackwell, 1989. Print.

Prelude

We Don't Want to Miss a Thing: Millennial Technologies of Participation and Intimacy

ANDREW MCALISTER

The twin muses of Def Leppard's 1988 hit "Armageddon It" (released on their 1987 album *Hysteria*) and Aerosmith's "I Don't Want to Miss a Thing" (from the 1998 Michael Bay film *Armageddon*) not only aptly reflect heavy rock's relevance to the apocalyptic; both songs also reflect key themes related to technologies of media delivery crucial to the proliferation of apocalypse narratives. "Armageddon It" combines the end times with the receiving of sensation, while "I Don't Want to Miss a Thing" speaks to our gluttony for that same sensation in the form of media information. Further, both draw on "cock" rock's longstanding undercurrent of sexual/romantic desire to evoke a companion emotion to our contemporary desire for more video, more story, more memes, more connection—intimacy. Desire for participation and intimacy—as well as the anxiety of deprivation indicated by the possibility of *not* "geddon it" or "missing a thing"—form crucial conditions of reception for apocalypse narratives. It is these conditions that contemporary and imminent technological developments in media delivery seek to satisfy (where extant) in order to effect capitalist expansion. Technological innovations in film, television, gaming, and computer power generally both feed, and feed on, our need/desire to consume apocalypse narratives, themselves so often inseparable from the horrors of unchecked/unregulated technology itself. This tautology is evinced in each storytelling medium in turn.

Commercial film is a critical site for examination of anxieties surrounding apocalypse and technology as its paradigm of theatrical experience embodies our longest-standing dynamic of technologically enabled social intimacy and participation. Film audiences participate in a common experience together in a darkened room, exposed to media designed to elicit a heightened emotional response. Further, as film consumption through theatrical exhibition has evolved according to technological and economic exigencies, the prospect of liberation from the physical medium of celluloid threatens profound recastings of our understanding of the medium's methods of signification in a way analogous to the psychic and social disruptions engendered by real or representational apocalypse. Liberation and anxiety go hand-in-hand, and commence with technological change.

Indeed, the film medium has seen extensive change in the last two decades as digital technologies have altered industry practice in production, distribution, and exhibition. Though few films have taken this to the extreme of *Toy Story* (1995), the first wholly computer-animated feature film, digital cameras like the Arri Alexa and the RED One and its successors have since become the norm in feature-film image capture. These cameras offer advantages in shooting ratio (the ratio between total footage shot and the running time of a finished film) and mobility and handling. Filmmakers can shoot takes more cheaply on digital storage media than on film, and realize further savings by avoiding film-related processing costs. The cameras are also smaller and lighter than traditional film cameras and allow for affordable multiple-camera setups and immersive shooting within scenes where it would be impossible to deploy and disguise full-size film camera setups.[1] Consumer-level Digital Single-Lens Reflex cameras, or DSLRs, like the Canon 7D and 5D Mark III—lightweight, ultraportable, and typically offering extraordinary image quality for under $3,000—increase this flexibility even more, and are often the camera of choice for commercial/industrial production and documentary shoots. While film is still the medium of choice for a number of notable big-budget filmmakers able to work on their own creative and technological terms (Christopher Nolan, J. J. Abrams, Paul Thomas Anderson), as well as a faction of low-budget filmmakers willing to work with 16mm film rather than accede to the digital trend (O'Falt), digital image capture is now the norm rather than the exception. Further, advances in computer-generated imagery (CGI) and its integration into live action sequences have made it possible for well-funded filmmakers to create practically *any* image that can be imagined.

Aesthetic debates over the meaning of this new normal for film imagery are in full flower. Traditional celluloid filmmakers and some critics argue for the "humanity" of the film image,[2] while others argue for the realization of a new "digital aesthetic" when contemporary digital technologies are used rhetorically to match visual tone and feel with appropriate narrative subject matter (Scheuermann 2). Economic motivations for these changes also work in several directions. While the trend toward digital image capture has put many lower-budget filmmakers on something closer to equal footing with high-capital productions, it has also undercut economies of scale for producers choosing celluloid, essentially forcing the hand of many producers toward digital in order to survive. Overall and over time, the growth of digital technologies favors manufacturers of cameras and distributors of feature films, in the former case by maintaining a market for devices that obsolesce much more quickly than traditional film cameras, and in the latter by reducing shipping costs for actual film negatives.

While digital image capture has more recently reached a tipping point, digital editing has been the norm in filmmaking for the better part of two decades. Nonlinear, nondestructive digital editing with systems like Apple Final Cut Pro, Adobe Premiere, and Avid affords filmmakers wildly expanded and inexpensive creative possibilities over the traditional cutting and assembly of film. These systems import digital and analog images into the digital domain for ease of manipulation. "Nonlinear" means that images need not be accessed by rolling deep into rolls of film to locate a desired take; these editing systems can find film segments anywhere within the body of imported footage and combine them with any other segment while adding digital special effects for the ability to preview a multitude of possible versions of a scene. "Nondestructive" means that if images have been captured on celluloid, no film is altered or destroyed in the digital editing process; after they are digitized, images can be endlessly combined and recombined, while the actual film elements can remain sacrosanct until or unless the producer prefers to create a celluloid screening print of the finished product. Further, several of these editing systems are inexpensive enough to be accessible to professionals and amateurs alike, including students. Other systems, like Apple's iMovie, are standard software on certain new computers.

Digital technology has wrought similarly profound changes in film distribution and exhibition. The most visible of these is the industry-wide conversion to digital projection, which has occurred over the last ten years. At the end of 2014, global conversion to digital screens stood at 89.8% of the worldwide total, or 127,688 screens (Vivarelli); as recently as 2009, over 80% of 120,000 screens worldwide were still equipped for 35mm projection only (Hancock). As a point of acceleration, this date is not coincidental, as 2009 saw the release of James Cameron's epic *Avatar*, which required digital projection to be presented in its 3D version.

Again, there are advantages to these changes both for established commercial entities and grassroots producers. Major studios have, for some time, hoped to realize the end of distribution of physical film prints both for immediate savings in shipping costs and as a larger move away from film in order to facilitate electronic distribution of product to new platforms and, to a lesser extent, to avoid rising silver costs (Geuss). Paramount was, in 2014, the first major studio to announce cessation of shipping 35mm prints of new releases. The new industry standard is the "DCP," or Digital Cinema Package—a hard drive about the size of a standard paperback book containing all files necessary for the digital exhibition of a film. The DCP can be plugged into a digital projection system to provide state-of-the-art picture and sound for countless screenings without the degradation endemic to actual film prints (Alexander and Blakely). Further, DCPs cost only about $150 to manufacture vs. $1,500 for a comparable film print. While the cost of conversion was immense (varying from $70,000–$150,000 per screen), exhibitors had little choice were they to survive. Major film studios participated in a subsidy program to alleviate some of the cost (Alimurung). At the other end of the spectrum, what is a question of reducing costs for established film distributors is a new point of access for independent producers. Digitally produced features and shorts are easily posted to YouTube, Vimeo, and other internet sources, including crowd-funding sites like Kickstarter and GoFundMe. Coupled with the consumer-level cameras capable of high-quality image capture and cheap editing software, both the means of filmmaking and access to distribution channels are accessible at unprecedented levels.

Not all digital technologies, however, are used only to make the status quo more stable and less expensive. In addition to now-familiar formats like 3D and IMAX, filmmakers and exhibitors continue to explore technologies that allow for improved images and more all-encompassing viewing experiences. Some filmmakers are exploring the higher frame rate of 48 frames per second (fps)—double the conventional film rate of 24 fps—offered by some digital cameras. These filmmakers believe the higher rate results in a more "immersive" quality (Scheuermann 3), more realistic motion scenes, and a more convincing 3D effect (Lowe). For exhibitors, a major new viewing enhancement is *haptics*, "the technology which brings tactile or force-feedback to users" (Danieau 23), sometimes referred to as "4D," and most commonly encountered today as D-Box seats in some theaters. These motor-driven seats—available at a premium ticket price—can be keyed to camera motions presented on-screen, or programmed to provide "haptic metaphors keyed to the semantics of the camera effect" (Danieau 23). In other words, they allow you to move like the camera, or physically to feel the totality of whatever the filmmaker would have you feel.

Collectively, these changes amplify participation both *experientially*, by offering a more immersive sensory viewing experience in theaters, and *culturally*, by facilitating less-expensive access to the means of film production than ever before. This participation, in turn, generates the cultural intimacy familiar to users of social media to document, publicize, and distribute one's identity across global networks through photographs and audiovisual images. Further, these tools facilitate a remix culture that can as easily be adapted to resistance as endorsement, increasing the degree of democratic participation available to individuals. Like the internet, digital film tools weaken the barriers between industry and consumer, allowing feedback between producer and audience and muddying the waters between supply and demand. In any case, such tools grant new levels of immediacy and investment in a traditional medium that heighten that medium's efficacy in delivering narratives of crisis, chaos, and doom.

If film finds itself technologically liberated, television has continued to expand temporally, by increasing the number of channels of endless flow, and physically, by blooming into greater ubiquity in social spaces. Both dimensions of expansion enlarge its cultural presence and cement its centrality to considerations of apocalypse. By normalizing sensory overload, this expansion prefigures a deafening silence in the event of failure of information infrastructure; and as Thomas DeZengotita has argued, by representing, condensing, narrating, and narrativizing—*mediating*—greater and greater amounts of our experience, it decreases our ability (or *radically* decreases our inclination, to the same effect) to engage and comprehend *unmediated* experience when necessary or inevitable (21).

Technological changes to television in recent years have both expanded the medium beyond its traditional borders and maneuvered it to remain the center of the screen experience in many households (and in consumer consciousness). The transition to digital TV (DTV) completed in 2009 has opened TV up to new realms, including more ubiquitous contemporary screening platforms like laptops, tablets, and smartphones. While the technology exists, there is still maneuvering for the circumstances of distribution. Broadcasters favor the proliferation of "mobile TV," which allows for direct access of scheduled, structured programming over mobile devices (National Association of Broadcasters), as opposed to streaming content via the internet, which effectively empowers consumers to bypass broadcast content entirely. In other words, mobile television is like having a TV with you wherever you go, while streaming offers you the entire internet (including programming many broadcasters already make available via the web) wherever you go. Who needs the former when you have the latter, and for that matter, why not both?[3]

Both, in fact, *are* offered by a new generation of broadband TVs that allow users to stream internet content through their televisions, a capability previously offered by add-on devices like Roku and Apple TV, and more recently Google's Chromecast and Amazon's Fire TV Stick. These TVs serve the purposes of hardware manufacturers by obviating the aftermarket devices and concentrating consumer interest on a single object of desire, and culturally, a single site of attention within the household. The traditional TV set becomes a multipurpose monitor—a trend exacerbated by the proliferation of home theater technology. Home theater systems provide a small-scale cinematic experience in one's living room by integrating a television and audio system, typically with "surround sound" programmed in 7.1 channels (left and right front speakers, left and right rear speakers, left and right surround speakers, a center channel speaker primarily for dialogue, and the ".1" of the equation, a restricted bandwidth subwoofer channel for bass frequencies). Combined with the overlapping rollouts of the DVD (which Rosenberg notes has been in steep sales decline since 2008) and Blu-Ray (DVD's successor, but now also losing the battle with downloaded media) formats, the means to bring intense audiovisual spectacle to one's home are readily available. There may be a point of stasis for domestic spectacle: despite the increasing number of feature films being released in 3D, it is uncertain (leaning toward unlikely) that 3D technology will take root as a new feature of an increasingly standardized home theater setup. Most TV manufacturers are diminishing their 3D offerings in favor of sets offering "4K" resolution (roughly four times the pixel rate offered by HDTV), although, as with 3D television, there is very little programming available at this stage of early adoption (Simpson). Few other developing technologies seem to offer profound improvements to the TV viewing experience. The success of 3D without viewing glasses seems unlikely if its be-goggled predecessor indeed fails. The integration of virtual reality (VR) headsets (e.g., Oculus Rift and Samsung VR) and binaural sound (the creation of spatially "real" soundscapes through headphones using surround sound encoding) seems likely to *change* the dynamic of TV viewing, rather than enhance it. Gesture control (Ihlwan) of TV sets seems a gimmick at best, and "designer" TV sets like Samsung's Armani edition (Ihlwan) promise cachet, but no better picture quality.

In the absence of substantial changes to the viewing experience (or perhaps in the interim until 4K takes hold), a welcome change in recent TV consumption has been viewer control over content, both proscriptive and empowering. Regarding the former, all televisions manufactured since 2000 have been required to feature the "V-chip" that can be programmed to restrict objectionable content. Of the latter, this period has seen the proliferation of digital video recorders, or DVRs, that allow users to record and manipulate programming—and avoid advertisements. DVRs can be programmed to seek and record according to viewers' tastes, in essence creating a customized "TVscape" of programming that exclusively panders to individual tastes in entertainment, news, and politics. Such an individualized TV viewing menu is an example of what technology critic Farhad Manjoo refers to as "selective exposure," or manipulating one's information intake to flatter and reinforce one's worldview. On the level of entertainment, this may be nothing more than a recipe for another satisfied TV customer, but it can also serve as a perfect filter for those who prefer to reinforce an isolated, or partisan, or even paranoid worldview (Manjoo 30). Viewers can thus participate in creating their own reality, while risking isolation from dissenting views or even credible news information. You might welcome the apocalypse; you might even have been planning for it—but it could happen and you might not even know it.

Gaming, with its longstanding locus in homes since moving out of public arcades, enjoys a more variegated, less monolithic relationship with technological progress than film or television. Consequently, its many technological developments have led to unquestionable economic and demographic expansion, but no clear consensus on format, distribution, or software hegemonies to come. As a kind of tribalism, this is not without resonance with potential postapocalyptic realities. Ironically, gaming's intrinsic interactive nature has both engaged more users in simulated apocalyptic survival scenarios than have more traditional media, *and* channeled those scenarios through interfaces arguably further removed from the means of actual postapocalyptic survival than those offered by older media's ability to dramatize.

At $67 billion, 2013 global consumer spending on video games nearly doubled that spent on cinema ($34 billion), as it had done for the five years prior; and, after a slow climb, spending on video games finally eclipsed the $65 billion consumers spent on audio media (McKinsey 10). Moreover, digital spending on games (online and mobile) overtook spending on boxed-console and PC games in 2010, and now accounts for 67% of total global spending (McKinsey 8). Clearly, gaming is a cultural force of exceptional economic agility.

Not surprisingly, gaming is also as much a collection of communities as a "medium" in traditional terms, and indeed, its technological developments have often met with entrenched communal/tribal responses. Part of the reason for these responses is that developments yet to come are in many ways already in place, and many offer the possibility of "disruption" of gaming orthodoxy (such as it is). Mobile gaming is a legacy primarily of the Nintendo Game Boy of the 1980s. Today mobile gaming is disdained by many gamers (Plummer), yet it is also unabashedly proclaimed to be "the future" by others (Hudson). Console gaming, presently dominated by Microsoft's Xbox One and Sony's Playstation 4, is either yesterday's news (Plummer)—or not, depending mostly on users' ease in accessing content (Hudson). Online gaming—one of the most important gaming developments of all time, leading to the rise of MOGs (multiplayer online games) and MMORPGs (massive multiplayer online role-playing games) like *World of Warcraft*—is either an important cultural link to online communities (Crawford, Gosling, and Light 11) or an opportunity for endless "microtransactions" where players must "pay to unlock" game secrets and new levels instead of "playing" to unlock them, as in the past (Duwell). Gestural (popularized by Nintendo's Wii system in 2006) and voice control are gimmicks (Duwell)—but they connect us to rituals grounded in religion and magic (Adams), and they drive sales.[4]

On other points, there is more agreement. Disc-based games seem to be on the wane. Sony and Nintendo planned (but did not complete) a joint venture to equip the Super Nintendo Entertainment System with a CD-ROM drive in 1991, but the impetus from this effort resulted in Sony's offering of the original Playstation with CD capability (Goldberg 3). This was essential to the liberation of games from limited storage.[5] Digital distribution of game content is the way of the future, and may have as a standard feature technological impediments to "gamer lending culture" (LaBoeuf). Role-playing games (RPGs) and shooter games, especially player-versus-player (PvP) games, have driven development of the medium and are still dominant. As Harold Goldberg says, "PvP made these games more adult, more real, and ultimately, produced a kind of thrilling togetherness that mimics life during wartime" (4). And technology, rather than giving rise to game innovation, is being harnessed primarily to monetize every aspect of the pastime. According to Ron Duwell, "Our corporate gaming world has 'innovated' a whole new landscape of revenue and ways to drain money from video games, and it has even put it on the forefront of gameplay design as well. Charge people to keep their games fresh, turn games into a shallow 'one time only' experience, so they have to buy new games quicker."

Leavening that pronouncement somewhat, Duwell also says, "I believe in procedural generation as a true '8th generation' gameplay movement. It worked for *Minecraft*"—but the economics of the medium are unavoidable, unavoidably formative of the gaming experience, and inextricable from the state of the gaming art.[6] As Kristina Hudson puts it, "The cost to make a console game is so expensive that publishers have reduced the number of titles being developed. Less titles in this hit-driven business means an increased risk of missing the mark of what consumers really want to play. This of course leads to less innovation in game play and storytelling which leads to more sequels with there being a community already built around an existing title. This is where the indie developer becomes an important part of the video game ecosystem. They bring more variety and innovation to the platforms at fractions of the costs." The game development costs for the major companies that Hudson alludes to are considerable: developing *Grand Theft Auto V* cost an estimated $100 million (Larkin). The real challenge to independents, however, is finding distribution for their games—a situation analogous to that of independent filmmakers providing distinctive voices as alternatives to highly capitalized, therefore risk-averse studios, and then having to fight for widespread distribution of their work.

As for the present state of gameplay, console gaming thrives on the Xbox One and Playstation 4, and (for a more general audience) on Wii and Wii U.

"Next Gen" consoles are expected to provide a noticeable but brief spike in the popularity of the configuration.[7] PC gaming abides with increasing online entanglements, including *de rigueur*, sometimes "first-day" microtransactions. Mobile gaming dwells on everyone's smartphone. Disc-less, exclusively digital distribution (for consoles, not just for PCs, as with the popular game distributor Steam), along with unlimited-storage cloud-based gaming, and the extension of 4G LTE (long-term evolution) networks by wireless providers (Plummer) are on the horizon. These innovations are likely to be accessed through broadband-capable TV sets using apps, such as Sony's PlayStation Now, created by makers of traditional consoles. Possibilities for seismic disruption include developments in virtual reality (VR) like Oculus Rift and Samsung VR, wearable technology like Google Glass, facial recognition (not just for making avatars, but for sensing players' emotions and adjusting gameplay automatically), and "augmented reality" (game worlds that incorporate aspects of players' real-world environments for increased verisimilitude), all presented with 4K visuals (Walton, Fenlon). Augmented reality especially would seem to offer extraordinarily effective means for delivery of visions of the apocalypse. Its inescapably participatory "final fantasy" could be as intimate as the investment in the player's surroundings, and as grandiose *or* quotidian as that player's daily existence.

Media technologies are only one part of the picture. Technologies for telling apocalyptic stories exist alongside non-media technologies that continue to develop through means sometimes apparently benign, but when necessary, justified by political/military urgency. More technologies than just those of entertainment and recreation exacerbate and exploit apocalypse anxiety. Although the chapters in this volume center on narratives from film, television, and gaming, a review of these media would be remiss to neglect two technological phenomena arguably more responsible for visions and anxieties of apocalypse than these three combined. One is the sheer proliferation of computing woven into contemporary existence, practically taken for granted as a utility, and in its value and description as "connectedness," both signified and delivered to our persons by the ubiquity of cell phones. Whether one's preferred tech dystopia is that of malevolent computer networks, like Skynet in the *Terminator* films, or that of the infrastructure deprivation depicted in *The Walking Dead* TV series, we are acculturated in Western societies to extraordinary access to extraordinary amounts of information, a situation that presents a positive capability—but also a severe deprivation in times of crisis. For cultural critic George Trow, a variety of this kind of deprivation pertains already even without an apocalyptic scenario, as a neurosis arising from no middle ground between the "grid of one"—personal intimacy—and the "grid of two hundred million"—the community of American TV watchers (48–49).

In effect, and despite the exact technological means, all the media discussed in this essay have colonized cell phones as the most available, most convenient, and most intimate site of garnering audience attention short of wearable devices. As such, cell phones are not just where the rubber meets the road of delivering any kind of information—entertainment, public safety information, troop movements—to our minds, they have become like the car itself: something we wear as much as use, something we think we cannot live without, something that delivers to us the ability to be at our chosen sites of our being, even as they deliver us as consumers to car makers, gas companies, insurers, and advertisers. What phones can deliver to us is incalculable, but *how* they deliver *us* as an audience assigns them pride of place as the premier technology of both our enlightenment and our exploitation. Our attention, our whereabouts, our intimate histories are harvested by data commerce companies and state surveillance agencies, if not without our perfunctory consent, too often without our having truly "opted in" to the furthest uses to which our data is put; as we pay for the privilege, our "service providers" meter our usage, effectively charging us to provide them with a valuable commodity. *Metered access to something we think we cannot live without* suggests the metaphor of addiction, with the relatively sterile benefit of convenience filling the role of sensory pleasure.

The same convenience informs another of our technological relationships as well. Cell phones may be the way we happily mediate ourselves, but in the realm of unmediated experience, we cannot fail to reckon drones as the totem technology of the delivery of apocalypse, both for their deadliness and feckless ease of use. Whether delivering consumer goods, strategic battlefield images, or actual ordnance, drones offer us insulation both from scrutiny and from the harm they may do while delivering their payload. Like any apocalyptic technology, they depend on the conscience of the user to be employed constructively. The remove that drones offer their operators from the consequences of their use enables and explains the cold pragmatism of our increasing acceptance of drones, and the darker irony of their adaptability for both conquest and commerce. As the cell phone brings the world of information to our fingertips, so do drones form the tendrils by which we visit our global acts of empire on other peoples, even as our human victims remain as abstract to us as the celebrated elements of our ethos: freedom, equality, democracy. By contrast, using drones for more instantaneous indulgence in consumer goods seems more benign, but arguably extends the power of their controllers by appearing to lessen the technology's threat. Business as usual may seem like the lesser of two evils, but drones deliver the unwanted with the wanted, for sender and receiver alike. We have the technology to deliver images of apocalypse, and apocalypse itself, but preventing it is the responsibility of the craftspeople, not the tools they create.

NOTES

1. Parts of Marvel's *The Avengers* were shot with Canon 7Ds precisely to exploit their ability to provide immersive footage during battle scenes (Alexander and Blakely). Jonathan Glazer's *Under the Skin* (2013) relied on multiple digital cameras hidden in the interior of the vehicle driven by actress Scarlett Johansson for much of the film (Glazer). And musical dance sequences in Lars Von Trier's *Dancer in the Dark* (2000) were realized using dozens of tiny digital cameras hidden on-set (Von Trier).

2. Manohla Dargis argues, "We're not talking about the disappearance of one material—oil, watercolor, acrylic or gouache—we're talking about deep ontological and phenomenological shifts that are transforming a medium" (Dargis and Scott).

3. Neither traditional nor cable broadcast has a monopoly on content creation, as evinced by successful forays into the production of original programming by Netflix (*Orange Is the New Black, House of Cards*) and Amazon (*Transparent*). As McKinsey puts it, "A number of media owners who control consumer access platforms have shown an appetite for moving into content provision, whether by acquiring rights, a pre-existing library or acquiring content production. These players potentially have the power to disrupt the more traditional author-producer relationship" (5).

4. Harold Goldberg has noted, "A lot of core gamers complain the simplicity makes these offerings [Wii games and Xbox games with Kinect software] annoyingly lackluster. But that doesn't stop people from buying motion-based games, does it?" (4).

5. Of the DVD drive in Sony's Playstation 2, Sam Houser, of Rockstar Games, says, "The amount of storage on a PlayStation 2 DVD opened up so many possibilities for storage and graphics and characterization. It literally changed everything" (qtd. in Goldberg 4).

6. "Procedural generation" is content created algorithmically rather than manually in response to gameplay.

7. Consoles had 78% of gaming activity in 2008, and 31% in 2013. The figure is expected to rally to 40% when "Next Gen" popularity peaks in 2017, and steadily decline thereafter (Plummer).

WORKS CITED

Adams, Ernest. "50 Greatest Game Innovations." *Businessweek* 5 Nov. 2007: n. pag. *Bloomberg.com*. Web. 20 July 2015.

Alexander, Helen, and Rhys Blakely. "The Triumph of Digital Will Be the Death of Many Movies." *New Republic* 12 Sept. 2014: n. pag. Web. 19 July 2015.

Alimurung, Gendy. "Movie Studios Are Forcing Hollywood to Abandon 35MM Film but the Consequences of Going Digital Are Vast and Troubling." *LA Weekly* 12 Apr. 2012: n. pag. Web. 21 July 2015.

Crawford, Garry, Victoria K. Gosling, and Ben Light. "The Social and Cultural Significance of Online Gaming." *Online Gaming in Context*. Eds. Crawford, Gosling, and Light. New York: Routledge, 2011. 3–22. Print.

Danieau, Fabien, et al. "Toward Haptic Cinematography: Enhancing Movie Experience with Haptic Effects Based on Cinematographic Camera Motions." *Technicolor Innovation in Motion* Summer 2014: 23–40. Print.

Dargis, Manohla, and A. O. Scott. "Film Is Dead? Long Live Movies." *New York Times* 6 Sept. 2012: n. pag. Web. 21 July 2015.

DeZengotita, Thomas. *Mediated: How the Media Shape Your World*. London: Bloomsbury, 2005. Print.

Duwell, Ron. "Innovation and Refinement in Video Gaming: Are There Any New Ideas?" *TechnoBuffalo*. TechnoBuffalo LLC, 24 July 2014: n. pag. Web. 23 July 2015.

Fenlon, Wes. "Gaming in 4K: The Future Is Now, If You Give Up 60 Frames per Second." *PC Gamer* 28 July 2014: n. pag. Web. 21 July 2015.

Geuss, Megan. "Celluloid No More: Distribution by Film to Cease by 2013 in US." *Ars Technica* 9 June 2012: n. pag. Web. 19 July 2015.

Glazer, Jonathan. Audio commentary. *Under the Skin*. Dir. Glazer. Lionsgate, 2014. DVD.

Goldberg, Harold. "The 25 Greatest Breakthroughs in Video Game History." *Ign.com*. Ziff Davis, 30 Jan. 2012: 1–4. Web. 18 July 2015.

Hancock, David. "Digital Projection Grows with 90 Percent Penetration of Cinema Screens This Year." *Ihs.com*. IHS, Inc., 17 July 2013: n. pag. Web. 20 July 2015.

Hudson, Kristina. "10 Things You Need to Know About Video Games." 2 Mar. 2015: n.pag. *Washingtontechnology.org*. Washington Technology Industry Assn., 2 Mar. 2015: n.pag. Web. 17 July 2015.

Ihlwan, Moon. "TV Technology: The Latest Innovations." *Bloomberg.com*. 3 Apr. 2009: 1–21. Web. 17 July 2015.

LaBoeuf, Sarah. "Gamer Culture Will Suffer if Next Gen Blocks Used Games." *Gamesradar+*. 8 Feb. 2013: n. pag. Web. 18 July 2015.

Larkin, Megan. "Advancing Video Game Technology May Be Too Realistic." *Columbia Science and Technology Law Review* 15 Oct. 2013. 16 (Fall 2014): n. pag. Web. 15 July 2015.

Lowe, Kinsey. "Cinema's Digital Takeover: The Decline And Fall of Film As We Have Known It." *Deadline Hollywood* 4 Feb. 2012: n. pag. Web. 20 July 2015.

Manjoo, Farhad. *True Enough: Learning to Live in a Post-Fact Society*. Hoboken: Wiley, 2008. Print.

McKinsey & Company. "Global Media Report 2014." Sept. 2014: 1–25. *McKinsey.com*. Web. 20 July 2015.

National Association of Broadcasters. "Innovation in Television." 2015: n. pag. Web. 17 July 2015.

O'Falt, Chris. "Sundance: In a World Gone Digital, Indie Filmmakers Reach for 16mm." *Hollywood Reporter* 20 Jan. 2014: n. pag. Web. 15 July 2015.

Plummer, Quinten. "A Look at Innovative Tech Driving the Impending Demise of the Game Console." *TechTimes* 5 Nov. 2014: n. pag. Web. 19 July 2015.

Rosenberg, Eli. "DVD Sales Dive While Netflix Soars." *Atlantic* 12 May 2011: n. pag. Web. 19 July 2015.

Scheuermann, Brett. "Film vs. Digital: How David Fincher Has Adapted to Survive in Hollywood." *WhatCulture.com*. 26 Jan. 2013: 1–4. Web. 17 July 2015.

Simpson, Connor. "3D TV Is Dead." *Thewire.com* 6 Jan. 2014: n. pag. Web. 20 July 2015.

Trow, George. *Within the Context of No Context*. New York: Atlantic Monthly Press, 1981. Print.

Vivarelli, Nick. "Almost 90 Percent of the Planet's Movie Screens Are Now Digital." *Variety* 6 Feb. 2015: n. pag. Web. 17 July 2015.

Von Trier, Lars. Audio Commentary. *Dancer in the Dark*. Dir. Von Trier. 2000. New Line, 2005. DVD.

Walton, Mark. "The State of 4K Gaming in 2015." *Ars Technica* 26 May 2015: n. pag. Web. 15 July 2015.

The South Will Rise Again

Contagion, War and Reconstruction
in The Walking Dead,
Seasons One Through Five

ANGELA TENGA

In AMC's *The Walking Dead*, the South is a physical and political land-scape where the zombie plague dramatizes issues related to the history of North-South division in the United States. In particular, the series draws on the popular understanding of the Civil War (1861–1865), the role of slavery in American history, and the persistence of a residual barrier between the North and the South in the popular imagination. Exploiting the zombie's symbolic range as a versatile figure of enslavement, invasion, alienation, and reverse migration, the series not only recalls the struggle of the South to establish its independence, sovereignty, and distinct identity, but also reconstitutes the South as a site of victory and dominance.

One source of the zombie's popularity has been its flexibility as a metaphor, and *The Walking Dead* documents Peter Dendle's view of this "mythological creature that has proven itself consistently resonant with shifting cultural anxieties" (45). Discussing the appeal of the zombie to American audiences in the early twentieth century, Kyle Bishop argues that the notion of zombification as "a repressive ideological apparatus" found a ready audience in the United States of this time: "slavery had been an essential part of the United States economic and social system for many years, and the wounds of the Civil War and a largely failed attempt at reconstruction would have still been fresh and sensitive" (59–60). In the early twenty-first century, despite substantial social and political change, the zombie—or "walker," as it is known within *The Walking Dead* universe—still has the power to speak to audiences about the ancestral wounds that gave it its early relevance to American consumers. Indeed, one of its most compelling applications in the AMC series is its use as an instrument of ethnographic commentary, and specifically, as a means to explore the cultural identity of the American South.

According to James C. Cobb's study of Southern identity, the South began to benefit from a shift in the longstanding perception of Northern dominance in the last few decades of the twentieth century. Cobb suggests that the civil unrest of the 1960s, the disillusionment caused by the Vietnam War, the Watergate scandal, and the economic distress of the 1970s had a profound effect on the North, and many Southerners "could not resist the temptation to revel in the astonishingly swift demise of their region's old tormentor and would-be conqueror, the omniscient, omnipotent, and omnipresent North" (218). Cobb argues that the stigma of Southernness died as the South was reborn: "The region that had once been such a big part of the national problem now seemed poised to provide the solution, reincarnated ... and ready to show a humbled North the way to simpler, more peaceful times" (237). Despite this role reversal, Atlanta comedian Jeff Foxworthy would continue to joke that "in a lot of parts of the country ... [when] people hear me talk, they automatically want to deduct a hundred IQ points." The reaction to which Foxworthy humorously alludes suggests a lingering problem with respect to Americans' general perception of Southerners. As a narrative of the South, *The Walking Dead* displays a strong sense of place and participates in the ongoing renegotiation of Southern identity. Its role in restoring the Southern image is an important interpretive context for the series. The presentation of a world in which the North has been either eliminated or rendered irrelevant suggests that one outcome of the "civil" war between humans and zombies may be the ascendance of the South in a postapocalyptic Reconstruction.

The state of Georgia—an emblem of both antebellum glory and modern success—is prominent in both the series' fictional wasteland and its real-world production. Rick Grimes begins his bleak odyssey in a small town somewhere outside Atlanta, and the series is filmed in Georgia. As fans flock to filming locations, the dead are breathing new life into Georgia's tourism industry. One striking example is the revival of the town of Grantville, which languished with the decline of the local cotton industry. Its decaying remains became a natural backdrop for the series, which in turn has drawn thousands of visitors from around the world. Capitalizing on the popularity of the series, Mayor Jim Sells offers a tour in which he "explains where each scene from the 'Clear' episode ... was filmed" (Martin). Other Georgia towns have enjoyed similar revivals, such as Senoia, the site of the fictional Woodbury settlement. In response to the popularity of the series, fan groups have created web pages that offer details and maps for those who want to conduct self-guided tours. The city of Atlanta, though hardly in need of revival, is also an important geographic and narrative center for the series; many of its most visually impressive scenes have been shot in and around Georgia's preeminent metropolis. For example, the building that served as the Centers for Disease Control and Prevention (CDC) in season one is Atlanta's Cobb Energy Performing Arts Centre, while the memorable closing scene of "Days Gone Bye," in which Rick takes refuge inside a tank on the zombie-filled Atlanta streets, was shot "near the corner of Forsyth and Walton" (Hunter). Atlanta's Grady Memorial Hospital houses a sinister survivor group in season five and also connects the present narrative with Atlanta's storied past: Margaret Mitchell, who penned the Southern epic *Gone with the Wind*, died in Grady Hospital in 1949 (Brown and Wiley 266–67).[1]

In the era that *Gone with the Wind* commemorates, Georgia had a slave-based economy. As the birthplace of the cotton gin, the state also played a significant role in the history of slavery in the U.S. Eli Whitney's invention transformed the economy of the South, but also institutionalized slavery. Henry Louis Gates, Jr., has noted that "the invention of the cotton gin greatly increased the productivity of cotton harvesting by slaves. This resulted in dramatically higher profits for planters, which in turn led to a seemingly insatiable increase in the demand for more slaves." A powerful symbol of enslavement, the folkloric zombie was a being without awareness or will, a body reanimated through sorcery and commonly used for slave labor. This version of the zombie was "brought from Africa to Haiti with the slave trade," notes Bishop, while the "fascination with voodoo rituals and zombie practices" in the U.S. in the early twentieth century was fueled by the spread of stories of "reanimated corpses used by local plantation owners to increase production" (47). While later zombies in film and print would become ravenous eaters of human flesh and a menace to the human species, this folkloric version is a victim "who has had her identity and autonomy stripped from her, being converted to nothing more than an enslaved cipher" (Bishop 53). The folkloric zombie thus has much relevance both to slavery in the U.S. and to the historical conflict between the American North and South. In a sense, the return of the postapocalyptic undead to the former cotton fields of Georgia is a sort of homecoming for the zombie, a return to a site that symbolically connects it to the history of enslavement in the pre-emancipation United States.

The zombies of *The Walking Dead*, however, are no longer mere slaves, and the landscapes that they inhabit bear eerie similarities to scenes of a war-ravaged South. From the neatly wrapped corpses piled outside the hospital where Rick Grimes awakens in "Days Gone Bye" to fields strewn with the bodies of the dead, the carnage could easily be described in the terms applied to Civil War battlefields that were littered with "hideous numbers of dead bodies turning black and swollen" in the sun (Catton 119). Of particular relevance is the special significance assigned to the process of ruination in Megan Kate Nelson's study of the destruction wrought in the Civil War: the "interplay between the whole past and the fragmented present of Civil War ruins ... seemed to capture the moment of transformation from one time to another, from one material form to another" (2). Nelson's insight not only applies equally well to the apocalyptic landscape of *The Walking Dead*, but also provides a useful description of the undead themselves, especially those whose decomposition has not advanced far enough to render them unrecognizable. Characters who transform into zombies—such as Andrea's sister, Amy, or Carol's daughter, Sophia—visually embed both their currently monstrous and their recently human forms; they are all the more problematic because of their continuing resemblance to their former living selves. Bishop says that "this seemingly innocuous resemblance manifests visually what Freud calls the *Unheimlich*—an uncanny similarity between the familiar and the unfamiliar that makes such monsters even more disturbing and frightening" (95). The "ruination" of the physical body of the zombie effects a painful juxtaposition of the living and undead states, echoing and amplifying the story told by the ruins of their physical environment. Further, the walkers' predation on all living humans without discrimination—with no exceptions made for former relatives, friends, or neighbors—evokes another quality of Civil War devastation cited in Nelson's study: "Americans had made these ruins using the violent technologies of war.... Such ruins were self-inflicted and deliberately created" (2). The zombie provides a natural metaphor for the state of the human during times of civil war: people turn on their own countrymen, treating them as they might any other enemy and negating one of the presumed givens of civilized societies.

This combined symbolism situates Georgia's new war on a very old battlefield. Atlanta's role in the American Civil War was pivotal. As an important rail hub and one of the great cities of the South, Atlanta became an important strategic and symbolic target for the North. The city had in fact begun as the endpoint of a railway line, or "terminus"—a label that was applied as a proper name to the settlement in its early days and that *The Walking Dead* memorializes in the name of an alleged safe haven in seasons four and five of the series. This sinister community proves to be a site where cannibalism is practiced, so the "end of the line" pun embedded in its name also seems fitting. Atlanta was a major commercial center as well, and the victory of the Union forces led by General William Tecumseh Sherman is often cited as a watershed moment. Historian Albert Castel considers the Atlanta campaign "one of the most dramatic and decisive episodes of the Civil War," arguing that its outcome, if it "did not constitute a turning point in the struggle between the North and the South, definitely assured that this struggle would turn out as it did" (xii). Building on Castel's work, Richard M. McMurry cites the Atlanta campaign as the last of four great operations that "determined the military outcome of the American Civil War," arguing that the Northern army's "success in that last great operation marked the end of any rational hope that the Confederacy could establish its independence" (xiii–xiv). It is fitting, then, that *The Walking Dead* returns to the greater Atlanta area to revisit the question of Southern independence. The new "civil" war affords the South a second chance to separate itself from the North, which for all intents and purposes no longer exists as a geographic, political, economic, or social entity. By the end of season five, Rick and his group have reached Alexandria, but there is no speculation about points farther north—nor even a hint of interest in the possibility of their existence.

Although the North is barely a rumor in *The Walking Dead*, the newly sovereign South is populated primarily by the undead masses, who perform as proxies for freed slaves and racial Others during the difficult postwar era in a controversial neo-Reconstruction. Often described as a second civil war, Reconstruction exacerbated North-South tensions as Southern states were forced to support the enfranchisement of former slaves and follow federal rules in order to be readmitted to the Union. Southern states in the postwar era struggled with widespread resistance to federal policies that protected the new rights of freedmen, straining interracial relations. The zombie, returning from the dead to prey on the living, similarly refuses to "stay in its place" and disrupts the established hegemony. Moreover, the postwar South was not a uniform entity, and its diverse groups did not always get along. As historian Eric Foner writes, "White society was transformed no less fully than black, as traditional animosities grew more acute, longstanding conflicts acquired altered meanings, and new groups emerged into political consciousness" (5). Foner's observation applies surprisingly well to the human society of *The Walking Dead*, which presents a microcosmic glimpse of such issues. The conflict between Rick Grimes and Merle Dixon in "Guts," for example, suggests a clash of social groups and problematizes class relations as the lawman, representing the respectable middle class, subdues the "redneck," a term denoting the stereotype of "rural, lower-class whites who [are] aggressively ignorant, uncouth, and lawless and [show] no particular ambition to be otherwise" (Cobb 226). When Rick handcuffs the unruly rebel to a pipe and leaves him under guard on a rooftop, he reveals how dire circumstances can intensify old hostilities; unfettered by a larger culture of law, Rick is free to treat Merle as he sees fit, without worry about whether his actions are consistent with the requirements of his former profession. In other cases, characters develop a new awareness of their political selves. For example, Carol, formerly a fearful battered housewife, becomes a fighter, an independent thinker, a member of the prison group's governing council, and an agent of decisive action in tough situations—such as her controversial execution of eleven-year-old Lizzie, whose dangerous mental instability Carol judges to be irremediable ("The Grove"). Her awakening to a new self is both personal and political—an awareness that expands her understanding of herself as a politically viable individual.

Beyond these social issues, Southern states after the Civil War faced devastated infrastructures and severely depressed economies, with cities that were once "thriving centers of commerce" reduced to "smoking piles of brick" (Nelson 11). As a symbol of consumption in Western societies, the zombie often serves as "a reflection of modern-day commercial society, propelled only by its need to perpetually consume" (Lauro and Embry 99), but as *The Walking Dead*'s symbol of economic disorder in the postwar South, walkers frustrate attempts to rebuild and restore prosperity. Even long after Reconstruction ended, the South continued to suffer the economic effects of the Civil War, and contrasting images of an impoverished South and a prosperous North persisted in the popular imagination. *The Walking Dead* recalls and reverses this legacy of Northern dominance. To this end, the series frequently hints at distrust of both federal authority and the North with which that authority was, in the postwar South, commonly associated. For example, Atlanta's CDC, a potent symbol of federal power, is depicted as ineffective yet menacing. When Rick and his group arrive at the CDC in season one, the last surviving CDC scientist allows them to enter, discloses that the CDC has failed to find a way to counteract the zombie infection, and then reveals that the group is trapped inside a building that will soon self-destruct ("TS-19").

Given the popular equation of federal power with Northern dominance of a postwar South, it is not surprising that depictions of Northerners in the series sometimes reflect cultural stereotypes and suggest Southern supremacy. For example, certain characters who are not given specifically Northern back-stories still suggest, through their undisguised native accents, Northern regions. When those accents are coupled with stereotypical Northern traits, the characters can be viewed productively as stand-ins for the North. Andrea, for example, is not identified with any specific origin, but Canadian-American actress Laurie Holden's accent separates her from the clearly marked Southerners of the series (several of whom are portrayed by English actors), thus hinting at Andrea's background. That she is a civil rights attorney who loses her life through the Governor's machinations while trying to broker peace between the prison group and Woodbury evokes memories of the 1964 murders of civil rights workers James Chaney, Andrew Goodman, and Michael Schwerner in Mississippi. Dale Horvath, whose fictional origins are also obscure, is nonetheless marked as a Northerner by virtue of the accent of actor Jeffrey DeMunn, who hails from upstate New York. Dale's liberal political views set him at odds with the group—and especially with two men with pronounced Southern accents, Shane and Rick—when the fate of a prisoner is being decided in season two. Dale argues for a nonviolent solution, and when he is outvoted, he stalks off in anger and is eviscerated by a walker ("Judge, Jury, Executioner"). On some level, this is a fitting end for a character who allows emotion to override prudence; the outcome demonstrates his unsuitability for a world in which even a momentary emotional overreaction can have fatal consequences.

Dale's response is also driven by his persistent application of his old social conscience to postapocalyptic issues, which leads to his marginalization and inability to align with the prevailing values of his group; his violent and graphically depicted death, precipitated indirectly by his divergent political stance, is a narrative punishment of a stereotypically "Northern" worldview. Occasionally, characters who are more explicitly connected to the North also receive "deserved" punishments. For example, when strangers Dave and Tony arrive in the "Nebraska" episode, their distinctive accents immediately mark them as thugs, even before their ties to the Northeast and dishonorable intentions toward Rick's group are revealed. This initial impression is soon confirmed through their insistent inquiries about Hershel's farm, Dave's request to be treated to "a little Southern hospitality," and Tony's uncouth behavior (he urinates in a corner of the pub as Rick watches with disgust). These incidental hoodlums are quickly eliminated and easily overshadowed by strong men with Southern accents—including Rick, Hershel, and Daryl Dixon, whose very name echoes that of the traditional dividing line between the North and the South.

Historically, slavery was a notorious source of North-South division; today, the Mason-Dixon Line may suggest other divisive human-rights issues. In *Dead Man Walking*, Sister Helen Prejean cites evidence that suggests that insistence on the death penalty in Southern states is, on some level, an act of defiance against the federal authority that forced desegregation measures on the South (46). She notes that two-thirds of all U.S. executions take place in four states—Louisiana, Georgia, Texas, and Florida (49). If Prejean's 1992 statistics are updated and expanded, the argument strengthens: of the 1,411 U.S. executions since 1976, more than eighty percent have been carried out in the South ("Number of Executions"). As a proxy for the South and one of the nation's leaders in capital punishment, Georgia is an especially meaningful site for the center of the kingdom of the dead, where disagreements about the ontological status of the undead and the social necessity of execution often bear an uncomfortable resemblance to debates about executing condemned criminals. In the world of *The Walking Dead*, small groups of men still have the power to decide whether killing a man to protect their community can be a just action. This occurs, for example, when Rick and the group decide the fate of the prisoner Randall, a member of a rival group who might, if released, lead his group back to Hershel's farm to raid it and wreak havoc. Most of the group agrees that Randall must die, but after Rick unilaterally revokes the death sentence, Shane decides to finish the job. Randall's execution and subsequent reanimation give a double meaning to the notion of "dead man walking." While Randall's murder is part of Shane's plot to lure Rick to a secluded spot and kill him, Shane also believes that Rick has failed in his duty to protect the group; indeed, Shane has made this argument throughout most of the second season. Therefore, when Shane enacts the vision of justice determined by his social unit, he responds to a political crisis by defying the leader who disregards the voice of his people. However, Shane's actions are also those of a mob's henchman. His dual role as vigilante and legitimate executioner comments on the problematic status of capital punishment as an institution, hinting at questions not only about its justification per se, but also about related issues, such as fairness in its application. Such concerns are visually echoed when Lori finds Rick rigging a noose in the barn rafters prior to the group's formal agreement to execute Randall—evoking images of lynching (a practice commonly associated with the postwar South) and blurring the line between official "justice" and extrajudicial action.

In addition to their role as proxies for freed slaves and racial Others, the walkers of the AMC series capture the sense of the North as an intrusive entity in the postwar era. As invaders of spaces that traditionally were inhabited by a dominant group that is now struggling to restore its position, they recall the carpetbaggers who descended opportunistically on the postwar South. Their unwelcome arrival, exploitive activities, and infiltration of Southern society are translated into an infestation of monsters that literally feed on the people of the South. At the same time, the undead encountered by Rick's group presumably belong to the local population, so they double as scalawags who betray the South by too readily embracing Northern ways. Indeed, zombies embody qualities that reflect certain stereotypical Southern perceptions of the North. For example, Cobb cites a "'reverse migration' of blacks to the South" that took place after their experience of the "coldness and impersonality" of the North "helped to drive them back" (238). The notion of the industrialized North as a site of a soulless, mechanized life is reshaped in the form of the zombie, whose association with rampant consumption also connects neatly with a vision of the North as the home of many of the country's major commercial centers. Perhaps most telling of all is the idea of the zombie as a figure of both enslavement and the trappings of the North. The walking dead who return and threaten to change individuals into a loathsome Other are reminders of the dangers of another form of oppression: that of a culturally dominant North whose norms and values threaten to consume those of its Southern counterpart. As figures of "reverse migration," the undead represent a cultural infection as the ways of the North, carried back to the South by those who return, may infiltrate and corrupt traditional Southern ways.

To preserve and protect those Southern ways, *The Walking Dead* has assembled a collection of strong, dominant Southern men. In these men, the series accommodates and complicates a range of types and stereotypes. Hershel Greene (portrayed by Georgia-born actor Scott Wilson), owner of the farm where Rick and his group find sanctuary in season two, is drawn from "the familiar portrait of the [S]outhern planter as aristocratic, graceful, honorable, manly, and well-spoken" (Cobb 47)—though he lacks the aristocratic trappings that would, perhaps, render him harder for the average viewer to relate to and identify with. Rick Grimes (portrayed by English actor Andrew Lincoln) is the Southern "everyman." Strong, proud, laconic, capable, resourceful, protective of his family, and willing to get his hands dirty, he is a far cry from the inept Southern lawman figure popularized in an earlier age of American television. Rick rehabilitates the model found, for example, in fellow Georgian Rosco P. Coltrane, the bumbling sheriff of Hazzard County in CBS's *The Dukes of Hazzard*. The villainous Governor (played by English actor David Morrissey) is, at least superficially, the perfect Southern gentleman. Charming, polite, tactful, hospitable, and solicitous to guests, he has a smoothness and finesse that combine with his strong personal magnetism to make him popular with the opposite sex. That he is also a ruthless killer who will stop at nothing to achieve his goals positions him as a consummate politician—and, in particular, a Southern politician, a stereotype whose cultural heritage has both historical and popular roots. With his private "estate" and virtually undisputed authority, the Governor is rebuilding the Old South, where political power rested in the hands of a small number of powerful landholders—an American aristocracy. He also follows in the footsteps of notorious predecessors, such as Louisiana governor Huey Long, the model for fictional Southern politician Willie Stark of Robert Penn Warren's *All the King's Men* (1946). As charismatic populists, Long, Stark, and the Governor have much in common. Described as "[a]mbitious, aggressive, uninhibited, exceedingly colorful, and mesmerizing," Long was an ambivalent figure who "mixed frankness with hypocrisy ... compassion with savagery" (White x)—a description that could have been written of the Governor himself. And finally, perhaps the most powerful sign of an ascendant South is the prominence of fan favorite Daryl Dixon (played by Norman Reedus, a Floridian by birth), a model of the "reclaimed redneck." As Cobb notes, the label "redneck" reached a turning point when it "ceased to be a term of opprobrium and began to convey a fierce and even admirable resistance to American mass society's insistence on conformity" (226). With his trademark crossbow, angel-wings biker vest, and seemingly ever-present string of squirrels, Daryl is an icon of independence, resourcefulness, and strength, a vision of an undefeated and undefeatable South.

In 1939, the fall of the South was immortalized in one of Hollywood's most memorable films: *Gone with the Wind*, adapted from Margaret Mitchell's classic novel. In the popular imagination, that film permanently linked the state of Georgia—and its modern-day metropolis, Atlanta—to the glory of the Old South and to the first apocalypse that reduced it to ashes. The next apocalypse, argues *The Walking Dead*, will be even more destructive, yet a tough new self-reliant South will rise from its ashes, testing Gerald O'Hara's belief that "land is the only thing in the world worth workin' for, worth fightin' for, worth dyin' for, because it's the only thing that lasts" (*Gone with the Wind*). This South will survive a disease that very nearly destroys it and wrap its new wounds in much the same material that was used on soldiers in the Civil War. An infected South is the site of this series' exploration of wounds that don't heal, and its undead are not only reminders of horrors that graves cannot contain, but also alienated, disenfranchised Others that metamorphose into figures of reverse migration and cultural contagion. To effect the liberation of the South, the series erases the North and showcases Southern men as shapers of the brittle future that will follow the demise of a civilization that is once more "gone with the wind." Replacing a cultural narrative of defeat with a narrative of survival and independence, *The Walking Dead* casts a reimagined South as its true protagonist.

NOTES

An earlier version of this essay was presented at the thirty-sixth annual International Conference on the Fantastic in the Arts in Orlando, Florida (March 2015).

1. According to Margaret Mitchell House staff, the current Grady Hospital is not the same building in which the author died. That building now houses Grady Memorial offices.

WORKS CITED

Bishop, Kyle William. *American Zombie Gothic: The Rise and Fall (and Rise) of the Walking Dead in Popular Culture*. Jefferson: McFarland, 2010. Print.

Brown, Ellen F., and John Wiley, Jr. *Margaret Mitchell's* Gone with the Wind: *A Bestseller's Odyssey from Atlanta to Hollywood*. Lanham: Taylor, 2011. Print.

Castel, Albert. *Decision in the West: The Atlanta Campaign of 1864*. Lawrence: University Press of Kansas, 1992. Print. Modern War Studies.

Catton, Bruce. *This Hallowed Ground: A History of the Civil War*. New York: Vintage, 2012. Print.

Cobb, James C. *Away Down South: A History of Southern Identity*. New York: Oxford University Press, 2005. Print.

"Days Gone Bye." *The Walking Dead*. AMC. 31 Oct. 2010. Television.

Dendle, Peter. "The Zombie as Barometer of Cultural Anxiety." *Monsters and the Monstrous: Myths and Metaphors of Enduring Evil*. Ed. Niall Scott. New York: Rodopi, 2007. 45–57. Print. At the Interface/Probing the Boundaries 38.

Foner, Eric. *A Short History of Reconstruction.* New York: Harper, 1990. Print.
Foxworthy, Jeff. *The Best of Jeff Foxworthy: Double Wide Single Minded.* Rhino, 2003. CD.
Gates, Henry Louis, Jr. "100 Amazing Facts About the Negro: Why Was Cotton 'King'?" *The African Americans: Many Rivers to Cross.* PBS. WNET. 2013. Web. 3 July 2015.
Gone with the Wind. Dir. Victor Fleming. 1939. Warner Home Video, 2009. DVD.
"The Grove." *The Walking Dead.* AMC. 16 Mar. 2014. Television.
"Guts." *The Walking Dead.* AMC. 7 Nov. 2010. Television.
Hunter, Marnie. "'Walking Dead' in Georgia: Film Tourism Comes to Life." *cnn.com.* Cable News Network, 2 Mar. 2015. Web. 1 July 2015.
"Judge, Jury, Executioner." *The Walking Dead.* AMC. 4 Mar. 2012. Television.
Lauro, Sarah Juliet, and Karen Embry. "A Zombie Manifesto: The Nonhuman Condition in the Era of Advanced Capitalism." *boundary 2* 35.1 (2008): 85–108. Print.
Margaret Mitchell House Staff. Telephone interview. 28 May 2015.
Martin, Jeff. "'Walking Dead' Brings New Life to Ga. Town." *Associated Press.* 5 Oct. 2013. Web. 19 Aug. 2014.
McMurry, Richard M. *Atlanta 1864: Last Chance for the Confederacy.* Lincoln: University of Nebraska Press, 2000. Print. Great Campaigns of the Civil War.
"Nebraska." *The Walking Dead.* AMC. 12 Feb. 2012. Television.
Nelson, Megan Kate. *Ruin Nation: Destruction and the American Civil War.* Athens: University of Georgia Press, 2012. Print.
"Number of Executions by State and Region Since 1976." *Death Penalty Information Center.* 19 June 2015. Web. 3 July 2015.
Prejean, Helen. *Dead Man Walking: An Eyewitness Account of the Death Penalty in the United States.* New York: Vintage, 1994. Print.
"TS-19." *The Walking Dead.* AMC. 5 Dec. 2010. Television.
White, Richard D., Jr. *Kingfish: The Reign of Huey P. Long.* New York: Random, 2006. Print.

The Recuperation
of Wounded
Hegemonic Masculinity
on *Doomsday Preppers*

Tiffany A. Christian

Megan Hurwitt trains in the unused playground area of a local park in her hometown of Houston, Texas. Doing chin-ups and push-ups, jumping on rusty metal benches, she hones her strength and stamina in preparation for what she considers a probable future: the apocalypse. Featured on the premiere episode of the National Geographic Channel's *Doomsday Preppers* (2012–2014), Megan is one of several women showcased among male preppers. The term "prepper" is distinct from that of "survivalist" in that preparedness is perceived to encompass a wider variety of activities designed to protect against disruptions of daily life that range from the local to the global. On the other hand, survivalism often connotes only the more extreme practices and has a negative association for many people. Although some participants in the show may identify themselves as survivalists, the less potentially offensive term of prepper will be used here. And while disaster preparedness and survivalism are distinct concepts, in the context of this study they are used together to describe a culture in which individuals, anticipating one or more catastrophic scenarios on a variety of scales, are actively preparing for the resulting chaos they imagine may happen. While many of the women on the show serve in a supporting capacity to the "preps" of their husbands or fathers, Megan and others represent a growing trend in the traditionally male-dominated culture of American preppers: today more women are directly participating in disaster preparedness.

Doomsday Preppers, as one of several television shows taking advantage

48

of the resurging popularity of American secular apocalypticism, provides a medium through which these women preppers can be made visible. The presentation of their efforts encourages the notion of a larger general interest in preparedness that is individualistic as well as neutral with regard to gender, race, and other aspects of social location. The segments focusing on women seem to support the idea that preparedness is not only available but also desired by more than those viewed as stereotypical "survivalists." The mere presence of these women is meant to reassure viewers that the show understands "diversity" and recognizes the need for preparedness among all Americans.

But while the visibility of a few women preppers might tempt some viewers into a feel-good complacency with regard to social progress, a closer inspection of the performances of these women as preppers indicates a more complicated, conflicted message. *Doomsday Preppers* is built around the recuperation of "wounded" hegemonic masculinities. Many of the women on the show, whether they support the endeavors of male family members or take care of their own disaster preparations, are on some level participating in the recuperation of a masculine ideal that sees itself in crisis. Women's performances of disaster preparedness rely in large part on familiar narrative tropes common to apocalyptic scenarios. These tropes—widespread civil unrest and violence, competition for resources, and the need for self-reliance and/or a militaristic outlook on survival—allow hegemonic masculinities to regain and maintain control in postapocalyptic fantasies. Women preppers who question or even resist these tropes are often devalued in various ways by the show's presentation of their endeavors. And even when women are performing in accordance with the norms of the "survivalist" narrative, their efforts and even their status as women are still devalued through editing and narration, providing spaces for viewers to reject the women's prepping authenticity.

American survivalism has long been connected to hypermasculinity. As summarized by Anastasia Salter and Bridget Blodgett, the term "hypermasculinity" describes an exaggerated performance of masculine-identified characteristics and behaviors, particularly those deemed stereotypical by the culture. This exaggerated performance of qualities such as independence, physical strength, aggression, hierarchical ranking, and competition, among others, according to Salter and Blodgett and based on previous psychological research, coincides with the dismissal of or hostility towards displays of feminine-identified cultural traits (402). As an example of hypermasculine performance, contemporary survivalist narratives conjure up stereotypical images of white supremacists with military backgrounds stockpiling food and weapons in underground bunkers and aggressively practicing self-reliance, sometimes to the point of extricating themselves from society and living "off the grid." These narratives can be identified as hypermasculine in that they depend on extreme interpretations of masculine-identified traits, such as the ability to operate under difficult circumstances without succumbing to the "weakness" of emotion. When women are discussed in a survivalist context, they may described as displaying traits and behaviors, such as aggression, that are coded as "hypermasculine" based on their exaggerated nature. But more often in popular entertainment media that portray apocalyptic and postapocalyptic scenarios, the characters with the most authority are heterosexual white men who display these hypermasculine traits.

If particular constructions of hegemonic masculinity continue to be valorized in contemporary American society, how can masculinity be in crisis? In this sense, crisis is a perceptual phenomenon. Susan Jeffords, Sally Robinson, and Hamilton Carroll all discuss how, since the 1960s, the tensions created by civil rights and women's liberation movements have destabilized white male identity. Although masculinities are not homogeneous, the discourse of hegemonic masculinity and its associated representations remain relatively static (Ashcraft and Flores 4). This static, dominant, and generally invisible image of white masculinity was unmasked, as it were, during the social upheavals of the Cold War era, which undermined its ability to remain unmarked and thus normative (Carroll 7). Although the tensions instigated by the social movements of the 1960s impacted other groups such as women, people of color, and queer communities to a much greater degree, the focus of attention has remained on the so-called decline of the white male, where "an enduring image of the disenfranchised white man has become a symbol for the decline of the American way" (Robinson 2). The perception of masculinity in decline or even victimized, and the subsequent connection to the decline of the best of American ideals and values, thus creates a "crisis" of anxiety-producing instability.

In recent years and thanks in large part to national and global economic crises as well as continued ideological tensions exposed by oppressed groups, these feelings of victimhood have resurged among those who align themselves ideologically with hegemonic white masculinity. A current profound sense of visibility has left white males exposed. As such, they view the current "crisis" as neither just nor moral, but rather as a violent injustice wherein they feel their destabilization only as loss (Ashcraft and Flores 10). Ironically, it makes little difference whether or not the crisis of hegemonic masculinity is "real." It is the *perception* of realness that creates the authenticity of crisis. As Robinson tells us, "A crisis is 'real' when its rhetorical strategies can be discerned and its effects charted; the reality of a particular crisis depends ... on the power of language, of metaphors and images, to convincingly represent the sense of trauma and turning point" (10). The crisis is not just perceived to be authentic; authenticity is produced through the rhetoric of crisis.

The perception of loss in the decentering of hegemonic masculinity has led to efforts to recuperate that cultural authority in various ways. One such method of recuperation involves the forming of a collective identity that can then allow itself to claim victimization. Victimhood is established, according to Carroll, by appropriating the identity politics and language of the Other, including communities of color, queer communities, and women. These traditionally marginalized social groups, viewed through a patriarchal lens, can be seen as succeeding in the battle for hierarchical control, particularly over labor opportunities; the gains made by second-wave feminism, civil rights groups, and queer communities seem to come at the expense of white masculinity. As Carroll argues, global labor shifts are often understood at the micrological level such that "white men place responsibility for a broad series of shifts in labor opportunity at the feet of the women and people of color who have displaced them" (3). At the same time, the supposed success of Othered groups and corresponding failure of white masculinity provides an opportunity for white men to appropriate the discourse of difference used by these threatening Others in order to express a sense of victimization. The ability of white masculinity to appropriate those discourses and redefine itself in the face of perceived crisis is, Carroll says, a privilege of white masculinity and functions to maintain that privilege (10). This appropriation manifests in popular culture as well as in cultural practice. Through this performative appropriation, and using the very same liberatory language that has been used to decenter it in the first place, those who identify with hegemonic masculinity can claim difference (and victimhood via difference) and thus recuperate its hegemony (Carroll 8).

Wounded hegemonic masculinity also seeks to regain its cultural authority by appealing to those deeply entrenched traditional masculine ideals of toughness, self-reliance, and aggressive competitiveness. Jeffords describes this process as "remasculinization," which entails "a revival of the images, abilities, and evaluations of men and masculinity in dominant U.S. culture" (xii). However, because of the indelible marks left by the women's rights and civil rights movements, recuperation involves more than traditional remasculinization. Robinson reminds us that the point of recuperation is to redefine white men in ways that better situate them to dictate relations of power. Since traditionally Othered groups have become more visible in recent decades, their supposed decentering of white masculinity has opened spaces for resistance to hegemonic male privilege. Thus, in order for decentered white men to be able to regain cultural authority, they must incorporate aspects of Othered groups. With regard to gender, this may include an acknowledgment of the necessity of and even the preference for such stereotypically feminine ideals as collaboration and self-sacrifice. In this way, "male power is actually consolidated through cycles of crisis and resolution whereby men ultimately deal with the threat of female power by incorporating it" (Robinson 10). In the context of disaster preparedness as a gendered cultural belief system, the incorporation of female power encompasses both some acknowledgement of the need for collaboration as well as the participation of women in the remasculinization of survivalism and/or the failure of femininity in the survivalist arena.

However, one of the most convenient ways for wounded hegemonic masculinity to reclaim control and authority continues to be through the symbolic annihilation of femininity in popular culture. In reality television, in particular, representations of gender are complicated through the prism of "realness." Rachel Dubrofsky has argued that reality television producers rely on the notion of surveillance to present participants as truly authentic: "Participants need to show, on camera, who they really are—that they are authentically, on camera, the same person they are (ostensibly) in their own lives" ("Surveillance" 117). At the same time, however, this supposed authenticity is manipulated throughout production, from casting to editing. Dubrofsky notes in a 2012 interview that show producers maintain strict control over who is selected for participation. In that process, there are "certain logics about how the action of the series unfolds that will privilege certain displays over others" ("096"). As a result, despite participants' supposed authentic behavior, reality television remains very much a constructed space.

In his discussion of the long-running contest show *Survivor*, Christopher Wright argues that the presentation of such shows as "real" can impact audiences much more greatly than fictional shows. Because viewers are presented with content explicitly billed as "reality," embedded ideologies that the participants present are normalized, seeming more natural than on a show that is billed as fiction (Wright 3). The notion that audiences tend to engage critically with these shows on a much lower level than they do with full-fledged fiction is somewhat simplistic since the explosion of reality television in recent years has made some patterns of manipulation more obvious. However, while audiences' engagement with these shows is not as passive as Wright seems to imply, his point still has some validity. On the level of ideology, the performances of the actors and their situations, as well as the editing of the show, can reinforce existing paradigms. Thus, while audiences may individualize showcased preppers and disagree with the way these people are being represented, other markers of representation may remain invisible and thus continue to affirm gender hierarchies.

In each episode in the first season of NatGeo's *Doomsday Preppers*, a number of individuals or groups (typically three) are showcased in a demonstration of their disaster preparedness. The show's season one opening monologue—repeated at the beginning of each episode—works to emphasize the "reality" of the show: "Across the country, there is a growing darkness, a belief that the end of days is near. Ordinary Americans, from all walks of life, are taking whatever measures necessary to prepare and protect themselves from what they perceive is the fast-approaching end of the world as we know it" (*Doomsday Preppers*). Highlighting the ordinariness of these preppers suggests to audiences that these are indeed real people and that, even when the cameras go away, their preparation efforts continue. The preppers then discuss what specific apocalyptic scenarios they expect and the preparations they have undergone in order to survive catastrophe. These preparations usually include practicing the technique of "bugging-out"—a military slang word to describe a quick retreat from a dangerous area but that can also include, in the survivalist context, moving to a previously secured location such as a cave or bunker—and building "bug-out bags" or portable emergency supply kits (also called "go bags"). Preparations can also include intensive food storage, weapons training, and scouting for or building safe locations for the most extreme emergencies. Many preppers also learn "primitive" skills, including pre-modern fire making, DIY weaponry, and traditional medicine such as harvesting aloe vera plants for burns. After demonstrating the extent of their "preps," preppers are assessed by what the show calls a team of "practical preppers" in a segment called "Expert Assessment." This team of experts provides the preppers with ideas for improving their overall preparedness score. The show then does a brief follow-up with each prepper to determine whether the assessment team's suggestions have been implemented.

A survey of the segments in season one reveals that the majority of preppers showcased are male. Some segments may be considered ambiguous by showcasing husband and wife teams as well as families. However, by using the interviews within each segment to determine which prepper is given the most focus, I have found that men outnumber women by almost three to one. These men, by and large, fit within a certain stereotypical perception of survivalists, which recalls Dubrofsky's argument about casting logics: they tend to be in their forties or older, they are white, they identify as heterosexual, and some of them have military backgrounds. Many could be categorized as middle class, and they often stress that prepping is a lifestyle that they have chosen. Some work alone while others involve their wives, children, grandchildren, and other family members or friends. In such scenarios, the white male prepper often serves as the manager of the group and doles out responsibilities to the others. And in many of these cases, the show makes it apparent that prepping began as the white male's idea, and other group members participate with varying degrees of willingness.

The women who participate in disaster preparedness on the show are presented in various (sometimes conflicting) ways. Some women attempt to represent themselves as providing an alternative to the stereotypical prepper narrative of aggressive isolation ("bugging out") in that they are looking after their communities and attempting to form collaborative networks. These few examples contrast with more normative representations of the highly masculinized narrative tropes associated with survivalism, including aggressive competition, displays of toughness, hierarchical methods of maintaining order and control, and a notion of the necessity of self-reliance and independence, with all of these elements used as indicators of strength. When women display prepping behaviors that go against these masculine norms, the show uses subtle ways of devaluing their feminine performances, primarily through the editing of footage and interviews. When women do participate heavily in masculine performances of prepping, *Doomsday Preppers* complicates their performances and seems to want to demonstrate to viewers that those performances will never be good enough.

Almost from the beginning of the series, we see the conflicts in women's performances of prepping. In the second episode, viewers are introduced to Kellene Bishop, who is first shown cooking in her kitchen. She is described as a "bubbly housewife" with "a reputation for being able to whip up a gourmet cuisine in a flash" ("I Hope"). As the narrator tells us that she fears an economic collapse, images of cooking and food continue. Viewers are told that she considers herself a "foodie" (someone interested in fine dining), and her preps include storing tons of gourmet food (as opposed to MREs or basic rations). Highlighting Kellene's interest in storing gourmet goods presents her as overly consumerist and thus ultra-feminine. Her husband, Scott, is also somewhat feminized through his interest in the luxury of eating well when he should be more concerned with "toughing it out." The show's producers do attempt to help Scott recuperate his masculinity, however, when he is shown working out on a punching bag and taking the lead in doing practice sweeps for intruders around the home.

Kellene, despite her feminine performance of overly civilized life in the kitchen, also participates in the project of recuperating wounded hegemonic masculinity through her performances in shooting and in self-defense. She is shown practicing with a firearm, and the self-defense classes she runs with her husband are not used to build a network for the postapocalypse, but rather so that these women can manage their own individual survival ("I Hope"). The masculinized aggression associated with using firearms is something that is recognized by many women preppers, as Becky Brown, another featured prepper on the show, demonstrates: "I don't have a gun. I'm a girl, I'm feminine, I'm not supposed to love guns, right? But you get in a different mentality when you're protecting your family and your home and the things that are most important to you. When the government takes over, I will need to know how to shoot a gun" ("Friends Can Become Enemies"). This complicated statement seems to equate femininity with a lack of love for firearms, which themselves serve as a symbol for violence. Becky also implies that the ability to use a gun somehow requires a "love" for guns, and thus a love for violence. In order to force herself to learn about weaponry, Becky feels it necessary to discard femininity with its supposed inherent antipathy to violence. Femininity becomes devalued once again in the context of disaster preparedness, this time by the prepper herself.

Even with these attempts at performing masculine norms, however, women preppers continue to be undermined by the show's editing. For instance, when Kellene shows off one of her guns, the "peashooter," NatGeo tells viewers in a caption that the peashooter is a relatively weak weapon. From this, viewers receive the message that Kellene is either unwilling or unable to handle a more useful or powerful weapon; thus, her attempts at performing masculinity fail on some level. As another example, episode nine showcases Janet Spencer of Helena, Montana, who is preparing for an attack on the nuclear stockpile in nearby Great Falls. Her primary prep of food storage, meant to assist survivors fleeing the attack, is undertaken with a certain amount of subterfuge because her husband does not approve. In order to prove her sanity, she consistently emphasizes in interviews that she understands how "crazy" her creative storage techniques may seem; nevertheless, the show provides something of a Frankenbite that frames and devalues her testimony. (The term "Frankenbite" is defined by Kevin Arnovitz as the editing together of disparate clips into a seamless presentation that is meant to "manufacture" character or "story.") In its splicing together of the various places Janet has stored her supplies, along with a dramatic "race against time" aspect (since she can only prep while her husband is away), *Doomsday Preppers* allows for the interpretation that Janet's prepping may indeed be a little "crazy" despite her protestations ("Close the Door").

Perhaps one of the most memorable women to be featured in season one is Megan Hurwitt, who exemplifies both the recuperation of wounded hegemonic masculinity through her own behavior as well as the devaluing of femininity through the manipulation of "reality" television. In the premiere episode, she is introduced to viewers as a "Houston party girl." Although she is also described as independent, she is noted as loving her cats, her car, and "cocktails with friends," once again highlighting a superficial and consumeristic identity ("Bullets"). She is also shown swinging around a stripper pole (fully clothed) in her apartment. Visuals such as these potentially allow viewers to dismiss her preps, to take both her and her plans less seriously.

But Megan cannot be so easily dismissed. Sturdily built with wide shoulders that are emphasized as she walks and sporting a no-nonsense ponytail for the entirety of her segment, she exudes confidence in her preparations for bugging out of Houston in the event of a worldwide oil crisis. She also performs as aggressive and competitive, both of which are coded as traditionally masculine. For Megan, disaster preparedness is very much a competition: "When the shit hits the fan, I'm gonna be fitter than you are!" She also describes herself as a "machine" who is preparing to fight her way out of Houston when the time comes ("Bullets").

Perhaps one of the most disturbing aspects of Megan's performance is shown when she tells a story about another woman who mocked her prepping efforts. As the story unfolds, Megan performs a shoulder dance on camera to celebrate the idea that the other woman will starve to death ("Bullets"). This act of celebration serves, in effect, to dehumanize the other woman in the story. Megan sees her as weak for not taking preparedness seriously, and that point of view is performed in a stereotypically masculine way by celebrating her own strength and devaluing the other woman's feminine weakness. In this way Megan participates, with whatever level of consciousness, in recuperating wounded hegemonic masculinity. She makes clear her dismissal of femininity more than once when she discusses how to cope with catastrophe as a woman: "You just have to make sure they hear authority in your voice. You wanna make sure they understand, 'I am *not* your average woman. I will pop a cap in your ass, and you're not taking my shit'" ("Bullets"). What is an "average" woman in Megan's view? Whatever it is, it is rejected in favor of a more masculinized representation, one that is self-reliant and competitive, and that includes the threat of violence.

Despite Megan's performance of stereotypical hypermasculinity, her framing on the show continues to devalue her efforts and her performance. When she is shown practicing her bug-out route through Houston, she gets tired, makes frustrated comments, and ultimately takes much longer to reach her destination than she wished. Again, though it was a first trial run for her escape route, its experimental nature can be overlooked when confronted with visuals of her obvious exhaustion. Also, the assessment team makes a point of emphasizing several weaknesses in her prepping, including her lack of sufficient food storage, despite her stated plan of staying in the apartment for just a short time. But for casual viewers, this assessment may seem valid and thus prove again how ill-prepared she is, despite her bravado. Ultimately, Megan's masculine performance does not provide her with much of a buffer against the devaluing of her femininity.

While many of the women preppers on the show subscribe at least in part to a more masculinized view of preparedness, such is not the case for all. *Doomsday Preppers* has showcased women who actively resist the stereotypical performance of prepping, though these moments of rupture are tightly framed as a devaluing of those ideals. One such case is that of Kathy Harrison, described by NatGeo as a liberal from the northeastern United States who loves cooking, gardening, and playing with her children ("I Hope"). Her prepping is decidedly different from the norm. In addition to gardening and canning, her larger goal is to create a community network in the event that a large earthquake hits the area. For Kathy, this sort of collaboration, often considered a more "feminine" trait, is vital to survival—and violence is not. To that extent, her preps do not involve weapons at all. This performance of disaster preparedness is presented by the show as not just less valuable, but even dangerous. The lack of security for her home is assessed by the "experts" as a liability in the event of a disaster. But despite the supposed risks, Kathy stands firm against suggestions that she weaponize her home or create a more secure border. Hers is one of the few instances where a display of feminine-coded strength creeps into the show.

While Kathy's resistance is directed at the dismissal of her style of disaster preparedness, Narin Frank resists the very essence of what survival means. In addition to one man, Narin is one of only two women in season one who can be reliably identified as a person of color: she is the Cambodian wife of Bradford Frank, a medical doctor prepping for a widespread bird flu pandemic. At first, Narin's resistance to her husband's preps is framed as petty and may be interpreted as racist in that NatGeo focuses on her when she complains about the amount of money Bradford is spending on food and medicine storage ("It's Gonna Get Worse"). While other preppers mention how much money they spend on their preparations, generally there is little emphasis on economic details. Narin's focus on money, then, is atypical and provides a space in which to code her behavior based on stereotypical ideas about Asian and Asian-American women. Also, visuals of Narin doing dishes while Bradford explains which medicines they should reorder place her squarely in the domestic space, and in a way that is out of her control. As much as she objects to their house filling up with canned goods, there is nothing she can do about it.

However, within this segment there is an unexpected dramatic turn. Viewers are informed that Narin Frank is a survivor of the Khmer Rouge massacre, managing to escape from a prison camp at age nineteen to become the lone survivor of her family ("It's Gonna Get Worse"). Hers is a nightmare scenario that few Americans can comprehend, let alone relate to. But despite allowing viewers a tiny glimpse into her horrific past, the narration still manages to chide Narin somewhat for her disapproval of her husband's preparations, suggesting that because she has been through this trauma, she *should* understand her husband's actions rather than asking him to rely on her experience. That she does not rely on him is a shortcoming on her part, or so the framing of this incident seems to suggest. Certainly, Bradford shows little interest in taking Narin's suggestions or her knowledge into consideration, preferring instead to override her objections. The segment provides an extended scene where Bradford is installing ballistic glass over his regular windows. As NatGeo tells us, his efforts in the name of security need to be valued: "Bradford is determined to keep his family safe, even if they don't appreciate his efforts" ("It's Gonna Get Worse").

Eventually, however, Narin's resistance has an effect on her husband. He takes his wife and daughter to a site he is considering for their bug-out location: a deep cave. Inside, Narin is visibly uncomfortable. She tells her husband that during her time as a refugee, she had to hide in many caves and that being in one now brings back memories of those terrible days. Bradford finally tells NatGeo that he was unaware of his wife's fear of caves and that, despite his excitement, he might seriously consider finding another location ("It's Gonna Get Worse"). Of all the women involved in *Doomsday Preppers* who either prep themselves or assist in the preparations of a male family member, Narin Frank is one of the very few who manage to actively resist the survivalist narrative. She does this by forcing her husband to step away, if only briefly, from the culturally scripted masculine performance of "survival" that is spread through American popular culture—and to visualize a world of which he had previously been blind. In a show that touts the authenticity of its players, Narin reframes authenticity by sharing a story of actual survival.

Unfortunately, women like Narin Frank are rare on *Doomsday Preppers*. And in subsequent seasons, the show has heightened the extremism by presenting fewer women, showcasing instead more men who represent the survivalist stereotypes: tough, independent, "hardcore" white men, many with military backgrounds, who value self-reliance and relish the idea that, in a postapocalyptic universe, aggression will be critical to survival. As much as some women preppers may have contributed to the recuperation of wounded hegemonic masculinity by subscribing in some way to the survivalist narrative, the National Geographic Channel may have decided that it does not need "diversity" so much after all, particularly when women performing these masculine ideas can never seem to perform well enough to satisfy the demands of hegemonic masculinity.

WORKS CITED

Arnovitz, Kevin. "Virtual Dictionary: A Guide to the Language of Reality TV." *slate.com.* The Slate Group, 14 Sept. 2004. Web. 30 Dec. 2014.

Ashcraft, Karen Lee, and Lisa A. Flores. "'Slaves with White Collars': Persistent Performances of Masculinity in Crisis." *Text and Performance Quarterly* 23.1 (Jan. 2000): 1–29. EBSCOHost. Web. 7 Dec. 2013.

"Bullets, Lots of Bullets." *Doomsday Preppers.* National Geographic Channel. 7 Feb. 2012. Television.

Carroll, Hamilton. *Affirmative Reaction: New Formations of White Masculinity.* Durham: Duke University Press, 2011. Print.

"Close the Door, Load the Shotgun." *Doomsday Preppers.* National Geographic Channel. 3 Apr. 2012. Television.

Doomsday Preppers. National Geographic Channel. 2012–2014. Television.

Dubrofsky, Rachel E. "Surveillance on Reality Television and Facebook: From Authenticity to Flowing Data." *Communication Theory* 21.2 (2011): 111–29. *Communication & Mass Media Complete.* Web. 22 May 2015.

_____. "096: Interview with Rachel Dubrofsky—Author of 'The Surveillance of Women on Reality TV.'" Interview by Ben Myers and Desireé Rowe. Critical Lede. Podcast. N.p., Aug. 2012. Web. 22 May 2015.

"Friends Can Become Enemies." *Doomsday Preppers*. National Geographic Channel. 28 Feb. 2012. Television.

"I Hope I Am Crazy." *Doomsday Preppers*. National Geographic Channel. 7 Feb. 2012. Television.

"It's Gonna Get Worse." *Doomsday Preppers*. National Geographic Channel. 27 Mar. 2012. Television.

Jeffords, Susan. *The Remasculinization of America: Gender and the Vietnam War*. Bloomington: Indiana University Press, 1989. Print.

Robinson, Sally. *Marked Men: White Masculinity in Crisis*. New York: Columbia University Press, 2000. Print.

Salter, Anastasia, and Bridget Blodgett. "Hypermasculinity & Dickwolves: The Contentious Role of Women in the New Gaming Public." *Journal of Broadcasting & Electronic Media* 56.3 (2012): 401–16. Web. 21 May 2015.

Wright, Christopher J. *Tribal Warfare: Survivor and the Political Unconscious of Reality Television*. Lanham: Lexington, 2006. Print.

The Last Non-Judgment
Postmodern Apocalypse
in Battlestar Galactica

Stephen Joyce

Midway through season two of the acclaimed 2004–2009 science fiction series *Battlestar Galactica*, humanity teeters on the brink of self-destruction. The Cylons, artificial life-forms that can pass as human, have all but wiped out the human race in a devastating nuclear assault. The survivors, in a motley fleet of spaceships clustered around the outdated *Galactica*, have unexpectedly reunited with the battlestar *Pegasus,* captained by the fearsome Admiral Cain. The survivors' joy at the reunion is short-lived when they discover that Cain intends to impose brutal military control over the fractious, divided civilian population. President Laura Roslin concludes that Cain poses as much of a threat to the civilian fleet as the Cylons and tasks Commander Adama of the *Galactica* with the job of murdering his superior officer (one of fewer than 50,000 remaining human beings) for the good of humanity. As the *Galactica* and the *Pegasus* prepare to engage in a civil war that will shred any final hope of survival, Adama turns to the one being aboard who can understand the complexities of guilt and compulsion that drive his decision making—his enemy, the Cylon Sharon Valerii, who in an earlier incarnation had tried to assassinate Adama by shooting him twice at close range. In a moment that may stand as the defining statement of the first two seasons of *Battlestar Galactica*, Sharon repeats back to Adama his own words from the day of the apocalypse, but now with a coda that rings devastatingly true: "You said that humanity never asked itself why it deserved to survive. Maybe you don't" ("Resurrection Ship, Part II").

Ever since the first broadcast of its miniseries (2003), *Battlestar Galactica* has won widespread praise for its depiction of flawed but believable characters struggling through a postapocalyptic labyrinth of moral complexity that does not allow for neat resolutions or sentimentality. The creators intentionally used a science fiction format to dramatize important post–9/11 themes, such as terrorism, torture, and the balance between liberty and security during a time of crisis. In his *Series Bible, BSG* creator Ronald D. Moore wrote that "the Cylons *in our midst* should be a constant, lurking threat" (33, emphasis in original). Moore went on to note, "How the people react to this threat among them will be one of the primary storylines of the entire series—what will be their version of the Patriot Act?" (33). Accordingly, the series has often been analyzed as a running commentary on the War on Terror. Mike Milford and Robert C. Rowland describe *BSG* as a "situated ideological allegory" that is "neither monosemic nor fully polysemic ... but is limited by the pretextual knowledge of the audience" (540). Thus, Rikk Mulligan views the character of Admiral Cain as "an extension of the American use of the military in the Middle East, presidential disregard for the autonomy of world governments, and the imposition of American cultural norms and liberal democracy in name only" (63), while Brian Ott interprets the Cylon occupation of New Caprica that opens the third season as "an unmistakable metaphor for the U.S. occupation of Iraq" (22). Although the show's creators actively encouraged allegorical readings in their public comments, purely allegorical interpretations can lead to a problem when trying to understand the increasing dissatisfaction of fans with the show's direction from the beginning of season three to the series finale. Chris Dzialo argued that "*BSG*'s self-consciously balanced narrative resonated with a polarized body politic from 2004–2006, but at the present moment (mid–2007) seems to be struggling to enunciate a less-balanced form in order to find its audience in these arguably more unified times, when a sizeable majority appears discontented with George W. Bush and the war in Iraq" (172). Yet it is unclear from Dzialo's argument why *BSG*'s audience, which preferred a balanced narrative during a time when public debate was driven by simplistic binaries of good and evil, would then turn away from balanced narratives in a political environment of arguably greater unity, nor how this shift interacts with the internal logic of the show's development.

I argue that the shift in *Battlestar Galactica*'s reception after season two lies in how the narrative changed from a postmodern to a classical apocalypse and that this move fundamentally undercut the entire premise of the first two seasons, leading to increasing dissatisfaction among the show's fans. Moreover, this shift does not directly mirror the political environment but often runs counter to it. In 2003, when the Bush administration promoted certainty and a clear moral division between good and evil, *Battlestar Galactica* dramatized ambiguity and moral confusion; however, when the U.S. became bogged down in the occupation of Iraq with no clear goal or ethical purpose, *Battlestar Galactica* offered a narrative of increasing certainty with more defined lines between good and evil. From the perspective of understanding apocalyptic narratives in modern culture, *Battlestar Galactica* thus offers an unparalleled comparative viewpoint on the defining features of both classical and postmodern apocalyptic narratives and their different appeals.

Battlestar Galactica begins with the near-total destruction of a human civilization spread across twelve planets; in images repeated in the opening credits of each show, we watch from space as mushroom clouds blossom across the surface of the Earth-like Caprica, an eerily beautiful eruption of technological power come back to haunt its creators. The show thus taps into one of our most modern fears, the possibility of a nuclear holocaust. Yet what makes *Battlestar Galactica* a postmodern apocalypse is that the end of the world is only the beginning of the story. In classical apocalyptic narratives, "we project ourselves ... past the End, so as to see the structure whole" (Kermode 8), and apocalypticism's appeal is that what seems like chaos "has a discernible structure and meaning in relation to its End, and that this End is the product not of chance, but of divine plan" (McGinn 36). The word "apocalypse" does not refer to the end of time but to the revelation that comes once history has ceased and assumed a fixed shape. It is through this revelation, the *aletheia*, that classical apocalyptic narratives offer hope alongside the end of all things. Yet in postmodern apocalyptic narratives, Armageddon provides no consoling revelation. Like Hamm and Clov in Beckett's *Endgame*, we find the world may end without offering up the *aletheia* that makes sense of all suffering. This presents a major quandary in *Battlestar Galactica*'s first two seasons, when the characters must find not just a way but also a reason to go on living when the universe offers no moral justification for the annihilation of their civilization.

The difference between classical and postmodern apocalyptic narratives is made clear near the end of season one when President Roslin becomes convinced of the literal truth of an ancient religious prophecy and believes she is the dying leader spoken of in the scrolls of Pythia—the one who will lead humanity to a new home on the missing thirteenth colony, Earth. Although *Battlestar Galactica*'s human civilization is mostly identical to that of the contemporary United States, one major difference lies in its polytheist religion, which views time as cyclical rather than linear. As multiple characters intone throughout the series, "All this has happened before, and all this will happen again." The scrolls thus operate as both history and prophecy, recounting in the rich but vague symbolism typical of religious apocalyptic narratives both the founding of the Twelve Colonies and the coming apocalypse that will initiate the cycle anew. Yet, as is typical of *BSG*, even a classical apocalyptic narrative becomes a source of division rather than unity as it cleaves the fleet into believers and skeptics. Unlike Roslin, Adama believes

Earth is merely a useful myth, a way of maintaining cohesion within the fleet. As Bernard McGinn argues, such *a priori* readings of apocalyptic narratives make use "of the already established apocalyptic scenario to interpret current events and thus to move men to decision and action" (33). Situating the destruction of the colonies as the origin point of the foundation myth gives many of the survivors a sense of hope and purpose, but equally there are those who think it madness to follow the cryptic words of ancient texts. The tensions boil over at the end of season one, when Roslin interferes with Adama's orders by sending his best pilot on a quest for a religious relic—and Adama terminates her presidency. In the ensuing confusion, the fleet splits between believers and doubters, and the attempt to reunify the fleet becomes one of season two's major story arcs.

The classical apocalypse, by giving form and meaning to history, not only reveals the present's place in the divine plan but also separates the good from the wicked. Stephen O'Leary views apocalyptic narratives as "symbolic resources that enable societies to define and address the problem of evil" (6). This culminates in the Last Judgment, a moment at the end of time when "the good and the evil will be sorted into their respective axiological and spatial categories, the former judged worthy and therefore admitted into the New Jerusalem, the latter judged unworthy and cast into the lake of fire" (Pagano 72). Apocalypticism thus offers not simply meaning but also vindication and clarity, replacing "the moral epistemological murkiness of life as it is with a post-apocalyptic world in which all identities and values are clear" (Berger 81). Indeed, this was the frame into which the Bush administration sought to cast 9/11, as an apocalyptic event that revealed a world of "moral certitude, of either/or, and of good vs. evil" (Ott 24). It is here that *Battlestar Galactica* breaks dramatically from both traditional apocalyptic narratives and the politics of the War on Terror, for not only does the end of the world offer no transcendent meaning, but it also fails to divide good from evil as it increasingly blurs the boundaries between human and Cylon, between ally and enemy.

The opening episode of season one, "33," establishes the show's moral complexity. Relentlessly pursued by the Cylons, the fleet is forced to make a faster-than-light jump every thirty-three minutes. When the episode begins, the crew has executed 237 jumps over 130 hours, and the strain is written across the faces of the sleep-deprived crew. However, on the next jump, a civilian vessel called the *Olympic Carrier* is accidentally left behind. As recriminations fly, the crew realizes that this time the Cylons have not found them and they begin to suspect that Cylon agents aboard the *Olympic Carrier* relayed the fleet's location after each jump. When the *Olympic Carrier* suddenly returns, it heads directly for *Galactica* and refuses to respond to radio contact. The situation openly parallels a 9/11 type situation: what would you do if a passenger vessel, with suspected enemy infiltrators aboard, suddenly headed directly for a major military target and refused to answer all hails? But *BSG* never offers a satisfactory resolution. Roslin and Adama decide to destroy the vessel, killing all 1,345 people aboard in order to protect the fleet, yet this action is never represented as the morally correct decision. As Ott puts it, "*BSG* explores moral ambiguity. But rather than attempting to resolve this ambiguity, the show prompts reflection on the contexts that produce it, encouraging viewers to judge for themselves" (24). Time and again the series challenges viewers with impossible dilemmas; in the pilot, when the assembling civilian fleet is spotted by Cylon scouts, they must choose between leaving immediately and abandoning thousands of people or risk everyone being killed when the Cylon strike force appears. Roslin makes the decision to leave but is then told by her aide Billy "that the little girl you met earlier, Cami, her ship can't make the jump." As the crew prepares to flee, the radio is full of desperate messages begging "you can't just leave us here!" and we see Cami playing with her doll on one of the ships left behind as the Cylons close in. By focusing on the victim of Roslin's decision, we are encouraged to question her judgment even as the presence of the Cylons reinforces the logic of her choice. In *BSG*, it is impossible to separate good from evil as evil acts must be committed for the greater good and as the series develops the human characters are forced to ask how much of their humanity they are willing to sacrifice to preserve humanity.

If *Battlestar Galactica* undermines the belief that the good are wholly good, then it also challenges depictions of the enemy as wholly evil. The initial comparison between Cylons and Islamic terrorism has been explored by Tiffany Potter and C. W. Marshall, who argue that "*BSG* initially maps an Islamic identity onto the unknown, religiously driven, robotic culture that carries out a seemingly unprovoked attack on the series' knowable human population" (62). Yet through the character of Sharon "Boomer" Valerii, a Cylon sleeper agent in the colonial fleet, the series complicates the view of Cylons as a unified, fanatical enemy. Boomer is a respected pilot aboard *Galactica* who slowly begins to suspect what the audience already knows, that she is actually a Cylon. Yet Boomer is initially unaware of this fact and continually struggles against strange impulses and memory blackouts. The complex positioning of Boomer as an unaware enemy places the viewer in the confusing position of sympathizing with her character's fear and anxiety while simultaneously fearing for the fleet if she remains undiscovered. After the original Boomer is killed in retaliation for the attempted assassination of Adama, the episode "Downloaded" in season two shows us a resurrected Boomer on Caprica isolating herself from her fellow Cylons, overcome with guilt for the human friends she betrayed. Meanwhile, another version of Sharon Valerii, a self-aware Cylon model later given the codename "Athena," voluntarily becomes a prisoner aboard *Galactica* in order to bring to term the hybrid human-Cylon child she has conceived with a colonial officer, Karl "Helo" Agathon, thus initiating multiple boundary crossings between ally and enemy, between human and Cylon, and between any clear distinction between good and evil. The reversal becomes complete in season three, when the Cylons occupy New Caprica and the human characters fight back through suicide bombings and assassinations, thus turning the Cylons from coded Islamic terrorists to the United States military imposing American rule in Iraq. As Matthias Stephan writes, "This blurring of the lines of audience identification calls attention to the tactics of each side, as both sides exhibit nurturing and brutally violent behavior, at times, and neither side can be easily identified as good or evil, right or wrong, for very long."

Moral ambiguity is also reflected in *Battlestar Galactica*'s signature visual style, which destabilizes the traditional omniscient invisible narrating eye that seamlessly follows the action without ever calling attention to itself. In the *Series Bible*, Moore emphasizes that the "first thing that will leap out at viewers is the dynamic use of the documentary or cinema verité style. Through extensive use of hand-held cameras, practical lighting, and functional set design, the battlestar *Galactica* will feel on every level like a real place" (1). Yet the visual style also goes far beyond creating a documentary feel. The camera pans and zooms erratically, often cutting to imprecise close-ups that leave key details outside the frame in a way that breaks the traditional conventions of narrative film. Even if the characters are bewildered by moral dilemmas, we as an audience expect the camera to show us their perplexity from the stable vantage point of the omniscient narrator. In *Battlestar Galactica*, however, not only are the characters perpetually disoriented in an ethical and epistemological labyrinth, but even the omniscient narrator often does not know where to look. The camera as omniscient narrator has as much difficulty following the action as the characters have deciding what to do, and this visual confusion fundamentally destabilizes our certainty as to what the truth is and where the moral high ground lies—if it even exists at all.

Joshua Gunn and David E. Beard argue that "faced with the denial of resolution characteristic of the immanent apocalyptic, we suggest that the rhetor and audience suffer a destabilized sense of self akin to the debilitating experience of confronting a sublime object" (270). In traditional apocalyptic narratives, the imminent end clarifies the identity of all, separating those who understand and work towards the divine plan from the heretics and unbelievers. In the postmodern apocalypse, not only is it impossible to distinguish good from evil, but the inability to see an end beyond the permanent state of crisis and flux destabilizes the subject's sense of self. In *Battlestar Galactica*, this issue runs throughout the series as characters wonder about the identity of the Cylons in the fleet. In turn, this speculation leads several characters aboard *Galactica* to question their own identities, most notably the scientist Gaius Baltar, who secretly hopes he may be a Cylon. It was Baltar who originally gave the Cylons access to the human defense systems and thus allowed the surprise attack that wiped out the Twelve Colonies; but if he were really a Cylon, then "I would stop being a traitor to one set of people and be a hero to another" ("The Passage"). Either way he would have a narrative that defined his identity, but in this postmodern apocalyptic scenario, it is the not knowing that destabilizes Baltar's sense of self. Whereas classical apocalypticism defines exactly who we are and what roles we must play, in the postmodern apocalypse, the absence of meaning destabilizes not only narratives of history but also the identity of its agents, leaving us only the twin demons of doubt and dread.

Originally, then, *Battlestar Galactica* was structured around a postmodern apocalypse in which Armageddon has already occurred without providing structure and meaning to the present's position in history, or separating the good from the evil, or providing a fixed narrative that offers clear identities to the confused, struggling characters. In the final two seasons, however, the show pivoted from a postmodern to a classical apocalyptic narrative, and it was this change in the show's basic premise, rather than shifting public political sentiments, that caused many fans to become disappointed with the series' final trajectory and ending.

After the escape from New Caprica, the show resolves the long-running tension regarding the prophecies as *Galactica* searches for the Eye of Jupiter, which will point the way to Earth. The discovery of the Eye, a nova thousands of years in the making that just happens to occur as *Galactica* arrives, removes any doubts that there is a divine plan. As the prophesied signs come true, even skeptics come to believe in the will of the gods and so much of the indeterminacy surrounding the survivors' fate vanishes. One of the keys to *Battlestar Galactica*'s initial dramatic power was that it depicted "a war fought *between* apocalypses, between the realized apocalypse of the nuclear annihilation of human civilization and the potential apocalypse of the ending of the human race" (Stevenson 113). The suspension between postmodern and classical apocalypse generated the show's distinctive ambiguity. Yet the revelation that the characters really are part of a divine plan broke this delicate balance. For many fans, this was the most disappointing creative decision in the show's evolution. Sam Miller argues that "the problem is a simplistic god, an ultimate benevolent power who is guiding everyone to a happy ending," while Brad Templeton regards the show's biggest failure as the revelation that "God did it." Further, Robert Bland criticizes the way the introduction of the divine plan removes agency from the characters. Bland believes that "RDM [Moore] & Co. not only violated the tacit agreement between storyteller and fan, but they exploded the internal engine that had been propelling *BSG* forward since its inception: its characters."

With the revelation of the divine plan, the characters also become divided into good and evil, but rather than mapping these categories onto human/Cylon, the righteous are those who further the divine plan and the wicked are those who obstruct God's designs. Much of the show's moral complexity is thus removed as characters can increasingly be defined as good or evil, while the more fixed narrative also stabilizes the identities of all. Athena, the self-aware version of Sharon Valerii who is the mother of the human-Cylon hybrid child Hera, sides with the humans and becomes an officer in the colonial fleet, thus creating a fixed identity for herself once she defines her duty as protecting Hera to further God's plan. As Julie Hawk puts it, the two most evident traits of the various Cylon Sharons "are her need to situate herself within a coherent narrative, even if that means compartmentalizing her psychic remainder in order to keep the narrative functional, and her insistence that she have the right and the ability to make her own choices. In short, she is compelled both to discover her self and to create her self" (7). Yet the ambiguity surrounding Boomer and Athena's identities was essential to the first two seasons. In season one, we watched Boomer struggle with the horrifying realization that she was not who she thought she was. When Athena comes to *Galactica* in season two, we wonder if she is deliberately manipulating the emotions of those around her, particularly her former lovers, Chief Tyrol and Helo—and we wonder what her ultimate goal is. Once the design of God's plan starts to become clear, so, too, does Athena's identity, and the story becomes an affirmative account of self-realization that actually diminishes the character's dramatic potential.

As the show developed, then, it pivoted to a classical form of apocalyptic narrative that undercut the ambiguity that characterizes the postmodern apocalypse that had been the core of the show's dramatic conflict. *Battlestar Galactica*'s evolution thus, ironically, ran counter to the popular political narratives of its time. When the Bush administration propounded certainty and righteousness after 9/11, the show dramatized its opposite, but as the nation became disillusioned by the murky realities of military occupation and torture, *Battlestar Galactica* moved towards a narrative that emphasized certainty and resolution. Although *Battlestar Galactica* often makes easily decoded comments on the War on Terror, we should be wary of interpreting these as simple reflections of social concerns. Rather, fiction often imagines the thing we lack. In a time of messianic certainty, *Battlestar Galactica* embraced fear and confusion in a thrilling postmodern apocalyptic scenario; when the times mirrored the show, the show fell for the siren song of clarity and purpose, becoming its own Book of Revelation by dissipating the qualities it had revealed best.

Works Cited

Battlestar Galactica. Dev. Ronald D. Moore and David Eick. Universal, 2004–2009. DVD.

Beckett, Samuel. *Endgame.* 1957. London: Faber, 1958. Print.

Berger, James. *After the End: Representations of Post Apocalypse.* Minneapolis: University of Minnesota Press, 1999. Print.

Bland, Robert. "In God We Rust: Final Thoughts on *Battlestar Galactica.*" *Tor.com.* Macmillan, 14 Apr. 2009. Web. 26 Oct. 2014.

Dzialo, Chris. "When Balance Goes Bad: How *Battlestar Galactica* Says Everything and Nothing." Potter and Marshall, *Cylons* 171–84.

Gunn, Joshua, and David E. Beard. "On the Apocalyptic Sublime." *Southern Communication Journal* 65.4 (2000): 269–86. *Taylor & Francis Online.* Web. 28 Dec. 2014.

Hawk, Julie. "Objet 8 and the Cylon Remainder: Posthuman Subjectivization in *Battlestar Galactica.*" *Journal of Popular Culture* 44.1 (2011): 3–15. *Wiley Online Library.* Web. 28 Dec. 2014.

Kermode, Frank. *The Sense of an Ending: Studies in the Theory of Fiction.* 1967. London: Oxford University Press, 1968. Print.

McGinn, Bernard. *Visions of the End: Apocalyptic Traditions in the Middle Ages.* New York: Columbia University Press, 1979. Print.

Milford, Mike, and Robert C. Rowland. "Situated Ideological Allegory and *Battlestar Galactica.*" *Western Journal of Communication* 76.5 (2012): 536–51. *Taylor & Francis Online.* Web. 26 Oct. 2014.

Miller, Sam J. "Not in Our Stars: The Betrayals of the *BSG* Finale." *Galactica Sitrep.* 16 Apr. 2009. Web. 26 Oct. 2014.

Moore, Ronald D. *Battlestar Galactica: Series Bible.* 2003. Web. 26 Oct. 2014.

Mulligan, Rikk. "The Cain Mutiny: Reflecting the Faces of Military Leadership in a Time of Fear." Potter and Marshall, *Cylons* 52–63.

O'Leary, Stephen D. *Arguing the Apocalypse: A Theory of Millennial Rhetoric.* Oxford: Oxford University Press, 1998. Print.

Ott, Brian. "(Re)Framing Fear: Equipment for Living in a Post-9/11 World." Potter and Marshall, *Cylons* 13–26.

Pagano, David. "The Space of Apocalypse in Zombie Cinema." *Zombie Culture: Autopsies of the Living Dead.* Ed. Shawn McIntosh and Marc Leverette. Lanham: Scarecrow, 2008. Print.

"The Passage." *Battlestar Galactica.* Sci-Fi Channel. 8 Dec. 2006. Television.

Potter, Tiffany, and C. W. Marshall, eds. *Cylons in America: Critical Studies in* Battlestar Galactica. New York: Continuum, 2007. Print.

_____. "Remapping Terrorism Stereotypes in *Battlestar Galactica.*" *Muslims in American Popular Culture.* Ed. Anne R. Richards and Iraj Omidvar. Westport: Praeger, 2013. 61–72. Print.

"Resurrection Ship, Part II." *Battlestar Galactica.* Sci-Fi Channel. 13 Jan. 2006. Television.

Stephan, Matthias. "*Battlestar Galactica*: Not Your Father's Sci-Fi." *16:9* (in English) 10.46 (June 2012). Web. 26 Oct. 2014.

Stevenson, Gregory. "Apocalyptic War in *Buffy the Vampire Slayer, Angel, Supernatural,* and *Battlestar Galactica.*" *Small Screen Revelations: Apocalypse in Contemporary Television.* Ed. James Aston and John Walliss. Sheffield: Sheffield Phoenix Press, 2013. 96–117. Print.

Templeton, Brad. "Battlestar's 'Daybreak': The Worst Ending in the History of On-Screen Science Fiction." *Brad Ideas* 13 July 2009. Web. 26 Oct. 2014.

"33." *Battlestar Galactica.* Sci-Fi Channel. 14 Jan. 2005. Television.

The Emergence
of the Lost Apocalypse
from *28 Days Later*
to *Snowpiercer*

MARK MCCARTHY

Writing on the apocalypse made personal, Neil Gaiman noted, "There's no big apocalypse. Just an endless procession of little ones." One could point to the anticlimactic passing of Y2K or the end of the Mayan calendar as some of the more public but ultimately inconsequential "apocalypses" that have helped sustain our collective interest in the End Times. Television is currently peppered with shows of almost every format focused on the end of the world, from educational to reality to fiction. In film our interest is no less intense as filmmakers continue to bring "the end" to life. Although its popularity remains unabated, the form of the apocalypse in popular fiction has undergone a dramatic shift. Recent film and television treatments have begun to formulate an apocalypse that is markedly different from that of the last apocalyptic film cycle in the 1990s. In films like *Deep Impact*, *Armageddon*, and *Independence Day*, the apocalypse is simply an event to be overcome. These films represent a hopeful version of the apocalypse, showing us that when faced with the end of the world, "humanity's overriding task is to fathom the hidden patterns that reveal the true temporal and spatial contours of reality," allowing "humans to discern the proper avenue to follow..." (DiTommaso 225).

Post–9/11, however, the popular apocalypse has taken a pessimistic turn, evolving into something I call the "Lost Apocalypse." This vision of the end times is defined by a sense of fatalism that emphasizes the impotence of human action in the face of impending destruction. These narratives are situated in a world not far removed from our own and focus on a core group of survivors making their way through dangerous and shifting environments. There is an overarching sense of uncertainty and fear that is never resolved, suggesting that, in the long term, human survival is not possible. What, then, has changed, allowing the Lost Apocalypse to take hold? As Western society reorients itself to the future, films like *28 Days Later* (2002), *28 Weeks Later* (2007), *Dawn of the Dead* (2004), *Land of the Dead* (2005), *Children of Men* (2006), and *Snowpiercer* (2013) embody the growing sense of anxiety that comes with this change. They present worlds where death is imminent, tragedy is unavoidable, short-term survival is the best outcome one can hope for, and revelation will not bring salvation. No longer imagined in terms of progress, cultural narratives about the future are marked by uncertainty, fear, and danger. A quick scan of recent news headlines reveals that Ebola is once again an imminent threat to civilization, terrorist groups lurk at our borders, and all manner of storms have been upgraded to super-storm status. The twenty-four-hour news cycle frames the world at large through disaster narratives, contributing to a perpetual state of collective uncertainty. The result is a sense of anxiety that feeds off the anticipation of the next threat. This anxiety is not caused by any singular event; instead, it is made up of a number of contemporaneous discourses that intersect in such ways that concepts like risk, fear, and threat become affectively real, acting upon the individuals, institutions, and narratives that make up society so as to engender *more* fears and reproduce this aura of anxiety. According to the philosopher and cultural theorist Paul Virilio, fear is no longer an ephemeral state; it has become "an environment, a surrounding, a world" (14). Once a temporally and spatially localized event that could be identified, quarantined, and overcome, fear has become a defining characteristic of society that resonates throughout it.

The worlds of the Lost Apocalypse encapsulate an understanding of our contemporary society put forth by the works of Virilio, as well as sociologists Zygmunt Bauman and Ulrich Beck. Although their works are distinct, all of these scholars trace societal shifts that foster a general sense of anxiety. One major change is an abandonment of the notion that society can rely on the institutions of the past (for example, the government or the medical establishment) as sources of security. According to Bauman, the result is that the government can no longer safeguard a society that has grown increasingly wary that any federal institution has the power to provide protection from the onslaught of external threats—both enumerated and unknown (25). This is in part due to a sense of openness fostered by an increasingly globalized society where these established institutions lack the control necessary to provide stability or security, as well as media narratives that emphasize vulnerability at every turn. Responsibility has thus shifted to the individual who must be "always on," looking towards the future to guard against potential dangers. Bauman goes further, suggesting that it is unreasonable to believe that we can close ourselves off. In short, one cannot protect against an "outside" that no longer exists (6).

Further exacerbating this sense of anxiety is that society is also increasingly unable to find security through stability. Virilio suggests that society is entering a new nomadism, defined by "repeated exodus" (64). Humanity is swept up into a peripatetic state of being. Aided by communication technologies that allow you to feel at home anywhere, the value of any given location is de-emphasized, making movement more likely. Society is in the midst of a "mass claustrophobia" that is beginning to envelop it: "That is why movement, escape, exodus become permanent phenomena. The only solution now is to move constantly or flee definitively" (Virilio 67). This emphasis on motion, both technological and physical, is encapsulated in Virilio's concept of "accelerated reality," or the instantaneous nature of reality where events have become delocalized in such a way that when an event like a terror attack occurs, people across the globe are affected in real time. The immediacy produced by this constant state of motion and connectivity does not allow time for reflection, instead calling upon the "conditioned responses produced by emotion" (Virilio 31). For Virilio, anxiety and fear are produced because the cycle of action-reflection-reaction has been replaced by action-reaction. This reactive, and at times preemptive, orientation is partially the result of a new way of understanding risk.

Ulrich Beck argues that Western society has moved away from an empirical understanding of risk, where past indicators were used to make predictions about the future (e.g., actuary tables). Instead, society is focused on "manufactured uncertainties" that refer to an indeterminate future characterized by what *could* happen (216). We have "reverse[d] the relationship of past, present, and future" so that "the past loses its power to determine the present" (214). Further, risk is not simply the possibility that a chosen action will result in an undesirable outcome (the classic definition), but rather it has become a discourse unto itself that positions the world in an "intermediate state" of the "no-longer-but-not-yet" (213). The focus is thus on the future as breeding ground of an indeterminate number of new and dangerous threats.

These conceptual shifts in how society frames and understands the world at large have led to an aura of anxiety that manifests itself through pessimism, fear, loneliness—and the frenetic narratives of the Lost Apocalypse. In these worlds safety is still promised in the spaces that contemporary society looks to for security, comfort, or guidance. Survivors risk their lives to make their way to malls, hospitals, churches, and military installations that promise refuge from the death and terror that surround them. What they inevitably find is that these spaces are no safer than the open road and that fellow survivors are some of their most dangerous enemies. Much of the narrative in *28 Days Later* follows the flight of a core group of survivors from infested London to a militarized country estate that promises safety and "the answer to infection." Selena, Jim, Hannah, and Frank are in constant motion, fleeing the city and fighting their way through the zombie-like infected, notable for their violent, animal-like behavior—and their extreme speed.

The film constantly reminds you that any promise of respite is a cruel joke. Jim's journey through London is shown through extreme long shots that show how alone he is. Lulled by the silence that has overtaken the once bustling city, Jim approaches an abandoned Mercedes before the quiet is destroyed by the shrill pierce of the car's alarm. Jim slowly begins to learn the scope of the situation as he reads through newspaper headlines about the refugee crisis created by Britain's "mass exodus." Shortly after, Jim stumbles into a church littered with corpses. Looking out, he says "hello" just loud enough to rouse the living infected, including a priest who chases him out into the dark streets. It quickly becomes clear that for Jim and the hundreds of dead that line the pews, this space that promised refuge is anything but safe. Even times of rest are marked by frantic danger as Jim's sleep is tainted by nightmares that rival his reality. These scenes evoke a sense of instability, danger, and somnolence, bringing to life Bauman's idea of "the permanence of transitoriness" that threatens both the refugee and those who inhabit the spaces that migration flows through (47). Movement in this sense is as corrosive as it is constant.

Time and again, the theme of perpetual motion presents itself in the Lost Apocalypse as the survivors are lured by the supposed safety of a given locale only to be thrust into danger again. Conversely to the focus on one individual at the beginning of *28 Days Later*, its sequel, *28 Weeks Later*, opens with a small band of survivors eking out an existence in a country cottage just before they are attacked by a horde of infected. As they are attacked, one of the survivors, Don, abandons the others in a frantic attempt to get away. He is soon reunited with his children in the "green zone," a militarized section of London set up by the American military. The children avoided the initial plague event and have been living in a Spanish refugee camp ever since. Their rest is short lived, as the safety of the green zone is soon shattered and the remaining survivors are forced again to flee. The children, Tammy and Andy, have barely settled into their new home when they decide to return to their real pre-crisis home. This flight, first on foot and then on a "stolen" moped, sets into motion the rest of the film's action. Upon arriving home, they soon realize that this supposedly abandoned, and thus safe, space is where their mother (an almost asymptomatic carrier of the Rage virus) has been hiding. All three are brought back into the green zone where the mother infects Don, who goes on a violent rampage infecting untold others. The safety of the green zone has been shattered, and the English refugees (healthy and infected) are herded into yet another "safe space" underground. The infected quickly tear through the others, causing a mass exodus into the streets on the Isle of Dogs. The rest of the film follows the children and their companions as they flee both the infected and the U.S. military (the soldiers tasked with killing anything that moves). The children's flight continues through the streets, parks, and subways to what we are finally led to believe is a helicopter trip across the English Channel. The final chilling moments are shaky shots following a horde of infected as they emerge from a French subway tunnel, the Eiffel Tower in the distance, a terrifying realization of Virilio's prediction that we will soon be caught between constant motion or unending flight.

Snowpiercer (2013) takes motion as a central theme more directly. In this film, the last surviving members of humanity reside on a train, positioned as a perpetual motion machine that circles the Earth. After humanity's failed attempt to combat climate change renders the Earth a frozen wasteland, the Snowpiercer acts as a futuristic Ark. The key to sustaining its operation is its continuous journey around the Earth's now connected rail lines; the train must remain in motion in order to sustain life, or as the children sing in one scene, "What happens if the engine stops? We'll all freeze and die." The train's population is stratified between extreme poverty and opulence, creating a friction that the narrative attempts to resolve. After the train's authorities commandeer several children, the protagonist, Curtis, leads a charge towards the engine car in order to wrest control from Wilford, both the inventor of the train and its autocratic ruler. The group of "tail dwellers" fight their way from car to car, each moment of rest shattered by increasingly violent attacks that force them forward. In fact, each moment of respite becomes increasingly surreal. Take, for example, the mid-journey lunch of sushi that is prepared for the insurgents under the fish-filled glass walls of the aquarium car. It soon becomes apparent that it is not just the train forced forward in perpetuity; so, too, is this group of revolutionaries. When Curtis confronts Wilford, the narrative reveals that this is not the first time that the inhabitants of the back cars have made this violent journey, that, in fact, it is part of a repeated culling. Both the circuitous route of the train and the repeated (yet thus far impotent) revolutions serve as metaphors for the exhausting pursuit of progress. This sort of progress offers no place of rest or goal to be achieved, but is instead indicative of a life of motion for motion's sake, or as Virilio states, our understanding of progress has changed so that we are "constantly preoccupied with progress and perpetually *occupied* with it" (47, emphasis in original). The by-product is a cultural anxiety that comes with this paradigm of progress. It ensures that we are constantly gripped by feelings of being "always behind," always catching up (Virilio 47).

The protagonists of the film *Children of Men* also find themselves in constant flight. Set in a world that is dying because fertility rates have dropped to zero, the storyline follows the disillusioned Theo as he attempts to smuggle a young West African immigrant named Kee out of Britain to safety. Kee is vital to the world's survival because she is pregnant—the first pregnant woman in eighteen years. Theo and Kee make their way through various spaces that promise shelter (safe house, cabin, refugee camp) as they attempt to rendezvous offshore with a ship (aptly named *Tomorrow*) that promises to take Kee to real safety. Throughout the film, Theo and Kee are allowed to catch their breath just long enough for any sense of security to be shattered by violence and a push forward. One such scene shows Theo letting his guard down for the first time as he and Julian, both his ex-wife and leader of the militant immigrants rights group, the Fishes, reminisce through a party trick where they shoot and catch a ping pong ball in their mouths. Seconds after they begin, the group is ambushed and Julian is dead. The pace and tenor of this scene are repeated throughout the film, with relatively brief scenes featuring moments of intimate human connection cut short by encroaching violence and the impetus to flee. The illusion of safety is framed as a requisite precursor of the violence that keeps Theo and Kee in constant motion.

The search for safe spaces is also at the heart of *28 Days Later*. The film plays against the assumption that conventional institutions offer the protection that we are assured they do. Churches are dens for the infected, "homes" are nothing more than nostalgic traps as they are either easily breached or sites that promise a slow death through attrition, and the military (what is left of the old world government) is in the service of protecting themselves over others. When the survivors arrive at a military compound, they are welcomed; however, shortly thereafter, they are told of their "reward": Selena and Hannah, as the only women survivors, are to be systematically gang raped by soldiers primarily in the name of maintaining morale. The promised return to normalcy is not in the form of rebuilding society, but in the subjugation and sexual abuse of these women so that the soldiers might carry on. In the end, Selena, Jim, and Hannah fight their way to survival and remind us of a lesson of the Lost Apocalypse: trust is reserved for those closest to you since everyone else is a potential threat and likely enemy. Or, or as the season three tagline of *The Walking Dead* proclaimed, "Fight the dead. Fear the living."

This sense of mistrust is repeated throughout Lost Apocalypse narratives. In the millennial remake of *Dawn of the Dead*, each survivor approaches the next with a sense of mistrust. The action begins when Ana's husband is infected by a bite to the neck from their young neighbor. Ana is driven from her home, and we are shown that the safety the home represents is illusory as zombies tear through the suburban neighborhood. In her first encounter with fellow survivor Kenneth, Ana is greeted with a shotgun leveled at her face until she can prove she is alive. Shortly after, other survivors shoot at Ana and Kenneth before they all decide to join together. On the surface, these reactions may seem like simple exercises of caution, but the interaction with other humans encapsulates the relationship between discrete groups of survivors in these films. Barely surviving a series of zombie attacks in the mall, the five original survivors are greeted by several mall security guards, with guns drawn, who tell them to "find someplace else." After begging for refuge, they are treated like prisoners until they overtake their captors during an argument about "letting the wrong ones in."

This message resonates through the films of the Lost Apocalypse, and like the mall in *Dawn of the Dead*, "safe" spaces become the physical manifestation of the desire to separate oneself from the always dangerous Other. These spaces bring to life the sense of security that border spaces are meant to evoke. Conceptually, however, the border has shifted from liminal space to the locus of advanced flows of people, ideas, and capital. Borders have become increasingly permeable due to geographical instability, economic disparity, free trade agreements, communication technologies, and other phenomena that we collectively term globalization. As a cultural site, national borders are no longer seen simply as spaces of differentiation; they have become rearticulated in the face of changing global structures and flows (Shome and Hegde 174). The concepts of inside and outside have been drastically reshaped to the point that it becomes increasingly difficult to draw distinctions between the two. For reasons ranging from policy changes to advancements in information technology, threats emanating from job insecurity, terrorism, or biological contagion are at once global *and* local issues. Bauman asserts that this openness (perceived and realized) is responsible for a societal sense of vulnerability that begets an atmosphere of anxiety. As a result, risk, fear, safety, and security have become commoditized. The potential violent actions of others are used to sell everything from gated communities and tasers to sport utility vehicles, "And so it is personal safety that has become a major, perhaps even the major selling point in all sorts of marketing strategies" (Bauman 12).

These strategies are at play in *Land of the Dead* (2005). A major part of the narrative focuses on the marking and policing of space, specifically of the luxury high-rise Fiddler's Green and the shantytown that surrounds it. In one particular scene, a commercial plays in the background. In an attempt to capitalize on the power of exclusion in pre-apocalypse Pittsburgh, the advertisement boasts that Fiddler's Green is "Bordered on three sides by mighty rivers.... There is a difference between our place and other places. If you can appreciate that difference ... why not join us at Fiddler's Green?" This pitch, just as effective in both pre- and postapocalyptic Pittsburgh as it would be in many parts of the United States today, relies on a manufactured sense of security created through the mobilizations of real and virtual borders. Jan Aart Scholte explains that "Until recently, social geography across the world had a territorialist character" that took shape by way of the mythical border that simply "refers to a line on this map which divides tracts on the earth's surface from each other" (47). The pre-apocalyptic Fiddler's Green epitomizes this character by emphasizing the natural physical barriers of "three mighty rivers" as a stand-in for the real exclusionary mechanisms of class and economics. These mechanisms are no less powerful after the apocalypse, when Fiddler's Green continues to exclude the undesirable, in this case any non-white or poor survivors—forcing them to live as human shields in the shantytown that buttresses the Green.

Given that life in these films has been reduced to a frantic dash from one tragedy to another, the question then becomes, "To what end?" In short, the answer is not a happy one. The films of the Lost Apocalypse are marked by a sense of pessimism that stands in stark contrast to the apocalyptic films of previous decades. There is no salvation on the other side, no society worth rebuilding. Instead, the narratives are left open-ended, revealing just enough of the future as if to say "good luck." Take the final scene of *28 Days Later*, featuring Selena at a sewing machine refashioning the hand-chosen dress that she was to have been raped in. On its own, this scene may seem innocuous, but knowing Selena's personal journey, it hints at something darker. As an audience, we witnessed her transformation from the strongest survivor into this paragon of domesticity. Through her virtual castration (the soldiers strip her of her machete and masculine clothing while sexually taunting her) and the threat of rape, Selena shrinks to make room for Jim to assert himself as the patriarch of their cobbled-together family. *Children of Men* closes on a seemingly ambiguous note when, in the final moments of the film, Theo succumbs to bullet wounds just as the rescue ship makes its way through dense fog to rescue Kee and her newborn child. This ending may point to a hopeful resolution, especially given the ship's name (*Tomorrow*) and its fortuitous timing. I would suggest, however, that the images and events may be just as indicative of a bleaker outcome. The structure and content of this final scene point back to earlier moments of respite that immediately preceded acts of violence followed by frantic flight, suggesting that this cycle will continue. The narrative reality is that this young girl is apparently the only human out of billions not stricken by infertility. Moreover, throughout the film Kee is as much a political pawn as she is a medical curiosity, and her "rescue" by boat suggests that like her past, her future will be defined by transience. Even the cinematography maintains the atmosphere of hopelessness that pervades the film. The same blue-gray tones saturate the screen; the dense grimy fog limits visibility to a few yards, recalling the claustrophobia of the earlier urban scenes; and the ship is no more than a fishing vessel dwarfed by the massiveness of the sea. Like other futureless apocalypse texts, *Children of Men* explores the tension between forced inertia and claustrophobia to represent a general sense of anxiety in Western culture at large.

The final moments of *Snowpiercer* capitalize on this tension even more. In the last few scenes the narrative takes on a not so thinly veiled critique of the "one percent," as the film's antagonist, Wilford, explains to Curtis the need to manufacture fear and uncertainty to maintain order and keep people in their pre-ordained places. Wilford's speech signals a clear indictment of the attitudes, institutions, and structures responsible for the recent real-world financial crisis, as well as the inequities of late capitalism at large. Shortly after, a makeshift bomb blows open the train, causing a giant avalanche that knocks most of the train cars down a mountain and buries the rest. The first car has made it through the disaster with Yona and Timmy (one of the stolen children) intact, seemingly the only survivors of the massive Snowpiercer. After fashioning some snow boots for both and a remarkably well fitting fur coat for Timmy, they step out into the snow and catch sight of a polar bear in the distance before the film fades to black. True to fashion for the Lost Apocalypse, on the surface this ending is hopeful. It would seem that Yona's father, Nam, was right; not *all* life was destroyed, and stepping foot outside of the train is not an instant death sentence. Yet clearly, Yona and Timmy are ill equipped to survive in the frozen wasteland, and even if they survive long enough for Timmy reach puberty, the repopulation of the Earth would require a Genesis-like miracle. More than a final call towards the suspension of disbelief, these final moments represent both a rejection of the exploitation of late capitalism and an inability (or unwillingness) to imagine any alternative.

Finally, the most overt example of an unwillingness to provide closure can be found in the final moments of the remade *Dawn of the Dead*. Ana, Kenneth, Nicole, Terry, and Chips (the dog) make their way by boat to an island in the middle of Lake Michigan. Their perilous flight, it would seem, has paid off—that is, until their fate is intimated through a series of scenes interspersed within the credits. These last moments, presented in the style of a camcorder recording, show their arrival on the island—where they are promptly attacked by a fresh horde of zombies. The camcorder falls to the ground, and while the ending is technically left open, given that they are now stranded on an unfamiliar island with no functioning boat to help them escape, we may assume that we have witnessed their last frantic moments. In these final scenes, like those of all of our examples, we are robbed of the satisfaction of closure. What remains is an avoidance of either a radical re-imagination of our world or its complete destruction. Just as the procession of real and manufactured crises in Western society mingles optimism and anxiety (in the anticipation of respite and the next threat respectively), these films end with just the slightest amount of hope mixed with the grim reality of these situations. The pessimistic inaction of the Lost Apocalypse makes real the aura of anxiety produced by the narrative of threat that is privileged today. An exhausted reflection, these films seem to suggest that at the end there will be no bang, no whimper, but rather an exasperated shrug that encapsulates a desire for change and the lack of will to make it happen. In that shrug, we, too, experience the perpetual tragedy that is the Lost Apocalypse.

Works Cited

Armageddon. Dir. Michael Bay. Buena Vista Pictures, 1998. Film.

Bauman, Zygmunt. *Liquid Times: Living in an Age of Uncertainty*. Cambridge: Polity Press, 2007. Print.

Beck, Ulrich. "Risk Society Revisited: Theory, Politics, and Research Programmes." *The Risk Society and Beyond: Critical Issues for Social Theory*. Ed. Barbara Adam and Joost van Loon. London: SAGE, 2000. *Open WorldCat*. Web. 7 Dec. 2012.

Children of Men. Dir. Alfonso Cuarón. Universal Pictures, 2006. Film.

Dawn of the Dead. Dir. Zack Snyder. Universal, 2004. Film.

Deep Impact. Dir. Mimi Leder. Paramount, 1998. Film.

DiTommaso, Lorenzo. "At the Edge of Tomorrow: Apocalypticism and Science Fiction." *End of Days: Essays on the Apocalypse from Antiquity to Modernity*. Ed. Karolyn Kinane and Michael Ryan. Jefferson: McFarland, 2009. 221–41. Print.

Gaiman, Neil. *Signal to Noise*. 2nd ed. Illustrated by Dave McKean. Milwaukee: Dark Horse, 2007. Print.

Independence Day. Dir. Roland Emmerich. Twentieth Century Fox, 1996. Film.

Land of the Dead. Dir. George Romero. Universal, 2005. DVD.

Scholte, Jan Aart. *Globalization: A Critical Introduction*. New York: St. Martin's, 2000. Print.

Shome, Raka, and Radha Hegde. "Culture, Communication, and the Challenge of Globalization." *Critical Studies in Media Communication* 19.2 (2002): 172–89. Web. 3 Nov. 2013.

Snowpiercer. Dir. Bong Joon-ho. RADiUS-TWC, 2013. Film.

28 Days Later. Dir. Danny Boyle. Fox Searchlight, 2002. Film.

28 Weeks Later. Dir. Juan Carlos Fresnadillo. Twentieth Century Fox, 2007. Film.

Virilio, Paul. *The Administration of Fear*. Los Angeles: Semiotext(e), 2012. Print.

The Walking Dead. Created by Frank Darabont. AMC. 2010 to present. Television.

Going Viral in a World Gone Global

How Contagion *Reinvents the Outbreak Narrative*

DAHLIA SCHWEITZER

Global and near-global pandemics are nothing new. However, the specific connection between globalization and disease transmission is new, as is the presence of a hysteria-inducing, disaster-driven news-media culture. Beginning with AIDS and its African mythology, then with other diseases, including SARS, Ebola, and H1N1, there has been an emphasis not merely on the way disease is transmitted, but also on the way information is being communicated. Another crucial factor is that not only do poor countries lack the ability "to monitor outbreaks and isolate and care for victims of an epidemic," but also, as Charles Kenny notes, the World Health Organization's budget has been in steady decline since 2011, with a little less than $500,000 spent per African country. Kenny also points out that "the U.S. Centers for Disease Control had a 2013 budget of $45 million for global disease detection and response—3 percent of what the country spends on baldness treatments each year." The increased compression of the world has created a ticking time bomb, with epidemics poised to strike and travel, making their way around the world before the world even knows what is happening.

Unsurprisingly, filmmakers and writers, whether consciously or subconsciously, have responded to this potential crisis. Films like Steven Soderbergh's *Contagion* (2011) depict the now traditional outbreak narrative in which the Centers for Disease Control (CDC) and the World Health Organization (WHO) struggle to keep up with a terrifying epidemic, demonstrating both the failure of global boundaries and our anxieties surrounding the revelation that these constructed barriers are not as real as we wish them to be.

In contrast, older films like *Outbreak* (a 1995 movie in which an Ebolaesque virus spreads from Africa to the small American town of Cedar Creek) and both the 1971 and 2008 versions of *The Andromeda Strain* (wherein a team of scientists try to isolate and neutralize a deadly organism from outer space that causes fatal blood clotting) paint a localized understanding of the world that feels dated by comparison. Nothing literally leaks in *The Andromeda Strain* (since the victim's blood turns into powder), and the leakage is minimal and geographically contained in *Outbreak*. In *Contagion*, however, the boundaries themselves leak.

Other contemporary disease/disaster media narratives depict different permutations of this new globalized narrative. For example, *World War Z* (2013) depicts zombies almost taking over the world. In the televised series adapted from Guillermo del Toro and Chuck Hogan's *The Strain* trilogy, a virus turns people into vampires and spreads throughout New York before devastating the world. Finally, the long running *Resident Evil* franchise (2002–16) explores the gory repercussions following the release of a deadly bio-weapon created by the Umbrella Corporation. In these texts and others, the traditional outbreak story has morphed to reflect contemporary anxieties evolving like viruses themselves, character tropes of vampires and zombies fusing with the biological model of viral infection, all existing in a liminal state between living and dead, and all existing now on a global scale.

The various permutations of the contemporary outbreak narrative reveal an awareness of the permeable boundaries between the personal body and the body politic, between nations, and between "ordinary" people and potentially "dangerous" disenfranchised groups, often perceived as sources of contagion, in addition to reflecting the cultural trauma that comes as a response to the realities of global contagion. These contemporary anxieties are representative of this new type of trauma, a product of our current globalized world and the epidemics that can—and do—infect it. *Contagion* and its contemporaries demonstrate the increasingly globalized nature of disease and its inevitable integration into—and impact upon—contemporary life.

In *Contagion*, the original source of the virus is left unrevealed until the end of the film. All we know initially is that it is first spread by Beth Emhoff, who transports the virus from Hong Kong to Chicago, where she has sex with an old lover, before heading home to her son and husband in Minneapolis. Her symptoms quickly worsen, and she dies suddenly, mere minutes into the film. Shortly thereafter, her son also dies. Her husband, Mitch, is mysteriously immune, but, unfortunately, like Cedar Creek, his town is quarantined so that he and his daughter cannot leave. Unlike Cedar Creek, however, where the residents are well-behaved, Mitch's town descends into chaos and looting. The National Guard merely prevents people from going in and out but does not maintain order within the town itself—a far cry from the Guard's official mission of duty and service. In this situation, the Guard does not want to get involved because entering the city means possible—likely—contamination. But the National Guard also does not enter because its members do not care about the residents. Security does not mean protection but *containment*, keeping the infected away from the uninfected. The infected are written off as worthless, and all that matters is keeping them inside. The National Guard shields the borders while the disease rages within, demonstrating one of many instances where the military and the medical come together, while also making visible the permeability of boundaries, both on a body level and on a political level. Biological security becomes political security.

Security—and how to maintain it—is a pervasive theme in all contagion narratives. The traditional understanding of contagion hinges precisely on the dangers of close contact, underscoring a literal threat for bodily boundaries, but contagion can also be seen as a metaphoric threat for larger, national boundaries. T-cells (try to) defend our bodies much as soldiers (try to) defend our borders. When governments turn to a nuclear bomb as their final recourse, there is a collapse of scale that underscores the intertwining between military/government and health. This is the relationship between a minuscule and personal war on a virus inside your body and a massive and impersonal war on the bodies of the infected, the physical and external manifestation of the virus's handiwork. In both *The Andromeda Strain* and *Outbreak*, the government's response to the respective epidemics is to threaten to blast away the infected area with a nuclear bomb. In *Resident Evil: Apocalypse*, the second film in the series, the all-controlling Umbrella Corporation actually does this, annihilating Raccoon City. When the virus is localized, a nuclear bomb is considered a viable option, having gone from being the ultimate threat to being the lesser of two evils. Even if it is the wrong move—which all the films emphasize that it is, largely because of the innocent civilians caught in the blast—it still goes from being the unthinkable to being a seemingly reasonable Plan B. This not only demonstrates the sheer magnitude of the virus and the inability of authorities to deal with it on a more humane level, but also emphasizes the fusion between military and health services. This fusion is made insidiously explicit in the first *Resident Evil* film, where the Umbrella Corporation is a global leader in both healthcare and military equipment, significantly bio-warfare items. In season one of *The Strain*, a computer virus is created to knock out power and destroy the infrastructure of New York City. While not nuclear annihilation, this is still debilitating to a contemporary society heavily reliant on technology and power. In *Contagion*, as in *World War Z*, the disease has gone too far, infected too many people, for a nuclear solution. A single nuclear bomb would no longer solve anything. You would have to blow up the world.

Contagion depicts the urgency with which the Department of Homeland

Security (DHS), the WHO, and the CDC try to determine if the virus is a bioweapon, where it came from, and how to stop it. The efforts of all these agencies (or networks) are in opposition to those of Alan Krumwiede. A conspiracy theorist, he posts videos and essays about the disease on his popular blog, his accusations going "viral," leading to actual riots, a metaphor for the rapid and even toxic spread of information in our contemporary society. Networks, seemingly secure and pervasive, appear to be no match for viruses, either literal or metaphorical. As a one-man source of interference, Krumwiede condemns the government for inaction before being exposed as a tool for a company selling Forsythia, a supposed cure for the virus.

Eventually, the CDC manages to identify a potential vaccine. To bypass the time it would take to complete official drug testing through government-mandated safety protocols, Dr. Hextall heroically injects herself with the vaccine before visiting her virus-ridden father. Once the vaccine's efficacy is confirmed, the CDC begins to distribute it through a lottery system. By this point, the global death toll has reached twenty-six million.

The film's final sequence interrupts the otherwise linear progression of the film to flash back to the very beginning, gradually revealing the virus's origin. First, a bulldozer for Beth Emhoff's company razes a tree for an unexplained demolition project, sending displaced bats flying over a pig farm, where a bat drops a piece of fruit. This fruit is then eaten by a pig that is shipped to a restaurant to be cooked, where a Chinese chef with poor hygiene habits spreads it to Beth Emhoff by shaking her hand. The last moments of the film emphasize its critique of global corporate capitalism and environmental destruction with strong racial and gender inflections. Interestingly, pinning the blame on these two figures, the dirty Chinese and the cheating blonde, feels heavy-handed and ideologically suspect, especially for a film otherwise devoted to accuracy and realism.

The emphasis on accuracy in *Contagion* is especially relevant, and not only because it is in marked contrast to the overly simplistic disease vector from which the virus originates. Unlike other films in the disaster genre, *Contagion* is not a fantastical film with an implausible or futuristic scenario. Rather than being typical science fiction, it is a fictional film about science— and a highly realistic one at that. Disaster and science fiction films and series are often characterized by excess, e.g., asteroids hurtling towards Earth or a man turning into an insect. *World War Z* and *The Strain* paint spectacularly melodramatic portraits of apocalyptic futures full of zombies, vampires, and destruction. *Contagion* is much more minimalist and realistic—and that is precisely why it is so chilling. Its accuracy of detail enhances the realism, not only in its scientific terminology but also in the design of its laboratories and the presentation of preventative gear and equipment. The removal of most traces of fantasy arguably heightens "the engagement with reality and with the experience of trauma" (Hallam 234). This *could* happen, the film seems to say, emphasizing data, numbers, maps, and scientific terminology. The film details not merely what could happen but also *how* it will happen. Or, as *Contagion* screenwriter Scott Z. Burns says, "I was certainly aware there were other pandemic movies, but I wanted to do one that really felt like what could happen…. The point of view of people within that field isn't 'If this is going to happen,' it's 'When is this going to happen?'" (qtd. in Douglas). *Contagion* is not about the distant future but about a possible today.

Another crucial element of the outbreak narrative is "Othering," which functions as a way of trying to establish boundaries to create a semblance of protection. Steven Pokornowski has argued, "The privileging of military and medical authority in the drive for security [suggests] that to sympathize with the other—be it a virus, a zombie, or just a different human—is deadly" (218). Even more crucially, Priscilla Wald had earlier observed that outbreak narratives themselves either "promote or mitigate the stigmatizing of individuals, groups, populations, locales (regional and global), behaviors, and lifestyles … [reinforcing] the almost suspicious belief that national borders can afford protection against communicable disease" (3, 8). Disease is consistently imagined as a foreign threat, and, since the Cold War era, "disease language" has been used in military contexts and vice versa. In most contagion narratives, the virus comes from the outside in, either from outer space (*The Andromeda Strain*) or from "uncivilized primitives" or even actual primates in Africa or Asia (*Outbreak, Contagion,* and *World War Z*). Donna Haraway has theorized, "In the face of the disease genocides accompanying European 'penetration' of the globe, the 'colored' body of the colonized was constructed as the dark source of infection, pollution, disorder, etc., that threatened to overwhelm white manhood (cities, civilization, the family, the white personal body)" (219). Diseases are often blamed on an unfortunate group, while modernization is offered as the antidote to the diseased and dangerous relics of primitive space and behavior. Thus, outbreak narratives offer not only a way to reflect on how a disease might spread but also a way to place blame.

However, this is where *Contagion* complicates matters, indicating shifting understandings of both modernization and globalization. In *Contagion*, the disease may originate in "dirty" Asia, but it is brought back to America by a blonde with immoral behavior. Its "root" cause can be traced to the action of an American company and its transmission to none other than the company's Global Operations Manager, the whiter-than-white Beth. Lindsay Hallam writes that in the slasher films of the 1980s, "made just as the AIDS epidemic was beginning, having sex is a sure fire way to get yourself killed," while in a torture porn film, "the worst thing you can do is go travelling" (231). In *Contagion*, it appears, the worst thing you can do is have sex *while* travelling, and the second-worst thing you can do is travel. If Beth had just stayed home, none of this would have happened. If an American company had not torn down forests in Asia, none of this would have happened. If the Asian chef had washed his hands or worn gloves, none of this would have happened. But the worst villains are the greedy corporation and the cheating spouse, both of whom ignore their respective boundaries. Even the chef, however, lets the pig's blood travel out of the kitchen and onto Beth's hands. *Contagion* shows the repercussions of disrespecting boundaries by exposing consequences, by making visible the constant and impossible-to-control flow of bodies, goods, and information in our twenty-first-century life.

The invisible made visible is seen repeatedly in outbreak narratives. Wald observes, "Outbreak stories convey … the ability to make the unseen world appear. Visual technologies, from electron microscopes to epidemiological maps and charts, are an important part of the outbreak narrative … express[ing] the ambiguous geography of an interconnected world" (37). Viewers see not only the virus but also the paths the virus takes, the actual transmission of the disease as it is traced, studied, and (possibly) neutralized. In *Contagion* and *Outbreak*, we have shot after shot of charts visualizing the virus's spread, reminders that globalization has only exacerbated the speed with which disease—and panic—can travel in a world reimagined "as a geography of bounded zones of containment, protection, and vulnerability" (Magnusson and Zalloua 7). Most alarming, however, is that despite this emphasis on making the invisible visible, technology has limits. Digital models may help identify the virus, but they cannot reveal the economic, political, and social forces behind it. Caetlin Benson-Allott has referenced a chilling scene in *Contagion* in which Dr. Ian Sussman sits in a café, staring at the objects around him—a counter, a cookie, a glass—seeing them as the contagious surfaces they are. He is not "accessing any new visual information; rather he recognizes the insufficiency of computer-generated imagery to explain this medical disaster" (15).

Human networks have become "conduits of viral destruction," with air travel, in particular, making "especially apparent the intricate networks of human existence and human interdependence" (Wald 4, 22). Epidemics have collapsed time and space since the mid-nineteenth century, "rendering seemingly stable geopolitical and biological distinctions tenuous, if not moot" (Cohen 17), but this kind of collapse has become even more pronounced in the twenty-first century, as technology persistently shrinks the world and changes our relationship to it. Ed Cohen argues that "[t]hese viral narratives challenge us precisely because they seem to revise, or 'rewrite,' the ways we like to make sense of ourselves as agents in the world" (17). *Contagion* and *World War Z* truly emphasize the frightening speed with which a virus can spread from one end of the world to the other, the intricately interlocked way in which the world now functions.

At the same time that global networks allow for (and encourage) the rapid spread of disease, they also enable the identification of these same diseases, as well as facilitate the dissemination of vaccines and/or antibodies. However, as depicted in *Contagion*, *Outbreak*, and *World War Z*, these international infrastructures also reflect the tensions between increased globalization and government regulation, between the local and the national as well as between the national and the global. Even though the films may have "happy" endings ("happy" being a relative term since the death tolls are anything but), these narratives expose how faulty existing regulations or infrastructures can be when it comes to dealing with any large-scale threat. Yet these narratives simultaneously remind us that infrastructure, the "global linkage across organizations, professions, and populations" (Magnusson and Zalloua 9), may be the only thing that can save us. Michel Foucault argues that "the concept of public health was formative for modern society, and epidemics were important because they manifested the need for protection in the form of regimented social behavior" (qtd. in Wald 18). Outbreak narratives may imply that there is not *enough* protection or regulation. After all, lapses in both are what allow disease to spread.

There is a strong emphasis in many outbreak narratives on the role humankind plays either in causing the virus or spreading it, stressing the repercussions of our abuse and disrespect of the natural order of things. In *Contagion*, for instance, the virus is a direct result of excessive development, corporate greed stripping animals of their natural habitat. The global scale of the virus is a demonstration of just how easily viruses can travel thanks to modern life and the impossibility of any sort of realistic quarantine. In many ways, the film is an examination of the "development" of civilization. The history of civilization actually parallels the history of disease. As humankind grows more sophisticated, so does disease. As humans develop, they find more ways to exploit the Earth and its animals—and often end up paying the price. In his explanatory sequence, at the end of the film, Steven Soderbergh is not subtle. Globalization and modern living may have led to medical and technological advances, but they have also stripped away traditional food sources, both from people and animals, forcing both to eat what they would not normally eat as their traditional habitats are destroyed in the interest of capitalistic advancement. Environmental trespass breeds disease.

Films like *Resident Evil* and *World War Z* readily identify the infected, their "othered" status always apparent. Zombie films make the identification absolutely clear. *Contagion* is, arguably, a zombie film without zombies. After all, zombies are metaphorical equivalents of the fear of contagion and the loss of personal autonomy. Beyond this, Kyle Bishop argues, "Because the aftereffects of war, terrorism, and natural disasters so closely resemble the scenarios of zombie cinema ... [these scenarios have] all the more power to shock and terrify a population that has become otherwise jaded by more traditional horror films" (11). *Contagion* focuses on the aftereffects of a virus almost as terrifying as a zombie apocalypse. But at least in *Contagion*, the dead stay dead, allowing Soderbergh to make more complex statements about how the living respond not only to infection but to infected people. As Brent Bellamy explains, the film is "a study in global circulation, picturing the spread of the disease, press conferences, international and multinational video conferences, and ultimately, global circuits of capital in the form of commodity shipments earlier in the film and vaccine shipments later on" (119).

Certainly, other outbreak texts also function on a metaphorical level. *Resident Evil* engages with our fears of bio-terrorism, with the possibility that a deadly virus could get in the hands of the wrong people. There is also the possibility of error. Bill Albertini has noted that "one of the primary, if underexamined, genre conventions of the outbreak narrative is the common failure of the containment" (443). The more complex and deadly our weapons become, biochemical or otherwise, the greater the repercussions of a mistake or a leak. *World War Z*, as Jesse Kavadlo contends, "is not, in the end, about zombies. It is, of course, about people.... And so we see a story of struggle and sacrifice. In doing so, the 'Zombie War' depicted specifically evokes AIDS, civil war, nuclear strikes, geopolitical shifts, massive displacement, natural disaster, and more" (168). As Pokornowski writes, "Perhaps the reason that the zombie and the virus are so intimately bound to one another and so prominent in the cultural imagination is that they embody ... [a] spreading tendency toward threatening, unfamiliar changes. We can think of these narratives of bioinsecurity as preoccupied with anxiety about a shift in the social order" (229). Outbreak narratives in the millennium terrify us by demonstrating how quickly our world could go awry. In the blink of an eye, a virus travels from one body to the next, from one country to the next, decimating and destroying. We isolate ourselves with the hope that modern medicine and modern governments can save us, when the fear lurking within, the fear exposed in all these stories, is that when it gets this bad, nothing will save us.

Of all the outbreak narratives, *Contagion* is the one most like a cautionary tale, unfolding not as a thriller but with painstaking precision. Day two, day three, day ten—they all unfold one at a time, the death toll clinically calculated and recorded. There is no race to the cure. There is no hero or heroine who needs saving. The danger here is so massive, the death toll so enormous, that there is no way to process it on an emotional level. What would it even look like to have millions dead? Where would the bodies go? Where would food come from? How would we survive? The questions are large, theoretical, and impersonal—making *Contagion* an educational film. Yet it also reaches its audience in a way many entertainment films do not. As director Steven

Soderbergh said, in an interview shortly before the release of the film, "There's no way you can watch this movie and not be aware of what you touch…. There's no escape" (qtd. in Michals). This is what we are doing, Soderbergh seems to say in his film. This is what is happening.

In order to understand the transmission of viruses, the world needs to be recognized as a complex and interlocked system where barriers are just as ineffectual at keeping viruses *out* as they are at keeping viruses *in*. In the twenty-first century, the threat of contagion is no longer held over a singular body or a singular location but over a *transnational* body. In all the outbreak narratives, quarantine and containment are emphasized—but also fundamentally ineffectual. Our increased awareness of our vulnerability and of the deadly ramifications of our increasingly networked world makes contagion narratives all the more relevant. The directors and writers of these narratives have managed to crystallize and advance a whirlwind of complex phenomena, capturing the repercussions of the networked world in which we live. Global health and security have now become intertwined issues, threatened by the seemingly constant risk of worldwide infection. Globalization infects, and we see this in stories where boundaries are insecure and able to be transgressed, regardless of whether the infection is literal or metaphorical. In turn, in a viral fashion, these narratives potentially can lead to an increase in pandemic reporting, making us all the more on the lookout for juicy news and dramatic retellings. While some theorists argue that watching a film of something awful decreases one's sensitivity, films like *Contagion* serve to *increase* our awareness of infectious disease and our vulnerability to it. Along the same lines, the CDC has a "Zombie Apocalypse Defense Plan" as a means of better educating the public about mass disaster and contagion. Learning how to plan for these contingencies is the real point of the exercise, not the specific scenario. While outbreak narratives may be fictitious entertainments, more of them than just *Contagion* may serve an instructional purpose. Public responses to real-life outbreaks like Ebola and AIDS not only reflect cultural fears of contagion and disease but are also determined partially, and significantly, by the internal logic and workings of film and television narrative.

The popularity of images of contagion has resulted from the genuine need to find effective strategies for responding to infectious disease outbreaks, even as the increase in infectious disease outbreaks has led to the popularity of portrayals of contagion. Anxiety is both displaced, through a proliferation of outbreak narratives with tidy endings, and exacerbated, as evidenced by the recent Ebola panic, which bordered on hysteria even though it was never a significant threat to America. The viral spread of outbreaks is now metaphorically connected to the "viral" spread of digital communication and information (bad or good, true or false). Meanwhile, globalization's penetration of boundaries becomes a metaphor for the pathogenic spread of "foreign elements." During the November 2014 campaign season, former senator Scott Brown, running for another senate seat out of New Hampshire, managed to pull all these metaphors together in one dizzying array, predicting that ISIS terrorists would sneak in via "porous" boundaries to spread Ebola.[1]

Today, with travel and technology bringing us closer together through arrangements that are both more compact and more complex than ever before, a potential pandemic feels inevitable. There is no longer an "other" to be quarantined—and even if there were, how and where would the "other" be quarantined? There are no prophylactics big enough or strong enough, no impenetrable barriers left. So what happens after the disease gets in? If fear and panic spread like a virus, how do we manage the world? If this kind of pandemic is truly inevitable, humankind must look beyond the crisis to the aftermath.

NOTE

1. In an interview with WGIR radio that was captured by the New Hampshire Democratic Party, Brown was asked whether he favored travel restrictions on some passengers in and out of West Africa. He replied, "We need a comprehensive approach and I think that should be part of it. I think it's all connected. For example, we have people coming into our country by legal means bringing in diseases and other potential challenges. Yet we have a border that's so porous that anyone can walk across it. I think it's naive to think that people aren't going to be walking through here who have those types of diseases and/or other types of intent, criminal or terrorist. And yet we do nothing to secure our border" (qtd. in Sargent).

WORKS CITED

Albertini, Bill. "Contagion and the Necessary Accident." *Discourse* 30.3 (Fall 2008): 443–67. Print.

The Andromeda Strain. Dir. Mikael Salomon. A. S. Films, 2008. Film.

The Andromeda Strain. Dir. Robert Wise. Universal Pictures, 1971. Film.

Bellamy, Brent. "Contagion." *Science Fiction Film and Television* 6.1 (Spring 2013): 119–23. Print.

Benson-Allott, Caetlin. "Out of Sight." *Film Quarterly* 65.2 (Winter 2011): 14–15. Print.

Bishop, Kyle William. *American Zombie Gothic: The Rise and Fall (and Rise) of the Walking Dead in Popular Culture.* Jefferson: McFarland, 2009. Print.

Cohen, Ed. "The Paradoxical Politics of Viral Containment; or, How Scale Undoes Us One and All." *Social Text* 29.1/106 (Spring 2011): 15–35. Print.

Contagion. Dir. Steven Soderbergh. Warner Bros., 2011. Film.

Douglas, Edward. "Interview: *Contagion* Writer Scott Z. Burns." *Coming Soon.* Coming Soon, 6 Sept. 2011. Web. 21 Dec. 2014.

Hallam, Lindsay. "Genre Cinema as Trauma Cinema: Post 9/11 Trauma and the Rise of 'Torture Porn' in Recent Horror Films." *Trauma, Media, Art.* Ed. Mick Broderick and Antonio Traverso. Newcastle upon Tyne: Cambridge Scholars Publishing, 2010. 228–36. Print.

Haraway, Donna. "The Biopolitics of Postmodern Bodies: Determinations of Self in Immune System Discourse." *American Feminist Thought at Century's End.* Ed. Linda S. Kaufman. Cambridge: Blackwell, 1993. 199–233. Print.

Kavadlo, Jesse. "War on Terror: Amending Monsters After 9/11." *Humanities Review* 6.2 (Spring 2008): 165–76. Print.

Kenny, Charles. "The Ebola Outbreak Shows Why the Global Health System Is Broken." *Business Week*. Business Week, 11 Aug. 2014. Web. 21 Dec. 2014.

Magnusson, Bruce, and Zahi Zalloua. *Contagion: Health, Fear, Sovereignty*. Seattle: University of Washington Press, 2012. Print.

Michals, Susan. "'Contagion' Director on Washing Your Hands." *Wall Street Journal*. Dow Jones, 8 Sept. 2011. Web. 21 Dec. 2014.

Outbreak. Dir. Wolfgang Petersen. Warner Bros., 1995. Film.

Pokornowski, Steven. "Insecure Lives: Zombies, Global Health, and the Totalitarianism of Generalization." *Literature and Medicine* 31.2 (Fall 2013): 216–34. Print.

Resident Evil. Dir. Paul W. S. Anderson. Screen Gems, 2002. Film.

Resident Evil: Apocalypse. Dir. Alexander Witt. Screen Gems, 2004. Film.

Sargent, Greg. "Scott Brown: Anyone with Ebola Can 'Walk Across' Our 'Porous' Border." *Thewashingtonpost.com*. The Washington Post, 14 Oct. 2014. Web. 4 Dec. 2014.

The Strain. Created by Guillermo del Toro and Chuck Hogan. FX. 2014 to present. Television.

Wald, Priscilla. *Contagious: Cultures, Carriers, and the Outbreak Narrative*. Durham: Duke University Press. Print.

World War Z. Dir. Marc Foster. Paramount, 2013. Film.

The Second Coming of *Left Behind* and the Deglobalization of Christian Apocalypse

TIM BRYANT

In the 2014 remake of *Left Behind*, airline pilot Rayford "Ray" Steele's decision to return London flight PanCon 257 back to New York signals a dramatic denial of the global scope of Christian Apocalypse in contrast to the overall, globalizing claims of Tim LaHaye's and Jerry B. Jenkins's series. In an interview, Nicolas Cage explains that his own brother's faith inspired him to accept the lead role in the remake (Lee 22). Cage's celebrity status may also have been a factor in his casting, given the surge of participation in religious cinema by Hollywood actors during 2014: Kevin Sorbo in *God's Not Dead*, Russell Crowe in *Noah*, Greg Kinnear in *Heaven Is for Real,* and Christian Bale in *Exodus: Gods and Kings.* Approximating the apocalyptic vision of Crowe's Old Testament deluge and the spectacular plagues of Bale's *Exodus*, Cage's *Left Behind* finds itself caught between the ethos of such recent films' divine theatrics (in the tradition of Charlton Heston in the 1956 *The Ten Commandments*) and the proselytizing function of Sorbo's and Kinnear's more prosaic narratives. Glenn Shuck has identified the *Left Behind* franchise as emblematic of the contemporary fusion of Christian evangelism and an emergent "network culture" (1–2). Yet this most recent film also shies away from that fusion of secular technologies and evangelical faith. As a literal swerve toward and then away from international shores, the shape of Ray's boomerang flight signifies the conflicting directions the film wishes to take toward mass popularity and moral purpose—resulting in a spectacular failure to merge religious instruction and popular cinema. This struggle is yet another stage in the saga of the *Left Behind* franchise, its popular narratives of Christian Apocalypse having failed to take full flight past the original book series into other media outlets.

Left Behind imagines a confrontational Second Coming of Christ and catastrophic End of Days based on pre-millennial dispensationalist interpretations of the Biblical Apocalypse expressed in Old and New Testament prophecy, especially the Book of Revelation. The original twelve-book series narrates the efforts of those "left behind" (after the instantaneous and global disappearance of worthy believers) to fight for Christ against the Antichrist, incarnated on Earth as the politician Nicolae Carpathia. In the first book, *Left Behind: A Novel of the Earth's Last Days* (1995), the core group of characters—including Ray, his daughter Chloe, and globetrotting reporter Cameron "Buck" Williams—identify themselves as the "Tribulation Force" to signify their religious conversion and commitment to fight Carpathia during the prophesied seven years preceding Apocalypse. In the final book, *Glorious Appearing: The End of Days* (2004), Jesus appears in person to defeat Carpathia, casting him into Hell and ushering in the "Millennial Kingdom" as a thousand years of Heaven on Earth. Persuaded by the innumerable signs of Christian Apocalypse overtaking the world and Carpathia's infernal influence, the Steeles and Williams become holy warriors on a global scale throughout the series' creative renderings of Christian eschatology.

In contrast to secular science fiction television series premised on similar disappearances—e.g., USA's *The 4400* (2004–2007) and HBO's *The Leftovers* (2014 on)—*Left Behind* dispels narrative ambiguity in favor of moral assurance by grounding its storyline in adaptations of Biblical scripture. Indeed, various minor characters' guesses about the cause of the disappearances—"space aliens, germ gas, and death rays" (*Left Behind* 377)—prove feeble in contrast to the reasoning of the more spiritually and professionally minded protagonists. These adaptations, however creatively and necessarily they may depart from the Protestant tenet of *sola scriptura* (that "scripture alone" matters to salvation), nevertheless remain faithful in their intent to model in their narratives and effect in their readers a conversion to right belief. They may not be scripture, but they derive text, subtext, and context from it. This singular purpose remains consistent across a range of derivative media carrying the *Left Behind* name, including a young adult novel series (1997–2004), a trilogy of films starring Kirk Cameron (2000–2005), a ten-volume graphic-novel series (2002), authorized spin-off novels by Mel Odom (2003) and Neesa Hart (2004–2005), three additional prequel novels and one sequel novel by LaHaye and Jenkins (2005–2007), and four video games (2006–2011). All of these works refer to specific passages of prophecy from the Bible, intend to enact conversion, and assert a worldwide context as the arena of action. For example, in the franchise's series of video games—*Left Behind:*

Eternal Forces (2006), *Left Behind: Tribulation Forces* (2008), *Left Behind 3: Rise of the Antichrist* (2010), and *Left Behind 4: World at War* (2011)—players assume the roles of members of the Tribulation Force, fighting against the forces of Antichrist in major cities around the world. Angels fly above to lend aid while players fight in the streets. Despite the game manual's anxiously repetitive warnings that "salvation, not destruction, is the goal," the first and subsequent installments of the video game series feature a wide range of mundane weapons generically appropriate to action/adventure games (Jones 9). Players also fight spiritually by converting enemies to Christ, and may also pray for extra strength and healing. The game measures player success not primarily by the number of enemy combatants defeated, but by the number of non-player characters converted to Christ. As Marnie Jones notes, the *Left Behind* video games are infused with a conflicting message on the right means of conducting evangelic "holy war" via bloodless conversion or bloody violence (9).

The concrete effects of right belief emphasized by this kind of gameplay also persist from the original novels to the original film trilogy: *Left Behind: The Movie* (2000), *Left Behind II: Tribulation Force* (2002), and *Left Behind: World at War* (2005)—all featuring former child actor and born-again Christian Kirk Cameron as Buck Williams. In a pivotal moment featured in both LaHaye's first novel and Cameron's first film, Buck converts to right belief moments before attending a meeting in which the Antichrist Nicolae Carpathia murders two men and uses his supernatural powers to alter witnesses' memories of the event so that they recall it as a murder-suicide enacted by one of the slain men. Because of his timely conversion, however, Buck retains the true memory of the event, unbeknown to Carpathia, who continues to employ Buck in order to spread his influence through Buck's international news reportage. In a similar example of saving faith, in the third film of the original trilogy, President Gerald Fitzhugh miraculously survives and walks away from a fall off the top floor of a skyscraper after Carpathia ejects him via telekinetic defenestration. In both cases, faith preserves the minds and bodies of these evangelical warriors, whose work by definition carries global significance.

Despite these isolated acts of resistance, Carpathia retains a nearly unlimited range of influence, ascending to the post of Secretary-General of the United Nations before fully revealing himself as Antichrist. Although restricted to events from the first three books in the original set of novels, the film trilogy remains faithful to the series' global scope. Emphasizing the action/adventure and thriller genres of film with warfare and political intrigue, the series begins with Buck on assignment in a Middle Eastern country, the skies suddenly overcast by an impenetrable, global darkness that alludes to the fifth Bowl Judgment, one of seven plagues prophesied in Revelation 16. Buck's profession as international photojournalist supports the worldwide scope of action and universal application of Christian evangelism. As an international airline pilot, Ray presents another example of the secular professional whose duties functionally support the global context of the *Left Behind* narrative. The operations of these secular professions thus serve as narrative vehicles for the series' spiritual professions of faith.

With the exceptions of the bestselling novel series by LaHaye and Jenkins and its YA adaptations, however, this combination of secular and spiritual globalism has failed to capture a wide audience. While the manifold forms of American popular media have, historically, been effective vehicles for expressions of popular religion, *Left Behind* does not effectively translate its version of Christian evangelism (which joins visions of inevitable disaster to conditional hopes of redemption) into other forms. The derivative novels have not made bestseller lists outside specifically Christian publications. After a disastrous box office for the first of Cameron's films, the second two installments of the film trilogy were released directly to DVD. Of the four video games, the first three have been discontinued, and the fourth is available for free online. The graphic novel adaptation was canceled within its first year. After such commercial failures, the 2014 cinematic remake seems understandably hesitant to embrace fully the evangelical ethos of the past derivative media or its globalizing claims. Indeed, the remake retains the indispensable references to Christ, but removes all mention of Antichrist. Instead, it veers toward the dynamics of secular catastrophe reminiscent of 1970s disaster movies like *Airport* (1970), *The Poseidon Adventure* (1972), and *The Towering Inferno* (1974). The 2014 *Left Behind* attempts to communicate the sense of Apocalypse derived from scriptural precedent while appealing to a wider audience via the action-thriller ethos of a Hollywood blockbuster. Caught between two vastly divergent forms of fidelity—to Biblical prophecy and to cinematic artistry—the film chooses neither fully and thus fails to approximate the potential virtues of either. The recent return of *Left Behind* to the big screen signifies the struggles of Christian evangelists to craft their message within the tropes of an increasingly secularized popular imaginary of apocalypse.

The 2014 film retains the discourse of pre-millennialist Apocalypse while subduing its tone and conditioning its delivery in several ways. The first third of the film emphasizes the Steele family's melodramatic dissolution, which father and daughter blame on wife and mother Irene, recently converted to an unspecified form of evangelical Christianity. The divisive effect of the mother's religiosity materializes in a conversation with her daughter, a Bible lying on a table nearby while the two women speak. Chloe unintentionally insults her mother when she recounts how a "crazy woman" at the airport told her of the coming End Times. Later in the film, when Ray is puzzling out the cause of his passengers' sudden disappearances from the plane mid-flight, he sees "Bible Study" scheduled on a future date in a missing flight attendant's planner. The presence of scripture in these trace forms gestures to the film's subtext of Christian faith, far more muted here than in the original novels.

Occasionally, the film does convey the actual content of Biblical scripture. Upon discovering that his co-pilot is among those missing, Ray sees writ large on the co-pilot's wristwatch "John 3:16," referring to a Biblical passage often quoted by Christian evangelists: "For God so loved the world, that he gave his only begotten Son, that whosoever believeth in him should not perish, but have everlasting life" (KJV). Before the closing credits, "Mark 13:32" appears against a black screen, followed by the King James Version of scripture to which it refers: "But of that day and hour knoweth no man," reminding viewers that only God possesses knowledge of the inevitable Apocalypse. Taken together, these two passages present the threat of annihilation through human ignorance and the possibility of redemption through right belief. The moral dialectic of these Old and New Testament ethics should align well with the 2014 Christian action-thriller, wherein the most literal questions concern landing a plane and saving lives. As the film's central symbol, the narrative flight tries to remain airborne based on the thrilling premise of physical survival in order to extend the possibly less thrilling discourse of Christian conversion and its concern with saving souls. But the film never gets the mix of these two sets of concerns—literal survival and spiritual salvation—right. Instead, its final hour alternates between painfully protracted "conversion" conversations on the plane and a series of awkwardly miraculous heroics on the ground. The filmmakers may intend these two trajectories to merge at the film's end in order to confirm a subtextual continuity from action to redemption, but, instead, the film swerves off course.

Earlier, the film has prepared viewers for some sort of satisfactory closure through an oddly directed narrative focus on sex and romance. Arriving at the airport for the fateful flight, Ray removes his wedding ring in the parking lot and flirts with the vivacious flight attendant Hattie Durham. Having just flown in herself, Chloe witnesses the pair's flirtation and confronts her father about the long dissolution of her parents' marriage. Juxtaposed with this family melodrama is the more optimistic promise of romantic love in Buck's fortuitous presence at the airport—Buck, who falls instantly in love with Chloe. While the plot clearly judges Ray for his loss of faith in his marriage, the narrative simultaneously approves the conventional Hollywood romance of Chloe and Buck. The two couples are conveniently intertwined further when Chloe receives her father's tickets for a U2 concert and asks Buck, who happens to be on Ray's flight, to give them to him. Viewers discover later that Chloe has written inside the envelope containing the tickets, "Today is the saddest day of my life," indicating both her disappointment with her father and her own lack of direction, now that she no longer identifies with either of her parents.[1]

Despite the film's need to communicate both condemnation *and* support of easy romance, Chloe remains a complicated site of sexual morality and imagery. She is a nonbeliever, but also sexually innocent and overtly moral, disagreeing with both her mother's newfound faith and her father's lack of marital faith. Viewers' potential identification with Chloe's complicated moral character, possibly the most attractive option given her parents' moral extremes, is deflected by the camera's framing of her body, particularly her cleavage. Several overhead shots of the actress capture her in a state of dishevelment, revealing her brassiere under a loose-fitting blouse.[2] The rendering of Chloe as a sex object, albeit one that may appear tame by Hollywood standards, nevertheless complicates viewer identification when framed by the competing standard of Christian chastity. This ambiguous spectacle, which may yet claim its own innocence, stands in sharp contrast to the unequivocal moment when her brother, supernaturally taken, literally disappears out of his clothes while Chloe embraces him at the mall.

Chloe's ordeals after her brother's miraculous disappearance demonstrate Calvinistic notions of human depravity that underscore the series' overall fundamentalist morality. Fleeing the mall, she avoids innumerable, spontaneous acts of vandalism, looting, and violence perpetrated by the immediately crazed and confused shoppers. In the parking lot, she narrowly avoids being hit by a small airplane that lands in the parking lot and crashes into her father's car. Forced to proceed on foot, Chloe runs to the hospital (where she confirms the disappearance of her brother when an older patient tells her all of the children have disappeared), to her parents' house (where she confirms the disappearance of her mother by finding her jewelry on the floor of a running shower), and lastly to her church (where she confirms that her minister, who has been left behind, does not possess adequate belief).[3] At the end of her conversation with her minister, Chloe scoffs, "Listen to you? Why should I? You didn't even listen to you." Despite her own initial resistance to conversion, Chloe's episodic encounters "on the ground" gather the evidence and attitude necessary to push the cinematic narrative toward conversion. Nonbelievers are prone to atavistic ruin when left on their own, the innocent are preserved by divine intervention, and conventional religious leaders offer only structure without true faith. The pedestrian nature of Chloe's evidence-gathering and her snap moral judgments offer viewers a definitive, if reductive, perspective by which to reject all the trappings of a world now shown worthy of Apocalyptic ruin.

Chloe's symbolic trek up to this point is far more pedestrian than that of her father, whose symbolic flight looms overhead. The skeptical daughter's struggle over faith, however, reaches symbolic heights when Chloe decides to climb to the top of a bridge to talk to her missing mother. She confesses her own wrongdoing by holding her mother's faith responsible for the family's problems. In a montage of shots with the melodramatic song "Here on Earth" in the background, Chloe precariously braves the high winds and delivers her heartfelt confession. This over-determined moment of elevation raises Chloe above the level of non-believers and prefigures her eventual conversion. Her skeptical but judgmental character serves the purpose of conversion by modeling that process herself, intended to draw resistant skeptics toward belief.

Meanwhile, on the ill-fated flight PanCon 257, the passengers in first class, those not "good" enough to have already been taken, present a sampling of belief systems and moral failings that cast them outside the bounds of salvation. The most dominant of these is an aggressively angry gambler who bullies everyone, including a young girl, to compensate for his short stature. The young girl's mother, who is contemplating divorce from her abusive husband, later pulls a gun (stolen from the taken air marshal's seat) and threatens to shoot everyone—including herself. Other first-class passengers include a drug addict (who correctly identifies their situation as the Biblical End Times), a corrupt businessman (who shows potential for redemption by expressing love for his daughter), a Muslim (who denounces his fellow passengers for suspecting all Muslims of terrorism), a scientist (who believes in conspiracy theories and Area 51), and an elderly woman (who is demonstrably less kind than her missing husband). The latter half of the film generally ignores the passengers in coach, including several parents with missing children. The others remaining on the plane, in or near the cockpit, are the reporter Buck and the airline's Ray and Hattie. The film's narrowing focus on the class of characters near the front of the plane spatially implies a class-based hierarchy of redemption, with professionals in the lead. This implicit valorization of the professional, invested with comprehensive expertise in both business and belief, is another example of what Andrew Strombeck argues is the series' overall infusion of "neoliberal values—specifically, those around market rationality and the validation of global meritocracy" (168). Even though those left behind are, by definition, flawed, they merit primacy of redemption through their professionally sanctioned efforts. In this way, "professional skills" of the select few come to "meld with one's Christian identity" (Strombeck 177).

In a scene unique to the 2014 remake, Pancon 257 narrowly avoids a head-on collision with an unmanned jet. After noting the resultant damage to his plane and dropping fuel supply, Ray decides to turn around and land in New York, effectively canceling out the narrative's international scope. Although the original *Left Behind* novel and film adaptation contain a similar decision to return the flight to Chicago, here that decision is catalyzed by a most unlikely mid-air event that does not occur in those earlier versions. In the first novel and first film adaptation, the decision not to continue on toward London does not diminish the international scope of action; in the remake, it reframes the narrative as one far more insular and safer in scope. Consequently, viewers' attention is restricted to the fate of an airplane flight that may end in disaster, its fuel supply aflame with the potential of being depleted before landing. This focus on an imperiled flight recalls the clichéd motifs of 1970s American disaster films, particularly *Airport* (1970). Moreover, the reversal of PanCon 257's trajectory matches the 2014 film's overall swerve away from the constant and explicit engagement with Christian evangelism in the original trilogy of *Left Behind* films. This adaptation distances itself, through both image and message, from its most important moral purpose, without gaining any substantial return in terms of dramatic novelty.

As the plane approaches New York City and its passengers and crew process the divine origin of the in-flight disappearances, the plotlines of the daughter and of the two men she loves converge. After several failed attempts, Buck, who joins Ray in the cockpit, succeeds in reaching Chloe through his mobile phone. The three briefly discuss Ray's plan to land in New York before the call cuts out. If the likelihood of this information-rich communication is not miraculous enough, Chloe instantly sets in motion a series of steps that will allow her to save her father's plane by herself, miraculously demonstrating multifaceted vehicular mobility and technological facility.[4] She runs along the street until she comes across a motorcycle, which she rides until commandeering an abandoned pickup truck. Reaching an unfinished construction site, Chloe supplies Buck with the coordinates of her location using the "compass app" on her mobile phone. She uses the truck to push away all obstacles and prepare the road to be a makeshift runway for PanCon 257. At one point, she removes a slow-moving road paver from the road by jury-rigging it to drive off the side on its own while she continues in the truck. Lastly, when her father tells her he needs to see the runway, she safely ignites and explodes a set of drums filled with flammable liquid. Upon seeing this pyre from the sky, Ray succeeds in landing the plane, even managing to lift the wing of the plane in order not to hit Chloe after her truck stalls in a ditch at the runway's edge. This incredible rescue ends when PanCon 257 stops, nose-to-nose with a tanker full of flammable liquid at the end of the miracle runway. The crisp execution of each step of this multi-stage sequence makes it too serious for enjoyment as camp, while the ridiculous spectacle of Chloe's sudden transfiguration into a supremely competent action hero is dramatically too over-the-top for the film's didactic intent. The film thus diverges from its moralistic goals without successfully approximating the generic super-heroics of the Hollywood blockbusters it tries to emulate.

After this final action sequence, the film returns to its emphasis on the dialogue of confession and belief, but this is a dialogue in which lesser characters do not partake on equal ground. Ray says, "You did a great job!" to Hattie before pausing and adding, "Hattie, I'm sorry." The disappointed flight attendant grudgingly acknowledges his words and walks away. Through their respective gestures, the pilot signifies that he may be worthy of salvation, the flight attendant—not. Likewise, the remaining passengers deplane frantically without any dialogue to indicate their own states of conversion. In contrast, Chloe gives her father his and her mother's wedding rings, which she had previously recovered from his car and their home. Father and daughter reconcile their differences through this symbolic affirmation of marriage and, by extension, of Irene's evangelical Christianity.

Despite the ambiguous state of faith of these passengers silently disappearing from the film, the spectacular framing of Apocalypse focuses in the final moment on Ray, Buck, and Chloe: the pilot, the reporter, and the woman who unites them. Standing side by side, the three leads view the New York City skyline aflame in the distance as fuel receptacles along the "runway" behind them explode. Buck says, "Looks like the end of the world," to which Chloe responds, "No not yet. I'm afraid this is just the beginning." The scene goes to black as the film's final song begins, with the refrain, "And you've been left behind. I wish we'd all been ready."[5] The film's two trajectories, of a 1970s-era disaster film and of a subdued adaptation of the *Left Behind* series' evangelism, coalesce in this final moment when, once again, viewers are gently given the warning that they had better believe righteously here and now, before the coming Apocalypse. Like the embattled franchise itself, *Left Behind*'s attempts to appeal to its audience while scaring them with threats of doom are persistent and persistently off-key.

The 2014 *Left Behind* has effectively repeated the commercial and critical failure of its multimedia predecessors. Two months after its October release, the film had earned a domestic gross of just $13.9 million, below its $16 million budget ("*Left Behind*," 2014). Moreover, initial critical reception was extremely negative. The film received a cumulative rating of "F" from *Entertainment Weekly* based on composite scores from leading film-rating sources: 54% at IMDb, 14% at MetaCritic, and 3% at Rotten Tomatoes ("Critical Mass" 56). One critic writes, "At best, *Left Behind* is shoddily made sensationalist propaganda—with atrocious acting—that barely registers as entertainment. At worst, it's profoundly moronic. Audiences, Christian or not, deserve better, and it's hard to imagine that the ham-fisted revelations in this schlock could serve any higher purpose" (Bahr). In the issue of the magazine dated the same day as the film's release, another *EW* critic enumerated several possible causes for the film's likely failure: that a Christian audience might be skeptical of Cage in the lead role, that audiences might experience "Rapture fatigue" due to the film's similarity to HBO's *The Leftovers*, and that the low reputation of the previous trilogy of films might preemptively turn away audiences (Lee 22).

Left Behind's repeated failures to extend its franchise past its literary origins run counter to the high popularity of secular apocalyptic narratives, first among them *The Walking Dead*, the cable television series (2010 to present) based on Robert Kirkman's graphic series (2003 to present). In 2013, when *The Walking Dead* averaged twelve million viewers per episode, it became the only show in the top fifty most-watched cable-television programs of all time that was not a live broadcast of a sporting event (Rice 26). But such visions as those of *The Walking Dead* focus for the most part on survival narratives, eschewing extended moralizing or compartmentalizing it in favor of the core elements of the action-thriller plot and stories based on the psychological drama of trauma. In contrast, *Left Behind* presumes scriptural prophecy as its dramatic precedent and remains beholden to those predictions. Zombie apocalypse narratives retain the advantage of serialized surprise with no obligation to moral justifications for whatever dramatic turns the shows' writers may imagine. The secular apocalypse suits the form of serialized drama in not forecasting its morals, while Christian Apocalypse, necessarily, must. There is no divide between internal states of being and outward survival in the secular apocalypse, but this is the very divide that *Left Behind* cannot seem to bridge. The evangelical franchise wants to envision Old Testament wrath and New Testament salvation, but cannot align the two within one consistent image. Instead, the film compartmentalizes internal debates about conversion within the external trappings of a disaster movie, ultimately swerving from the serious-minded implications of the former and fumbling at the artistry necessary to capture the latter. Although the concept of Apocalypse derives precedent from Christian scripture and practice, *Left Behind* as apocalyptic film has yet to find a place for its particular conversion narrative within the American popular imagination.

NOTES

1. The original film trilogy attempts to redeem romantic love through a double wedding at which the newly married protagonists confess their sins and dedicate their love to Christ (*Left Behind II: Tribulation Force*).

2. In contrast, righteous Irene wears a loose-fitting, inoffensive dress, and the adulterous Hattie wears a blouse and skirt so tight she appears ever on the verge of bursting forth from her uniform.

3. The disappearance and thereby presumed spiritual innocence of children indicates the series' consistent denial of the doctrine of Original Sin as professed in Catholicism and some strains of Protestantism.

4. Strombeck notes the original book series' embrace of "the technological products of multinational capitalism" in order to construct a more appealing, modernized image of Christian fundamentalism (165).

5. The opening lines of the original film trilogy—"How do you describe both a beginning and an end? We should have known better, but we didn't"—resonate with the moral culpability implied by the musical refrain of the 2014 remake.

WORKS CITED

Bahr, Lindsey. Rev. of *Left Behind*, dir. Vic Armstrong. *Entertainment Weekly*. 3 Oct. 2014: n. pag. Web. 8 Oct. 2014.

"Critical Mass." *Entertainment Weekly* 17 Oct. 2014: 56. Print.

Jones, Marnie. "'Spiritual Warfare' and Intolerance in Popular Culture: The *Left Behind* Franchise, the Commodification of Belief, and the Consequences for Imagination." *Studies in Popular Culture* 32.1 (Fall 2009): 1–19. Print.

LaHaye, Tim, and Jerry B. Jenkins. *Left Behind: A Novel of the Earth's Last Days*. Carol Stream: Tyndale House, 1995. Print.

Lee, Chris. "Nicolas Cage Has a 'Come to Jesus' Moment." *Entertainment Weekly* 3 Oct. 2014: 22. Print.

Left Behind. Dir. Vic Armstrong. Perf. Nicolas Cage. Stoney Lake Entertainment, 2014. DVD.

Left Behind II: Tribulation Force. Dir. Bill Corcoran. Perf. Kirk Cameron. Cloud Ten Pictures, 2002. DVD.

"*Left Behind* (2014)." *Box Office Mojo. IMDb.com*. 4 Dec. 2014. Web. 8 Dec. 2014.

Left Behind: Eternal Forces. Left Behind Games, 2006. Video game.

Left Behind: The Movie. Dir. Vic Sarin. Perf. Kirk Cameron. Cloud Ten Pictures, 2000. DVD.

Left Behind: World at War. Dir. Craig R. Baxley. Perf. Kirk Cameron. Cloud Ten Pictures, 2005. DVD.

Rice, Lynette. "*Walking Dead*'s Ratings Spook Basic-Cable Peers." *Entertainment Weekly* 19 July 2013: 26. Print.

Shuck, Glenn. *Marks of the Beast: The* Left Behind *Novels and the Struggle for Evangelical Identity*. New York: New York University Press, 2005. Print.

Strombeck, Andrew. "Invest in Jesus: Neoliberalism and the *Left Behind* Novels." *Cultural Critique* 64 (Fall 2006): 161–95. Print.

Corporate Abuse and Social Inequality in *RoboCop* and *Fido*

BILL CLEMENTE

The recent spate of crises around the globe may lead many to feel that the Four Horsemen of the Apocalypse gallop just around the next corner. From Ebola outbreaks in West Africa and the measles scourge in Disneyland to Putin's nuclear threats over the Ukraine, from war creep in Iraq and Syria to terrorist attacks in Paris, media reports make the most stalwart idealists falter. Postapocalyptic films often choreograph a catastrophic future to highlight contemporary concerns, and our new millennium has seen a proliferation of apocalyptic films feeding on ongoing American anxieties. The 2014 science fiction film *RoboCop* draws on distress triggered by diverse issues, from the militarization of the police to the unholy alliance of wing-nut media and global corporations. Earlier, the 2006 zomcom *Fido* paid homage to walking-dead traditions established by George Romero, whose zombie films bristle with social commentary and political criticism. *Fido* references multiple issues that continue to plague America, from soaring corporate profits made through perpetuating fears about security, to the growing disparity between the powerful super rich and the ever diminishing political influence of the middle class and the poor.

A reboot of the 1987 film with the same name, the most recent *RoboCop* clearly owes a great deal to the first installment in the series. But the 2014 movie also references contemporary areas of alarm, among them the ongoing militarization of police departments. This reality hit home by way of riots near St. Louis, Missouri, when the police weapons, attire, and vehicles called to mind not only local Ferguson law officers contending with rioters after the killing by a white police officer of unarmed black teenager Michael Brown

(August 9, 2014), but also battle-hardened soldiers in Iraq fighting well-armed Sunni insurgents in the streets of Fallujah during Operation Phantom Fury (November-December 2004), the bloodiest battle of the Iraq War. As Shane Bauer has observed, "Outfitting America's warrior cops, it turns out, is a major business." Bauer also points out that while the Department of Defense has made available over five billion dollars to police departments around the country, "Homeland Security has handed out grants worth eight times as much—$41 billion since 2002." These funds finance the purchase of all manner of equipment that SWAT teams increasingly use for mundane operations such as drug busts. "In all," Bauer notes, "the number of swat raids across the country has increased 20-fold since the 1980s...." The profits from the purchase of these military items likewise line the pockets of numerous corporations, from the LRAD Corporation's long-range debilitating noise device to the use of the Lenco Company's Bearcat armored truck, weapons the Ferguson Police Department purchased with Homeland Security grants (Kane).

RoboCop's opening sequence underscores the consequences of both the militarization of the police and the military's outsourcing to private firms such as the film's OnmiCorp, led by CEO Raymond Sellars. As the film begins, MGM's famous lion gargles instead of roars, paralleling the wing-nut host of *The Novak Element*, Patrick "Pat" Novak, who exercises his voice before his performance. The scene emphasizes the role media play in bolstering specific ideologies, in this case the push for militarized and mechanized crime control of the kind OmniCorp manufactures. As Peter W. Singer argues, this use of Private Military Firms blossomed in Iraq, where in 2005 "[m]ore than 60 firms [employed] more than 20,000 private personnel" to carry out various military functions, "roughly the same number as [were] provided by all of the United States' coalition partners combined." Many of these firms were private security firms that featured prominently in post-occupation policing throughout the country and in prisons such as Abu Ghraib.

Given "unprecedented access" by the general in charge of Operation Freedom Iran, Novak's crew goes on patrol in Tehran, where OmniCorp robots walk the streets to ensure security. The ED 209 and EM 208 mechanized devices, with air cover provided by OmniCorp drones, perform so-called "non-invasive searches" and protect "red assets" (e.g., human reporters and soldiers) in the name of making America safe by subduing threats abroad. Of the repressed Iranians, Novak says, "The honest people over there appreciate us." Significantly enough, none of the mechanized devices sport military insignia; instead, OmniCorp's logo emblazons the drones. While no harm comes to a red asset, an Iranian suicide bomber and a small group of insurgents sacrifice their lives to destroy the robots, concluding with an ED 209 dispatching in a blaze of bullets a young boy who wields a knife.

On his show, Novak argues that all the countries of the world use

OmniCorp's technology for domestic security—except the United States. While praising OmniCorp's Raymond Sellars as a true American, Novak excoriates U.S. Senator Dreyfus, author of the Dreyfus Act, which forbids the use of robots for civil law enforcement. In league with OmniCorp's interests, Novak seeks to alter the 70% approval rating for the Dreyfus Act by eroding robophobia. Dreyfus represents a left-wing version of Novak's right-wing nut, for while he opposes the use of robots in the United States, he says nothing of the repression throughout the world where, one assumes, robots limit personal freedom while inflating OmniCorp's profits. Meanwhile, Sellars hungers for the missing American market that "bleeds" his company of an estimated $600 billion in potential revenue.

The film likewise questions corporate science, for Sellars tasks the brilliant scientist Dr. Dennett Norton to create a crime-fighting cyborg from the shattered body of Detroit policeman Alex Murphy, grievously wounded in an explosion designed by corrupt fellow officers to kill him. With his robobody, Murphy will eventually ferret out the corruption in the police department, and Norton's rehabilitation work will ultimately represent the positive side of the cyborg premise, that of the posthuman rippling with possibilities for a better future. In the words of N. Katherine Hayles, "In the posthuman, there are no essential differences or absolute demarcations between bodily existence and computer simulation, cybernetic mechanism and biological organism, robot teleology and human goals" (3). The film depends on the familiar trope of the robot's longing for emotion, for to erase human consciousness and get Murphy up to the killing speed of OmniCorp robots, Norton initially represses the human part of Murphy the cyborg. Murphy's wife, however, eventually triggers memories and emotions that allow him to overcome the system Norton implanted in Murphy's brain, allowing Murphy both to solve the mystery of who blew up his body and to stop Sellars permanently. At the film's conclusion, he is able to reconnect with his wife and child—after altering the "technical" looking black armor upon which Sellars insisted to silver, suggestive of a brighter future.

Earlier in the film and after being armed with information from police computers, Murphy's cybernetic brain crashes, forcing Norton to deplete his patient's dopamine levels in an attempt to delete Murphy's humanity. Now seemingly a robot with a human face, Murphy manages to drive down Detroit's crime rate by over 60% and approval rates for the Dreyfus Act to 50%. Manipulated by Novak and, one assumes, Sellars's corporate lobbyists, Congress revokes the legislation (though the President will eventually veto the revocation when the truth about OmniCorp again reshapes public opinion). The information denied both Murphy and society points to one of the many dangers the posthuman world of the cyborg poses. As Donna Haraway explains in *Simians, Cyborgs, and Women*, the cyborg's power finds reference

in the metaphor of C³I—command-control-communication-intelligence—
"the military's symbol for its operations theory" (176). Haraway also notes,
"The biggest threat to such power is interruption of communication" (176),
which occurs when Norton eliminates the human element of the operational
equation. Once Murphy connects again with his emotions, however, he
becomes fully functional and reveals police and politicians' involvement in
Sellars's operations. When Sellars seeks to hide the truth by demanding that
Norton kill Murphy, Norton refuses. Science, after all, can possess a conscience.

The growing divide between the powerful and the powerless—discussed
at length by Thomas Piketty in *Capital*, wherein he investigates wealth distribution over the past few centuries in various European countries and the
United States—finds reflection in the need in *RoboCop* to keep information
about political, corporate, and police corruption from the general public.
Piketty argues that the gap "is largely the result of an unprecedented increase
in wage inequality and in particular the emergence of extremely high remu-
nerations at the summit of the wage hierarchy, particularly among top man-
agers of large firms" who fight aggressively to maintain this growing
imbalance (298). The revelations Murphy's actions reveal to the public undermine profit and unsettle those in powerful positions who would otherwise
remain beyond the reach of justice. This same equation plays out with respect
to the way in which laws such as "stop and frisk" unfairly target poor minori-
ties at the same time that major white-collar criminals often escape with
impunity. Matt Taibbi has pointed out that although many honest people
work to ensure the equality before the law that characterizes a free democracy,
underneath that surface is "a florid and malevolent bureaucracy that mostly
(not absolutely, but mostly) keeps rich and poor separate through thousands
of tiny, scarcely visible inequities" (9). Consequently, far too many poor people live in fear of losing government assistance simply by filling out forms
incorrectly. At the same time, only a few major players in the financial institutions responsible for the monetary fraud that has brought near financial
ruin to many countries have faced prosecution. As Murphy's actions indicate,
putting a human face on justice is both daunting and dangerous. He prevails
partially because those who try to gun him down have terrible aim. Justice
is as fragile as the double tap to the head that would crush the cyborg's circuits.

In his voracious pursuit of profit and control in the name of security,
OmniCorp's CEO shares many traits with *Fido*'s Jonathan Bottoms, Zomcon's
heartless security chief. Both Sellars and Bottoms and the companies they
represent show no compassion; they think only in terms of profit and power.
Henry Giroux's comments about what he describes as zombie capitalism
and politics make this very point with respect to what he sees as a growing

authoritarianism in the United States: "What we are currently witnessing in this form of zombie politics and predatory capitalism is the unleashing of powerfully regressive symbolic and corporeal violence against all those individuals and groups who have been 'othered' because their very presence undermines the engines of wealth and inequality that drive the neoliberal dreams of consumption, power, and profitability for the very few" (37). This notion of corporate zombies provides the bridge that connects *RoboCop* to *Fido*.

A Canadian film directed by Andrew Currie, *Fido* offers a tactical combination of guts and giggles to highlight a number of essential concerns in the contemporary United States, from the definition of family to the dangers posed by the economic and political clout of large corporations. Currie's film also formulates a response to Sarah Juliet Lauro and Karen Embry's argument that the zombie's "dystopic promise is that it can only assure the destruction of a corrupt system without imagining a replacement" (96) because the zombie seldom offers a resolution. While this assertion certainly applies to George Romero's early films, *Fido*, while forging connections with the original *Night of the Living Dead* (1968), alters Romero's first film dramatically. In Currie's film, the zombie apocalypse failed, and humanity subsequently surrendered its freedom to Zomcon, a huge corporation that appears to control the entire country.

The film announces its connections with *Night of the Living Dead* at the onset, when children in elementary school watch a Zomcon propaganda video that features black-and-white footage from the recent Zombie Wars, footage that resembles clips from Romero's genre-busting zombie film. *Fido's* main narrative takes place in white-picket-fenced Willard, the name of the nearest town to the farmhouse in which the main characters in *Night of the Living Dead* perish. But in this alternate cinematic universe, the mise-en-scène elements do not take their source from the turbulent years of the late Sixties, when Romero's film hit drive-in theaters. Willard presents instead what seems to be an idealized suburbia of the Eisenhower years—until viewers realize that the pastel colors, large-finned cars, manicured gardens, and cocktail dresses shroud the reality that defines Zomcon.

The school's propaganda video underscores the reality of what Naomi Klein argues can happen when large firms and governments take advantage of political or environmental crises to, among other things, privatize everything from mines in Chile to public schools in New Orleans. Tranquil Willard mirrors the privatization strategy Klein describes: "an ever widening chasm between the dazzling rich and the disposable poor and an aggressive nationalism that justifies bottomless spending on security" (18). When Jonathan Bottoms visits the children in their classroom to reinforce his company's importance, for example, he tells the youngsters, "Without Zomcon we'd all be dead."

The trope of the radiation plague-created zombies from Romero's first zombie film persists in *Fido*—but with a twist. Dr. Hrothgar Geiger discovered that zombies die from blows to the head and/or cremation; he likewise invented the Geiger collar, which suppresses the zombie's desire for human flesh. The collar also provides the film with its running joke that equates zombies with dogs who must be leashed in public. In the world of Willard, therefore, zombies become the "disposable poor" who allow the citizens of the town to live middle-class dreams that disguise nightmares. Like *RoboCop* but in a more graphic display, *Fido* presents a postapocalyptic community that "not only exposes," in Aalya Ahmad's words, "but destroys entrenched systems of power feeding on racism, patriarchy, gross inequality and other institutionalized follies" (ch. 10).

In all-white Willard, the zombies provide the only "people" of color. In this manner, "zombie gray is the new black" (Ahmad, ch. 10). Zomcon itself thrives on the fear sown throughout the community that justifies the need for the intense security the company provides as well as the comforts it sells at a high price. To this end, what Steven Shaviro writes about Romero's horror films applies, though in less obvious ways, to *Fido*: "Romero's zombies seem almost natural in a society in which the material comforts of the middle class coexist with a repressive conformism, mindless mumbling, media manipulation, and the more blatant violence of poverty, sexism, racism, and militarism" (3). At the school, for example, outdoor education consists of learning how to shoot rifles at targets while the children chant, "Head shots are the best; in the brains but not the chest." The same school includes as well a pair of bullies, Zomcon cadets, brown shirts, who terrorize the introspective Timmy Robinson. Helen Robinson, Timmy's mother, purchases the zombie Timmy will name Fido, even though her husband, Bill, has a zombie phobia attributed to his having had to kill his father in the Zombie Wars. That war also made Jonathan Bottoms a hero for his 500-zombie tally that began with his first kill, his Uncle Bob, whose head he keeps in a jar in his "war room."

A nationalist in terms of supporting what the ubiquitous Zomcon flag and symbols represent, Bottoms feels nothing for people, including his wife and daughter. He tells the Robinsons that he could take his wife's head off in a second. Without irony, Bottoms claims that having feelings would make it "harder to pull the trigger." Bottoms is also rapacious, a living dead person in league with a company that controls media, markets, the military, and the zombies themselves, the latter a commodity the company sells as slave labor. For business reasons, therefore, Zomcon does not attempt to kill off the zombies who continue to dwell in the wild zones outside the containment fences that surround Willard.

In its mindless pursuit of power and profit, Zomcon itself suggests the corporate zombieism described by Henry Giroux. This company that teaches children to fear also teaches them to distrust even the elderly, who will turn into zombies at their death. As Bottoms says, "I hate old people." Bottoms and Zomcon represent something Kim Paffenroth argues regarding Romero's zombies: "For Romero, it is not the zombie's bite that turns us into monsters, but materialism and consumerism that turn us into zombies, addicted to things that satisfy only the basest, most animal or mechanical urges of our beings" (*Gospel* 55). Zomcon's fence ensures profits and control not only of the zombies but also of Willard's citizens.

Although its primary homage is to *Night of the Living Dead*, *Fido* also has ties to other Romero movies. In *Land of the Dead* (2005), Romero lashes out at corporate America in the form of Fiddler's Green, where CEO Kaufman's elite dwell and figuratively feed off those who serve him for the security he offers. This film increasingly aligns its zombies with the people in the enclave who must live a life suffused with sickness and poverty; eventually, the sentient zombie Big Daddy organizes his fellow walking dead and upends Fiddler's Green, freeing the impoverished citizens. In Currie's film, the irrepressible Scottish actor/comedian Billy Connolly brings life to Fido, who, though inarticulate, shows more humanity than do most people in Willard. *Fido* likewise moves from the flesh-eating monsters of Romero's films and returns in important respects to the Haitian zombie as depicted in W. B. Seabrook's *The Magic Island* (1929), Zora Neale Hurston's *Tell My Horse* (1938), and (to a degree) Victor Halperin's *White Zombie* (1932), the film that birthed the Hollywood zombie.

While not a classic horror film, *Fido* preys delightfully on what the horrified Barbara bemoans at the conclusion of the 1990 remake of *Night of the Living Dead*: "They're us. We're them and they're us." Fido's entrance into the film underscores this point. Portrayed as the typically passive wife associated with 1950s patriarchal society, Helen visits the Bottoms household to welcome the family—Jonathan, his wife Dee Dee, and their daughter Alexia—and discovers that the new head of security has numerous household zombies. So to keep up with appearances, she chooses to ignore her husband's phobia and buys a zombie.

Husband Bill's fears and obsession with death inform this microcosm of the post–Zombie Wars society and mark a distinguishing feature of how Currie manipulates the traditional Hollywood zombie Romero unleashed. The Canadian film returns to the zombie source described by Seabrook in a chapter of *The Magic Island* titled "Dead Men Working," wherein complacent zombies labor in the sugarcane fields owned by Hasco, the Haitian-American Sugar Company. In Romero-influenced zombie films, in general, characters fear getting attacked and killed by zombies. In the world of forced labor Seabrook describes, however, people fear becoming zombies, which provides an apt metaphor for the mechanical and constant labor that wears down the poor for their entire lives. As Bishop writes, "If the ultimate fear for those who believe in voodoo is to become a zombie, then the analogous fear of the imperialist is to become a slave" (ch. 2). For example, Bill Robinson, like pretty much all citizens over the age of twelve, totes a pistol. Fear of becoming a zombie takes control of Bill's life. At night, he reads *Death* magazine and toils at his job to provide for a "headless" funeral, replete with a Zomcon head casket, so that his family will not come back as zombies. He likewise drags his family to headless funerals, taking pride in the fact that he *slaves* to keep up on payments for the death insurance policy from Zomcon that only the wealthiest can afford.

Bill obviously lives a rather dead life, a zombie existence of going through the mechanical motions. When as a rite of passage to manhood, he gives Timmy a pistol, Bill adds that Timmy must stop having feelings, for the boy mourns the loss of Fido, carted off by Bottoms to work in Zomcon's factory. And when Helen tells Bill what everyone else (including Fido) has already noticed, that she is pregnant, Bill responds woefully that he cannot afford death insurance for a fourth person. In many respects, Bill Robinson passes through the years working to avoid what he has figuratively already become.

Billy Connelly's Fido delivers and triggers both the film's hilarity and its thoughtful smiles. In Romero's *Land of the Dead*, the camera sutures with the zombie to reveal its gaze, a technique that fuses a bond between the zombie and the viewer. Thus, in *Land of the Dead*, the viewer appreciates Big Daddy's rage, sympathizing with the zombie's plight. With respect to Fido, however, Helen and Timmy go a step further, openly empathizing with Fido, suggesting that they can place themselves in the zombie's position. In fact, Timmy tells his father, "I'd rather be a zombie than dead." And Helen tells Bill to get his own funeral: "Timmy and I are going zombie."

Fido's insinuation into the family triggers changes, giving Timmy confidence and motivating Helen to break the patriarchal chains that stifle her. In effect, Fido resembles the stray dog that eventually wins the family's heart. And, yes, Fido plays Lassie. When the brown shirts tie Timmy to a tree and deactivate Fido's restraint collar, one of the bully brothers clumsily shoots his brother. And instead of killing Timmy, Fido attacks the shooter, leaving Timmy unharmed. When Fido's debilitated fingers cannot undo knots, Timmy sends him to get Helen, who utters the words all Lassie fans expect: "Fido, where's Timmy? Is he hurt?"

While directing Helen to Timmy's location through a series of grunts and hand waves, Fido glances at the pistol Helen has pulled from her purse. She looks at Fido and asks whether he would attack her. Fido's gentle gaze returns to Helen, and he whimpers quietly, causing Helen to blush and whisper, "Oh Fido," for he looks with obvious tenderness not at her pistol but her thigh. At another juncture, Helen affectionately cups Fido's cheek after Bill orders him tied to a tree, telling Fido that she wishes she had met him before he died. Fido's affection for Helen grows throughout the film as he becomes more firmly entrenched in the family: he dances with her when Bill will not; he wears one of Bill's suits to a funeral; he occupies Bill favorite seat; he wins Timmy's heart and Helen's affection. In a scene where Bill, with typical inattention, abandons his family to play golf, Helen brings cool drinks to her "boys," Fido and Timmy, who wash Bill's car. As she approaches, the camera reveals Fido's vision of the beautifully soft-focused Helen, whose slow-motion gait registers the zombie's loving appreciation and romantic inclinations— abruptly interrupted when Timmy sprays him with the hose.

Fido assumes the place of the father figure, similar to the re-imagined role of the Terminator in *Terminator 2,* the fearsome robot who will not harm or allow harm to come to Sarah Connor's ten-year-old son, John. Thus Fido not only rescues Timmy from the feckless brown-shirt bullies but also eventually kills Jonathan Bottoms, who had enslaved Fido and who attempted to throw Timmy into the clutches of the zombies in the Wild Zone. Like the romantic attraction between Helen and Fido, the idea that a zombie could assume the role of protective father clearly indicates the way this film reverses the abjection and the uncanny essential to traditional zombie films. This reversal finds, perhaps, its most memorable instance not in the affection Helen and Fido share but in an even more romantic relationship. At the film's conclusion, Mr. Theopolis, the former head of security at Zomcon who lost his position for fraternizing with the strikingly attractive young zombie Tammy, kisses her gently, turning the uncanny on its head by making the unfamiliar familiar. Theopolis helps Timmy gain access to Zomcon, where the factory full of chained zombies slaving in the gloomy metal shop is reminiscent of the Haitian zombies mindlessly grinding sugar cane in the factory Murder Legendre operates in the Halperin brothers' *White Zombie* (1932). "Legendre's factory," Bishop argues, "is an appalling hyperbole of the further limits of a capitalist system: he owns not only the means of production but the labor force as well" (ch. 2).

The film's conclusion offers a modicum of hope for what might be, in Paffenroth's words, "a wiping clean of all the capitalist filth that has accumulated in the U.S., to start over with some post-racial, post-capitalist community founded on equality and more humane values" ("Zombies" ch. 1). After the zombie outbreak at Zomcon, the Bottoms family, the Robinsons (Helen, Timmy, and Fido), Mr. Theopolis, and Tammy gather in the Robinsons' yard. Killed by Bottoms, Bill Robinson lies at peace, his head separated from his body. In the yard Timmy and Fido play catch, and an elderly person enjoys a game of checkers with a zombie. Jonathan Bottoms is now a zombie, and his daughter, Alexia, tells Timmy, "It's kind of cool. And he's much nicer now." Meanwhile, Mr. Theopolis, instead of using Tammy as arm candy, dotes on her. And Fido, surrogate husband and stepfather to Timmy and his newborn sibling, reaches into the baby carriage and gently strokes the youngster's soft cheek. Smoking a cigarette, he glances at Helen, who smiles coyly at Fido's contented grunt of a laugh. And so the microcosm of Willard's altered society offers an integrated mixture of domestic relations. In Currie's rendering of the familiar horror genre, the zombie, representing the return of the oppressed, does indeed offer a potential resolution for conflicts the film addresses, promising Paffenroth's "community founded on equality and more humane values" ("Zombies" ch. 1). This ending is in keeping with the hopeful image that concludes *RoboCop*, with the cyborg Alex Murphy, a Detroit Police Department badge emblazoned on his armor, bonded emotionally with his wife and son.

WORKS CITED

Ahmad, Aalya. "Gray Is the New Black: Race, Class, and Zombies." Boluk and Linz ch. 10.

Bauer, Shane. "The Making of the Warrior Cop." *motherjones.com*. Mother Jones and the Foundation for National Progress, 23 Oct. 2014. Web. 1 Nov. 2014.

Bishop, Kyle William. *American Zombie Gothic: The Rise and Fall (and Rise) of the Walking Dead in Popular Culture*. Jefferson: McFarland, 2010. Ebook.

Boluk, Stephanie, and Wylie Lenz, eds. *Generation Zombie: Essays on the Living Dead in Modern Culture*. Jefferson: McFarland, 2011. Ebook.

Fido. Dir. Andrew Currie. Lionsgate, 2006. Film.

Giroux, Henry A. *Zombie Politics and Culture in the Age of Casino Capitalism*. New York: Peter Lang, 2011. Print.

Haraway, Donna. *Simians, Cyborgs, and Women*. New York: Routledge, 1991. Print.

Hayles, N. Katherine. *How We Became Posthuman*. Chicago: University of Chicago Press, 1999. Print.

Hurston, Zora Neale. *Tell My Horse: Voodoo and Life in Haiti and Jamaica*. 1938. New York: Harper, 2009. Print.

Kane, Alex. "Ferguson Is Big Business: How Companies Are Profiting from Public Crackdowns." *salon.com*. Salon, 24 Aug. 2014. Web. 26 May 2015.

Klein, Naomi. *The Shock Doctrine: The Rise of Disaster Capitalism*. New York: Picador, 2008. Ebook.

Land of the Dead. Dir. George Romero. Universal, 2005. Film.

Lauro, Sarah Juliet, and Karen Embry. "A Zombie Manifesto: The Nonhuman Condition in the Era of Advanced Capitalism." *boundary 2* 35.1 (2008): 85–108. Print.

Night of the Living Dead. Dir. George Romero. Walter Reade, 1968. Film.

Night of the Living Dead. Dir. Tom Savini. Columbia, 1990. Film.

Paffenroth, Kim. *Gospel of the Living Dead: George Romero's Vision of Hell on Earth*. Waco: Baylor University Press, 2006. Print.

_____. "Zombies as Internal Fear or Threat." Boluk and Linz ch. 1.

Piketty, Thomas. *Capital in the Twenty-First Century*. Cambridge: Harvard University Press, 2014. Ebook.

RoboCop. Dir. Paul Verhoeven. Orion Pictures, 1987. Film.

RoboCop. Dir. José Padilha. Columbia, 2014. Film.

Seabrook, W. B. *The Magic Island*. New York: Harcourt, 1929. Print.

Shaviro, Steven. *Cinematic Body*. Minneapolis: University of Minnesota Press, 1993. Print.
Singer, Peter W. "Outsourcing War." *Brookings* Mar./Apr., 2005: n. pag. Web. 4 Oct. 2014.
Taibbi, Matt. *The Divide: American Injustice in the Age of the Wealth Gap*. New York: Spiegel & Grau, 2014. Ebook.
Terminator 2: Judgment Day. Dir. James Cameron. TriStar, 1991. Film.
White Zombie. Dir. Victor Halperin. United Artists, 1932. Film.

We Go Forward

An Inquiry into The Hunger Games and Other Class-Based Dystopias in Millennial Cinema

LENNART SOBERON

Dystopian societies are currently fashionable in cinema. The young adult market has been rocked by dystopian science fiction films of varying commercial and artistic quality: e.g., *The Host* (2013), *Divergent* (2014), *The Giver* (2014), *Maze Runner* (2014), and *Insurgent* (2015). At the core of this recent trend lies the sweeping success, both in terms of box office and cultural significance, of the adaptations of Suzanne Collins's *The Hunger Games* series. Collins's dystopian Panem can best be described as a hybrid of numerous historic and fictional regimes, channeling elements from Caesar's Imperial Rome to Lucas's *THX: 1138* (1971). Now that *The Hunger Games* has been firmly established in the cinematic landscape, it is time to take a critical look at these cultural products by placing this franchise and its setting in perspective with other films, both old and new, within the genre.

In a classical sense, almost all dystopian films are part of the science fiction genre. These films strike a balance between spectacle and societal criticism and are defined by the ideas they pose or reflections they offer. Tom Moylan makes the claim that one of SF's central tendencies is "to re-create the empirical present of its author and implied readers as an 'elsewhere'" (5). Keith Booker has also pointed out that science fiction is very much "a genre of ideas," a genre that "can cast new light on social and political phenomena that we experience every day" (266–67). Since its inception, science fiction has provided imaginative explorations of contemporary social and political issues. These narratives deliver warnings about technology gone rampant, scientific mishaps, humanity's violent nature, and mankind's inevitable self-destruction. Perhaps no category of films in this wide genre has proven more interesting in offering reflections of the world we live in than that of dystopian SF. This subgenre first popped up in the cinematic landscape after the events of World War II and has been present ever since (Moylan and Baccolini 4). The starting point of these narratives is often an apocalyptic event that drastically reshapes the world, providing a much needed reset for civilization. The existing structures have been done away with, and mankind is free to restructure whatever is left. Films with a postapocalyptic setting are mainly interested in how humanity handles this clean slate.

The apocalypse can be considered not only in a literal sense but also in a more figurative manner. As such, the apocalypse does not have to be a natural catastrophe, a nuclear war, or anything that decimates the world population, but may also refer to any significant event (or series thereof) that radically alters the socio-political modes and structures of the past. Of great importance are the magnitude and impact of this societal transformation. Any apocalypse leaves the world as we know it seemingly beyond recognition. By this definition, an apocalypse can be a political revolution or a major technological advancement. As Jörn Ahrens has noted, "[T]he apocalypse can be seen as a particular narrative that describes a process of transformation resulting from crisis" (53). Most of the societal forms of organization that arise from the rubble of such an apocalypse are shown to be dark and merciless constructions. Barbaric communes, totalitarian regimes, and corporate constructs are plentiful and tell stories of oppression and injustice. In effect, the genre is never short of settings that defy the imagination, yet despite their often unrealistic and contrived nature, these civilizations reflect our own world in a number of ways. Franklin, for one, has described the dystopias of contemporary science fiction films as "mirror[ing] the profound social decay we are experiencing" (31). These films not only tell a story through their narrative, but more importantly through the social environment of their setting. As such, these films do not always result in action-packed battles against alien creatures or in spectacular space voyages; more often, they revolve around social structures and the effects they have on the individual. Among the effects of these more developed stages of societal restructuring are issues of class struggle.

Dystopian narratives not only often offer insight into living conditions in alternate realities, but they also suggest that the injustice displayed in these fictional settings is disturbingly similar to that of our current society. Moylan refers to this subgenre as a "critical dystopia," a fictional narrative that works by way of warning (188). Raffaella Baccolini has observed that a "utopian core" can be recognized in these narratives (qtd. in Lacey 106–07). Thus, these products can be treated as a site of resistance. According to Annette Kuhn, the content of these science fiction films reflects "social trends and attitudes of the time, mirroring the preoccupations of the historical moment in which the films were made" (10). In the reflective model that Kuhn discusses, films are treated as sociological evidence of sorts. Another cultural instrumentality here adopted is that these products relate to the social order through the mediation of ideologies. These alternate realities demonstrate the ways society looks upon itself, possibly enacting, supporting, and resisting certain ideologies in the process.

In this way, an apocalyptic event can function as both an instrument and a metaphor. Often only referred to, or seen in a film's prologue, the apocalypse is a pretext to create dystopian settings. As Barton Palmer has stressed, these imagined times "are essentially 'characterized' by their advancements in science," in the sense that the introduction of a certain element has radically altered the face of history (171). This particular advancement, or adjustment, serves as a conduit for the ideological attitude within these cautionary tales. As such, these stories can be perceived as containing a statement about the dangers of this societal restructuring and its origins.

Throughout more than half a century of Hollywood blockbusters and avant-garde works alike, narratives of human distress in dystopian societies have reflected the societal struggles of the time. During the Cold War, the fear of Communism and nuclear annihilation resulted in a series of films clearly displaying the Communist threat and the results of coming under Soviet rule (Sanders 68). The dystopias presented here corresponded greatly with the perception and fears American citizens had about life under Soviet rule. Films such as *Invasion of the Body Snatchers* (1978) give a clear impression of this climate of paranoia and the fear of foreign infiltration. Domestic social change in the U.S. also did not go unnoticed in these films. Corresponding with political unrest concerning the civil rights movement and the growing racial struggles in 1960s America, *The Planet of Apes* saga "emerges [as] a liberal allegory of racial conflict" (Greene 72).

Yet it was not until the 1980s that this special brand of science fiction truly thrived. As Moylan and Baccolini claim, "In the face of economic restructuring, right-wing politics and a cultural milieu informed by an intensifying fundamentalism and commodification, sf-writers revived and reformulated the dystopian genre" (2). A new series of films satirized our consumption-driven capitalist society by showcasing a series of corporate dystopias such as those in *Blade Runner* (1982) and *Robocop* (1987). Stephen Prince even stated that the future world these movies conjured was "non-apocalpytic," that they "represented not a radical, violent break with the present but rather an extension [of it]" (336–37). The problems, structures, and power relations all featured in these fictional universes were but modern conditions projected into the future. The 1980s were the Reagan years after all, a time of unrestricted capitalism, increased defense spending, and corporate concentration. As Moylan notes, "It was in this era of economic restructuring, political opportunism, and cultural implosion that dystopian narrative reappeared within the formal parameters of sf" (186). Concerns about the nation's future and the growing disparity of wealth were ever present within the American populace. American paranoia regarding the Soviets was replaced by a deep distrust of national media, uncontrolled corporations, and a corrupt political body. The dystopian films of the time share a thematic resemblance, one where capitalism and grand commerce have gone rampant and are on the verge of collapsing. The films showcase governmental or corporate totalitarianism, where rigid class inequalities and the structures that support them are at the heart of the story. In these spaces, profit is power and the individual is estranged from that in which he/she operates. Taking into account that these films saw their high point in the neoliberal climate of the Thatcher/Reagan era, it is important to note that these types of critical dystopias are all but limited to one particular place in time.

In the last few years, a new cycle of anti-capitalist dystopias, inspired by and complementing on the envisioned spaces of 1980s SF cinema, has reached the screen. These films offer a gloomy view of late capitalism. Despite being situated in a postapocalyptic world, the social order and organizing structures of the dystopias prove similar to that of contemporary Western society. Since no other films of the genre have been as popular as *The Hunger Games* movies, the first three installments of the franchise (i.e., *The Hunger Games*, 2012, *Catching Fire*, 2013, and *Mockingjay—Part 1*, 2014) can be used as prime examples of the elements that define class-based critical dystopias in millennial film.

Curiously, *The Hunger Games*'s fictional totalitarian state of Panem is a particularly tricky society to identify. Panem has been perceived to be a large number of things, but despite being in many ways a mash-up of past historical and fictional regimes, it is hard not to read this fictional universe as at least partially inspired by the existing inadequacies of contemporary Western society. Through huge economic gaps, political rhetoric, and brutal force, the nation keeps its districts' subjects in check. The Capitol symbolizes the upper class and controls the twelve districts, each one representing a certain rank within the nation's workforce. This class disparity is thus defined by a difference in wealth and a central inability to escape one's societal predisposition. Each inhabitant is restricted to the limits of his/her district and the chances there provided. As it goes, every district is assigned a specialized industry (agriculture, livestock, etc.) and provides specific products to the Capitol. Most people within the districts are both physically and economically unable to escape these restrictions; thus, most people play the part they have been assigned to play.

The mise-en-scène elements and visual style of the films support this distinction between, for example, the underprivileged District 12 and the wealthy Capitol. Class disparity is also very much related to the physical space. The films show the presence of what David Desser has referred to as a "politicized production design" (84). There is a dialectic distinction expressed in the special patterning of the film's various locales. The aesthetics of District 12 clearly evoke the Depression-era photography of Dorothea Lange, depicting a rural region scarred by both industry and poverty. Color has seeped out from the frame, leaving mostly different shades of brown and grey. The inhabitants of this alternative future possess technology, clothing, and tools that would seem outdated even today. All this is in stark contrast to the Capitol, which is presented through extreme colors and general debauchery. This decadent setting contains extravagantly dressed characters with luxurious lifestyles in a futuristic cityscape. It is not so much an improvement on the life in District 12 as it is 12's polar opposite. In terms of the semiotics of these two spaces, there is a distinctively different connotation to the defining aspects of District 12 and the Capitol. Some kind of heroic association with community, poverty, and nature is juxtaposed to that of egotism, excess, and city. This is how these particular classes are identified: one an exploited community of rural workers, the other an overindulged bunch of thrill-seeking hedonists. The inevitable struggle between these two extremes lies at the heart of the critical dystopias within millennial cinema.

Underpinning the capitalist nature of such dystopias is their oppressive ideology and controlling apparatus. In Panem, the dictatorial President Snow is the all-powerful head of state. Since the nation is already under dictatorial rule, the only goal of this regime is to remain in control. How this control is achieved cannot, therefore, be left neglected. As with most dystopias, the hegemonic order within Panem is based on what Moylan and Baccolini had earlier described as "Gramscian principles of both coercion and consent" (5–6). In practice, a militant police force (ironically called Peacekeepers) controls the populace through oppressive violence, and a regulated system of economic inequality maintains the status quo. The social order is thus regulated by the state apparatus and economic structures, but to keep the people in check, a third, discursive power is present. Diverting spectacles such as the Hunger Games provide the "bread and circuses" aspect of the government's control. The Games symbolically sustain the existing order by annually reminding the districts who's in control and why resistance is ill-advised. Regarding the first aspect of physical control, the state utilizes surveillance technology and Peacekeepers to oppress its subjects. The amount of control present in Panem expresses the fear of the Foucaultian principle of the panopticon (Garriott 164). This systematic surveillance exists both internally and externally. Not only are all residents confined to their own district, but hidden surveillance cameras make the population live in a near-constant state of paranoia. Inhabitants of District 12 are denied the means to protect themselves, and any sign of resistance is met with cruel punishment, exemplified by Gale's lashing for the crime of poaching.

Another structure keeping the population in check is the socioeconomic stratification within the individual districts. According to Sean P. Connors, the divide between merchants and miners is a "class structure, intentionally erected and sustained by the Capitol, [that] works against the interests of the individual districts by perpetuating social inequities and pitting their citizens against each other" (95). As already made evident, the class divisions and matching power relations are socioeconomically based; therefore, the Capitol's denial of tools and functions needed to improve the grim conditions in the districts can be seen as a second technique of oppression. Not only is the technology utilized in the districts vastly inferior to that of the Capitol, but food is so scarce in certain districts that starvation is common. Impoverished, the oppressed are too preoccupied with survival even to consider revolution. Power lies with a select few, and, with the exception of a few victors in the Hunger Games, there is little upward social mobility. Life in the Capitol is one of deliberate excess, with the upper class having products, tools, and chances closed off from those not belonging to their circles. One striking example is transportation. High-speed trains and hovercraft run through all districts but are accessible to only a select few citizens. Thus, the underprivileged majority is literally immobile when it comes to escaping their societal predisposition. Inhabitants of the Capitol are also exempt from the reaping of tributes; the sole basis for this privilege is their place of birth. Capitol residents lead a more luxurious life and are exempt from the violence and hardships faced by the rest of Panem. Privileges are defined by their exclusivity, and in Panem these are almost entirely dependent on place. Despite the inner hierarchies of the Capitol, being a citizen alone grants you unmatched benefits. In theory, almost the only way for an ordinary district nobody to be given a place within the upper class is to win the Hunger Games. It's here that the third discursive element comes into play.

As President Snow tells Seneca Crane in the first *Hunger Games* film, "Hope. It is the only thing stronger than fear. A little hope is effective. A lot of hope is dangerous. A spark is fine, as long as it's contained." Snow thinks that the population of Panem will tolerate injustice and inequality when it's presented in a comforting narrative. He believes that if everyone fears both punishment *and* the loss of what "little hope" they have been given by the Capitol, most people will resist rebellion. This idea is referenced in the regime's propaganda broadcasts. Peeta's propo shows, featured in *Mockingjay–Part 1*, all stress the current state of things as being the lesser of two evils. Continuously, the subjects of the state of Panem are exhorted to stay in their place and obey. These structures are reinforced by a doctrine that stresses the present divide to be both necessary and natural. The earlier war between the districts and the Capitol is used as a reminder of why change is undesirable. All inequalities are justified through this collective history; even the reaping of tributes finds its origins in this "deserved punishment for a stab in the back" mythical narrative. Therefore, the Hunger Games and their nationwide broadcast work within the regime's double discourse: one of symbolic punishment (for the districts) and one of popular diversion (for the Capitol). Fear and a little hope keep the less privileged of the districts in check, while the Capitol enjoys a culture of consumption. This corresponds with Louis Althusser's notion of commodity fetishism as a concealment of capitalist exploitation (130–31). The bread and circuses function of the Games is presented in a fashion akin to contemporary American media culture. Viewers engage with the program by supporting tributes with supplies, and the director searches the battlefield for drama (e.g., the star-crossed lovers narrative of Katniss and Peeta). This engagement, together with the sardonic TV host interviewing the tributes and providing commentary for the Games, paints a picture not too different from that of the present reality TV landscape.

At their core, these millennial dystopian narratives are about class struggles, about characters refusing to accept their given position and fighting to escape their preordained class or to destroy the system altogether. The narratives often situate their protagonist near the bottom of the social ladder, the hero's struggles echoing that of the 99%. Too, these narratives often start with the lead characters taking the grave injustices that dominate their world for granted. The protagonists are only trying to stay afloat in a harsh reality; however, in classic Hollywood fashion, a tragic event turns the protagonist into an active hero. The selection of Prim as tribute forces Katniss out of her passive state into the active role of first tribute, then victor, then Mockingjay. The personalizing of injustice makes Katniss more aware of the chains she's been born with and eventually inspires her to rebel, ultimately serving as the symbol of a revolution of the people against their unjust rulers. In a way, these dystopian films tap into a deeply ingrained American myth, one that Booker considers to be "a vision of individual resistance to systematic oppression that dates back to the American revolution" (257). Yet in another way, they are narratives propagating collective action as the solution to the ailments of our millennial era.

In this respect, a break with past dystopian films is noticeable. In films of the 1980s, the narratives' societies provide a setting in which the hero is mostly bent on completing his mission, whereas millennial dystopian films have more of a focus on the usurping of the system and its vested values. Characters such as Robocop, Rick Deckard, and Douglas Quaid are confronted by existing inequalities, but they do not stop operating within the constructs of society. These 1980s films are also characterized by a certain degree of cynical nihilism. As Stephen Prince observes, "The future these films conjured contained many attributes of their era, but hope for a better tomorrow was not among them" (340). However, in the millennial films, new energy surges through the genre. Moylan and Baccolini state that this recent body of work "makes room for a new expression of the utopian imagination" (7). Past critical dystopian narratives mostly ended on an ambiguous note and left us with the hero realizing the democratic deficiencies of his society, while at the same time remaining undecided of his place in the world. However, millennial dystopian narratives seem far more straightforward in their delivered resolution, presenting protagonists who at the end of their personal journey continue to engage actively in rebellious struggle for societal change. In *The Hunger Games* Katniss first comes to terms with the grave injustices present in her district at the hands of the Capitol. Her first big battle is one on a personal micro-level by competing in the Hunger Games and fighting to survive, thus undermining the authority of President Snow. In the next installments, however, this battle is transposed to a macro-level in which she becomes the sign of the protests against the regime, resulting in her becoming the best-known symbol of the revolution that will abolish or transform the established classes.

This trend toward active change is noticeable in a wide series of millennial movies. Films such as *In Time* (2011), *Cloud Atlas* (2012), *Elysium* (2013), *Divergent* (2014), and *Snowpiercer* (2014) all heavily romanticize the resistance factions and the guerrilla-like battles they wage against an oppressive regime. In *Mockingjay–Part I*, the resistance faction is, however, a more ambiguous lot. Despite their claims being fair and their cause just, they employ many of the same propaganda techniques as does the Capitol. In need of a heroic face for the revolution, President Coin and her main advisor, Plutarch Heavensbee, use Katniss as a propaganda tool to persuade the people to fight back. But Katniss has already been misused as a propaganda instrument in the Hunger Games, and she now clearly suffers from Post-Traumatic Stress Disorder. Even so, the rebel alliance of District 13 manipulates her into serving as their symbol. A series of embedded propos in which Katniss is used to stress "why we fight" employs classic propagandistic techniques (emotional appeal, enemy vilification, heroic associations, etc.) to enhance the righteousness of the rebel cause. Katniss's personal guilt and stress are hidden beneath her Mockingjay persona.

The elements discussed in relation to the class-based critical dystopia of *The Hunger Games* series can all be applied to a variety of films of recent years. *In Time* deals with a future in which time has become a global financial currency, resulting in the poor growing old while the rich stay young. The central class-dialectics expressed herein are those of young and old, but also those of the opposing aesthetics of the inner city and the urban suburbs. One storyline in *Cloud Atlas* matches its classes to the identity of humans and clones. Since the latter are forbidden to go beyond their workspace, the indoors is associated with oppression and the outdoors with freedom. In *Elysium*, Earth has become something of a third-world country in itself, with the wealthiest percentage of the population having retreated off-world to the space colony of Elysium. Along with the rich basking in luxury, a techno-magical machine also provides the upper class with healthcare for any illness. *Divergent* proves to be yet another class-based dystopia, in which a futuristic society is divided into multiple tribe-like factions. This systematic classification is based on the perception of people's defining characteristics and permanently determines every individual's place in society. Needless to say, this class division is supported by a preordained hierarchy. At the bottom of the social ladder is the Factionless, a category of casteless individuals stripped of all forms of status and security. But perhaps the most overtly anti-capitalist narrative and the most striking visual metaphor for the clash between classes is that of *Snowpiercer*. Here an apocalyptic winter has forced the last remaining survivors of humanity to live in a perpetually moving train. The train is divided into a series of carriages suited for three central classes—or, in the words of the film's Thatcher-inspired authority figure Mason, "First Class, Economy, and freeloaders." By linking the class logic of capitalist society to that of public transport, the film provides a clear setting in which the rudimentary inequalities of our contemporary society are easily demonstrated. The journey from the back of the train towards the front becomes an analogy for the difficult rise in social hierarchy. Here the discursive element pops up again. Throughout the story the heroic back-passengers are reminded to stick to their place, their oppressors claiming that these structures are natural and that opposing them would be dangerous to the established order. Outside the frame, the train has already experienced a number of failed revolutions; nonetheless, back-carriage passenger Curtis Everett leads his peers in a kind of blitzkrieg to the front of the train. "We go forward," he proclaims, not stopping for anything until the front is reached.

These films all feature the same narrative structure, wherein an individual takes on a central figure of authority within a class-composed capitalist regime. By the end of these films, the existing order is disrupted. This can happen only by the destruction of the very mechanisms that are responsible for the imbalance. At the end of *In Time*, the protagonist causes a crash of currency. In *Snowpiercer* the only way to disrupt the present structure is to stop (and crash) the train. *Elysium* also ends with the destruction of the titular space colony (including the scientific wonders that it holds) in hope of returning to a more egalitarian restructuring of society. This radical collapse of the dominant societal structures usually ends with the future uncertain and the film's ending open. Baccolini recognizes this as another core aspect of the critical dystopia, stating that "critical dystopias reject the conservative dystopian tendency to settle for the anti-utopian closure invited by the historical situation by setting up 'open endings' that resist closure and maintain the utopian impulse within the work" (18). Dystopian thrillers have long been a platform for left-wing critical thinking, causing Prince to describe such films from the 1980s on as "a critique and a portrait of capitalism run amok" (340). The recent cycle of critical dystopias seems to be a continuation of this trend, only with a stronger utopian impulse, suggesting a glimmer of hope or a solution for a better world to be found in a call to arms against the institutions and structures that form the basis of oppression.

Works Cited

Ahrens, Jörn. "How to Save the Unsaved World? Transforming the Self in *The Matrix, The Terminator,* and *12 Monkeys.*" *Media and the Apocalypse.* Ed. Kylo-Patrick R. Hart and Annette M. Holba. New York: Peter Lang, 2009. 53–66. Print.

Althusser, Louis. *Philosophy of the Encounter: Later Writings, 1978–87.* Brooklyn: Verso, 2006. Print.

Baccoloni, Raffaella. "Gender and Genre in the Feminist Critical Dystopias of Katherine Burdekin, Margaret Atwood, and Octavia Butler." *Future Females, the Next Generation: New Voices and Velocities in Feminist Science Fiction.* Ed. Marleen Barr. Boston: Rowman and Littlefield, 2000. 13–34. Print.

Booker, Keith. *Alternate Americas: Science Fiction Film and American Culture.* Westport: Praeger, 2006. Print.

Connors, Sean P. "I Was Watching You, Mockingjay: Surveillance, Tactics and the Limits of the Panopticonism." *The Politics of Panem.* Ed. Connors. Jefferson: McFarland, 2014. 85–102. Print.

Desser, David. "Race, Space and Class: The Politics of Cityscapes in Science-Fiction Films." *Alien Zone II: The Spaces of Science-Fiction Cinema.* Ed. Annette Kuhn. New York: Verso, 1999. 80–96. Print.

Franklin, Bruce H. "Visions of the Future in Science Fiction Films from 1970 to 1982." *Alien Zone: Cultural Theory and Contemporary Science Fiction Cinema.* Ed. Annette Kuhn. New York: Verso, 1990. 19–31. Print.

Garriott, Deidre Anne Evans. "Performing the Capitol in Digital Spaces: The Punitive Gaze of the Panopticon Among Fans and Critics." *Space and Place in* The Hunger Games: *New Readings of the Novels.* Ed. Garriott, Whitney Elaine Jones, and Julie Elizabeth Tyler. Jefferson: McFarland, 2014. 163–83. Print.

Greene, Eric. *Planet of the Apes as American Myth: Race and Politics in the Films and Television Series.* Jefferson: McFarland, 1996. Print.

The Hunger Games. Dir. Gary Ross. Lionsgate, 2012. Film.

Kuhn, Annette. Introduction. *Alien Zone: Cultural Theory and Contemporary Science Fiction Cinema.* Ed. Kuhn. New York: Verso, 1990. 1–14. Print.

Lacey, Lauren J. *The Past That Might Have Been, the Future That May Come: Women Writing Fantastic Fiction, 1960s to the Present.* Jefferson: McFarland, 2013. Print.

Moylan, Tom. *Scraps of the Untainted Sky: Science Fiction, Utopia, Dystopia.* Boulder: Westview Press, 2000. Print.

_____, and Raffaella Baccolini. *Dark Horizons: Science Fiction and the Dystopian Imagination*. 2003. New York: Routledge, 2013. Print.

Palmer, Barton. "Imagining the Future, Contemplating the Past." *The Philosophy of Science Fiction Film*. Ed. Steven M. Sanders. Lexington: University Press of Kentucky, 2007. 171–90. Print.

Prince, Stephen. *A New Pot of Gold: Hollywood Under the Electronic Rainbow, 1980–1989*. Berkeley: University of California Press, 2002. Print.

Sanders, Steven M. "Picturing Paranoia: Interpreting *The Invasion of the Body Snatchers*." *The Philosophy of Science Fiction Film*. Ed. Sanders. Lexington: University Press of Kentucky, 2007. 55–72. Print.

Snowpiercer. Dir. Bong Joon-ho. Moho Films, 2013. Film.

Determined About Determinism

Genetic Manipulation, Memory and Identity in Shaping the Postapocalyptic Self in Dark Angel and Divergent

MAX DESPAIN

In the postapocalyptic worlds of the television series *Dark Angel* (2000–2002) and the films *Divergent* (2014) and *Insurgent* (2015), the heroines are young women dealing with issues of genetic determinism while developing their own sense of self in a dystopian world. The popular but unscientific belief that genes are the singular determining factor in behavior suggests that coded memory in the story world's heroines' DNA will govern their behavior. But tangled with that coding are the socially acquired memories and community memories that include pre-apocalyptic media such as art and film. The heroines in these productions operate in imaginatively limitless worlds for viewers, because the apocalyptic events have made these worlds both recognizable with and completely different from our own. The social and cultural fissures created by the apocalyptic events require this kind of memory to bridge the gap. Both the *Dark Angel* television show and the *Divergent* series films, by way of considering multiple sources of identity formation, address American concerns over how technological experimentation can become a catastrophic force that could destroy our optimism for the future. The narratives' women, emerging from adolescence and forming identities after apocalyptic events, engage our cultural anxieties not only about social memory, but also about the hidden memory suggested in genetic determinism. And in proving themselves capable of operating beyond their inscribed genetic programming, they give our present-day society hope for a seemingly hopeless future.

The rising popularity of dystopian television and film is merely one symptom of growing popular fears about our future as the human race. These shows join a long tradition in utopian/dystopian literature addressing different forms of determinism. Cultural critic and historian Russell Jacoby suggests that the upswing in "anti-utopian" speculation comes from "the dwindling force of the modern imagination. History affects not only elections and wars, but the way we think and imagine" (xiii). Dystopias, then, are not only a likely popular genre but also a unique place to work out social apprehensions. When those fictional dystopias are directed primarily at young adult audiences, they open unique critical spaces to interact with social worries in a personal way that mirrors larger social realities, such as large-scale institutional manipulation and personal choice.

Critics of both children's and young adult literature and media tend to accept the unavoidable duality in the target audience. U. C. Knoepflmacher and Mitzi Myers, editors of a special edition of *Children's Literature*, have observed that the young adult category of production is ideal material for both adults and children. They note that in writing a "dialogic mix of older and younger voices … [a]uthors who write for children inevitably create a colloquy between past and present selves" (vii), tying in the inseparable quality of memory and young adult production as well as the link between older and younger audiences. Adult creators and authors must remember their own adolescent experiences when producing these narratives, predictably making that same connection for adult consumers identifying through memory with a younger version of themselves.

Acknowledging at least dual viewership and layers of interpretation in a diverse audience allows critical consumers of young adult cinematic narratives, and often their source books, to find the content more palatable by writing it off as "kids' stuff" while at the same time applying increasing complexity and interpretation to these visual and literary texts. In reality, this distance opens opportunities for both adult critical and adolescent formative exploration in areas including serious political inquiry and our darkest fears about identity. Even when Jack Zipes reminds his readers that there was "always a utopian element in children's literature from its beginnings" (ix), he also argues that dystopian fiction naturally evolves from utopian fiction because the pursuit of perfection can "lead to rigid if not totalitarian societies" (xi). Arguments about young adult literature naturally extend to other media intended for the same audience. Lacking the gravitas assigned to many purely adult genres, cinematic YA creations are free to shift paradigms and indict the present through their unwavering gaze on these fractured examples of the future. In his introduction to a collection of essays on utopias, Dominic

Baker-Smith observes that the "imagined world is still so linked to our 'real' world as to suggest the possibility of movement between the two. It is almost a definition of a utopian work that it should be contagious, that is to say designed to infect our reading of our world" (1). Keeping in mind Zipes' insistence on the relationship between utopian and dystopian works, we can extrapolate the same movement Baker-Smith suggests for utopias between a fictional dystopia and our own reality. In other words, these future-focused media narratives contain characters and commentary that should influence our present-day efforts to avoid dystopian futures.

The relationship between genes and memory in a postapocalyptic society draws attention to the idea of a better world before the apocalypse, one that existed before the genetic manipulation that is often a symptom of unethical government institutions. The memories of a happier time match with Martin Conway's discussion on autobiographical memory, that consistent, internal narrative we construct of ourselves. In the context of identity, Conway claims that our internal narrative is "a record of times when the self was not threatened or stressed and when the goals and plans of the self ran smoothly and were attainable. Consulting this record can sustain the self during periods of threat, stress, and alienation" (25). Although Conway's example is about immigrants escaping to America from war, dystopian characters experience that same threat, stress, and alienation. Inevitably, dystopian characters deal with their trauma through the perception that the pre-apocalyptic world holds the key to their autobiographical selves: their identities. Their present-day oppressive dystopias cause them to seek out the more complete and, as such, more satisfying sense of self out of their pasts. Our dystopian protagonists emerge from societies that believe that self is determined by the genetic codes they hold, but they gain memories that feel personal through historical artifacts such as art or a remaining video, and they think these memories also influence their sense of self.

Alison Landsberg describes the actuality of coming by and retaining recollections from such visual media as "prosthetic memory," claiming that "the person does not simply apprehend a historical narrative but takes on a more personal, deeply felt memory of a past even through which he or she did not live. The resulting prosthetic memory has the ability to shape that person's subjectivity and politics" (2). The appropriated past, already filtered by the constructed narrative of television, film, or art, develops into memories added onto people's direct experience, shaping their personal sense of self by adding community obligations and a broader scope of values, often confusing individuals because of the fractured nature of their present-day social frameworks. Characters such as Max from *Dark Angel* and Tris from *The Divergent Series* struggle with a private sense of identity that sometimes conflicts with behavior they are expected to exhibit as members of their postapocalyptic societies.[1]

Max Guevera is a genetically superior soldier who was created in a Manticore laboratory in Washington State, prior to the electromagnetic pulse that is an apocalyptic event for America. Implanted in women and birthed on site, Max, along with the other X-5 soldiers, knows no other upbringing but a strict military education and physical training. At nine years old, most of the X-5s seize an opportunity to escape, but they are separated in the effort to avoid recapture. We understand about these events from flashbacks in the present-day television series featuring nineteen-year-old Max, whose singular purpose has been to find other escaped X-5s. Viewers watch her develop an American identity that must form a bond with pre-apocalyptic times, even if she was a Manticore prisoner when the electromagnetic pulse occurred. In one particular episode ("Art Attack"), Max's closest friend and partner, Logan Cale, insists they save a Norman Rockwell painting from being sold overseas. Doing so accentuates prosthetic memories in Max's identity formation. The Rockwell painting was initially stolen along with artwork by Jackson Pollock and Nancy Kintisch, and the latter two paintings have ended up in Johannesburg and Riyadh. Representative of the time before the Pulse and America's slide from superpower to third-world country, these artworks are pieces of culture and memory for Logan. When Max retrieves the Rockwell painting from a safe on a Korean ship, she spends a moment studying the image. Later, Logan impresses on Max how important these artifacts are for American identity by complaining how the Baseball Hall of Fame ended up in Kyoto. Logan adds, "One day this depression will be over and when it is, it would be nice if there was something left." Because she was locked in the laboratory at Manticore until just months before the Pulse, Max does not share Logan's affinity for an American identity. She must use this glimpse of the past, preserved in a painting, in order to value an American identity as something worth appropriating. Through artifacts, Max can share a collective identity with Logan, thus aligning their motives for working together against evil forces in their society.

The *Divergent* series follows Beatrice "Tris" Prior as she negotiates an unusual society sorted by personality factions that becomes recognizable as taking place in the postapocalyptic city of Chicago. Operating with nearly no historical information, viewers must accept the present-day differences from our own reality and wait to learn more about the causes that created the unfamiliar circumstances of this world. Different from Max Guevara, Tris is the example of personal options in the face of genetic determination. The delayed knowledge of Tris's genetic determination is one of the most important suspense points in the series, a point revealed only at the end of the second movie. Initially, Tris is told to use her personal resolve from a teacher who is giving a handed down narrative or memory about choosing a faction. Early in the movie, an Erudite teacher explains how a "personality" test should assign her students the correct faction for their type; however, the instructor informs them that "it is your right tomorrow, at the choosing ceremony, to choose any of the five factions regardless of your test results" (*Divergent*). The founders of this community know that genetic makeup should determine their members' factions, yet the tradition offered to their adolescents allows for alternatives. Choice points to the possibility that people can decide to override their genetic instructions, particularly to improve or act in moral ways.

Hints in the movie suggest that, by the end of what will be a four-film franchise,[2] the core issue is genetic determinism. Tris illegally seeks out her Erudite brother and confronts Jeanine Matthews, their leader, who sees Tris as a threat because she suspects that the young woman is Divergent. Chastising Tris for breaking the rules, Matthews reminds her of the dictum "Faction before blood," noting that she understands this dictum goes against fundamental human nature to place some other organization before the family unit. She identifies human nature as a weakness, insisting, "I think human nature is the enemy. It's human nature to keep secrets, lie, steal, and I want to eradicate that. That's how we'll maintain a stable, peaceful society." Matthews's belief that human nature can be exterminated points to genetic determination as the foundation for their community and the basis for the factions, discounting the possibility that people can behave from moral motivation as opposed to a predetermined genetic code. Much the same as Max, Tris is the physical manifestation of a memory, of the times before the Purity Wars, except in Tris's case, all people had her "pure," unmanipulated genes and the manipulation brought about the apocalypse.

Beyond their own apprehended, prosthetic memories, both Max and Tris are expected to operate in the unique social structures of their dystopian worlds. Again, at the opposite ends of the spectrum, Max negotiates a chaotic post-electromagnetic pulse environment in Seattle while Tris copes with the strictly regimented, post–Purity War experiment in what used to be Chicago. Both are examples of women navigating social structures, working towards some kind of change for the better. Long ago, Maurice Halbwachs pointed out that social transitions are impossible to disentangle from memory, arguing that individuals are necessarily enclosed in "families, religious groups, and social classes" (182). Those social structures hold identities based on traditions and a collective memory that instructs individuals in proper behavior. In each case, genetic manipulation suggests that the characters are preset to act individually by a powerful programmed influence in the unseen double-helix of their DNA. The heart of genetic determinism then is whether or not these women's personal moral codes and resolve can override their genetic coding to allow them to choose their roles as influential actors in their societies. Perhaps more important is whether or not they should fit into society or develop a new society that improves upon their current postapocalyptic condition.

Despite the technological capacity to produce genetically enhanced humans, the larger concern in each heroine's case is who decides what enhancements should happen and what good genes look like. Economic and social theorist Jeremy Rifkin writes about both our aspirations and fears regarding genetic engineering, observing that "we appear caught between our instinctual distrust of the institutional forces and our desire to increase our own personal options" as he considers the questions about both the positive possibilities for genetic changes and the negative consequences of that power in the wrong hands. Who decides what right looks like? For Max, it is Dr. Sandeman, a disgruntled member of a cultish eugenics organization. Sandeman defects from the group, forms the government-run Manticore, and becomes her creator. His use of animal DNA within his mostly human subjects defines his split with the Conclave, a secret cult which prides itself as a pure breeding project. Rifkin's reference to "institutional forces" resonates here when the scientist's experiments become the government's next attempt at creating an assassin force. Similarly, Tris is a much later example of government decision making gone wrong. Early institutional efforts to eliminate undesirable human characteristics through genetic manipulation resulted in the Purity Wars, destroying America as we know it now. In the dystopian future, discrimination fades to one major schism: genetically pure versus genetically impure. In each case, Max and Tris represent genetic coding from before the apocalyptic event, making them, in some ways, the physical memory of the failed attempts at governmental intrusion in genetic manipulation. When the science of changing genes does not succeed in improving human existence, the only hope is that genetic determinism is a false popular belief and that our heroines can rise above their biological coding.

The heroines in these bleak fictional environments are woman warriors sharing characteristics that win us over to their creators' intentions about genetic determinism versus self-determination. That women are the powerful heroines in these dystopian worlds reveals a subversive quality in both series. Addressing the controversial concept of eugenics, the people at the government-run Manticore who choose to enhance Max genetically, making her a transgenic X-5, could have just as easily required her to be male. The army of X-5s, most of whom did not escape Manitcore, includes all genders and races as if these are no longer categories for discrimination. Similarly, while Tris's size and strength give her troubles in training, she is not criticized for being a woman in the Dauntless faction, and the other faction members are of all races and genders. In fact, the creators' purpose in showing racially "blind" future societies while engaging with genetic determinism supports social scientists' understanding that "race is an invented social grouping [that] was confirmed by genomic studies of human variation, including the Human Genome Project, showing high levels of genetic similarity among people of all races" (Roberts 789–90).[3] This sophisticated insight suggests that viewers should pay close attention to the genetic argument presented in these imagined dystopian futures. If these series' creators and writers recognize the need for a change and insist on flattening major socially constructed discriminations based on race and gender, their treatment of genetic manipulation should reveal the same complexity.

Ultimately, we learn that both women are genetically different from the others around them: Max because she has been purposefully altered, and Tris because her genes are defined as pure. Each is a dystopian Eve, not fruitful by reproduction, but productive because of her genetic code. This important plot element opens up each of these narratives to examination through the lens of identity trepidations: what latent character traits are hidden in our DNA and how do current practices of genetic manipulation reveal the possibilities for frightening aberrations that could result in world destruction? Both narratives show the trajectory of the tenuous relationship with the science of genetics. Max is a super soldier capable of inhuman feats, partly because she shares DNA with animals, yet she experiences seizures because the genetic manipulation is imperfect. Tris represents the opposite end of the spectrum: a person whose genes have naturally healed themselves, an example of "re-emergence" after a national-level genetic manipulation experiment goes wrong. The violent behavior in genetically manipulated humans caused the Purity Wars, producing the apocalyptic conditions that are her present-day dystopian world.

The presence of genetic manipulation in these young adult dystopias points to a question circling science for centuries. People try to comprehend the past through the present, so they have hypothesized whether or not a memory of the past could exist in our present-day genetic code. In the nineteenth century, scientists were willing to hypothesize that if we inherited facial features from our ancestors, we could possibly inherit those ancestors' memories as well (Otis xi). Nineteenth-century psychologist Théodule Ribot argued that "Man inherits from his ancestors certain modes of sensation and of thought, and therefore is disposed to their will, and consequently to act as they did" (345). And if this mode of scientific thought lost favor in the next century, Emily Singer's 2009 article in *MIT Technology Review* shows that Lamarckian ideas of evolution (the idea that acquired characteristics can be passed on to offspring) have gained new footing in the millennial era. She reports that a study "found that a boost in the brain's ability to rewire itself and a corresponding improvement in memory could be passed on." With some possibility that inherited behavioral traits can include environmental factors, the focus on genetics in both *Dark Angel* and *Divergent* also suggests the likelihood that ancestral memories from before apocalyptic events could exist in our heroines' DNA. In fact, Max's genetic manipulation drives the antagonist's plot in the second season, and Tris's divergence (later understood as a genetic difference) is proof that this link is important.

Max's transgenic DNA makes her a manifestation of the time before the Pulse. In season two of *Dark Angel*, the episode entitled "Medium Is the Message" exposes a long-term eugenics program that trumps the pre-apocalyptic government experiment with Manticore. With a feeling of secrecy and supremacy that alludes to the "Illuminati," the Conclave has used selective breeding to create superior physical specimens who plan to rule the world. Max and Logan accidentally uncover the Conclave when a woman calls for help with her kidnapped son. The twist is that this woman is the unwitting breeding partner to Max's season two nemesis, Ames White, a member of the Phalanx, and a purist in his belief that genetic manipulation is taboo. When White is about to kill his breeding host wife, as is traditional in the Conclave, she asks, "What are you?" He replies, "I am the future." White is a member of a powerful underground cult whose intention is world domination. When Max thwarts White's attempt at murdering his wife and engages him in a fight, White's words reveal his institutional discrimination: "Transgenic scum. You think those geeks with their chemistry sets and their gene banks and their greasy little paws are the future?" There is no room for the pre-apocalyptic government experiments in the Conclave future, and because the new discrimination is based on genes, there is no room for diversity either. Max is a tangible reminder of a past who can be read as a memory that is unacceptable to White and his exclusionary intentions. In the spirit of most young adult narratives, Max's tenacity as a morally sound character who defeats immoral villains suggests that her identity transcends her transgenic makeup, providing viewers hope that personal concepts of identity can triumph over genes.

By the end of the *Divergent* film, the audience understands that Tris's unusual qualities allow her complete choice in a way that only other Divergent members of the community have. Free from a mind-controlling serum, Tris can stand up against Matthews when she recognizes that the new government Matthews will run will be even more discriminatory than the oppressive regime being overthrown. When Matthews uses a serum to control Four (Tris's boyfriend), she remarks to Tris: "Amazing, isn't it? Everything we think of what makes up a person, thoughts, emotions, history, all wiped away by chemistry." Yet again, we see Tris break this chemical control through independent behavior by holding a gun to her own head and engaging Four's fear response, which overrides the serum's control. Ultimately, when they escape to a train after stopping the genocide, Tris muses, "We have nothing. We have no home, no faction. I don't even know who I am anymore." But her viewers know who she is: the hope for a future free from immoral leaders ruling with totalitarian methods because people like Tris and her friends will stop the injustice.

The 2015 release of the second film in the series, *Insurgent*, only solidifies the argument that Tris is capable of thinking for herself beyond socially constructed efforts to manipulate genes and control people through chemistry. *Insurgent* opens with Matthews' broadcast on screens around the community, lying in her recorded message about the attack on Abnegation. She insists that the community has to "confront the element that threatens to poison us from within," and that they must "take a stand against Divergents." She makes the prescient statement that "Divergents will destroy our society unless we destroy them," failing to understand that her society just might need to fail. Earlier, in *Divergent*, Matthews wants to eradicate human nature because of weaknesses such as lying and stealing, yet she is engaged in just those faults to hold her community together. By the end of the film we understand why Matthews' efforts need to fail and the community should not remain as it has been.

The movie raises questions about what is "normal" when, in a Candor drug-induced test called a simulation, Tris says, "I can't help but think if I was normal, we would all be together." Shortly after this sim, her brother Caleb visits her cell to explain how he is willing to sacrifice his own family member to preserve what is best. He sides with "normal" when he tells Tris, "You are living proof that the Divergent problem is out of control," but also that "no one thinks it's your fault you were born that way." Tris's comment and Caleb's explanation both show how they believe the community they grew up in seems "right" or "normal" to both of them and that a problem resides in Tris's biological makeup. But when Tris manages to unlock the box their founders left them, only because she is Divergent and can transcend all the factions, the message inside reveals that their entire city is the furthest thing from normal.

An unnamed woman, apparently a founder of this city, provides a recorded message from the past. The message is an explanation about how the society in the city walls originated as an experiment to try and recover the humanity that mankind outside the walls had lost. This obscure reference to lost humanity hints at the more thorough explanation of the source of the Purity Wars that we can expect to be in the upcoming movies, based on what we have learned in the books. The woman claims that her people have "all but destroyed" the world outside the city. She explains that the faction system was the founders' way of preserving peace in this community, but that they hoped that some people would become able to "transcend these factions"— and that these people, the ones that Tris's society calls Divergents, would be vital to all of humanity's survival.

Now the choices that Tris has been able to make, choices that manage to override society's and science's best efforts to contain people, become understood in a new light as desirable traits. Tris finally can turn on Jeanine Matthews and tell her, "You were wrong about us [Divergents]. We were never the problem. We're the solution." The film closes with the community streaming towards the walls to the recording of the woman from the box telling them, "Mankind waits for you with hope beyond the wall." Film viewers might be encouraged to read the sunlight spilling across the moving forms as a promising moment for the beleaguered members of the city. Four tells Tris, "You changed everything." The two remaining movies in the series should demonstrate just how prophetic his words will be.

Again, true to the young adult genre, the audience experiences optimism. And those people unable to wait until 2017 for the last film in the franchise will read ahead to learn the full extent to which genetic determinism caused the apocalyptic Purity Wars and became the ruling consideration in this dystopian society left in their wake. Tris represents the genetic traits of our current moment, a moment that is far from a utopia, but better than the imagined future in *Divergent*. She is an artifact that gives viewers confidence that we have the capacity to make right choices now, no matter our genetic makeup.

Notwithstanding that more than a decade separates the *Dark Angel* television series and the cinematic adaptations of the *The Divergent Series*, the plot similarities involving young women protagonists whose genetic makeup is the primary pivot for their identity in postapocalyptic worlds show the enduring cultural anxieties being played out in contemporary narratives. Ultimately, each character's memories, as much a physical quality in their DNA as those apprehended through their environment, play a major role in producing identities that are the driving force of the plots in each script. These young women's struggles to emerge from adolescence with a formed sense of their identities while negotiating a chaotic postapocalyptic world emphasize American concerns about remaining connected with our past while negotiating an uncertain future.

Notes

1. I am writing with the assumption that curiosity will require viewers of *Divergent* the film to consume all of the book series, including *Insurgent* and *Allegiant*. I discuss the source of the apocalyptic event and the basis for the factions but do not give all of the social structure for the trilogy.

2. The final novel, *Allegiant*, will be split into two movies scheduled for March releases in 2016 and 2017; therefore, these films are not discussed in this paper.

3. Roberts eloquently interprets the data on page 215 in Joseph Graves' book, *The Emperor's New Clothes: Biological Theories of Race at the Millennium*.

Works Cited

"Art Attack." *Dark Angel*. Creators James Cameron and Charles H. Eglee. 20th Century Fox Television, 2000–2002. DVD.

Baker-Smith, Dominic. Introduction. *Between Dream and Nature: Essays on Utopia and Dystopia*. Eds. Baker-Smith and C. C. Barfoot. Amsterdam: Rodopi, 1987. 1–4. Print.

Conway, Martin. "The Inventory of Experience: Memory and Identity." *Collective Memory of Political Events: Social Psychological Perspectives*. Ed. James Pennebaker, Dario Paez, and Bernard Rim. New York: Psychology Press, 1997. Print. 21–45.

Dark Angel. Creators James Cameron and Charles H. Eglee. 20th Century Fox Television, 2000–2002. DVD.

Divergent. Dir. Neil Burger. Summit Entertainment, 2014. Film.

Graves, Joseph L. *The Emperor's New Clothes: Biological Theories of Race at the Millennium*. New Brunswick: Rutgers University Press, 2003. Print.

Halbwachs, Maurice. "The Social Frameworks of Memory." 1925. *On Collective Memory*. Ed. and Trans. Lewis A. Coser. Chicago: University of Chicago Press, 1992. 37–189. Print.

Insurgent. Dir. Robert Schwentke. Summit Entertainment, 2015. Film.

Jacoby, Russell. *Picture Imperfect: Utopian Thought for an Anti-Utopian Age*. New York: Columbia University Press, 2005. Print.

Knoepflmacher, U. C., and Mitzi Myers. "From the Editors: 'Cross-Writing' and the Reconceptualizing of Children's Literary Studies." *Children's Literature* 25 (May 1997): vii. Print.

Landsberg, Alison. *Prosthetic Memory: The Transformation of American Remembrance in the Age of Mass Culture*. New York: Columbia University Press, 2004. Print.

"Medium Is the Message." *Dark Angel*. Creators James Cameron and Charles H. Eglee. 20th Century Fox Television, 2000–2002. DVD.

Otis, Laura. *Organic Memory*. Lincoln: University of Nebraska Press, 1994. Print.

Ribot, Théodule. *Heredity: A Psychological Study of Its Phenomena, Laws, Causes, and Consequences*. 1875. Trans. Merwin-Marie Snell. New York: D. Appleton, 1903. Print.

Rifkin, Jeremy. "The Biotech Century: Genetic Commerce and the Dawn of a New Era." *Ars Electronica* 1999. n. pag. First published in *Maclean's* 4 May 1998. Web. 18 May 2015.

Roberts, Dorothy E. "Race, Gender, and Genetic Technologies: A New Reproductive Dystopia?" (2009). Faculty Scholarship. Penn Law: Legal Scholarship Repository. University of Pennsylvania Law School. Paper 1421. Web. 19 Oct. 2014. 783–804.

Singer, Emily. "A Comeback for Lamarckian Evolution?" *MIT Technology Review* 4 Feb. 2009. Web. n.p. 19 Oct. 2014.

Zipes, Jack. "Utopia, Dystopia, and the Quest for Hope." *Utopian and Dystopian Writing for Children and Young Adults*. Ed. Carrie Hintz and Elaine Ostry. New York: Routledge, 2013. ix-xii. Print.

The Apocalyptic
Mental Time Travel Film

Erasing Disaster in Edge of Tomorrow
and X-Men: Days of Future Past

RYAN LIZARDI

Apocalyptic narratives are often about time, or more specifically, about a lack of enough time to address impending doom: witness the split-second escapes in the film *2012* (2009) and the perpetual lack of time to prepare for impending threats on AMC's *The Walking Dead* (2010 to present). The particularly harrowing problem of not enough time has been solved by another genre, the time travel story, which allows for retries, revisions, and the reliving of crucial narrative moments. A variation of the time travel story known as mental time travel is an underexamined facet of this complex genre. Mark A. Wheeler, Donald T. Stuss, and Endel Tulving first posited this term to describe reliving "experiences by thinking back to previous situations and happenings in the past and to mentally project oneself into the anticipated future through imagination…" (331). When applied to media narratives, mental time travel becomes a genre mashup that deals with characters traveling to and within the past to a different point of their lives by inhabiting their own consciousness. Bodies do not travel, but minds do, so there are no time machines in these stories. The appeal of this form of time travel in apocalyptic media narratives is the characters' ability to retain knowledge and memories about the future while reliving and changing the past enough to erase disaster or, at the very least, to save themselves.

In 2014, films that dealt with mental time travel rose in prominence. A few of these films focused on apocalyptic storylines, with the alien invasion in *Edge of Tomorrow* and the destructive war of *X-Men: Days of Future Past* headlining this trend. This focus on mediated disaster erasure can be exam-

134

ined in three parts: an analysis of filmic examples and the narrative mechanisms they employ, an investigation of scenes of disaster and pain in order to find repetition and erasure, and finally, a synthesis of these elements in hopes of positing a shift in symbolic control over the apocalypse into the mind of the individual and away from authorities and institutions. Where these sources of salvation are perceived to have failed—in narratives and in the real world—the answer provided by media is to trust a self who has complete control over his or her internal mental world.

Fear of disaster, destruction, and annihilation by aliens or giant robots is a common modern and postmodern media theme, and examining the different modes of how this fear is dealt with can help us understand contemporary American culture. If media about the apocalypse and its destructive wake implicitly "bring our focus of attention to concerns about a world undergoing cultural change" (Holba and Hart x), then what cultural changes does a shift to internalized mental time travel speak to? What fears are assuaged when our protagonists have the literal ability to relive past moments to save the future? If "the fear stemming from any prophesized apocalypse emphasizes 'the' ending and de-emphasizes the new beginning" (Holba and Hart viii), then perhaps it is simply the desire to erase the problems of today with the benefit of hindsight. Not that all mental time travel media narratives are apocalyptic, nor is the mental time travel conceit new. Notable non-apocalyptic examples include *Groundhog Day* (1993), *The Butterfly Effect* (2004), *Source Code* (2011), and *About Time* (2013). These examples have contributed to the mental time travel narrative device, but *Edge of Tomorrow* and *X-Men: Days of Future Past* present a mediated rumination on the understandable human feeling "if only I would have" when things go apocalyptically wrong.

In *Edge of Tomorrow*, the male protagonist, Major William Cage, relives the same day over and over while learning how better to defeat a world-destroying alien race. Like a video game, every time Cage dies, his day begins again; however, he retains his memories from previous "attempts." He finds and trains with the only other person to have experienced this phenomenon, Sergeant Rita Vrataski—also known as the "Angel of Verdun" for her unexplainable past heroics. Cage and Vrataski are on a quest to destroy the "Omega" alien to incapacitate a network of aliens who can also relive days for optimal battle results. In *X-Men: Days of Future Past*, Wolverine's consciousness is sent back in time by Kitty Pryde to change events that lead to a destructive war in his present. Wolverine both inhabits his own body in 1973 and retains his future memories. While in the past, Wolverine recruits the young Professor Xavier and Magneto; however, he must also bring onboard Quicksilver, whose mutant ability is to move so fast as to render time immaterial, thus manipulating a world that ostensibly stands still.

Appropriately, Quicksilver listens to Jim Croce's "Time in a Bottle" (1972) while moving at super speed—a cinematic signal to viewers that time is irrelevant for this character. This group is tasked with stopping the Sentinel program, which involves robots that sense mutants and adapt to fight their abilities. The films may be different in structure (*Edge*'s Cage repeatedly travels one day while *X-Men*'s Wolverine travels just once yet spans decades), but the idea of wanting to gain enough control to prevent the destruction of humanity is the same in both films.

In an age of video games, the normal procedure for a dead digital hero is simply to rematerialize at a prior point in gameplay. Presumably, the player is now more mentally equipped to succeed, knowing what tasks are in the immediate future. While mental time travel may appear more complicated and less palatable to popcorn audiences well-versed in time travel that often includes machines (such as Doc's DeLorean in *Back to the Future* [1985]), the concept of consciousness traveling back in time is more familiar to a generation of gamers. After all, everyone knows that, in games at least, you get a do-over. Chris Nashawaty of *Entertainment Weekly* pointedly describes *Edge* as "one of those time-loop thrillers where a reluctant hero has to relive the same events over and over, videogame-style, learning a little more each time..." ("Edge" 62). Cyclical looping until a character gets it right is often the crux of these films, and it points towards a cultivated desire in the audience to maintain control over a situation that seems impossible the first time around.

The trend towards this mental time travel narrative mechanism has not gone unnoticed by the popular press. In analyzing the number of versions of the same day in *Groundhog Day* and *Edge of Tomorrow*, Lindsey Bahr notes that *Groundhog* repeats at most thirty-five times, while *Edge* loops twenty-three times (62–63). Bahr says that these numbers "reflect onscreen loops" (62), but this distinction severely minimizes the number of days that are implied rather than shown within the narratives. These "implied days" affect the way the audience perceives Cage as a protagonist, especially in light of the video game characteristics evident in his role as hero. Cage clearly relives his day hundreds of times, evidenced through quick editing of duplicated actions as well as the beleaguered look on his face when he fails. The audience progresses with Cage like a video game player and shares his experiences. But every time he gets further in his quest/day (almost like a new level in a game), the audience is also given the sense that Cage has already been there many times. This implies a wealth of "attempts" not shown on screen. Janet Murray also noted this video game-like feature of mental time travel films in discussing *Groundhog Day*, as well as previous examples of repetition like *It's a Wonderful Life* (1946) and *Rashomon* (1950). Murray argues that because of its "simulation structure, *Groundhog Day*, though it has none of the shoot-'em-up content of videogames, is as much like a videogame as a linear film can be" (36).

We get only one "attempt" at real-life events, and if at the end of life we are left with regrets about situations we could not control or decisions we were not sure about, the past cannot be changed. Researchers have often found deathbed regrets to contain feelings of "guilt" and worry about things left "undone" (Edwards et al. 760), while other experts discuss more general and existential concerns about "*not having lived a life true to themselves*" (Ware 39, emphasis in original). What these regrets have in common is an inability to go back and change the past. Protagonists of the mental time travel film avoid this problem by rehashing failed actions. In *Edge*, the key for Major Cage is to memorize precise and complex movements. Although Vrataski lost the ability before Cage attained it, she is still the best person to train him. They go over motions like "stepping left, ducking right," while Vrataski excoriates Cage for "not being specific" enough during their training sessions (as each time for her is the first time). Cage repeats and learns the steps to fight an enemy that has the same ability to repeat and learn. *X-Men* not only connects to *Edge* in that it has an enemy, the mutant-hunting Sentinels, able to learn and adapt on the fly, but also in that Wolverine benefits from the hindsight of his own experiences as well as the experiences of the mutants who prepped him in the present. When visiting the younger versions of Professor Xavier and Beast, Wolverine is able to parlay his previous experiences with the older versions of these characters to smooth over the initial confusion over who he is and why he is there. It helps that Wolverine knows details about these two, and is able to say things such as "You and I are going to be good friends…. You just don't know it yet." *Edge*'s Cage uses more immediate repetition to learn from his mistakes, while Wolverine learns over a longer timeline.

An interesting dichotomy emerges in the relationship between learning from one's mistakes and being able to change the future. If Cage must step left and then duck right, how much choice and influence does he have? In re-executing failed movements with compensating corrections, perhaps he merely reaffirms the agency of the invading aliens as he adjusts to their actions, which in turn have been adjusted to compensate for our actions. Is Beast from *X-Men* correct when he says that "time is immutable"? Channeling Heidegger, Corey Anton says that "[f]reedom is inseparable from futuralness," defined as "existence that moves toward the will-have-been past" (189). More pointedly, Anton says that "the past, as past, is irrevocable" and "all the things we did not do, none now could have been done" (189–90). These films present a dialogue about fate and the ability—and real life's inability—to control or change the past. In movies about aliens and mutants, that subtext seems evocative of deep cultural fears. Through these apocalyptic erasure fantasies, we avoid the uncomfortable notion that the "future is actually the past: it is the past to which we currently are in the process of sentencing ourselves" (Anton 190).

The familiar apocalyptic media narrative of a world on the brink of destruction only to have the crisis averted at the last minute still occurs in science fiction, with examples like *Armageddon* (1998), *Sunshine* (2007), and even *The World's End* (2013). Missing within this scenario is the actual final apocalyptic destruction, implying that to suffer through the final destruction is to move beyond the point of no return, whether this is from the perspective of the characters or the world as a whole. The mental time travel narrative fixes this apocalyptic point of no return (and any pleasure derived from seeing ultimate destruction realized) by providing the opportunity to do anything over that went wrong the first time around. Perhaps the most famous example of this corrective time travel occurs in *Terminator 2: Judgment Day* (1991), when the Terminator is sent back in time to erase an on-screen, explosive apocalyptic park scene that initially ends in nuclear destruction and skeletons hanging from fences. In this case, avoiding such destruction takes the concerted effort of a rebel force in the future and time warps, but contemporary apocalyptic media narratives retain destructive scenes while shifting the onus of eventual time-travel-assisted avoidance to the individual's mind and lived experience. In *X-Men*, Sentinels are destroying all mutant-kind, and although initial scenes depict many mutants fighting against this unstoppable force, the solution to their plight is eventually reduced to the powers of one individual mutant, Kitty Pryde, to send back another individual mutant, Wolverine, to change the past and avert the apocalypse. Prior to the mental time travel, only Kitty Pryde's survival matters, and during the mental time travel, Logan's survival becomes primary along with Kitty as present-day conduit. In fact, not only will the other mutants have the timeline in which they fought erased, but they will also never know there was a worldwide Sentinel fight to begin with. Wolverine mentally time traveled at the behest of the surviving mutants, but in the end only he knows the full extent of what the future could have been.

If the key to the time travel apocalyptic film is the ability to experience disaster and then subsequently avert it—a destructive having one's cake and eating it too—then the mental time travel apocalyptic film takes this dynamic a step further by individualizing the experience of pain and the redo to erase it. In most mental time travel narratives, apocalyptic or not, this is achieved by resetting protagonists' timelines through their experiences of death. These characters die (and often feel the pain of death) over and over, only to end up back where they started. Perpetual repetition of torture and pain would likely be unbearable without a clear path of escape, as a "being could not be free if it were held fully in an atomistic and linear sequence of 'nows'" (Anton

189). Even in the comedic *Groundhog Day*, Bill Murray's character, Phil, attempts suicide a number of times in his efforts to break a perpetual day cycle. As a dark comedy, *Groundhog Day* does not linger on the pain it presents, but at least some of the methods of death appear to produce extreme levels of discomfort.

In *Edge of Tomorrow*, Major Cage dies horrifically on the field of battle through explosions, bullets, and fire—and every time, he jolts awake and clutches the afflicted area of the deathblow. Cage feels his face burn in his initial death/reset, and grabs his chest when shot the second time around. His first death is also a form of sacrifice, as he intentionally uses a mine as a shield in order to kill one of the larger invading aliens, whose dripping blood turns out to be the key to Cage's mental time travel. Cage then embarks on his hundreds of redos, with every one punctuated by death. When he breaks his leg in a training session with Vrataski, she suggests they just reset; then she shoots Cage. He tries to plead with her to stop, presumably because he will feel the acute pain of the bullet even if the consequences are not permanent. Eventually, Cage loses the ability to reset, thereby raising the stakes of his final "attempt" with no redo potential. When things inevitably go wrong, he tells Vrataski that "we've been through worse"; however, technically, during his time loop cycle, only he has been through worse. Vrataski's experience with her own countless deaths is more removed from the audience's experience, since the Sergeant's deaths are never shown or described in detail.

X-Men's mental time travel has a more complicated relationship to time and relived actions. Both the audience and the characters are still subjected to scenes of apocalypse, but mental time travel is presented in a longer form than daily looping. In earlier attempts at apocalypse erasure, the mutants must stall an attack by the Sentinels to give Kitty Pryde enough time to send someone's consciousness to the past in order to avoid being in the specific moment of attack. Besides Wolverine, the rest of the mutants must endure continuous pain and deaths that ultimately will never happen, but are nonetheless shown to the audience. We watch as Iceman is decapitated and Storm is impaled in slow motion, only to discover these events will not "count" in the changed future. A complicated conceit, *X-Men* has Kitty Pryde explain this version of mental time travel to Wolverine as an audience surrogate: "Basically, your body will go to sleep while your mind travels back in time. As long as you're back there, past and present will continue to coexist, but once you wake up, whatever you've done will take hold and become history. And for the rest of us it'll be the only history we know. It'll be like the last fifty years never happened. And this world, this war, the only person who will remember it is you."

Kitty knows they cannot keep avoiding disaster, and so, as a more permanent solution, Wolverine's consciousness is sent back in time. Although he does not die and then resurrect over and over again as Cage does, in this venture his healing factor means he must endure symbolic "death repetition" as he is shot, impaled, and drowned only to regenerate. In discussing small changes in the past that have big effects, Mark Rose says that "[b]lindly we contribute to the chain of cause and effect that operates through time, and blindly we suffer" (105). Unlike other mental time travelers, such as *Edge's* Cage or even *Groundhog Day's* Phil, Wolverine is comparatively blind as to whether his actions will cause the desired effect in the future. When Cage rolls under a truck and is flattened, he awakens immediately and learns to adapt for the next time. Wolverine, however, understands his goal is to prevent the Sentinel program by convincing Mystique not to murder a key mutant opponent, but he does not know whether he will be successful. At one point, his actions lead to the very Sentinels he was trying to prevent being set loose. Without the instant feedback that other mental time travelers experience, Wolverine might wonder if all of his subsequent actions are moot. Should apocalyptic events still "take hold" after his actions, will he be faced with an even worse scenario than the one he left? In effect, Wolverine trades repeated daily suffering for blindness to the moment and for a comparative lack of control.

In real life, we are often blind to the moment and also do not have control over big global events, while mental time travel represents a mediated attempt to fulfill "if only I could have" thoughts. Jörn Ahrens argues that "[t]he representation of the hero who mightily saves the post-apocalyptic world is deeply bound to the belief that man can shape his future..." (64). With consistent warnings of terrorism and ecological disaster, coupled with political deadlock, apocalyptic mental time travel films present an interesting contemporary commentary on placing faith in the individual to shape the future, a shaping that goes beyond simple disaster avoidance. Mental time travelers have the ability to erase and fix apocalyptic events that have already occurred, which speaks directly to most people's relationship to disasters. Something terrible happens, and, assuming we were not directly connected to the events, we are left without much control over the current state of affairs. The heroes in our mental time travel films reverse this dynamic as they serve not only to restore control over the current state of disaster but also to erase the apocalypse altogether. This is a powerful individualistic message in the face of a world where the single person may feel disempowered.

Describing the turmoil of the 1970s and the subsequent increase in apocalyptic films, Nashawaty argues that the decade provided "the psychic topsoil where doomsday visions not only took root but blossomed and thrived" ("A Brief History" 25). A similar fertile ground exists in today's cultural landscape, with contemporary apocalyptic visions speaking to nurtured fears about terrorism, ecological disasters, and biological diseases. What is different in mental time travel films is the manner in which these problems are narratively solved. The apocalyptic mental time travel film uses the immense power of the individual not to avoid disaster but to control and reverse it. The power is in the mind of the individual, and pointedly not in the hands of officials, authorities, or institutions because they have all failed the protagonists. Avoiding world-ending disaster in prior narratives like *Armageddon* is very different than *Edge* or *X-Men*'s erasure as the mental time travel films benefit from hindsight, which is often all we have in the real world.

In *Edge*, millions have died and humans have only one victory to hang their hats on. The situation is dire. Before entering battle for the first time, Cage is told by his Master Sergeant that "tomorrow you will be baptized in the crucible of battle" and, prophetically, that he will be "born again." Countless scenes of pain, death, and disaster are revisited over and over on the beach battleground, but when Cage defeats the Omega, he not only avoids further battles but also inexplicably erases roughly the previous thirty-six hours. In the case of *X-Men*, the erasure is even more extensive. When Wolverine, young Professor Xavier, and young Beast successfully change the events that led to the Sentinels' creation, not only are future wars avoided but also decades of disasters are erased. Even characters who died in previous films, like Jean Gray and Cyclops, return because they never died. The individual protagonist in the apocalyptic film "has to shape a future after the suddenness of catastrophe invades" (Ahrens 54), but in the apocalyptic mental time travel film, the future and the past are shaped by erasing the catastrophe entirely. As Professor Xavier describes it, the plan is to "end this war before it ever begins."

Themes of choice, fate, and the fear of final disaster run throughout the apocalyptic mental time travel film. Fredric Jameson argues that science fiction's "deepest vocation" is to "demonstrate and to dramatize our incapacity to imagine the future..." (153), but the mental time travel film assuages some of these fears by allowing a glimpse of the future and then granting the control to change it. The rhetoric of inevitability persists, but in the end the ability to enact change is affirmed, perhaps because an immutable future is too scary to imagine. Of course, certain movements and deaths do remain unchanged throughout *Edge*, despite the significant alterations made by Cage. What remains unchanged still speaks to the future's finality. Time travel media narratives often deal with immutability, from *Doctor Who*'s tenth Doctor discussing unchangeable events that are "fixed in time" in the 2009 episode "The Waters of Mars" to Doc Brown opining that November 12, 1955, "inherently contains some sort of cosmic significance" in *Back to the Future II* (1989). But when all-engulfing catastrophe is eventually erased in both *Edge* and *X-Men*, hope for the future is restored. We all fear a final death, and the apocalypse film affirms that a "strange fascination exists to depict the final disaster on Earth and the martyrdom of manhood" (Ahrens 53). In a world where every new disease, threat, or storm portends a coming doom according to the media, the idea of the end of the world is fascinating and scary. *X-Men* posits that "war is inevitable," yet its end presents a changed history and a momentary erasure of disaster (until the inevitable sequel). While the media-driven fear of apocalypse is reaffirmed for the audience, simultaneously the hope in an individual and internalized solution is also nurtured. The power of "if only I could have" is all these protagonists need.

Works Cited

About Time. Dir. Richard Curtis. Translux, Working Title Films, 2013. Film.

Ahrens, Jörn. "How to Save the Unsaved World? Transforming the Self in *The Matrix, The Terminator,* and *12 Monkeys.*" Hart and Holba 53–66.

Anton, Corey. "Futuralness as Freedom: Moving Toward the Past That Will-Have-Been." Hart and Holba 189–202.

Armageddon. Dir. Michael Bay. Touchstone Pictures, 1998. Film.

Back to the Future. Dir. Robert Zemeckis. Universal Pictures, 1985. Film.

Back to the Future II. Dir. Robert Zemeckis. Universal Pictures, 1989. Film.

Bahr, Lindsey. "Let's Do the Time Loop Again." *Entertainment Weekly* 13 June 2014: 62–63. Print.

The Butterfly Effect. Dirs. Eric Bress and J. Mackye Gruber. BenderSpink, FilmEngine, 2004. Film.

Edge of Tomorrow. Dir. Doug Liman. Warner Bros., 2014. Film.

Edwards, Adrian, et al. "The Understanding of Spirituality and the Potential Role of Spiritual Care in End-of-Life and Palliative Care: A Meta-Study of Qualitative Research." *Palliative Medicine* 24.8 (2010): 753–70. Web. 14 Jan. 2015.

Groundhog Day. Dir. Harold Ramis. Columbia Pictures, 1993. Film.

Hart, Kylo-Patrick R., and Annette M. Holba, eds. *Media and the Apocalypse.* New York: Peter Lang, 2009. Print.

Holba, Annette M., and Kylo-Patrick R. Hart. "Introduction." Hart and Holba vii–xiv.

It's a Wonderful Life. Dir. Frank Capra. Liberty Films, 1946. Film.

Jameson, Fredric. "Progress Versus Utopia; Or, Can We Imagine the Future?" *Science Fiction Studies* 9.2 (1982): 147–58. Web. 9 Sept. 2015.

Murray, Janet H. *Hamlet on the Holodeck: The Future of Narrative in Cyberspace.* Cambridge: MIT Press, 1997. Print.

Nashawaty, Chris. "A Brief History of the Cinematic Apocalypse." *Entertainment Weekly* 4 July 2014: 24–27. Print.

_____. "Edge of Tomorrow." *Entertainment Weekly* 13 June 2014: 61–62. Print.

Rashomon. Dir. Akira Kurosawa. Daiei Motion Picture Company, 1950. Film.

Rose, Mark. *Alien Encounters: Anatomy of Science Fiction.* Cambridge: Harvard University Press, 1981. Print.

Source Code. Dir. Duncan Jones. Vendome Pictures, 2011. Film.

Sunshine. Dir. Danny Boyle. DNA Films, 2007. Film.

Terminator 2: Judgment Day. Dir. James Cameron. Carolco Pictures, 1991. Film.

2012. Dir. Roland Emmerich. Columbia Pictures, 2009. Film.

The Walking Dead. Created by Frank Darabont. AMC. 2010 to present. Television.

Ware, Bronnie. *The Top Five Regrets of the Dying: A Life Transformed by the Dearly Departed.* Carlsbad: Hay House, 2012. Print.

"The Waters of Mars." *Doctor Who*. BBC. 15 Nov. 2009. Television.

Wheeler, Mark A., Donald T. Stuss, and Endel Tulving, "Toward a Theory of Episodic Memory: The Frontal Lobes and Autonoetic Consciousness." *Psychological Bulletin* 121 (1997): 331–54. Web. 14 January 2015.

The World's End. Dir. Edgar Wright. Universal Pictures, 2013. Film.

X-Men: Days of Future Past. Dir. Bryan Singer. Twentieth Century Fox, 2014. Film.

In the Flesh
The Politics of Apocalyptic Memory

FRANCES AULD

In the Flesh presents zombies as figures of empathetic horror, rather than the zombies created by a mindless virus in films such as *World War Z* or the rotting mega-consumers of *The Walking Dead*. In the BBC Three series (later aired in the U.S. on BBC America), the risen dead, called "rotters" or "the Risen," are capable of being brought back to their mostly human senses through government-instituted drug therapy. While on the drug, the Risen slowly reclaim their humanity from monstrosity, perhaps reclaiming their soul as a function and activity.[1] They also echo twenty-first-century men and women returning from war: processed, counseled, and medicated before being returned to their lives. The zombies are even given the physical camouflage of contact lenses and make-up, as well as the psychologically comforting mantra, "I am a Partially Deceased Syndrome sufferer and what I did in my untreated state was not my fault" (season one, episode one).[2] Like real soldiers going home, they strive to create a post-trauma life that cannot ever quite be the original, pre-war experience (Paulson and Krippner 3–4). These zombies face discrimination, and they live in a liminal state forever separated from those who have not experienced what they have. Their memories are the basis for the empathy that allows them to return to life; however, their specific memory of being among the rabid dead remains a difference even greater than their undead flesh.

The first episodes of *In the Flesh* revolve around the experiences of Kieren Walker as he reintegrates into the small town of Roarton, Lancashire, his home, as well as the scene of his birth, death, and resurrection. His "second life" as a Partially Deceased Syndrome sufferer (PDS) has an intense political focus, because Kieren's side (the zombies) lost the war. In addition, his beloved best mate, Rick Macy (and the stimulus for Kieren's suicide), died as a soldier in Afghanistan after being driven to war by parental homophobia. The meaning (or lack of meaning) in both the UK soldier's and the protagonist's deaths is a strong sub-theme in the first season's episodes. However, all the PDS sufferers enact some sense of the lost soldier returning home, fighting the memories and feelings associated with their wartime actions. The series clearly signals the real illness Post-Traumatic Stress Disorder (PTSD) with the naming of the fictional "PDS."[3] The first episode begins with Kieren's flashback to his pre-medicated, undead-self killing a young woman in the local supermarket. Kieren's experience of apocalypse is as much his memory of performing atrocious acts as a zombie as of having physically risen from the dead in a cataclysmic reversal of nature.

In the larger, post-rising world, living humans celebrate their survival in the struggle with the untreated, flesh-eating dead, whom the living still hunt for bounty. These feral zombies are worth £40 if shot and £80 if they are undamaged by the hunter. At the beginning of the series, members of the Human Volunteer Force (HVF) drink free at the local pub as hero militia, even as their destruction of the risen dead is framed by the knowledge that they were (and perhaps still are) executing individuals who *could* have been brought back to human consciousness. Members of the Roarton HVF militia, like the Risen, are guilty of genocide of the "Other," made valid at the time by the individuals' need for survival. The HVF militia stopped the undead from killing and eating the townspeople, but the risen dead were killing and eating the townspeople to fuel their own bodies. The violence of each side is validated as necessary for their survival as individual components of their communities. Characters on both sides were doing what they had to do. In season one, episode two, the Risen Amy Dyer explains, "We were in survival mode." As critic Steven Pokornowski recognizes, contemporary zombie narratives often reduce all life to what he calls "bare" life, in which the sanction of violence works to critique our culture's social ethos (41–42). *In the Flesh* certainly evokes the problematic decisions surrounding the last decade and a half of war. As fictional as the zombie scenario is, the survivors' whatever-was-necessary statement marks the metaphorical truth of the series; it also marks the genuine tension of a twenty-first-century Western culture full of traumatized veterans of the wars in Iraq and Afghanistan, what Brigadier General Stephen Xenakis called "the postwar epidemic that has already begun" (9). Like real-world trauma survivors, these fictional survivors have experienced multiple kinds of corporeal vulnerability and have been both politically and physically transformed by the experience. What *In the Flesh* promises and delivers is the point of view of the zombie. Point of view is the hallmark of Dominic Mitchell's narrative: his BBC America Series' tagline is "Zombies from the other side." In the first season, the PDS survivors' side is the experience of their poignant and problematic return home.

The series' narrative begins after the 2009 apocalyptic war of undead and human; now, zombies-turned-back-to-neighbors are being released to their families. A cure has been found for the undead's rabid behavior, but no one can forget what occurred. Viewers come to know both sides of the war (both the HVF militia's and the undead Risen's response) through the lens of memory. The sense of cataclysm resonates through both sides' survivors. Kieren stands in the doorway of his sister's bedroom, hearing her fight zombies in her dreams, unable to help her any more than he can erase his own memories of being a killer. These zombies are not the "unstoppable hoards" cited by Kyle Bishop in *American Zombie Gothic*, although both zombies and survivors share the zeitgeist of the post 9/11 wars (11–12). These sentient undead lead far more complicated "lives" than George Romero's living dead, as do those human beings sharing their world with reclaimed, thinking, feeling corpses. The humans' experiences are further complicated in the second season, when a politically radical portion of the Risen, the Undead Liberation Army (ULA), begins terrorist activities.

Cultural fears of terrorist activity as one of the foundational aspects of early twenty-first-century zombie cinema have been cited by Philip Simpson, among others (29).[4] However, in contrast to Simpson's identification of *The Walking Dead* as "the retreat from the never-ending geopolitical perils of the post 9–11 world..." (38), *In The Flesh* focuses on both zombies and the living working to function in a world whose apocalyptic scars are hidden by makeup and contact lenses. In the scene in which Kieren (the reclaimed zombie) watches his sister (the former zombie hunter) sleep in an average teenage girl's bedroom, the decor is contemporary and recognizable. Almost all of the landscape of destruction is internal, and the BBC series does not seem interested in retreat; instead, this narrative forces the viewer to see a world still running on advanced capitalism, even after a cataclysmic event. The world of *In the Flesh* is a politically and economically familiar enough model so that viewers see the "camouflaged" undead all the more distinctly. In the second season, when the Risen stop wearing their physical camouflage, there is no psychic place to retreat for the humans. The Risen reframe the already complex issue of terrorism and violence as they embody both perpetrator and victim, refusing to shield the living from the reality of their shared present and their grisly past.

Apocalypse, according to *In the Flesh*, was not the rising of the dead come to destroy the living or the living's execution of their miraculously risen friends and family. The real, damning, and ongoing disaster is the irresistible hunger to make sense of all survivors' actions and the corruptive, corrosive, and inescapable memories of what both sides did to survive. In this way, the first season can be read as an essay into the reintegration of twenty-first-century veterans returning from deployment in Iraq and Afghanistan with memories that continue to destabilize their lives, while the second season questions their ability to become "cured" of their experiences. Like real men and women living with the caustic experience of wars in Iraq and Afghanistan, characters like Kieren work to negotiate their memories and, to some extent, their actions as a kind of disease or syndrome that the national government insists can be controlled and hidden.

In the Flesh tells the story of zombies who killed people. Robert Kirkman's *The Walking Dead* focuses on the suffering of all still living humans—exemplified by Rick Grimes, the beleaguered but still breathing deputy sheriff. This American zombie classic, both as graphic novel and television series, explores the painful postapocalyptic decay of the *human* population, with no emotional gravitas apparent in the infected once they have completely turned. The humans' losses extend well beyond the physical destruction of their world. Their losses are deeply psychological, as well as social (see Dawn Keetley's anthology, *"We're All Infected"*). In the cable television series, the humans' response to various traumas is the crux of the larger narrative. Humans no longer fit inside the ethical and social expectations of the modern and postmodern eras. Yet as in Romero's seminal *Night of the Living Dead* (1968), human survival in *The Walking Dead* is still clearly privileged over that of the formerly human.

In contrast, *In the Flesh* evokes empathy for the undead, even when it inspects their most grotesque atrocities. The British series focuses on the traumatic guilt of the aggressor in battle, rather than the pain of the surviving victims. Human losses are not glossed over, however. The series begins with the brutal death of Lisa Lancaster, including the protagonist's consumption of her brain. When the rehabilitated Kieren later goes to his victim's family to try to explain that she will not be coming back, he struggles with the potential destruction of their hope as the cost of his confession of murder. This perspective, the point of view of the PDS sufferers, is in some ways far more complex that of the surviving humans in *The Walking Dead*. While both have survived apocalypse and both have been remade through the furnace of the war to survive, *The Walking Dead*'s humans have a basic protective insulation of innocence that the re-humanized of *In the Flesh* lack. The Risen must exist with the pervasive knowledge that they were the instruments (if not the cause) of brutality to their neighbors, mass death, and the unhinging of the world's society.

The PDS survivors' flashbacks are not even the fantasy nightmares of the surviving humans. They are memories in which the "dreamers" reenact the consumption atrocities required for their survival after rising from their graves. This is a terrible intimacy that the humans, either observers or protectors, cannot comprehend. The Risen hold the memories of neither guns nor bombs, but the teeth of human carnage. They awoke as weapons *in the flesh*. Even when their own brains stop cycling through these memories into their present, they must live within the geography of their previous destruction. Kieren returns to the graveyard in which he was buried after his suicide, ducking under and through the razor wire and biohazard tape. He is the walking biohazard, conscious of his continued excision from the living, even as he wears make-up and contact lenses to pass. When he meets another zombie (his former hunting partner, Amy Dyer) in the graveyard, Kieren is so terrified of her that he stabs her with a piece of rebar. Whether he fears her as a zombie or a human being is not clear. As a human, she might kill him for being a "rotter," and if she is the Risen, he fears her wild hunger, even as he remembers his own.

The Risen are not, cannot be, human again. Their loss of human life occurred prior to their re-birth as zombies. Their re-found sentience is further complicated by their earlier loss of genuine human life. For the undead of *In the Flesh*, the rising was a one-time, inexplicable event without any sense of their victims returning as zombies. Whether by war, disease, accident, or suicide, each of the Risen has been to the grave, and that experience alone puts them in a separate class, something they actually share with those they killed. They are veterans of death, and even if they had not become the instrument of slaughter, their pre-rising knowledge is a barrier to their acceptance by the rest of the (human) world.

Even without the draw of a political or ethical response to their treatment, the PDS sufferers come together to be with those who have a first-person understanding of both death and rising. Like other trauma survivors, particularly veterans, the Risen find comfort in the presence of others of their kind. Both Simon Monroe (newcomer to Roarton) and Amy are involved with the ULA, and even Kieren looks for an undead voice to help him understand his experiences. "I was once where you are now. Frightened. Confused. Filled to the brim with guilt," says the online figure whose voice has been modified even as his face is obscured by a black hood decorated with a skeleton (season one, episode one). This Undead Prophet supports a second rising that requires the sacrifice of Kieren Walker. Like the innocent local Rave organized by the Roarton Risen, the ULA and the Undead Prophet offer some chance for the Risen to be in the company of others who share their vocabulary of experience and undead memory. Once again, the fictional survivors behave in ways that match the needs of real Gulf War veterans. In their 2007 examination of PTSD, Daryl S. Paulson and Stanley C. Krippner cite contemporary therapy for combat veterans suffering from the nightmares associated with their traumatic experiences: "A group can serve as a 'safe haven' where clients feel comfortable revealing frightening nightmares, share hidden dilemmas, experience emotional reactions in a supportive environment" (130). Trauma survivors do come together to articulate and explore the psychic experiences of their previous physical and emotional traumas with others who share the reality of war memories. In the series, the ULA's attraction for Kieren is natural for him as a trauma survivor even as it creates suspense through the plot twist of an extremist faction bent on Kieren's final death.

In the first season, the sense of constant bombardment of their difference is paradoxically heightened by the cultural necessity for PDS survivors to pass as physically human. When the government insists that all homes harboring a survivor be marked with spray paint, it is the "PDS" inscription on Rick Macy's garage door that causes his murder. The painting of a word on his home makes the veteran's father unable to believe the make-up and contact lenses on his undead son. When faced with Rick's experience in Afghanistan, his father destroys the Risen warrior rather than live with his son's past. Survivors *must* paint their faces and bodies and wear contact lenses to hide their eyes as social contract. But the Risen's medication is what allows them to retain their rationality and hold on to their personality and consciousness. This internal, normalizing agent benefits the user, unlike the topical disguise that comforts the society in which the user exists. Society wants skin to look a certain way; it demands survivors hide the cause of their experience. People do not want to know what the Risen have done, what they have seen, or who they have been. PDS survivors must hide their eyes; their society resists looking into the eyes of those who have killed to survive. Even by the end of season two, a bar patron quietly tells her companion that she is sickened by the eyes of the "rotters." Medicated into rationality and appropriately disguised, survivors are treated as second-class citizens or worse. In season two, Kieren learns that after a non-rabid human killed ten of the Risen, the judge who gave sentence modified the man's time in jail because the Risen are only half-people. Their very status as members of the society is abrogated by their past. Like contemporary veterans, their actions in war, as well as their experiences and memories of war, are indelible components of their identity. The Risen are seen as the crimes they have committed, even as they are simultaneously silenced when they attempt to talk about the pre-treatment atrocities they visited on friends and family. In a particularly ironic turn, Kieren's father insists that he sit at the table and pretend to eat meals with his family. At the same time that Kieren must simulate human behavior, his family does not want to hear him discuss what he actually did as an unmedicated zombie.

In the Flesh further evokes the reality of PTSD when Kieren is asked in a therapy session about how it feels to rejoin society; he identifies his extreme guilt. One of the complicated aspects of the rhetoric of PTSD when it occurs in veterans damaged by both the violence they have witnessed and the violence that they have performed is that the status of individuals with PTSD is that of victims, even when a portion of their trauma is based on the acts that they performed. This conflation of victim and perpetrator is as paradoxical as it is genuine. In the first episode of season one, Kieren says, "I am a zombie and I killed people." But when he takes responsibility for the violence he committed against others, Kieren is redirected by his counselor, and he repeats the appropriate message: "I am a Partially Deceased Syndrome sufferer and what I did in my untreated state was not my fault" (season one, episode one). In season two, his physician asks him to repeat his affirmation; he looks in the mirror and quickly says, "I am a Partially Deceased Syndrome sufferer and that's not my fault" (episode one).

In the establishing shots of the series, the small rural English village of Roarton is displayed as a place of empty fields and worn buildings, without the human presence or domestic energy of an active community. This place clearly bears the scars of a disaster with buildings tagged by the phrases "HVF" and "rotters." These inscriptions, combined with the desolate imagery, signify that this community has suffered extreme violence and is continuing to do so. This is a place of post-traumatic stress. Part of the measure of this experience is the examination of what sociologists call "chronic community disorder," particularly in communities marked by lower socioeconomic status and those with residents who lack mobility: "Neighborhood studies now regularly include measurements of physical decay termed 'visible disorder' by Sampson and Raudenbush (1999)" (qtd. in Frankenberg et al. 500). When the Victus (Pro–Living Party) government representative MP Maxine Martin asks the Vicar how the townspeople are dealing with the loss of a former resident to a ULA attack, his response is "We're very resilient people" (season two, episode one). The term "resilient" may be especially telling, as the concept of Iraq and Afghanistan veterans' resiliency is a component of contemporary preparedness training to help mitigate troops' potential for PTSD.[5]

In the first episode of the series, Kieren resists the idea that he will be put back in a predominantly human society when he is sent home to Roarton. He clearly fears his flashbacks for the emotional distress they cause him. When he explains this to the physician giving him his daily dose of neurotryptolin and preparing him to leave the zombie-holding facility, Dr. Shepherd is delighted. He praises Kieren with "You are feeling." This recognition that the PDS sufferers are moving from numbness to the experience of genuine, if intense, emotions recalls real veteran PTSD sufferers who experience a disconnect with their normal emotional state. Laurie B. Slone and Matthew J. Friedman recognize that veterans for whom "emotional expression is discouraged" in a war zone (59) may have difficulty reclaiming their emotions when they return to a civilian life.[6]

For the fictional sufferer of PDS, the key to both physical and mental healing seems to be time and consistent medication, although the marker of healing seems to be pain. Kieren experiences physical pain from wearing his contact lenses too long: "My eyes feel sore, which is odd because I'm not supposed to feel pain" (season two, episode one). His physician tells him that neuro-genesis (regrowing brain cells) means that some of the components he is regaining are pain receptors.

Kieren's physical pain is a corporeal marker of his changed "life"; however, the pain of his emotional scars threatens his very identity. Paulson and Krippner cite the experience of both trauma and political terror as "threats to self-identity at its very core" (19). Kieren's quest for his own identity is particularly poignant in the first season. Entering the bedroom that has been kept by his grieving parents just as he left it when he committed suicide, he glances at objects and reaches out to touch them, finally exploring a secret cache of photos and memorabilia focusing on his relationship with Rick, an Afghanistan war veteran who died in combat. Kieren's sister asks him, "What are you? ... Who are you? What's your name?" and he responds, "Kieren," to which she retorts, "Na, don't believe ya" (season one, episode one). Later, the Vicar stirs the humans of Roarton when he preaches that "They are not your neighbors, not your friends. They are all imposters, changelings of the highest order" (season one, episode three). The friends and family of both the Human Volunteer Force (HVF) and the Risen do not know how to deal with either group. Each side has committed violence against a being that was human but is unrecognizable as such within the battle scenarios of the Rising. Yet Kieren and the other Risen did not initially have a choice about destroying human life when, rabid and hunger-crazed, they clawed themselves out of their graves.

When the Risen begin to create their own political and cultural identity, they strike out as terrorists, reverting to their unmedicated physiology and unmediated violence to call for recognition of their presence and their rights. This violence, like both HVF Jem Walker's killing of the medicated, non-violent teenage zombie Henry and Maxine Martin's killing of Amy Dyer in the second season, is different than the killings of either side in the original battle for survival. These are casualties of the undigested trauma that each side experienced, flaring again in a format very consistent with real Post-Traumatic Stress Disorder. The veterans of each side are hyper-sensitized and fumbling with the reconstruction of their identities.

Sarah Juliet Lauro and Karen Embry recognize, in the figure of the zombie, a posthuman who is essentially fleshly, temporal: "The vulnerability of the flesh and the instinctual fear of its decay, as well as the dissolution of consciousness—all things that happen as we approach death—are suggested in the monstrous hyperbolic of the zombie as living corpse" (101). *In the Flesh*'s zombies, however, with their often guilt-ridden memories of a rabid past and optimistic, focused plans for a future, resist the limitations of the temporal category. They exist in a time continuum that includes past and future. Kieren knows he would be safer abroad, and so he is preparing to leave to study art in Paris; Amy Dyer falls in love with Philip Wilson, plans for a future, and is gleefully introducing him to her dead mother when Amy is stabbed into final death. The Risen also problematize the purely fleshly/carnal nature of the zombie in the imagination of the viewers as well as for the fictional humans in the series. What I call "carni-tas," the desire for sensual consumption, the feeding of fleshly, primitive appetites, is what the humans trapped in apocalyptic zombie fantasies typically fear from the zombies.[7] Early twenty-first-century zombie cinema models the audience's genuine fear that we, the humans, will be consumed, our essences lost to fuel another's essence, our unique selves gone at another's gustatory pleasure. But again, *In the Flesh* diverges. "Caritas," the love that feeds another without dissolution of either self, the heart-love that motivates someone to nourish another human being, is paradoxically apparent in the Risen multiple times. An unmedicated adult male, presumably the father, protects and comforts an unmedicated young female when the HVF comes after her. The presence of this emotion is more shocking in its implications than when Kieren steps into the line of fire to protect the zombie family from the HVF's guns or when the Risen strive to comfort one another at the final death of Amy Dyer. It is perhaps most eloquent when Kieren weeps at the death of Amy, his best friend. Like the beating of Dyer's heart when she stands with her human lover, it is a sign of something beyond *the flesh*.

Finally, perhaps the most optimistic comment that *In the Flesh* suggests about PTSD is made when Kieren, drugged with "Blue Oblivion" (the illegal substance that transforms the Risen back into their unmedicated state), struggles against the chemical trigger that he has been given. He resists sliding back into his rabid, violent state. His sentience, his rationality, and his personality overcome his impulse to react as if he were in a battle for survival. Zombie or not, Kieren reacts to his father with love rather than appetite. Kieren survives.

Notes

An earlier version of this essay was presented at the International Conference on the Fantastic in the Arts in March 2015 in Orlando, Florida.

1. Stephen Asma identifies the idea of a soul as function rather than substance in *On Monsters* (2009). He references both the Aristotelean and the medieval ideas of "soul" as activity as it relates to monsters (80).

2. Episodes of *In the Flesh* are untitled; therefore, they are identified in this essay by season and episode numbers. These numbers are not repeated in the Works Cited.

3. In 2012 Dr. Simon Wessely identified the PTSD rate for soldiers in the United Kingdom at about 5%, while the rate for United States soldiers ran at 15–20% (Wessely cited in Ritchie). The reasons given for this disparity were the relative age of British troops (older), the shorter duration of their tours of duty, and the fact that the majority of the troops did not serve in Iraq.

4. See Philip L. Simpson, "The Zombie Apocalypse Is upon Us! Homeland Inse-

curity"; also, Kyle William Bishop, *American Gothic Zombie;* and Steven Pokornowski, "Burying the Living with the Dead: Security, Survival and the Sanction of Violence."

5. Alison Howell writes, "In Western military contexts, and especially in the U.S. Army, PTSD is being parsed in the same two directions: on one hand through an increased emphasis on resilience, and on the other, through the biomedicalization of traumatic events in war, in particular through the diagnosis of mild traumatic brain injury (TBI) and what might be called the 're-physicalization' of trauma in military contexts" (220). She cites the model of taught or trained resilience as a current military preventative to PTSD.

6. Slone and Friedman discuss contemporary soldiers' mental skills sets for survival as "B.A.T.T.L.E.M.I.N.D." (56–62). This acronym is used by the U.S. Army to help reset soldiers' thinking when they return home since "the mindset necessary for survival in a warzone is usually quite different from the mindset that makes things go smoothly at home" (56).

7. The use of "carni-tas" and "caritas" as contrasting terms came to me through professors teaching medieval literature.

Works Cited

Asma, Stephen. *On Monsters: An Unnatural History of Our Worst Fears.* Oxford: Oxford University Press, 2009. Print.

Bishop, Kyle William. *American Zombie Gothic: The Rise and Fall (and Rise) of the Walking Dead in Popular Culture.* Jefferson: McFarland, 2011. Print.

Frankenberg, Elizabeth, Jenna Nobles, and Cecep Sumantri. "Community Destruction and Traumatic Stress in Post-Tsunami Indonesia." *Journal of Health and Social Behavior* 53.4 (2012): 498–514. Print.

Howell, Alison. "The Demise of PTSD: From Governing Through Trauma to Governing Resilience." *Alternatives: Global, Local, Political* 37.3 (2012): 214–26. Print.

In the Flesh. Created by Dominic Mitchell. Seasons One-Two. BBC Three, BBC America 2013–14. Television.

Keetley, Dawn, ed. *"We're All Infected": Essays on AMC's* The Walking Dead *and the Fate of the Human.* Jefferson: McFarland, 2014. Print.

Kirkman, Robert, and Tony Moore. *The Walking Dead.* Berkeley: Image Comics, 2004.

Lauro, Sarah Juliet, and Karen Embry. "A Zombie Manifesto: The Nonhuman Condition in the Era of Advanced Capitalism." *boundary 2* 35.1 (2008): 85–108. Print.

Paulson, Daryl S., and Stanley C. Krippner. *Haunted by Combat; Understanding PTSD in War Veterans.* Plymouth, UK: Rowman & Littlefield, 2007. Print.

Pokornowski, Steven. "Burying the Living with the Dead: Security, Survival, and the Sanction of Violence." Keetley 41–55.

Ritchie, Elspeth Cameron. "Why Is the UK's PTSD Rate So Much Lower Than the U.S.'s?" Battleland: Military Health. *Time.* 26 June 2012: n. pag. Web. 15 Jan. 2015.

Romero, George, dir. *Night of the Living Dead.* Image Ten-Laurel, 1968. Film.

Simpson, Phillip L. "The Zombie Apocalypse Is upon Us! Homeland Insecurity." Keetley 28–40.

Slone, Laurie B., and Matthew J. Friedman. *After the War Zone: A Practical Guide for Returning Troops and Their Families.* Philadelphia: Da Capo, 2008. Print.

The Walking Dead. AMC, 2010 to present. Television.

World War Z. Dir. Marc Forester. Paramount, 2013. Film.

Xenakis, Stephen N., and Matthew J. Friedman. "Understanding PTSD." *Wilson Quarterly* 36.1 (Winter 2012): 8–9.

In Search of a New Paradise and the Construction of Hell in *The 100*

CEREN MERT *and* AMANDA FIRESTONE

In the not-too-distant-future, a young woman carefully scratches charcoal drawings onto a concrete floor and the walls surrounding it. The images are of plants, fish, insects, and birds; some are clearly recognizable while others are not. There are also drawings of human-made monuments like the Great Pyramids and the Arc de Triomphe. The artist, seventeen-year-old Clarke Griffin, has never physically seen any of the things she draws because like everyone she knows, she has been confined to a space station floating high above Earth for her entire life. Her renderings are only small representations, tokens of the planet left behind nearly a hundred years ago as a result of nuclear holocaust.

This is the opening scene of *The 100*.[1] The show debuted on The CW in March 2014 and follows the complex social issues and anxieties of several groups surviving in this postapocalyptic storyworld. Ark, the slowly failing international space station above Earth, is home to a near totalitarian society where even the smallest infractions are cause for a death sentence. One hundred teenagers, each imprisoned and slated for execution at eighteen, are sent to Earth, simply known as Ground, in order to discover if the planet is viable enough to sustain human life. If it is, members of Ark can return in order to rebuild society; if not, then the "expendable" teens are no great loss ("Pilot"). Clarke and those who survive the crash-landing quickly discover they are not alone. The descendants of the people who survived nuclear war, dubbed Grounders, are hostile. To further complicate matters, the group almost immediately implodes, creating two factions with dichotomous philosophies as to how this situation ought to be handled.

The first season closely follows the construction of characters' identities, including the affinities and animosities that ultimately create and represent some as Others. In this show, the distinctions between being from Ark or from Ground are crucial, but so are those among the social statuses of individuals from Ark. Too, the distinctions between the different genders and ages of the people—particularly as more "adults" arrive from the space station—are fundamental. Therefore, as part of the process of identity formation, the idea of representation is important. Representation, both as a concept and a sociopolitical issue, occupies a significant place within a wide range of academic fields; here, the cultural studies contextual framework in terms of identity supports the formation of the groups in *The 100*. Another concept that adds a layer of complexity to this analysis is the tension between utopia and dystopia. The people of Ark seek to rebuild the social contract post-catastrophe in an effort to achieve a utopia; inadvertently, they create dystopian conditions via laws and social mores designed for "the greater good." Thus, we contend that in the series (specifically in its first season), the search for and hopeful creation of a utopian world results in a dystopian one that is very much in line with the way the characters construct their self-identities, the identities of other people, and their representations of the Other.

Representation is a relatively ambiguous term. It can be used in denotative—defining—and connotative—implying—forms in any number of ways. As Jen Webb reminds us, "Representation is also fundamental to everyday life. People practice representation all the time because we live immersed in representation: it is how we understand our environments and each other" (2). For scholars, representation as a concept and analytical tool is understood through a variety of discipline-focused approaches. Stuart Hall breaks the concept of representation into two overlapping systems of meaning-making: the semiotic and the discursive ("Work of Representation" 19). Images, language, and the physical world simultaneously "stand in the place of" and "stand for" meaning in concrete and symbolic terms (19).

Some of Clarke's charcoal drawings "stand in place of" the plants that grow on Earth. Clarke's renderings are not the plants at all, but they nonetheless carry meaning to those who observe them. These drawings are her mental representations of Earth—probably created as a result of exposure to other representations about Ground like movies, songs, or books. Clarke sometimes talks aloud to herself about her living situation: "I was born in space. Have never felt the sun on my face, or breathed real air, or floated in the water. None of us have" ("Earth Skills"). The pictures that she has drawn in her cell stand in for the actual things and are "tweaked" according to her perceptions of the way Earth was before nuclear disaster. Clarke and others on Ark share a broadly similar conceptual map as a result of having a common culture and language, a way of making meaning within this community.

As Hall states, "Representation *is* an essential part of the process by which meaning is produced and exchanged between members of a culture. It *does* involve the use of language, of signs and images" ("Work of Representation" 15, emphasis in original). Semiotics, or the study of signs, can be a key way that language is deconstructed to understand how meanings are made. Clarke's drawings function as signs; they represent different plants, animals, places, and things. We can think about one such object, a book perhaps. If one utters or reads the word "book," all those who know the English language will have a mental representation of the object. This mental/visual image of the book in our mind is the concept of that word. This mental image varies from person to person and may be influenced by any number of things. The image may be the last book we read, a favorite book from childhood, an old book we once saw in a museum, etc. Although each person assumes a "different" book in her or his mind's eye, the language is such that it offers a general description that unifies the meaning of the word "book," perhaps as an object made of paper with many words printed on individual pages that reveal a cohesive amount of information. In this respect, language within the systems of representation holds a significant role, as it is through conceptual thinking that we have mental images of different objects, events, and people. In other words, concepts and images are brought together and expressed by the use of language; a common language is essential to communicate the translation of these thoughts, sounds, or images to others (Hall, "Work of Representation" 17–18).

Representation often works in tandem with the formation of identity, which Hall notes as the "process of subjectification to discursive practices, and the politics of exclusion which all such subjectification appears to entail, the question of *identification*" ("Who Needs 'Identity'?" 16, emphasis in original). It is "a process never completed—always 'in process'" (Hall, "Who Needs 'Identity'?" 16). Effectively, it becomes the progression of knowing oneself, one's subjectivity, in relation to how one makes meaning through language, specifically that which separates oneself as different from other people.

The people on Ark share a culture, history, and language. While it may appear these people have a common origin—Earth—each group within the community has differently historicized the past in relation to their material conditions. This clearly affects how they construct their own identities, depending on where each person is positioned within the communal hierarchy. When the one hundred young, now-former delinquents are sent to Ground, they immediately begin the process of constructing new identities in regard to their changed spatial arrangements. Already they were set apart from the general populace on Ark as criminals, held up as examples—representations—of lawlessness and the breakdown of society to others living on Ark; linguistically, they were singled out—identified—by being consistently referred to as "delinquents," further marking them as dangerous. But their arrival on Ground means that they are effectively free to create new lives, new identities that do not mark them as criminals but as anything else they might like to be (while still carrying the "baggage" of their prior identities). The rebellious leader Bellamy Blake explains his desire to break away from anything Ark-related. Bellamy says, "My people already are down. *Those people* locked my people up. *Those people* killed my mother for the crime of having a second child.... Here there are no laws. Here we do whatever the hell we want whenever the hell we want" ("Pilot," emphasis added). In tremendous agreement, the overwhelming majority of teens begin to chant "Whatever the hell we want!" to drive home their desire to create new identities that are not dictated by their prisoner statuses from Ark.

Bellamy's language sets up a clear binary between those sent to Ground, young criminals, and those remaining on Ark, specifically privileged bureaucrats who simply enforce laws without question. For Bellamy and many of the other teens, it's an Us versus Them scenario. This dichotomy extends to Wells Jaha and others like him, such as Clarke, who wish to remain in contact with Ark. This bifurcation in the group is in part due to the elevated privilege that Wells and Clarke enjoyed because their parents were key council members. In the few hours after the crash, these people have undergone radical restructuring of their identities and seek to represent themselves in new ways, particularly as they have the ability to do so without interference or oppression from Ark officials. Things quickly become both more problematic and complex as those identities must shift again at the realization that the teens are not alone on the planet's surface.

Though there is dissent among the teens based on their social status and political leanings, they do share the distinct commonality of Ark. Unbeknown to them, pockets of human beings survived the nuclear devastation and subsequent generations built new communities. Referred to as Grounders, these truly native people share few, if any, commonalities with the Ark teens; they grow up in clan communities speaking a language akin to Creole, and only certain members, warriors, are bilingual with English. While these traits are enough to mark the Grounders as different from the Ark explorers, it is their violent introduction in the pilot episode that seals the teens' perception that Grounders are not just different; they are dangerous Others.

The concepts of Difference and the Other are crucial. Hall explains that meaning-making is highly dependent upon recognizing what is different in terms of binary poles, but he adds, "Though binary oppositions—*white/black, day/night, masculine/feminine, British/alien*—have the great value of capturing the diversity of the world within their either/or extremes, they are also a rather crude and reductionist way of establishing meaning" ("Spectacle of the 'Other'" 235, emphasis in original). Hall further notes that a black-and-white photo is actually a misnomer because there is no total saturation of black or white hue; instead, the print is created with shades of grey. Additionally, he says that the poles of nearly all binary oppositions encompass relations of power where one extreme receives prestige and privilege over the other. Hall ultimately argues that we need Difference in order to construct a meaning of the world and self-identity. But Difference often is wrapped in the hierarchized power imbalances in such binaries. Plainly, we better understand and define ourselves by recognizing what we are not, and what we are not is something different, Other. The Other instantly comes with negative connotations as it is unfamiliar and perhaps difficult to understand or empathize with. Simultaneously, we name the Other through negative, unfavorable language and representation, and we also positively construct our own identity, which is through that difference between "we or us" versus "them" (Hall, "Spectacle of the 'Other'" 235).

The Ark teens and the Grounders become immediate enemies when Jasper Jordan, who travels with Clarke and several others to find Mount Weather (the original intended landing site for the dropship), is spectacularly speared through the chest by an as-yet-unknown assailant. The remaining party quickly returns to the makeshift camp to tell the others about the danger. For the Ark teens, the attack on Jasper is totally unprovoked, immediately making the assailant an Other, something to be feared and destroyed. Their collective assumptions about what Ground would be like—a potentially radioactive wasteland devoid of most life, especially human life—are quickly dashed as Clarke rather obviously states, "Everything we thought we knew about the Ground is wrong" ("Earth Skills"). And once again, identities must shift to accommodate these new realities and meanings as they are encountered.

While the Ark adolescents did not choose to be sent to Ground, the Ark Council's intention is that they should be the unwilling pioneers on this brave new world. The "adults" of Ark have inadvertently made the pioneers colonizers, and the indigenous inhabitants begin to act accordingly, seeing the Ark teens as a threat to their existence. Each group has judged the other as a danger, and while not impossible, creating cohesion between the Ark teens and Grounders is a tall order. At one point, the main protagonists try to create an alliance with Anya, the leader of the Woods Clan Grounders. Significantly, Anya says, "You started a war that you don't know how to end" ("Unity Day"). Anya's declaration alludes to the colonialist practice of invading "unknown" lands while disregarding the likelihood that this action will be perceived by the "conquered" group as a hostile trespassing. Toward the end of the first season, it becomes clear that—intentional or not—a war on Ground has started. While the aim was to find a paradise on Earth, a place where all the people of Ark could go to reestablish human society, the reality instead is a kind of hell, generated through the encounters and clashes between these Othered groups. This is solidified by the "us" and "them" representations each group constructs. To the Ark teens, Grounders are savages who booby-trap the forests with rudimentary (yet highly effective) technologies of death. Conversely, for Grounders, the Sky People—those from Ark—are equally as brutal, as evidenced by Bellamy's capture and torture of Lincoln, a Woods Clan warrior. Somehow both groups fail to recognize the worst in themselves, offering those behaviors as normalized means of protecting themselves as individuals or the community; yet they clearly identify similar tactics as barbarous traits in the Other. Representations of the self, the collective, and the Other are always in process, always becoming, and always fixed only temporarily because change is inevitable.

In *The 100*, as people left Earth when the nuclear devastation became apparent, their assumed hope was that the collective international space stations floating above the planet would be humanity's safe haven. When the stations joined together to become Ark, it was an opportunity to mold a society into something more idyllic. Humanity hoped that this new community could learn from the mistakes made on Ground and create something far better. However, the "new life in space" does not become a utopia. Instead, it brings its own problems, such as shortages of air, food, water, medical supplies, and so forth. Indeed, just as the dropship is launched, Clarke's mother, Abby, who is the chief medical officer for Ark, is sentenced to be "floated" (executed by being blown into space) because she has used more than the allotted medical supplies during a crucial surgery to save the life of Chancellor Thelonious Jaha. Laws (such as restricting the resources each person has access to) are designed to stabilize the society. When Abby initially calls for more anesthetic, one of her colleagues says, "We're way over the line…. You're asking me to break the law" ("Pilot"). Though she is already aware that the legal consequence of her action is execution, she replies, "Fine. I'll do it myself. Let them come after me" ("Pilot"). While the laws are in place to protect the welfare of the greater good, in this moment Abby's decision to use more blood and anesthetic for the Chancellor ultimately saves his life. This, in essence, is the tension between the binaries of utopia and dystopia: good intentions for the greater community while creating circumstances that clearly restrict and oppress that community.

Hence, Ark becomes an unpredictable and inhospitable place to live. In other words, the "advanced technologies" on Ark and the social laws created for that place eventually present its inhabitants nothing but devastation and despair. In a strange reversal, *The 100* portrays the hope of those living on Ark as an optimism that stems from a collective memory about the so-called Ground. Accordingly, Ground now represents the opportunity for a new civilization, the pursuit of or the desire to hold onto a utopian ideal, while Ark's residents live in (or have anxiety about the emergence of) a dystopia. In this sense, utopia and dystopia do not have to be mutually exclusive; even in a setting or context where dystopia is prevalent, such as that of *The 100*, it is still possible to chase the idea or emotional state of utopia.

Thus, we return to the crucial concepts of Identity and Difference. In both contexts—the burgeoning hell of Ark and the burgeoning hell of Ground—the people living there must reconcile who they have been, who they are becoming, and how they are going to maintain their social relationships through the inevitable changes. Fredric Jameson further examines the literary ramifications for "Utopian" and "Dystopian" worlds.[2] For him, texts that posit "Utopias" conceptualize social alternatives that are "a representational meditation on radical difference, radical otherness, and on the systemic nature of the social totality, to the point where one cannot imagine any fundamental change in our social existence which has not first thrown off Utopian visions like so many sparks from a comet" (Jameson xii). Plainly, in order to construct a stable social Identity, then it must be first rooted in notions of a society that is so radically Different that system appears implausible. Yet we are challenged since "even our wildest imaginings are all collages of experience, constructs made up of bits and pieces of the here and now" (Jameson xiii).

The notion of a "Utopian" totality, or closure (Jameson 4–5), assumes there is a point at which supreme perfection is achieved and movement toward that ideal is, to us, an expression of faith that believes the current reality can be transformed. Many of the inhabitants of Ark are very much invested in a belief that a better life, a utopia, is still a real possibility. Vera Kane, one of Ark's spiritual leaders, speaks to this as she waters a small tree— the Eden Tree—representative of her people's Earth origins and hopeful destination. She says, "Our ancestors built this Ark to be our salvation, but it's also our test. But we endure because we have faith. Faith that one day, generations from now, our people will return to the Ground" ("Murphy's Law"). Vera constructs a communal identity as she says "our people," a term that appears completely inclusive of all Ark residents. Of course, she is unaware that the delinquents were sent to Ground, and they *know* that it is not the utopia she likely envisions. Additionally, her linguistic inclusivity is at odds with the way Bellamy earlier constructs the Ark community through his use of "my people," meaning the working class, versus "those people," meaning privileged bureaucrats.

Vera's devout conviction is shared by a number of others and, as such, means they are willing to make the ultimate sacrifice. A handful of Ark officials, including Abby and Thelonious, know that life support is failing. Indeed, Abby's husband, Jake Griffin, was floated for collecting the evidence of the failure and attempting to make it public knowledge. Marcus Kane, a high-ranking council member and Vera's son, devises a population reduction plan, known as The Culling, where 320 people will be euthanized in an extreme measure to provide clean oxygen for the remaining inhabitants for nearly six months. This should provide just enough time to stabilize the air scrubbers for the return to Ground, though this, too, is problematic as there are not enough seats on the remaining dropships for all the people. As Thelonious grimly quips, "We are on the *Titanic* and there aren't enough lifeboats" ("Contents Under Pressure"). Abby attempts to stop The Culling by broadcasting the video that Jake intended to release. Unexpectedly, people come together and volunteer for euthanasia in order to give their loved ones, and by extension the rest of the community, a better chance for survival.

In this scenario, the people who volunteer for death hope that their loved ones will have the opportunity to find paradise. While it is never revealed what their individual beliefs or philosophies are, their sacrifice embodies facets of Jameson's theories connected to the Utopian program and the Utopian impulse (3). The Utopian program is enacted through "political practice" that ultimately "aims at founding a whole new society" (Jameson 3). For the volunteers, their decision is both personal and political, offering them a glimpse of, if not access to, the totality and closure—the perfection—that is achieved in the Utopian program. They recognize that their sacrifice benefits others, while their deaths are the ultimate totality.

However, Jameson's Utopian impulse is far more sinister and cynical. The Utopian impulse is characterized by "liberal reforms and commercial pipedreams, the deceptive yet tempting swindles of the here and now, where Utopia serves as the mere lure and bait for ideology" (Jameson 3). For the Ark's volunteers, there is nothing but hope that their loved ones will actually come close to that shiny future on Ground. Individually, we assume that all of them have someone who will grieve for them. Besides, not dissimilar to the *Titanic* disaster, the people more likely to perish when Ark fails are those from less privileged strata. Certainly, all of the Council members have the opportunity to flee to Ground. Volunteering for euthanasia does not radically change the circumstances of Ark, nor does it aid in reaching Utopia. Once more, the distinction between Bellamy's "my people" and "those people" speaks to how identity and representational privileges function. In this case, the Utopian impulse may seek to reach an ideal society, but, instead, it badly reshapes the future.

Utopia and dystopia are often presented as the extreme opposites of the same spectrum. And the opportunity to recognize one set of ideals is only accomplished by contrasting it with the acute differences of the other. As in the example of Hall's black-and-white photo, the existence of those two poles is in many ways purely symbolic since it is the density of the shades of grey, of the liminal space in between, that is truly representative of "how things are." So it is with Jameson's Utopian program and Utopian impulse: the first is about totality—the endgame—and the second is about segments of life—the present and immediate future. In the show, all of the characters encounter a range of utopian and dystopian experiences. While they overwhelmingly meet things that are squarely dystopian like violence, oppression, and corruption, there are certainly moments of awe, wonder, delight, and peace that more often categorize utopia. For example, when Abby lands on Ground, she is the first to leave her dropship, and like the teens who arrived before her, she steps onto the planet that she has been dreaming about her entire life. When Thelonious prompts her to describe what she sees through an intercom system, she says, "It's everything I've dreamed. So much green. There are trees everywhere. And water. And air. The air smells sweet. It's so beautiful. Thelonious, you should be here" ("We Are Grounders [Part 2]"). Simultaneously, in the main camp of the initial crash site, a bloody battle is happening in which Sky People and Grounders gruesomely kill one another. Abby experiences a facet of utopia while Clarke experiences a facet of dystopia.

In this moment, Abby accesses a fleeting Utopian totality. Her world has radically changed, for the better, and she is on the cusp of receiving the "new world" that she so concertedly fought for. But Utopia does not exist without the limits posed by people in the pursuit of reaching it. For instance, the implementation of strict order and punishment on Ark is *supposed* to be for the better of the social order. However, it is clear that rules "for the good of the people" can also produce results that are contrary to that ethos. Michael D. Gordin, Helen Tilley, and Gyan Prakash describe this problematic: "Despite the name, dystopia is not simply the opposite of utopia. A true opposite of utopia would be a society that is either completely unplanned or is planned to be deliberately terrifying and awful. Dystopia, typically invoked, is neither of these things; rather, it is a utopia that has gone wrong, or a utopia that functions only for a particular segment of society" (1). For the show's characters, going back to Earth is a probable solution in achieving utopia. In contrast, only three generations prior during the nuclear Armageddon, Earth was a dystopian hell. Nevertheless, this utopian ideal or method for maintaining human life again blooms its own dystopia. Bellamy's "Whatever the hell we want" vision of utopia, more aligned with the anarchistic, unplanned society, clearly unravels as the teens fight and murder each other to satisfy their individual desires. Then again, the Exodus Charter, the laws devised by the Council to be applied to the new settlement on Ground, is no better as it continues to enforce rules that ultimately cull people's individual freedoms.

Neither solution offers the promised symbolic heaven. In terms of identity and representation, former delinquents Bellamy, Clarke, and the others bear the burden of coming to terms with the necessity of rules in order to structure the community. The issues of who they are and how they represent themselves are crucial in how they will shape their new lives on Ground, where the environment, their enemies, and their interpersonal conflicts can be hell. But in all of that are the glimpses of utopia that drive them forward to carve out a little piece of that dream. And just when they each feel they have reached some stability, identities must change again as they face new experiences and challenges on the beautiful yet dangerous planet.

NOTES

1. This essay focuses exclusively on season one of *The 100*.
2. Jameson specifically capitalizes Utopia and Dystopia in recognition that these are "political issue(s)" though he writes about them in a literary capacity (xi).

WORKS CITED

"Contents Under Pressure." *The 100*. Warner Bros., 2014. Netflix.

Du Gay, Paul, Jessica Evans, and Peter Redman. *Identity: A Reader*. London: Sage, 2000. Print.

"Earth Skills." *The 100*. Warner Bros., 2014. Netflix.

Gordin, Michael D., Helen Tilley, and Gyan Prakash. Introduction. *Utopia/Dystopia: Conditions of Historical Possibility*. Eds. Gordin, Tilley, and Prakash. Princeton: Princeton University Press, 2010. 1–17. Print.

Hall, Stuart. "The Spectacle of the Other." Du Gay, Evans, and Redman 225–79.

_____. "Who Needs 'Identity'?" Du Gay, Evans, and Redman 15–30.

_____. "The Work of Representation." *Representation: Cultural Representations and Signifying. Practices*. Ed. Hall. London: Sage, 1997. 15–65. Print.

Jameson, Fredric. *Archaeologies of the Future: The Desire Called Utopia and Other Science Fictions*. Verso: London, 2005. Print.

"Murphy's Law." *The 100*. Warner Bros., 2014. Netflix.

The 100. Season One. The CW. Warner Bros., 2014. Netflix.

"Pilot." Season One. *The 100*. Warner Bros., 2014. Netflix.

"Unity Day." *The 100*. Warner Bros., 2014. Netflix.

"We Are Grounders (Part 2)." *The 100*. Warner Bros., 2014. Netflix.

Webb, Jen. *Understanding Representation*. London: Sage, 2009. Print.

The Apocalypse Will Not Take Place

Megamonster Films (Cloverfield, Pacific Rim, Godzilla) *in the Postmodern Age*

SHARON DIANE KING

The Apocalypse will not take place.

We are watching monster movies. We place the ticket stubs in our pockets or work the remotes in our hands. In the theatre, the scent of popcorn pervades; giggles and murmurs erupt through the cinematic sound and fury on the screen before us. At home the pause button calms; the close reach of bathroom and microwave reassures. And we know how it ends. The monsters will rage but not win. It is a given that we—humanity, the Earth, our civilization—will not be extinguished. The narrative in which we take the lead trumps all.

The Apocalypse will take place.

We are watching monster movies. Vast sums of money have been spent to ensure our belief in our own imminent destruction. The essence of American filmmaking is brought to bear: an action-adventure mode, an unabashedly realistic acting style, a showcasing of technological omnipotence in special effects. It is a given that we—the Earth, human civilization, our power of narrative—will be threatened with extinction. All resources are marshaled to make us buy and watch, hold our breath, cry out in terror.

From its opening sequence, the film *Cloverfield* (2008), with its found-footage format and bleak stamp "Property of U.S. Government," jolts the spectator; its designation of New York City's Central Park as a "former" place throwing viewers into tragic mode: pity for the loss, dread for what must have happened to cause it. The hand-held camera wielded inexpertly by the de facto point-of-view character Hud wrests control from the audience, its endlessly twisting angles churning stomachs, in some spectators even inducing vertigo (Happy Russia). The film's purported story—a banal record of a farewell party, interspersed with random clips of doomed lovers Beth and Rob, their halcyon day spent at Coney Island having been taped over—is hijacked some twenty minutes in, the focus violently wrenched away from its Rom-Dram roots into a grimly intimate, bewildering account of a monster's attack on New York City. The first image is the most shocking: the claw-scarred, severed head of the iconic Statue of Liberty, hurled savagely through the streets of the city, mayhem in its wake. Haunting, horror-inducing images now engage us relentlessly—blood spattering across the camera lens when the parasite-creatures attack bored waif Marlena, her eyes dripping blood before she perishes gruesomely; a wraith-white horse and carriage trotting driverless down a near-empty Manhattan street; the impossible tilt of Beth's nearly collapsed apartment building, from which Rob still must rescue her. For much of the film, we see only half-glimpses of the huge, ungainly Cloverfield monster devastating the city, its obscured form adding to the *unheimlich* terror it generates. If the home video is not "the last thing" he will see, as Hud insouciantly jokes at the start about the soon-to-depart Rob, it is simply because he and untold others—perhaps most of the world's population—never got a chance to view it. And though the footage cuts off on a happy note—"I had a good day," Beth smilingly tells Rob at Coney Island—there is no closure, no answers as the film ends. The army's "Hammer Down Protocol," set to wipe out Manhattan should the creature not be destroyed, may have occurred—or something far, far worse. We do not find out.

In a voice as deep and gritty as the breach he describes, the narrator of the more traditionally told *Pacific Rim* (2013) provides an origin myth for the Pacific Ring of Fire: giant alien creatures that are the first wave of colonization of the planet, stirring up from the depths through a vast undersea portal to wreak havoc on the Earth's crust. As the voiceover narration describes how humanity had been looking for extraterrestrial life "in the wrong direction," images of the awe-inspiring vastness of the stellar system dissolve into earthly horrors: a roaring *kaiju* (giant monster), an enormous insect-like creature, assaulting the beloved Golden Gate Bridge amid girders falling, automobiles tumbling, shrieking people running in panic, bombers raining down their inevitably ineffectual payloads. Clips of news reports display world leaders—including real-time President Obama—opining over the gravity of the threat, images of destruction spooling behind them: buildings in smoking piles of rubble, hazmat teams searching for victims, graphs of economic chaos as half the world's oceans become off limits. The narrator utters the names of coastal cities now lost—Lima, Seattle, Vladivostok—like those of fallen comrades; captions scrolling across news screens describe the terror of the infernal beasts bubbling to the surface: "Is this how the world ends?" The defense against these monsters vomited up from the deep is the program of the Jaegers, gigantic killing machines operated from the inside by a pair of mind-linked fighters and their off-site director. Scenes of the Jaegers' rapid superstardom and equally sudden horrific failures—one costing the narrator his brother—in the face of ever-strengthening *kaiju* attacks set the audience on a rollercoaster of emotions: relief, tension, uncertainty, dread. The audience grasps how bleak the prospects of this world are even before the opening title sequences, the under-girding theme music, and the real start of the film. The constant threat of doom—more cities falling, casualties mounting, defensive coastal walls tumbling like children's building blocks—does not lessen as the plot unfolds.

A disaster at a nuclear power plant in Japan serves as a foil for a personal tale of heartbreaking loss, forming the backstory to the 2014 iteration of *Godzilla*, the king of *kaiju* that over decades has morphed into, if not benevolence, at least into a lack of malevolence towards humanity. In 1999, lead engineer Joe Brody's research-driven warnings about the uncanny regularity of seismic activity near his nuclear plant go unheeded; his wife, also an engineer, is sent to check on the nuclear reactor. She is soon trapped during an earthquake and dies before Brody's eyes. His guilt-fueled paranoia drives him for fifteen years, culminating in his being brought before a scientific team researching alpha predator Godzilla and a strange dormant behemoth found in the ruins of the power plant, just as this insect-like MUTO stirs from its torpor. Shrieking its unnervingly grating rattle-cry, the MUTO exacts chaos both intimate—Brody's fatal injury, his Navy officer son Ford's imperiled family, a child separated from his parents spared from certain death by Ford's heroic actions—and global, as it devastates Honolulu, Las Vegas, and later (with the help of its mate), San Francisco. The audience again witnesses constructs emblematic of cultural and civic identity—a tranquil beach luau, skyscrapers on the Vegas Strip, the dragon gate of Chinatown—dominated and trampled, accompanied by panic-stricken mobs fleeing in every direction amid screams and resounding car alarms. Military strategies for nuclear annihilation of the MUTOs, at variance with the scientists' consensus, bring about disastrous consequences, as the gargantuan pair captures and gorges on the very warheads intended to destroy them. However, in a protracted battle that wipes out most of what remains of San Francisco, Godzilla prevails over the MUTOs. Yet the danger to humankind is only partially mitigated by this "dracos-ex-machina"; the "millions of lives" at risk are spared not because Godzilla was defending humanity but as a consequence of his territorial defense against MUTO encroachment. Humans may celebrate as the giant reptilian creature lumbers back into the sea, but the sense of peril lingers.

The Apocalypse will not take place.

From its nascent state, filmmaking has called attention to itself and its virtuality. In one of the earliest meta films, *Kid Auto Races at Venice*, Charlie Chaplin doggedly plants himself in front of the camera, upstaging and displacing the ostensible *raison d'être* of the film. The essence of the postmodern elaborates on this tendency, substituting "the signs of the real for the real" (Baudrillard 2) via electronic technologies and digital media, its modes simulation, self-referentiality, hypermediality. These are everywhere in evidence in these megamonster films, in which the threat of supermonsters dooming civilization is decentered and undermined by the very signs of its reality, the media-generated and media-driven narratives meant to describe it.

"People are going to watch this," clueless impromptu cameraman Hud insists in *Cloverfield*, yet the documentation of the horrific event attracts attention to itself even more than it establishes a record. From the start the footage calls attention to itself with large-print warnings of "Do Not Duplicate," reminiscent of films cheaply plagiarized for the black market. Well before the monster attacks New York City, Hud's camera lens has turned its voyeuristic male gaze on partygoers, leering at the ultra hip Marlena, listening in on the awkward, unhappy encounter between Rob and Beth—whose past intimate connection was fleeting at best—and the lightning-quick gossip that follows. When the monster strikes, Hud's reality-TV-style videorecording is immediately perceived as being of significance for future generations: a media spectacle yet to be realized, his grasp at virtual immortality. Thus, sometimes almost ludicrously, the camera never stops rolling no matter what the risk, no matter how grim or savage the scenario before him: "If this is the last thing you see, it means I died," he babbles incoherently in a video selfie. Hud's artless, inane commentaries, envisioning elaborate governmental conspiracies and bizarrely frightening scenarios as he stumbles along in the pitch darkness of the subway, repel and distract the more he records; he has no words to comfort Marlena, attacked and bleeding, in the hour before her appalling, bloody demise. Nor is his cinematic eye fixed on the monster; continuously the focus will veer off from the creature to the others watching it, who are coping with the havoc it has wrought upon them.

This movie purportedly about a giant monster attack is, then, really a movie about the experience of watching people experience a monster attack, a cinematic *ourobouros*, the tail/tale-devouring serpent. The threat to all life in New York, and possibly the planet, has become a mere backdrop to the story of unknown viewers watching as a party goes awry and two ill-fated lovers manufacture meaning out of their past encounter by finding each other one last time before they perish. Nor is it unrelievedly bleak: the humorous angle of mass media consumerism as a permanent condition of postmodern society plays out in a mob continuing to loot an electronics equipment store amid the monster's frenzy, in the Muzak still playing in the swank lounge of an upscale apartment building as yet undamaged. Hud's very name reflects the hyper reality intrinsic to the postmodern moment: an acronym for Heads Up Display, a mode of presenting data (for use in aircraft piloting computers, and video games) that allows users to not have to look away from what is before them. *Cloverfield*'s title itself bespeaks the subbing of the signs of reality for the real: the name was initially a placeholder that used producer J. J. Abrams's Santa Monica Freeway turnoff as a working title concealing the film that was in development. Once the film was completed, the title was given a backstory as the governmental name for the investigation of the creature. The false title remained to stand in for itself, a kind of cinematic meta.

Pacific Rim's hypermediality is evident from the first images onscreen: text definitions of two key foreign terms (Japanese *kaiju*, German *Jaeger*), their origins recalling the Axis enemies of yore and foreshadowing the ferociously intimidating enemies of the story, the giant *kaiju* monsters. These, we learn, are not one-of-a-kind creatures with personal motivations but are generic, spawned by the aliens as scout troops, set up to fail so that their masters can learn to win. The simulacral appearance of the *kaiju* (as well as the parasite-like ticks they carry) reflects their hypermediated origins, their form and designs reminiscent of dozens of other recent cinematic monsters, among them the *Cloverfield* creature and its parasites, and the prawn from *District 9*. Their very familiarity breeds, if not contempt, an odd level of reassurance: otherworldly they may be, but their appearance belies it, mitigating the horror an audience might experience. Similarly mediated are the giant robotic "Jaegers," puppet-master simulation suits eerily evoking doppelgangers, created to do battle with the *kaiju* being disgorged from the breach in the Pacific Ocean. The Jaegers also display an amazing range of appearances, shapes, unique features, dazzling colors, their likenesses reflecting a plethora of images from various media: *Transformers* action figures (children's toys, film and TV), Iron Man's radial-hearted suit (graphic novels, film), characters from *Robotech* (Japanese anime) and *Battletech* (video games), even *Star Wars*' storm troopers (film, toys). The A-I system of Gipsy Danger, the lead Jaeger, was given voice by the actress playing a main character in the video game *Portal*, a conscious directorial choice requiring permissions from the corporation owning the game (Nicholson). Quintessential constructs of virtual reality, the Jaegers are cinematically self-referential as well: their inhabiting paired operators are controlled by the "main brain," a coordinator giving audio directions, in a process that replicates motion capture for film. The duet-like inner operation of these enormous killing machines requires an exceptionally close mental bond for the pair inside, a kind of *Star Trek* Vulcan mind-meld enhanced with technology, so that the duo may be "in the drift" and work seamlessly together. The Jaegers' appeal to the audience, especially by world youth who recognize and identify with their imagery and processes, perfectly exemplifies the postmodern impulse toward any simulacrum that deters "every real process via its operational double, a programmatic, metastable, perfectly descriptive machine that offers all the signs of the real and short-circuits all its vicissitudes" (Baudrillard 2). How bad can the apocalypse be when one just has the urge to play with its toys?

The hypermediality of *Pacific Rim* pervades, constantly deflating the very sense of peril that it raises. Comic relief character and fanboy scientist Newton Geiszler sports tattoos of his favorite *kaiju* (ironically one that the film's point-of-view character, Raleigh Becket, has slain), guilelessly acknowledging his wish to encounter another specimen "alive" someday. This media-spawned dream comes true when he mind-links with part of a *kaiju* brain, a process that threatens to kills him and cause global annihilation when the creature takes from his consciousness to its "hive mind" nearly all the information needed to eliminate human resistance. Yet in their humor, the scenes with Geiszler being pursued, even licked by a *kaiju* (a scene of intimate violation weirdly derivative of scenes in *Alien*, *Jurassic Park*, and *Starship Troopers*), undermine much of the sense of dread. The superstardom of the Jaeger fighters, who are allowed to win the first wave of battles against the *kaiju* by the creatures' alien controllers, is also a phenomenon both created and fostered by the media. Victims of their own success, these global "rock stars" (as the audience sees in the flashback story) go on talk shows and make the proverbial cover of *Rolling Stone* as the duels-writ-large become political propaganda. Military victory is soon twinned with the triumph of mediated consumerism, the heroes becoming mere props to be trotted out before the world to sell goods (brightly colored children's shoes) and public attitudes ("winning"). And though the media's feeding frenzy seems to have been overcome when the Jaegers again rise to defend the planet from total destruction, the film's rhetoric subverts it: near the end, Pentecost, the commander of the Jaeger teams, gives a rousing speech proclaiming that the Jaegers will be "canceling the apocalypse," as if it were a TV series down in the ratings.

The MegaMonStar Godzilla, born of the nuclear terrors following World War II, has been elaborated by the media over the past sixty-plus years into a franchise, starring in innumerable films, TV series, toys, video games, graphic novels—even possessing his own theme music. He is his own meta. Thus to create some distance, to reinstate some of the awe, the 2014 *Godzilla* must needs reinvent him: the Monarch project scientists uttering his name as if it were unfamiliar, the shrieking crowds in his path not recognizing his well-known thundering tread. Even the protagonist's young son perceives Godzilla, in his mediated appearance on the TV news, merely as a "dinosaur" sprung to life. Morphing from a 1950s-era symbol of the nuclear threat to humanity (in the film referenced by footage of the Bikini Atoll's devastation) to a defender of sorts of the planet and its denizens, Godzilla has long been cinematically displaced as a symbol of the apocalypse. In the current film, the dimorphic mating pair of MUTOs fills this role. Yet while they terrify, some of their targets comically undermine them. Among numerous scenes of the MUTOs' civic devastation, we witness the iconic Tour Eiffel toppling; yet as the camera pulls back, the audience sees it is not the symbol of Paris that has fallen, but its counterfeit, the "Eiffel Tower Experience," part of the simulacra-city *par excellence* that is Las Vegas. Gamblers in the casinos remain focused on slot machines and roulette wheels, registering much more the loss of electrical power than the giant creature raining down destruction, perhaps attributing it to part of the "Las Vegas Experience." And in an homage to perhaps most archetypal simulation figure of all this "adult Disneyland," emergency crews break down the door of an elegant colonnaded suite to find the music of Elvis "The King" Presley still playing (aptly, "Devil in Disguise"), though the entire back portion of the building has been wrenched away.

Other "signs of the real" that are not real pull us away from a sense of catastrophe even as they draw us in. One of the standout performances of the film is that of the driven, desperate Joe Brody, with his no-holds-barred impulse to make sense of his wife's death despite the label of conspiracy theorist thrust on him, the isolation and alienation from colleagues and kin. Yet at the heart of the most emotionally wrenching scenes, the consummate acting power of Bryan Cranston hearkens back to his greatest role, that of the meth king Walter White in TV's *Breaking Bad*. Both characters are driven, nearly maddened figures who shake spectators to the core with their raw intensity; Cranston's film performance (despite the character's thin development) convinces in its resonance with his past body of work. Such hypermediality occurs elsewhere as well: Brody's poignant farewell to his wife, shut in behind sealed doors as the corridor fills with radiation, strongly evokes the tragic scene of Kirk bidding goodbye to Spock, shut in the radiation-filled engine room after saving the *Enterprise,* in *Star Trek II: The Wrath of Khan.* Simulation and dissimulation play their own doppelganger roles in *Godzilla*: the massive seismic activity that occurs in Japan and the Philippines, in the past and in the present moment of the film, are explained away as earthquakes, an assumption that the military encourages. Yet in each occasion the audience learns that the tremors stem from the awakening and emergence of the MUTOs, the convulsions being yet another form of simulation taken to be real. The quake is a lie.

The Apocalypse will take place.
     The horror of the Aurora movie theatre massacre in 2012 pierced the cinematic veil; we can no longer find refuge in our mediated imaginative cocoons. And outside the boundaries of the films, countless specters of anni-

hilation loom: unchecked global warming, savage terrorist groups like ISIS, deadly pollution from fracking, infectious diseases such as Ebola. Yet even within the films there is no shelter. Disinformation reigns. There is no certainty about the rationale for concealing the *Cloverfield* footage: if there appears to be some government in control, there is also apparently a governmental cover-up. This is equally the case in *Godzilla*, where the military is content to let the populace remain ignorant as long as possible, scientific documents are heavily marked "REDACTED," and presumed conspiracy theorist Joe Brody fights for fifteen years to find the truth, only to die upon its discovery. Nor, in these films, is much thought given to the poisonous legacies of pollutants within the military-industrial complex, or to the pleasant visages painted on the instruments of war. In *Pacific Rim*, the monumental pollution that helped terraform the Earth for the *kaiju's* easy conquest is exacerbated by the monsters' own poison, the "*kaiju* blue" that renders vast areas toxic to humanity. In both *Pacific Rim* and *Godzilla*, the thermonuclear detonations intended to fight the enemy leave their own slow toxins behind, a clear reference to the 2011 disaster at Fukushima; the MUTOs in *Godzilla* further remind us that our nuclear proliferation attracts our own demise. The giant toys that are the robot fighters in *Pacific Rim* are, like the real-world drones multiplying in our skies, hard to discern from those of video games: the ultimate triumph of simulacra. And though the menace to human civilization may be less with Godzilla, he is not, like his media relative Gamera, a friend to children: the tsunami in his wake wipes out part of Honolulu, and the Golden Gate Bridge, clogged with school buses, is clearly an obstacle in his path. Humanity remains exposed to danger.

And yet.

Megamonster films exist to entertain. They do so by shoring up the audience's tottering matrix of confidence in a future. The very presence of monsters that threaten gives confidence to spectators that they can defend themselves, staves off the terror that they perhaps cannot ultimately be master. For the most part, audience members do not see the nuclear radiation seeping into their daily lives, poisoning slowly and surely; they do not dwell on the global climate change that may terraform the Earth for no good purpose. They merely rejoice that some measure of humanity exists, even if it is an authoritarian one.

The deep rhetoric of the films themselves negates annihilation, though it is of little comfort. In *Cloverfield*, characters before and after the attack offer variants on Hud's statement to the parasite-stricken Marlena: "I know I should say something, but I don't know what to say." Confronted with the end, humanity has no words left; and the camera that spares nothing is the only thing spared. Simulation is all. The world of *Pacific Rim* offers a vision even more grim: if the Jaeger operators can "step into" each other's heads, they are also urged not to remember, not to wallow too deeply in memories. Intense recollections and bad remembrances will force them out of "alignment" and get in the way of their "drift" together; they must "rein in" their thoughts in order to complete their task. If we do not remember, we have not lost and do not lose. Perhaps this explains why the head of the conquering Gipsy Danger is so disproportionately small to the rest of the robot. Heads get in the way. In like manner, the scientists in *Godzilla* urge that the MUTOs be dealt with by the titular god-monster, who possesses the power of nature to "restore balance": "Let go and let Godzilla." Human efforts bring on disaster; they do not thwart it.

In truth, the "real" of human civilization has become irrelevant in this postmodern era. The apocalypse cannot occur on Godzilla's watch, or within the Jaegers' purview, because in the world of hypermediality and simulation, the end of human existence "has no relation to any reality whatsoever" (Baudrillard 6).

The Apocalypse will not take place.

Works Cited

Baudrillard, Jean. *Simulation and Simulacra*. Trans. Sheila Faria Glaser. Ann Arbor: University of Michigan Press, 1994. Print.
Breaking Bad. Perf. Bryan Cranston. Sony Pictures, 2008–2013. Television.
Cloverfield. Dir. Matt Reeves. Bad Robot Productions, 2008. Film.
Godzilla. Dir. Gareth Edwards. Legendary Pictures-Warner Brothers, 2014. Film.
Happy Russia [Gary Guillot]. "*Cloverfield* Makes People Sick!" Forum. *Omega Sector BBS*. TrekCore, 24 Jan. 2008. Web. 1 Sept. 2014.
Kid Auto Races at Venice. Dir. Henry Lehrman. Keystone Film Company, 1914. Film.
Nicholson, Max. "Del Toro Explains GLADOS Voice in *Pacific Rim*." IGN.com. Ziff-Davis, 7 Jan. 2013. Web. 8 Jan. 2015.
Pacific Rim. Dir. Guillermo del Toro. Legendary Pictures, 2013. Film.
Star Trek II: The Wrath of Khan. Dir. Nicholas Meyer. Paramount Pictures, 1982. Film.

Psychological Significance Within Postapocalyptic Film

Two Unique Approaches
to Adaptation

PATRICK L. SMITH

Cinema often creates storylines that depict the struggle of human beings in the most dire of situations, from which survival is unlikely unless unique solutions arise from potential chaos. Characters in these films reflect resilience and motivation amid great inner turmoil. The postapocalyptic film is certainly no exception, as the subgenre focuses on humanity at the brink of collapse due to tragic events that threaten the entire human race. Although these films vary by the source of crisis, there is a common thread of human responsiveness to an aversive environment. For instance, humans, in order to survive, must learn to adapt to their surroundings or they will inevitably be lost. And while the focus of postapocalyptic films implies imminent doom, this subgenre has thrived for more than a half century. In order to continue, newer films of this nature must be compelling to an interested audience. Plot development, character development, effective direction, and various elements of production are intended to invent stories that will captivate viewers.

The creative process for evolving the subgenre can be described in numerous ways, especially by methods that have been analyzed by the social and natural sciences. Postapocalyptic cinema shares a common thread in storytelling, as films gravitate towards the conflict humanity experiences when adapting to adverse environmental conditions. In terms of the natural sciences, human behavior can be likened to the observable actions of other animal species. This notion, known as behavioral functionalism, stems from the three major principles of Charles Darwin's classic natural selection theory, originally published in 1859. The first principle pertains to variability within animal species. No two organisms are completely alike, and their genetic makeup (that presumably guides behavioral tendencies) ranges among members of any species. The second principle further characterizes variation in a "survival of the fittest" paradigm, a term later coined by Herbert Spencer after his review of Darwin's work (see Spencer 444). Changes in the environment benefit variations that are able to adapt responsively to potentially fatal conditions (which cannot be reliably predicted by the specie). If an animal can adapt, then it can survive; if not, then it (and the variation it comprises) will become extinct. The final principle involves reproductive fitness, in which surviving specie members must reproduce in order for the specie to continue to exist. These Darwinian themes appropriately characterize universal behaviors like aggression and social attraction (Aronson 356). Interestingly, these same behaviors are often reliably observed in postapocalyptic cinema.

Although the natural sciences characterize the subgenre to an adequate degree, postapocalyptic interpretation benefits even more from the principles of the social sciences. When humanity is at the brink of collapse, good filmmaking attempts to project the emotional struggle during adverse consequences. Although the notion of a "stimulus-response" phenomenon is well studied among psychological disciplines, one of the most intriguing schools of psychology that addresses human conflict is psychoanalysis. Based on the works of Sigmund Freud, psychoanalysis explains how conscious behavior is an attempt to maintain subconscious equilibrium. Freud has been quoted as saying that "experiences can give the explanation for the sensitivity to later traumata and only when these memory traces, which almost always are forgotten, are discovered and made conscious, is the power developed to banish the symptoms" (Hall 48). This would suggest that human behavior is merely a product of subconscious remnants, and conscious behaviors are intended to minimize previously unresolved psychological tension.

In order to handle personal conflict within the environment, Freudian theory considers three psychic forces: the id, the ego, and the superego (Hall 22). The id, guided by the "pleasure principle," represents the primal qualities of human beings, and it is considered to be the evolutionary link to immediate, instinctive urges of pleasure and the avoidance of pain (Hall 39). As summarized by Calvin Hall, this component of humanity is the natural antagonist of the superego, which is guided by the principles of morality, fear of punishment, and social disapproval (46). However, the superego is also considered by Freud as irrationally based (Hall 48). With these two dynamically opposed forces beneath one's conscious existence, a third psychic force must link them to the reality of the environment. This third component, the ego, serves as a necessary regulator between the unconscious and the external world (Freud 3). Based on the "reality principle," the ego's role is to accommodate unconscious urges so that an individual can maintain a sensory-driven, conscious existence (see Freud 8). At any given point of reacting to the environment, these underlying forces can heighten tension and subconscious anxiety. To alleviate this anxiety, there are defense mechanisms, which are considered to be ego-driven devices that modify covert behaviors while one faces the subconscious tension. Moreover, defense mechanisms (e.g., denial, displacement, reaction formation, rationalization, regression, sublimation) serve as coping strategies, and they can effectively explain common, functional behaviors that are characterized by the social and natural sciences (Hall 85).

Conscious adaptation to societal pressures has been likened to the classic defense mechanisms that were initially proposed by Freud. For instance, Roy F. Baumeister, Karen Dale, and Kristin L. Sommer confirm the need for defense mechanisms like denial, reaction formation, and displacement in the social world as a means of adjusting to personal turmoil (1116). Although these researchers suggest that certain Freudian mechanisms need to be revised from their original presentation (e.g., displacement, or impulsive aggression, may be better defined as scapegoating behavior), they also clearly see the modern relevance of Freud's seminal work (1096). Defense mechanisms have also been linked to different personality dispositions, in which individuals who score high for personal neuroticism are likely to externalize personal defenses immaturely, such as displacing aggressive tendencies onto others (Furnham 732). Adrian Furnham states that outward coping behaviors may also be related to gender, in which males are more likely to show more primitive, immature behaviors when compared to women, who tend to channel personal conflicts towards more socially acceptable actions (729). These findings suggest that inner conflict from modern sociocultural pressures drives personal actions (Furnham 731), and that stereotypical behaviors (via defense mechanisms) serve as identifiable, adaptive responses for any animal, including humans. Although classic Freudian theory has been heavily questioned in terms of modern social significance, its fundamental themes still resonate within the field in terms of characterizing motivation and behavior.

In order to bring postapocalyptic film to life, proper depiction of human behavior is critical. The use of Freudian mechanisms within filmmaking does have empirical support. Alan Sugarman notes that the unconscious process of fantasy development as "a means of processing inner and outer experience, and communicating it, is an important mental function..." (177). Moreover, the crises from "the real world" can be a valuable source for engaging an audience, and, during extremely difficult social, economic, and political times, an individual can relate to projections of human crises in film. Lisa D. Butler and Oxana Palesh have observed that "many film directors and cinematographers skillfully use cinematic devices to convey and dramatize the dissociative experiences of their characters—and the force of these techniques may issue from the movie-viewer's personal knowledge of the relatively normative dissociative experiences related to traumatic or stressful life events" (65). The incorporation of realism into fantasy scenarios seems to be a popular source for apocalyptic storylines, but emotional outlets like laughter and humor can also be effective for projecting extreme personal conflict. For instance, Zvi Lothane states that "humor is confrontational, and confrontation is the opposite of gratification: it destabilizes the existing neurotic equilibrium by employing shock and surprise, and thus constitutes iatrogenic trauma that needs to be accepted, endured, and learned" (237). Lothane adds, "Analyzing jokes and telling jokes is one of the auxiliary techniques of the psychoanalytic method: it helps to lift representations, take hold of unconscious emotions, and fantasies, and enhance interpretation" (238). By this notion, filmmaking can satirize serious content while maintaining more lighthearted undertones to which the audience can relate. Regardless of the approach a filmmaker takes, an understanding of human psychology can be a desirable tool to create unique renditions of a well-established subgenre, in this case apocalyptic narrative.

In 2006, two films epitomized the aforementioned approaches to expand the subgenre. *Children of Men* (directed by Alfonso Cuarón) and *Fido* (directed by Andrew Currie) serve as innovative narratives within postapocalyptic media. These films are completely different in scope, but they are quite successful at projecting the hidden conflicts that drive actions within their characters. Moreover, each story can be described in terms of the way psychoanalytic theory depicts aversive conflict. *Children of Men*, an adaptation of the P. D. James novel *The Children of Men* (1992), explores the way society (in groups and as individuals) breaks down when a potential end of humanity is imminent. However, it also portrays individual resilience for the sake of keeping the hope of survival as a possibility. The other film, *Fido*, is more lighthearted in nature. *Fido* takes a satirical approach after a zombie apocalypse has occurred, and it focuses on stereotypical behaviors in any society during a continual environmental struggle. Despite their opposite emotional undertones, each film can be given merit for representing empirically driven behaviors through the actions of its characters.

Children of Men clearly depicts the human race in a crisis of extinction. However, the film is unique in the way it uses the principles of natural selection to describe adaptive conflict. Most postapocalyptic films tend to focus on a rapid environmental crisis that threatens to eliminate humanity (i.e., Darwin's second principle). *Children of Men*, however, suggests that the current environment does not pose a direct threat to extinction. Instead, the future of the human species and its ability to reproduce (Darwin's third principle) is the focus of peril. The film is set in the year 2027, when humans have lost a valuable natural resource that is necessary for its survival: children. The film's characters are aware of their loss, and the ongoing awareness of eventual extinction threatens the infrastructure of human society. One by one, nations begin to crumble, and the factions within each society make individuals turn against one another. For example, the setting of London has become an unstable community, in which "Fugees," or non-native residents, are hunted and placed in detention centers that resemble prisons during wartime. This segregated atmosphere is similar to the concentration camps in Eastern Europe during World War II, as the Fugees are met with harsh treatment by the governing British class. Furthermore, any resistance to the status quo is met with violence and death. There are also active dissenters working against the initiatives of the ruling class, and these groups (e.g., the Fishes) retaliate with equally excessive force. Throughout the film, the warring factions set a grim backdrop of collective tension, and they represent a collective response of the defense mechanism of displacement, which is defined as aggressive behaviors towards those who are not directly related to an underlying conflict. As a result, London becomes a literal war zone that claims innocent lives while not addressing the true problem.

Under such a severe crisis, many of the major characters display actions that are representative of Freudian defense mechanisms. The most notable of these characters is the film's protagonist, Theo Faron, who transforms his personality throughout the events of the film. Prior to these events, Theo was a passionate political activist in London, where he and his wife, Julian, strongly opposed the status quo of their own government. However, after their son, Dylan, died in the flu pandemic of 2008, Theo personally faced a particularly excruciating dilemma: how to handle the end of humankind. In the process, Theo changed his entire lifestyle, altering his idealistic views into a career that supports the bureaucratic view of England. This change in lifestyle clearly represents the defense mechanism of reaction formation, which guides actions that are directly opposite from one's subconscious (or previously expected) behaviors. By "selling out" from what he initially accepted as true, Theo completely changes his personal philosophy from what he strongly believed prior to his son's death. But when Theo is kidnapped by the Fishes, he encounters Julian, now his ex-wife and the group's leader, who wants his help transporting someone out of England. Inevitably, Theo feels compelled to help Julian, despite his not knowing that her passenger, Kee, is pregnant. During the short period that Theo and Julian are reunited, Theo shows another defense mechanism, regression, the reversion into a developmentally younger state. In numerous scenes, the couple's interactions, ranging from childlike bickering (e.g., who's grieving more appropriately over the loss of Dylan) to playful banter (e.g., playing a game of "catch" from mouth to mouth with a ping-pong ball), characterize this defense mechanism. Although Theo and Julian share a past, their reunion shows another one of Theo's coping strategies as his means of getting through tumultuous times.

When Theo does learn of Kee's unique pregnancy, he completely changes his actions to help a scared mother in the midst of potentially manipulative captors. When the moment of new hope presents itself, Theo begins to demonstrate a highly protective nature towards Kee and her unborn child, and he will do anything possible to ensure the safety of both—even though Julian is dead, betrayed and murdered by the Fishes. This shift in Theo's attitude represents another defense mechanism, sublimation, which is considered a sign of psychological maturity (see Hall 119). Sublimation requires an individual consciously to demonstrate actions that benefit society, actions that should show a selfless regard for others. Theo's drive compels him to accompany Kee to the ship *Tomorrow*, a vessel that will transport her child to the Human Project, a peaceful and mindful group attempting to repopulate the Earth. While this journey is filled with peril, Theo's desire to help the future of humanity does not waver, and he puts himself in harm's way so that the species has a chance to avoid extinction. Through these actions Theo eventually loses his life, but Kee and her child reach the end of their journey. As a sign of gratitude, Kee even names her newborn daughter "Dylan," in memory of Theo and Julian's lost child.

Although the development of Theo can be well-linked to psychoanalysis, other notable characters in the film also reflect common Freudian defense mechanisms. For instance, Theo's best friend, Jasper, has also suffered from the crisis of infertility and from subsequent political strife. Jasper and his wife, Janice, were both political activists, but their activism led them to experience personal turmoil, most notably the torture-induced catatonia suffered by Janice. In order to cope with these experiences, Jasper continually demonstrates regression (another defense mechanism) into a younger, more immature personality. As a former political cartoonist, Jasper continuously expresses juvenile humor during the most serious of circumstances. While driving through horrible scenes of chaos in the English countryside (e.g., violent rebel vandals, piles of burning animal carcasses, Fugee transports), Jasper lightens the mood with a childish "pull my finger" routine. He also attempts an "eating the stork" joke in reference to the infertility crisis, but gets frustrated when Theo does not appreciate the humorous attempt. Even Jasper's choices in music and recreational drug use throughout the film indicate a form of escapism to a simpler and less chaotic time from his youth. Jasper shows regression until his untimely end. Facing imminent execution for sheltering Theo and Kee, Jasper makes the decision to euthanize his beloved Janice by giving her the drug Quietus. He then confronts a group of angry Fishes by reverting to his "pull my finger" gag before being shot. Jasper's regressive humor is truly a coping mechanism against a traumatic backdrop, as his actions oppose the pain that he has experienced throughout his life.

Other characters, although serving smaller purposes to the plot of the film, also demonstrate psychoanalytical principles. For instance, Nigel, Theo's cousin and a high-ranking political official in charge of art treasures, represents the status quo of an imperial government. However, when Theo meets with Nigel, Theo questions the longevity of preserving historical art given the impending extinction of man. Nigel, in his response, implies that just "having" the art is more important than the societal need for preservation. This response clearly reflects a denial of the current crisis, as Nigel's main focus is to preserve the art from the past, regardless of whether there is a population that can appreciate it in the future. Nigel is responsible for the "Ark of the Arts," which is influential in maintaining such works as Picasso's *Guernica*, Michelangelo's *David*, and Banksy's *British Cops Kissing*. By preserving such timeless works, the film depicts Nigel as more interested in the past than in the struggles of the future. With its breadth of characters, *Children of Men* provides a sobering look at how human beings differentially struggle with our own existence in the face of adversity.

Fido is also an example of prominent psychoanalytical themes, this time in a film that uses satire as a vehicle within the postapocalyptic subgenre. In the wake of wars that lead to a convenient solution related to a zombie apocalypse, the film provides a humorous fantasy scenario that symbolizes common Freudian dynamics (id, ego, superego) and defense mechanisms that help in maintaining personal equilibrium. In *Fido*, Freud's concept of the primitive id is depicted by the presence of zombies, who are mindlessly driven by the "hunger" of self-gratification. The opposing symbol of the society-preserving superego is represented by a media-driven technology corporation (Zomcon) that attempts to control both the human society and the zombies. By enslaving the zombies and making them a resource for labor within the community, Zomcon controls everything, and any resistance can lead to an individual's ultimate demise (either by death or expulsion). As a result of this collective dynamic, the members of a small community remain in a constant state of tension. To live a "normal life," citizens must consciously endure the tension, and the film does an effective job of demonstrating how individuals demonstrate ego-driven behaviors for the sake of adaptation in an anxiety-driven environment.

In short, *Fido* takes place in an alternate universe, but more specifically, in a town called Willard (an allusion to George Romero's *Night of the Living Dead*). Although the town seems to be a peaceful community that is representative of the idyllic 1950s, the world in which Willard exists has recently recovered from great peril. Massive bursts of radiation turned the dead into zombies, and society needed to survive the "Zombie Wars." In response, Zomcon contained many zombies in designated outposts known as "wild zones," presumably keeping humanity safe from the threat of the walking dead. But as a corporation, Zomcon has also found use for zombies as servants of man. Zomcon technology literally enables humans to harness selected zombies as menial labor. Obviously, the citizens of Willard are indebted to Zomcon for its efforts. Hence, they are coerced into believing that zombies can be a beneficial part of life as long as the citizens can afford the exorbitant prices charged by Zomcon *and* these same citizens do not challenge the increasingly powerful governing body. Although the film follows the pursuits of Timmy, a young boy who does not necessarily follow the direction that most citizens of Willard take (e.g., he befriends his zombie in a "boy and his zombie" motif, similar to the "boy and his dog" portrayal in the classic *Lassie* television series), there is great significance in the way that members of the community cope with the dire circumstances of their existence. Thus, the true essence of the story focuses on how individuals handle the tension between two controlling and potentially dangerous and dichotomous forces.

On the surface, the townspeople of Willard are presented in a calm, peaceful manner, but this setting reflects collective denial of potential impositions from both a zombie takeover and the power-hungry Zomcon organization. This becomes evident at the beginning of the film when Miss Mills, a teacher in the Willard community, shows her class a short film that praises the company of Zomcon for its efforts in "making a better life through containment." Although it is a clear propaganda piece, Miss Mills simply praises the film and wants her children to acknowledge that "Zomcon makes the world a better place." The children blissfully oblige—except for Timmy, the protagonist of the story. This introduction of the Willard school, followed by shots of the community (and interspersed media clips assuring that Willard is the "safest it's ever been"), provide the viewer with a false sense of complacency, regardless of the horrific undertones.

The backdrop of *Fido* represents the underlying conflict, but the film generally revolves around the Robinsons, a middle-class family unit. Although the family seems normal, consequences from the Zombie Wars have taken a major toll on the Robinsons. For instance, Bill Robinson, the patriarch, has been scarred by his past. The film mentions that he had to "kill" his own father when the older man became a zombie after a normal death. As a result of this trauma, Bill has been living in a state of denial, and he does not consciously accept the reality of the new world after the Zombie Wars. He is deathly afraid of another Zombie War, but his underlying fears manifest themselves in irrational behaviors. Bill fixates on using his family's finances for proper funeral expenses so that no family members become zombies (i.e., ensuring that they are beheaded after death so remaining radiation does not "turn them" in the afterlife). He is also extremely disturbed when

Helen, his wife, purchases Fido, the film's title character. Bill remains at odds with Fido by torturing the zombie (via a shock collar) and distancing himself further from his family. These actions disturb his wife and son, Helen and Timmy, who deal with subconscious conflict quite differently.

Helen Robinson has also felt the effects of these tumultuous times. She tries very hard to be a devoted wife and mother, and she often makes personal sacrifices to maintain a happy medium within the family unit. However, she is very sensitive to the social norms that have resulted from Zomcon's stranglehold over the town, and she often becomes preoccupied with how things "appear" for fear of others' judgments. For instance, Helen becomes concerned with Timmy after he is bullied and almost shot by classmates for his skepticism regarding Zomcon. However, her major concern is with what people think of Timmy and his family. Helen is aware of the serious dangers that zombies pose (especially if Zomcon's technology of control were to fail), but the pressure of "having one's own zombie" strongly influences her. This is what initially led her to purchase Fido. In fact, she supported her decision by stating, "Isn't it wonderful? Now we're not the only ones on the street without one." Despite strong protests from Bill (whose denials makes him prefer that zombies stay as far from him as possible), Helen continues to make rationalizations about her decision. For example, she justifies zombie labor in terms of maintaining social status, as owning a zombie makes the Robinsons more prominent members of the community. And later, Helen protects both her son and her zombie by burning the bodies of the bullies who had tried to kill Timmy but who, instead, fell prey to their own ineptitude, Fido's wrath, and Helen's ability to drive her car over one of the zombified bullies as he lunged toward Timmy. Helen's actions, although impulsive, are consciously justified by excuses, and as a result, Helen prevents herself from feeling any further conflict about the events that have transpired.

The final member of the Robinson family, Timmy, seems to be most attuned to the crisis within Willard. He seems to understand both extremes that face the community, so he attempts to act accordingly amid the tension. Despite his youth, Timmy seems to have a mature outlook on the conflict. He understands the threat of zombies, but he is also doubtful of Zomcon's omniscience when it comes to containing the zombie threat. For instance, he is very critical of Mr. Bottoms, the head of Zomcon security in Willard. Intuitively wary of Bottoms, Timmy questions the total "control" that Zomcon has in terms of preventing more zombies rising from the dead. Bottoms seems annoyed by a question for which has no answer. From the beginning (and in contrast to Bottoms' cold disdain), Timmy treats Fido like a pet, and he loves his pet zombie unconditionally. Despite the potential dangers that Fido might pose to him if Zomcon's technology fails, Timmy nurtures a strong bond with Fido throughout the film. He protects Fido from the perception of servitude that surrounds the zombies; indeed, he comes to love Fido and believes his feelings are reciprocated. Although Timmy's view makes him a primary target of Zomcon for his "unnatural love of zombies," these sublimated reactions inevitably save him (and Fido) from personal demise. Towards the end of the film, Timmy's actions seem contagious, as the community comes to appreciate zombies less as slaves and more as personal companions. In fact, the film concludes with a neighborhood gathering of Timmy's "new family" (including Fido now as patriarch), the Bottoms family (whose zombified patriarch is now controlled by his daughter), and Mr. Theopolis (who is accompanied by his zombie girlfriend, Tammy). The conclusion therefore demonstrates how the remaining characters sublimate the conflict by simply adapting their lifestyles in somewhat healthy manners.

Neither film suggests an optimistic outlook for humanity. Instead, both *Children of Men* and *Fido* imply uncertain futures for the specie. Moreover, humans are not portrayed as having much free will, and their growth is dependent upon subsequent challenges beyond the reach of the film's narrative. Regardless of the uncertain futures of both London and Willard, both films thematically support the natural and social sciences that characterize them: life is an ongoing struggle to maintain a constant social equilibrium for the sake of survival. Although behavioral adaptation is not favorable for any individual that must face it, the ultimate consequence, if successful, is the preservation of the specie. *Children of Men* demonstrates that the unique actions of a few can perhaps save the human race despite overwhelming odds. On the other hand, *Fido* satirically suggests that a "solution" to an apocalypse still poses ongoing pressures within a society. Albeit with different approaches, both films demonstrate that human existence should never be complacent toward the natural environment. Furthermore, these films parallel psychoanalytical theory, which also suggests that the fate of humanity lies among a delicate balance of subconscious forces. If society gravitates towards the primal end of its psychic existence, then the essence of humanity will de-evolve into violent chaos. However, if society is led to a sense of dominant self-preservation, then any chance of psychological growth will be minimized. Although many could argue that such themes are applicable to an array of social problems in both art and life, the power of these two films lies in their ability to suggest underlying human behavior in crisis, and they serve as significant and unique progressions within the postapocalyptic subgenre.

WORKS CITED

Aronson, Elliot. *The Social Animal.* 7th ed. New York: Freeman, 1995. Print.

Baumeister, Roy F., Karen Dale, and Kristin L. Sommer. "Freudian Defense Mechanisms and Empirical Findings in Modern Social Psychology: Reaction Formation, Projection, Displacement, Undoing, Isolation, Sublimation, and Denial." *Journal of Personality* 66.6 (1998): 1081–1124. Print.

Butler, Lisa D., and Oxana Palesh. "Spellbound: Dissociation in the Movies." *Journal of Trauma and Dissociation* 5.2 (2004): 61–87. Print.
Children of Men. Dir. Alfonso Cuarón. Universal, 2006. Film.
Darwin, Charles. *The Origin of Species*. 1859. Ed. Philip Appleman. New York: Norton, 2002. Print.
Fido. Dir. Andrew Currie. Lionsgate, 2006. Film.
Freud, Sigmund. *Civilization and Its Discontents*. 1929. Buckinghamshire, U.K.: Chrysoma Associates, 2000–2005. PDF file.
Furnham, Adrian. "Lay Understandings of Defense Mechanisms: The Role of Personality Traits and Gender." *Psychology, Health, & Medicine* 17.6 (2012): 723–34. Print.
Hall, Calvin. *A Primer of Freudian Psychology*. New York: New American Library, 1954. Print.
James, P. D. *The Children of Men*. New York: Vintage, 1992. Print.
Lassie. Created by Robert Maxwell and Rudd Weatherwax. CBS/Syndication. 1954–1973. Television.
Lothane, Zvi. "The Uses of Humor in Life, Neurosis, and in Psychotherapy: Part 2." *International Forum of Psychoanalysis* 17.3 (2008): 232–39. Print.
Night of the Living Dead. Dir. George A. Romero. Walter Reade, 1968. Film.
Spencer, Herbert. *The Principles of Biology*. Vol. 1. New York: D. Appleton, 1898. Print.
Sugarman, Alan. "Fantasizing as Process, Not Fantasy as Content: The Importance of Mental Organization." *Psychoanalytical Inquiry* 28.2 (2008): 169–89. Print.

"To Err Is Human"

The Human Species and the Inevitable Apocalypse
in The World's End

MARY F. PHARR

Simon Pegg and Edgar Wright's *The World's End* (2013) is a cinematic twist on familiar millennial preoccupations. The last film in Pegg and Wright's Cornetto Trilogy (following *Shaun of the Dead* in 2004 and *Hot Fuzz* in 2007), *The World's End* relies on postmodern visual and storyline references to earlier cinema to keep its audience receptive to the new film's message, which uses comedy as the base for psychological rumination and science fiction speculation. Among the many homages within this film are allusions to the first two cinematic versions of *Invasion of the Body Snatchers* (1956 and 1978) and the first film adaptation of *The Stepford Wives* (1975). Of all the homages, however, the allusions to Robert Wise's *The Day the Earth Stood Still* (1951) have the most thematic importance, as they lead directly to the apocalyptic dilemma Pegg and Wright present at their film's conclusion. In effect, Pegg and Wright use the millennial obsession with the possible end of our world as a means of examining what is distinctive about humankind as a species. Their Britcom movie continuously attests to the human tendency toward anarchy as the price we pay for free will. In a controversial ending, the film further suggests that if apocalypse is an inevitable side effect of our unruliness, most of those who somehow survive the end of our civilization will still retain the tendencies that have both improved and endangered Earth. The film is a mixed message, to say the least—but it does argue for the uniqueness of the human species.

The World's End originated in its creators' awareness of the changes wrought by time in their own English hometowns, specifically the "Starbucking" that routinely homogenizes contemporary culture, "making everything look the same" (Pegg qtd. in Kang). The film begins with a flashback in which Gary King recalls "a heroic quest," actually a pub crawl he and four friends attempted in June 1990 in their hometown of Newton Haven, England. Five teenagers tried to drink their way through the twelve pubs that composed the town's "Golden Mile"; nine pubs in, the three bleary youths who were still standing opted instead to head for the hills and see the sunrise. Gary remembers watching the sunrise and knowing that "life would never feel this good again." And, as he bitterly announces to his therapy/rehab group twenty-plus years later, "It never did." The strikingly handsome, solipsistic young Gary has become a worn-out loser addicted to alcohol and cocaine, still solipsistic but now facing middle age without his old looks, without his old friends, and without evidence of public achievement or private happiness. He is not even misunderstood—just a "force of maddening irritation" (Pegg, Robinson Int.). And so Gary begins to define himself by a determination to finish the Golden Mile, as though completing an adolescent stunt will turn it into a life-changing quest that will restore his lost glory. As illusions go, this one seems more pathetic than Blanche DuBois's hollow hope of at-long-last love.

But it's not. As Calum Marsh has observed, "The fantasy scenarios that emerge throughout Wright's work represent attempts to redirect and repurpose frustrations and anxieties that lack a healthy, sustainable outlet in ordinary life. He's taking real, palpable pain and making something useful and wonderful and fun out of it." Gary is never a good man, but he is a natural leader looking for both adherents and action to relieve the incessant pain that is his life. For Gary, the Golden Mile is the path to authenticity in a world otherwise given to ersatz identities and capitalist conformity. Ironically, Gary is himself an inveterate liar, a trickster who uses half-truths to reassemble his former friends and followers: Peter Page, bullied as a youth, is now a family man mostly ignored by his family and a junior partner at a car dealership owned by his father; Steven Prince, never quite as handsome or dynamic as Gary, is a successful construction manager; Oliver Chamberlain, burdened as a youth with a birthmark on his face, is now a real estate agent (the birthmark surgically removed) in love with Bluetooth technology; and Andy Knightley, Gary's one-time "wingman," is a lawyer who has not talked to his former best friend for years.

Despite their estrangement from Gary, all four men respond to his call for a crawl—perhaps because it might provide a nostalgic return to their lost comradery but mostly because they feel sorry for Gary, who manipulates his old buddies with increasingly outrageous lies, culminating in his claim that his beloved mother has just died. Nobody can abandon a guy who just lost his mum. Thematically, the call works because it pulls the characters and the audience into a real quest, this one referenced by the names given to Gary and his retinue. Early on, Gary wryly recalls, "They called me 'The King.' Because that's my name—Gary King." Inevitably, the King must have his Page, Prince, Chamberlain, and Knight, and they must follow him. Moreover, as Pegg has noted of Wright and himself, "We're British, and the pub forms a very important part of our cultural heritage. And here the journey ends up being an Arthurian quest, while also representing the 12 stations of recovery" (qtd. in Alexander). Allan Massie once remarked that "two great themes may be discerned" in works associated with the Arthurian cycle: the quest for the Grail, wherein "the hero is tested till he proves himself fit to attain the goal," and "the story of Arthur's betrayal and failure," ultimately "the revolt of disorder against order" (xiv). Filmgoers may well see the irony linking an extended drinking game to a quest for the Holy Grail, but how many viewers will see the downing of beer in the crawl's first pub as the initial step in recovery? Yet it is the beginning of the end of the faux, homogenized world that Newton Haven—read Earth—has become. It is a test wherein the King and his followers must prove themselves not only fit rioters but also fit fighters, fit friends, and, finally, fit rebels. For as indicated by the riotous nature of the pub crawl quest, this rebellion represents human disorder against alien order. Moreover, despite its topsy-turvy nature, this ironic quest, like all quests, will require sacrifice and death.

Wearing a duster, Gary insists on taking his retinue back to Newton Haven in the Beast, a 1980s Ford Granada that has been rebuilt but that is still (like Gary himself) more derelict than classic. The Beast is not just the steed that carries the King and company into adventure; it is also a doppelganger and a contradiction: both the emblem of "the once and future king" and the sign of a man out of touch with the millennial world. Once the men behaving like boys reach The First Post, pub number one, it does not resemble the lively place they remember, and no one seems to recognize them—a disappointment made worse by Andy's refusal to drink anything stronger than water. Having given up alcohol years before, Andy grimly endures Gary's scorn for his sobriety. When the second pub, The Old Familiar, proves just as unfamiliar *and* just as bland as The First Post, Gary grows annoyed. Things do not improve when Samantha Chamberlain, Oliver's younger sister, drops by the pub on her way to meet friends. Back on that best night of his life, Gary had a quick sexual encounter with Sam in one of The Old Familiar's restrooms. But now, the still good looking and thoroughly self-possessed Samantha firmly rejects Gary's crass attempt to repeat history. Moving on, the men pass a huge humanoid statue the group dismisses as "modern art" and reach pub three, The Famous Cock. The bartender there actually remembers Gary—but only because he was long ago banned from the pub for life. As his friends beat a hasty retreat, Gary sneaks over to drink the dregs from the glasses of departed patrons, keeping the quest alive through desperation.

Gary is a narcissist who feels he is at a crossroads. Psychologist Phebe Cramer has stated that narcissists may use "seduction and exploitation" to "meet their own needs," (225), then rationalize consequences away, or "if this fails, they may revert to wishful fantasy or refuse to recognize disquieting information..." (226). For Gary, the disquieting information is the mounting evidence that he has lost whatever power he once held over Newton Haven and that he has only remnants of power over the friends whose adult lives he refuses to recognize. The wishful fantasy seems evident: that Gary's power will return if he completes the crawl. But the entire experience is beginning to wear on the others, stirring up the buried pain they felt as adolescents. At The Cross Hands, pub four, everyone but Gary listens intently to Peter's revelation about the misery he experienced as a teenager bullied by Shane Hawkins, an acquaintance who now shows up and fails to recognize his former victim. An increasingly irritated Andy urges the others to quit the crawl. When a phone call from Gary's still living mum exposes her son as a trickster, Andy's anger intensifies, and it looks as if the quest is off.

The World's End never stops being funny, but it is also replete with convincing demonstrations of the anxiety men feel as time and circumstance force them to renegotiate their identity in a world that equates masculinity with youth and power. Steven is inarticulate about the people (like Samantha) who matter most to him, Oliver is constantly overruled, Andy can barely contain his temper, and Peter is openly stressed out. In the pub's restroom, Gary is also on edge, and when a local teenager ignores his forced banter, Gary picks a fight. He slams the teenager against a urinal—and the teen's head pops off, spilling something like thick blue ink. At this moment, the movie swings into a cinematic mashup, equal parts Marx Brothers anarchy and apocalyptic science fiction. As Gary stares at what the King has wrought, an angry Andy rushes in to tell the trickster he's been found out; but within moments, the "corpse" reanimates, and a stylized melee breaks out between Gary's band and the ex-corpse's robotic friends. As Marsh notes, "The joke is that the presence of the robots, while obviously terrifying, actually alleviates the pain of the situation: The disappointment you feel when you recognize that nobody in your small hometown recognizes or remembers you is explained by the fact that, yes, they've all been replaced by robots." Faced with a physical and psychological challenge unthinkable in the dull reality of their adult lives, four of the five men fight like the nobles their names suggest. Only Peter hides. When the not-humans are temporarily vanquished, Gary's group decides to finish the crawl to avoid undue suspicion from the humanoids all around them. Just before they leave the pub, teetotaler Andy downs five shots in a row. The retinue is intact; the quest continues.

At pub five, The Good Companions, everyone tries to behave like the pub's name. All the pub names are indicative of their significance to the quest, and so, in The Trusty Servant, pub six, the group encounters Gary's old drug dealer, who nervously tells the good companions not to call the humanoids "robots" since that term originated in the Czech word for "slave." Oliver misses this encounter, having gone to the restroom—where the humanoids ambush him. Just as in the 1990 crawl, Oliver is the first to drop out. The man who loved technology has now become quite technically advanced; he's just no longer human. Yet when a pleased-looking "Oliver" rejoins the group, his companions fail to notice any difference. At pub seven, The Two-Headed Dog, the men again run into Samantha, who ignores Gary's warning about her twin-sister friends—until the admittedly creepy twins rise up against her. Fortunately, first Gary and then Steven arrive to tear the twins apart—which pretty much convinces Sam that something is wrong in Newton Haven. Steven takes advantage of the moment to tell Sam that he has always loved her but never felt confident enough to woo her. Meanwhile, his friends debate what to call the humanoids, finally deciding on the bland term "blanks." The intrusion of both romance and nomenclature into a bizarre crisis takes the film to a surreal level, but two things are certain: the group's meandering behavior is both funny *and* human. John Lloyd has suggested that laughter "makes us human," and in *The World's End,* laughter connects Gary's posse to the audience outside the screen. The blanks do not seem to need humor, but humans must have it to quell angst.

This blend of the surreal and the speculative is heightened in pub eight, The Mermaid, where blanks looking like hot teens from 1990 dance in a disco setting. By now, Andy and Gary are too drunk to think clearly, but Peter learns from another scared old man that something alien, known as "The Network," arrived in June 1990. Over the last twenty-plus years, The Network has replaced most of Newton Haven's citizens with an "improved" version of themselves. Pegg and Wright clearly reference *Invasion of the Body Snatchers* and *The Stepford Wives* with this notion of replacement, but whatever is at work in *The World's End* seems more intent on refashioning—really force-evolving—humanity rather than simply disposing of some or all of our species. The old man sums up the intrusion succinctly: "It's not an invasion. It's a merger." Psychologist Thomas Suddendorf has pointed out that human "minds have spawned civilizations and technologies that have changed the face of the Earth," but the ambiguity within the changes wrought is what concerns The Network, which seems (rationally enough) to wonder what anarchic Earthlings may bring in time to change the face of the galaxy. The old man also warns about the cost to humanity: "Trust, love, respect, desire replaced in the name of progress." Scared, the companions flee—but with no better plan than to make it to the next pub.

At pub nine, The Beehive, the friends query everyone's favorite teacher, Mr. Shepherd, who admits being connected to The Network but denies being a robot. Shepherd says, "It's about working together as one team," working with aliens who want to help us like "teachers" until Earth is ready to join "a vast community of worlds." It's a good spiel, but it does not stop Andy from smashing off half of the blank "Oliver's" head after noticing that "Oliver" has somehow reacquired his old birthmark. Andy's aggression causes Shepherd and his cohorts to stream piercing light from their eyes and mouths in an intense demonstration of displeasure at the unenlightened ways of human beings. This startling sight in turn ignites another melee, during which Andy (in a demonstration of anarchy) tears Shepherd's head off. Meanwhile, in his own interpretation of defiance, Gary finishes the pint his quest demands even as he helps Sam escape before rejoining the others as they flee a reconstructed Shepherd and his flock. Vastly outnumbered, the shrunken posse hides out and gives in to paranoia, which demands that each man show a scar he got after the alien invasion to confirm that he is unimproved and so a true human. Everyone does so except Gary, even after Andy has bitterly reminded him of the long-ago accident in which Andy was almost killed. Gary had pretended to overdose, causing Andy to drive recklessly while trying to get his friend to a hospital. The car crashed and Gary bolted—leaving Andy grievously wounded *and* in trouble with the law. Yet Gary still shows nothing. "I know I'm me," he cries, then repeatedly bangs his head against a post. The obvious pain that results "proves I'm human," according to Gary. "Proves you're stupid," according to Steven. After a moment's pause, everyone realizes that "stupid" equals human. Together, they run.

In the woods, they stumble upon Peter's old nemesis, Shane, who uncharacteristically tries to apologize to Peter for his adolescent bullying. Full of Dutch courage, Peter responds by punching Shane—but as in 1990, Peter Page will never finish the quest. Having wandered away, Peter's friends watch in horror as Shane's fellow blanks overwhelm Peter. Despite the horror, however, Gary declares they will reach the last pub even if it kills them. In response, Andy knocks Gary out, the loyal Knight ready to carry the King to safety. With hordes of blanks and the "Modern Art" statue (come to life like Gort in *The Day the Earth Stood Still*) chasing them, the companions try to get back to the Beast, parked behind The King's Head, pub ten. But while Andy and Steven struggle with the back door, Gary wakes up, downs a pint, and scurries away. Although Steven begs Andy to leave the man who once abandoned him, Andy follows his friend in need. In another observation on what constitutes the human species, Wright believes, "Our mistakes are what make us human" ("Completing the Golden Mile"). By this standard, Gary is quintessentially human. At pub eleven, The Hole in the Wall, Gary quickly drinks his pint just as Steven proves his own loyalty by crashing the Beast through the pub's wall. But the blank horde swarms close behind, forcing Gary to continue the quest on foot, resolutely followed by Andy.

At pub twelve, The World's End, Gary finds a pint waiting for him like the Grail he imagines it to be—but before he can quaff it, Andy knocks the pint out of his hand, telling him "You let me down, man." As they fight for control, Gary's envy of Andy's "perfect life" roils until Andy admits that his wife has left him. "I am trying to win her back," he adds. "God knows I am losing. But I will continue to fight, because that is how we survive." The narcissistic Gary, however, turns the subject of suffering back to himself, frantically pleading that the Golden Mile "is all I've got!" As their struggle continues, Gary's duster sleeves fly up, revealing bandages covering scars from a recent attempt at suicide. Andy stops fighting, asking instead, "Gary, mate, how can you tell you're drunk if you're never sober?" In most narratives, this telling question would turn the struggle from human against human into humans against their demons. But Gary continues to rail, saying that, for him, "Nothing happened" after June 1990. He starts to draw another pint— but before he can finish, the part about nothing happening changes.

An alien *ex machina* device slowly lowers the bar into an arena, with Gary and Andy surrounded by the (mostly blank) citizens of Newton Haven. An imposing voice emanating from a piercing light on high addresses "Gary King of the humans," making Gary humankind's designated defender. The voice says, "We are here to enable your full potential as we have with countless worlds across the galaxy." Said enabling is done by "appropriating" a "small percentage" of the planet's population, then using the replacement simulants to indoctrinate the planet into joining a galactic confederation. According to the voice, while there is some sacrifice (e.g., Oliver and Peter), there are also volunteer participants who "willingly combine" for "attractive incentives" like better bodies and selective memories. Blanks physically identical to the handsome young Gary and his 1990 friends are revealed, with the "Gary" blank suggesting, "Allow me to carry your legend forward." Gary responds by tearing the simulant "Gary's" head off while shouting, "There's only one Gary King!"

His choice made clear, Gary demands to know who is trying to "tell us what to do." The voice responds, "We are The Network, and we are here for your betterment," starting with most of the technological improvements of the last twenty years. When Gary remains stubbornly unimpressed, The Network asks him a loaded question: "Must the galaxy be subjected to an entire planet of people like you?" The question brings to mind the end of *The Day the Earth Stood Still*: after being killed by irrational humans, the resurrected Klaatu informs our planet that if we do not cooperate with the rest of the galaxy, Earth *will* be obliterated in the cause of wider peace. In Pegg and Wright's version, of course, the guardians of the galaxy prefer conversion to annihilation—unless removal of free will is itself annihilation. When Andy supports Gary, The Network observes that Gary "is a detriment to himself, just as Earth is a detriment to the galaxy," with both man and planet acting out "the same cycles of self-destruction again and again." Gary's comeback is that "it's our basic human right to be fuck-ups." He proves his point by trying to quote Alexander Pope: "To err is human, so, uh…." He shrugs. As The Network claims that two drunken men cannot speak for all humanity, Steven drops in, shouting "Three drunken men!" Andy then points out that less than a handful of true humans survive in Newton Haven, not much of a conversion success. Andy even gets The Network to admit that other penetration points have also resisted merger. Steven demands that The Network stop "Starbucking us." Gary adds, "Face it. We are the human race and we don't like being told what to do." The Network then asks, "Just what is it that you want to do?" Gary's response comes from Roger Corman's *The Wild Angels* (1966), by way of a sampling at the start of Primal Scream's "Loaded" (1990): "We want to be free! We want to be able to do what we want to do! We want to get loaded, and we want to have a good time." Massie says that "It may be that [the Medieval] Arthur, like the Christian God, demands more of human nature than men can bear" (xiv). In contrast, Gary, the postmodern Arthur, demands only what men desire. Deciding the argument is pointless, The Network tells the humans, "You will be left to your own devices." Abruptly, the aliens leave.

What they leave behind is an apocalyptic pulse that throws humanity back into the Dark Ages. It starts with the fiery destruction of The World's End, then of Newton Haven, and then of postmodern civilization. Gary and his retinue escape thanks to an example of Samantha *ex machina*, as Sam sweeps them up in her car and outdrives the inferno. Later, Gary mumbles "I'm sorry" as he watches the destruction spread, yet he has succeeded in his quest—not to drink twelve pints of beer but to return to a past that cannot be homogenized by image and technology. The alien pulse that both saves the galaxy from human folly *and* gives humans another chance to evolve in their own way on their own planet may seem almost positive when viewed against the grim fate awaiting Earth in *The Day the Earth Stood Still*. As David Edelstein said in his review, "How many apocalyptic sci-fi action extravaganzas leave you feeling as if the world is just beginning?"

Edelstein's question encapsulates the comedic base in *The World's End*, but it only suggests the narrative's ambiguity. In an epilogue, Andy tells the tale of the Golden Mile to postapocalyptic listeners gathered around a campfire. He notes that the pulse did not just destroy technology; humans died as well (among them Gary's mum). The technologically based blanks also shut down when the pulse struck, but later, they mysteriously rebooted, "looking for guidance" but finding mostly hatred and rejection from humans. Still, some blanks have rebounded. Although he wears a ghastly covering over the missing half of his head, "Oliver" is once again a real estate agent, while

"Peter's" family does not even notice he is no longer organically human. The apocalypse also facilitated some happy endings: Andy is back with his wife, and Steven and Sam are together as they might never have been before the pulse. Unfortunately, Andy does not know what happened to Gary, though he hopes Gary found happiness and friendship "beyond the bottom of a glass." The audience then sees what Andy cannot: Gary in his duster, followed by the four blanks derived from his 1990 posse. Through the smoke of the postapocalyptic world, they approach a pub that sports a crude "No Blanks" sign. Inside, Gary announces that he and his friends are on a quest and require refreshment: "Five waters, please." As the inevitable fight begins, the barman asks Gary who he is. He replies, "Me? They call me the King" as his acolytes literally light up—and the melee begins again.

Historian Yuval Noah Harari understands the import of cognitive dissonance to *Homo sapiens:* "Humans have an amazing capacity to believe in contradictory things." Certainly, *The World's End* is an active discourse on human contradictions. On the one hand, Gary is off alcohol and has found the friends of his past even as he retains his own doubtful autonomy. Earth no longer depends on either questionable technological advances or corporate-induced imagery. And no one is being manipulated into an alien merger that effectively precludes free will. On the other hand, the humans who died had no say in their sacrifice. Many more humans will have lives foreshortened by the after-effects of the pulse (e.g., the lack of basic health technology). And the cycle of self-destruction goes on. By its postapocalyptic conclusion, *The World's End* has become an unlikely yet moving rumination on the way the human tendency to court anarchy may make apocalypse inevitable, even as it gives whatever is left of humanity the energy to go on amid the ruins.

Works Cited

Alexander, Bryan. "With 'The World's End,' It's Last Call for a Comedy." *USA Today* 22 Aug. 2013: 7b. Print.

"Completing the Golden Mile." Bonus Feature. *The World's End.* Dir. Edgar Wright. Universal Studios Home Entertainment, 2013. DVD.

Cramer, Phebe. *Protecting the Self: Defense Mechanisms in Action.* New York: Guilford Press, 2006. Print.

The Day the Earth Stood Still. Dir. Robert Wise. Twentieth Century-Fox, 1951. Film.

Edelstein, David. "Invasion of the Pub Crawlers." Rev. of *The World's End,* dir. Edgar Wright. *New York Magazine* 11 Aug. 2013: n. pag. Web. 8 Apr. 2015.

Harari, Yuval Noah. Interview by Arik Gabbai. "What Makes Humans Different? Fiction and Cooperation." *Smithsonian Magazine* Feb. 2015: n. pag. Web. May 2015.

Invasion of the Body Snatchers. Dir. Don Siegel. Allied Artists, 1956. Film.

Invasion of the Body Snatchers. Dir. Philip Kaufman. United Artists, 1978. Film.

Kang, Inkoo. "*The World's End* Creators Simon Pegg, Nick Frost and Edgar Wright

Versus Starbucksification." *Village Voice* 13 Aug. 2013 New York ed.: n. pag. Web. 12 May 2015.

Lloyd, John. "What Makes Us Human? Our Innate Curiosity and Our Ability to Laugh." *New Statesman* 1 Aug. 2014: n. pag. Web. 20 May 2015.

Marsh, Calum. Rev. of *The World's End,* dir. Edgar Wright. *Slant Magazine* 11 Aug. 2013: n. pag. Web. 8 Apr. 2015.

Massie, Allan. Foreword. *King Arthur in Legend and History.* Ed. Richard White. 1997. New York: Routledge, 1998. xiii-xiv. Print.

Pegg, Simon, Edgar Wright, and Nick Frost. Interview by Tasha Robinson. "*The World's End* Director and Stars on Eternal Adolescence and Why Spoilers Don't Matter." *Dissolve.* Pitchfork Media Inc., 22 Aug. 2013. Web. 8 Apr. 2015.

The Stepford Wives. Dir. Bryan Forbes. Columbia Pictures, 1975. Film.

Suddendorf, Thomas. "What Makes Us Human?" Web blog post. *Huffington Post.* The Huffington Post.com, Inc. 9 Dec. 2013; update 8 Feb. 2014. Web. 15 Apr. 2015.

The Wild Angels. Dir. Roger Corman. AIP, 1966. Film.

The World's End. Dir. Edgar Wright. Writ. Simon Pegg and Wright. Focus Features, 2013. Film.

More Man Than Machine

The Construction of Body and Identity in Battlestar Galactica *and* Terminator: The Sarah Connor Chronicles

LEISA A. CLARK

As apocalyptic narratives, the millennial *Terminator: The Sarah Connor Chronicles* (2008–2009) and *Battlestar Galactica* (2004–2009*)* represent opposite ends of the spectrum: the former focuses on disaster prevention in the future, while the latter explores the aftermath of a multi-planets nuclear holocaust in the distant past. What they share is a connectivity of theme, wherein each series features cybernetic organisms crucial to both plot and character development. But at the heart of both shows are questions about identity and humanity: what makes someone human, and why does it matter? Does being a flesh and blood *Homo sapiens* automatically enroll one in the "human of the month club," or is something more required to make one human? Is it possible for a constructed being (cyborg) to be more human than a human?

With the unparalleled success of *Star Wars* in 1977, the late Seventies and early Eighties experienced an explosion of science fiction films and television series designed to capitalize on the audience's desire for more SF during the gaps between sequels. The first *Battlestar Galactica* (*BSG*) television series premiered in 1978, and the first *Terminator* movie appeared in 1984. What has allowed these two franchises to remain both culturally relevant and still popular with fans for over three decades is a united theme of human survival in the face of adversity. The type of apocalypse scenarios presented in the two series originally focused on the anxieties of the time. Richard Hatch noted that the 1970s was a time of "bad economy, double-digit unemployment, inflation, gas lines, and the Iran hostage crisis—a time when the world was looking for escapism" (1). The later changes in the rebooted *BSG*'s narrative structure reflected post–9/11 and millennial concerns, especially about technology. Uncertainty regarding technology had long been a staple of science fiction, which had but to look at science fact for inspiration. In the early 1980s, fear of sentient machines replacing humans seeped into the collective imagination as computers and robots were lifted out of the pages of Isaac Asimov and Robert A. Heinlein and into our schools, workplaces, and homes. Anxiety about intelligent machines, combined with the even older fear of a nuclear holocaust, is crucial to both the *BSG* series and the *Terminator* films. In the pilot episodes of both the 1978 and the 2004 *BSG* series, the Twelve Colonies are obliterated by Cylon ships firing weapons from space, ending in the nuclear-fueled conflagration of twelve planets. The driving force of the *Terminator* films is preventing this same scenario on Earth. The films' most memorable image is of children playing in a park, followed by a blinding flash of nuclear obliteration.

Another aspect of the modern and postmodern concern with machine life centers on the question of gender in intelligent machines. Donna Haraway has suggested that human beings must evolve past their original purpose, leaving behind the distinction between organic and inorganic in order to exist in a "post-gender world" (9). A cybernetic being need not rely on gender as a way of understanding identity, yet humans still create cyborgs in their own image, assigning not just primary sex characteristics but also imbuing in the machines socialized gendered behaviors that suggest that the cyborg's identity is directly influenced by the gender and human characteristics assigned to it. Female Cylons and Terminators are extraordinary in many ways "average" women cannot be simply by the physical (and often intellectual) limitations of an organic body. Clearly, the machines in both television series were constructed through the lens of the male gaze because the default science fiction audience is expected to be male—but there is something more subversive in the idea that a constructed perfect female body neither depends upon nor actually needs male approval/influence to become more human. Additionally, if little genetic difference exists between *Homo sapiens* and gorillas beyond minute mutations and if we are only a few evolutionary steps removed from brachiating across the forest, then perhaps what separates humans from other life forms is something extra that cannot be quantified: the belief in one's own existence and purpose. *Battlestar Galactica* and *Terminator: The Sarah Connor Chronicles* (*SCC*) deal with the question of "what makes us human" by setting their stories in apocalyptic worlds where machines have threatened to become the dominant species. That in both cases the cyborgs are designed to be human-like in construction, appearance, and behavior suggests the blurring of boundaries between the self-awareness that marks humanity and the programmed identities that delineate artificial intelligence. However, machines that appear human and are also self-aware

are still not human beings; in many ways, these sentient creatures are superior to their creators, allowing for the emergence of a new species.

Terminators and Cylons are both man-made AIs that have turned on their creators, albeit for different reasons. Haraway defines a cyborg as "a cybernetic organism, a hybrid of machine and organism, a creature of social reality, as well as a creature of fiction" (7). Like all *Terminator* narratives, *SCC* suggests that once machines became self-aware (the singularity), they recognized their own superiority and chose to annihilate the inferior humans. The Cylons of *BSG*, however, first rebelled against slavery under human overlords, then later planned to infiltrate and improve upon humans by combining Cylon and human DNA through reproduction. Inherent in the machines is a thought process whereby "techno-bodies are healthy, enhanced, and fully functional—more real than real" (Balsamo 5), representing an upgrade from the weaker biological bodies of humans. What Matthew Gumpert has noted of the similarities between Cylons and humans could also apply to Terminators and humans: "Cylons are like us; we are like Cylons. This could have been a liberating symmetry, an escape from the old notion of the self as something undivided, and distinct from other selves" (146). This core similarity creates a disconnect between what we *perceive* to be humanity and what humanity actually *is*.

If, as Haraway suggests, "The cyborg is a creature in a post-gender world" (9), then why are Cylons and Terminators so clearly gendered? In the late Nineties, Anne Balsamo discussed a *LIFE* magazine report from the Eighties illustrating replaceable body parts. The *LIFE* article itself considered the possibility of replacing one's body parts with mechanical versions in the future. The illustration presented in the article is of a male body, complete with "plastic penile implants and the plastic nonfunctional testicle" (Balsamo 7), but without comparable female-bodied options displayed. Balsamo notes that, within this article, "the relationship between reconstructed body parts and gender identity" (6), although malleable, is distinguishably male. This default to the male body implies that everyone is male, so perforce, women are "Other" because they are not male. In creating their cybernetic organisms, Cylon and Cyberdine machine builders both deliberately assigned recognizable physical sex characteristics and genders to their creations, but the Terminators were made devoid of any reproductive function. There is no valid reason for both male and female Terminators other than that they have been created to mimic and destroy humans. Yet the T-800 and 900 models are permanently gendered, and the T-1000 models may choose to exhibit the sex characteristics of whichever suits their needs. That machines meant to infiltrate human enclaves with the express purpose of destroying them should look human makes perfect sense; giving them identifiable male and female sexes and genders does not. The ability for a Terminator to move about in particular places and circumstances is not based on gender but on its appearance of humanity. There is no logical reason for Terminators to look both male and female, because humanity itself is the disguise and what is under the Terminators' clothing does not matter in respect to their missions.

Conversely, Cylons have bodies specifically designed to mimic human sex physiognomies. Arguably, aside from Cameron, a T-900 model, Terminators are not necessarily gendered at all, in that their actions are not strictly limited to the roles of the sexes they portray physically. Cylons, however, clearly follow the discourses of gendered behaviors and expectations for their overt sexes, especially the females D'Anna (Three), Sharon (Eight), and Caprica (Six). Anthropologist Mary Douglas argues that "the social body constrains the way the physical body is perceived. The physical experience of the body, always modified by the social categories through which it is known, sustains a particular view of society" (65), and it is through this lens that the cyborg sexual identity is produced and maintained. For decades, feminists and queer theorists, such as Judith Butler, have suggested that gender is a social construct not solely limited by biological function. Sex is based on chromosomes, and on internal and external sexual organs; therefore, gender stereotypes are oversimplified but strongly held ideas of the expected behaviors of men and women based on perceived biological differences. Butler further contends that we do not have a choice about performing gender; our only choice is how that performance is manifested—how we will perform our gender each day, and what rules structure and control that performance (312). Gender stereotypes are based on the conventions for how male-bodied and female-bodied individuals "should" behave in one's culture, and this behavior and these conventions are learned, rather than innate. Stereotypes play out in a number of performed acts: from dressing in particular clothing to the jobs one chooses to work to how one interacts with the food that is necessary for survival. But the gender expectations that are reproduced by humans are mimicked by Cylons and Terminators in very different ways.

Any discussion of cybernetic organisms must consider not just the literal creation of the cyborg body but also its social construction. Since Cylons and Terminators were deliberately constructed to interact with humans, a reading of their bodies through the lenses of feminist theory and cultural anthropology suggests that they are gendered because humans assume they are—or should be—and treat them accordingly. In *SCC*, the Terminator Cameron looks like a teenaged girl, and that identity should de-sexualize her in some ways (as an unattainable minor); however, Cameron's clothing choices and the way her body moves (a by-product of actress Summer Glau's ballet training) disrupt the narrative. Cameron may behave in an asexual manner, but her body is clearly female, which is also true of the female Cylons. This certainly suggests that producers may still assume adolescent boys and male nerds are the primary audience for SF. If women are not science fiction's stereotypical audience, then it is easier for the female actors who appear on SF shows to be objectified for their appearance, which is often conflated with the characters they portray. Portrayals of actresses as obtainable objects feed into the imaginary narrative that forces female characters to be gorgeous and sexually available.

Over time, the roles women have played on SF television shows and in SF films have often been contentious and tethered to the social mores of the times when the shows and films were produced. Women have often been almost invisible and "[i]f presented at all, they were depicted in the traditional stereotypical roles of wife, mother, and homemaker. Women beyond these roles were evil, stupid, childlike, or a combination of these" (Ginn 27). The human women of *SCC* and *BSG* attempt to subvert this paradigm: Sarah Connor is a gun-toting, bomb-making warrior, and Kara Thrace is a cigar-smoking, alcohol-swilling badass; however, even as the humans challenge gender norms, the Cylons and Terminators reinforce them. Of the twelve known Cylon models (one has already been destroyed before the start of the *BSG* series), only five are female. Susan George notes, "While on the surface these new Cylons fulfill some of the promise evident in Donna Haraway's vision of cyborg identity, the Cylons, especially the female models, also embody our culture's fear and love of technology" (160). In more than one way, they are perfect machines who look like perfect humans. All five female Cylons are extraordinarily beautiful by Western standards, and four appear young and healthy. Only the character Ellen Tigh seems somewhat older, perhaps over forty, but she is still an overtly sexualized character, who is later revealed to be the "mother" of the skin-jobs. By contrast, the male-bodied Cylons vary greatly in age and appearance, from Number One/Cavil (a curmudgeonly grandfather type) and Saul Tigh (drunken, careworn, and middle-aged) to Galen Tyrol (whose working-class body is certainly not as buff or well-sculpted as some of his human counterparts on the *Galactica*). Overall, the male Cylons are more "average" in appearance when compared with the female Cylons.[1]

The first time we meet Number Six in the *BSG* 2004 reboot mini-series, she is wearing knee boots and a short red dress with a slit in the front. Next, we see Six in a clearly sexual relationship with Gaius Baltar; again, she is in the ubiquitous red dress, but now one that is even more revealing of her female body. Her body is a tool for Baltar to use. Her red dress immediately evokes Western notions of "fallen women" represented in over a thousand years of art, e.g., in Mary Magdalene's red hair and red attire, shown in works such as Giotto's *Resurrection (Noli Me Tangere)* (1304–1306), Benson's *The Magdalene Reading* (1525), and Caravaggio's *Penitent Magdalene* (1597). Over the four seasons of the show, Caprica Six develops into a nuanced character whose mission becomes to protect and to nurture the first Cylon-human hybrid baby, as well as to preach the concept of peace between the two species; however, her mission is often undermined by her presentation as a sexualized object of desire. The Model Six in Baltar's mind is constantly providing sexual encounters and performing sensual acts, effectively forcing the audience to see Caprica Six in the same way.

Arguably, female Terminators and Cylons are young and beautiful because older women have less value in a patriarchal culture that often defines women by their ability to give birth. This view is shared by humans and Cylons alike in *BSG*, as illustrated by Cylons Simon and Leoben, who run a breeding program on Caprica. Although not patriarchal in its intent, President Laura Roslin's decree criminalizing abortion (because reproduction is one of the only assured methods of ensuring the survival of humans) still forces women to be mothers, even if they do not want to be pregnant. Although this decision is not made lightly and is driven by practical necessity, the only laws about reproduction are aimed at the woman's right to choose. No clauses banning birth control or requiring men to take responsibility for babies are added to the decree, meaning that it places the obligation for childbirth and childrearing primarily on women. From a cultural standpoint, the humans are fairly egalitarian: there are men and women in every job on the *Galactica* and on the Twelve Colonies—but only women can become pregnant and give birth, and this does produce limitations on women by default. Cally and Tyrol, for example, never seem to share equal responsibility for baby Nicky: Tyrol works longer hours and has more responsibilities, so when Nicky is not in a day care center, Cally is the one caring for him on a day-to-day basis. After Cally dies, Tyrol does not seem to have any qualms about turning the baby he has raised over to his true, biological father.

When Simon/Number Four heals the human Kara Thrace after she is injured in season one, he suggests that she is more valuable as a viable womb than as a Viper pilot since the human race is on the verge of extinction. This concept horrifies Kara, who considers her vocation as a pilot to be fundamental to her identity ("The Farm"). In contrast, Caprica Sharon, whose mission is to seduce Helo and become pregnant by him, emphatically describes "procreation" as "one of God's commandments" ("The Farm")—even though the Cylons have proven incapable of conceiving until the hybrid pregnancy. The missing element, some Cylons believe, is love. Although this question is never satisfactorily answered, some Cylons believe that without love as part of the equation, conception cannot take place, so Sharon is purposely placed in situations of trauma and danger to speed up the process of building a relationship with Helo (who believes she is not only human, but the same Sharon he knew on the *Galactica*). A more insidious aspect of this Cylon declaration to "be fruitful and multiply," even though it seems they cannot do so, is the "baby machine farm" on Cylon-occupied Caprica. The Cylons' desperate attempts to produce a sustainable fetus through implantation of unwilling human hosts with Cylon gametes horrifies Kara, who destroys the building and kills the women, rather than allow the Cylons to continue the program. Unlike the Terminators, who demonstrate no reproductive biological urges, the Cylons are driven to produce offspring that will both expand and extend their existence beyond the seven skin-job models created by the Final Five. Conversely, fully human offspring allow the human species to continue to exist—and to record memories and histories of their progenitors. Cylons can resurrect upon death and Terminators can reboot, so this need for Cylons to produce children must have a purpose beyond the basic biological impetus to propagate the species.

The Cylons often act in ways that humans define as evil, but for many of the Cylons, these bad deeds (directed by God) will bring about good changes in the human race (even save them physically and spiritually). The birth of Hera heralds the dawn of a new age—a new species—combining human individualism, uniqueness, and mortality with Cylon strength and monotheistic morality. Hera is a new being, a savior of sorts, because she proves that Cylons can continue to exist even in the absence of a Resurrection ship. This becomes even more important when a combined Cylon and human task force destroys the Cylons' resurrection capabilities, and when Cavil wants to dissect Hera to find out why she exists. Cavil cannot see Hera as an individual being, but instead views her as "a half human, half machine object of curiosity." As Baltar argues in response, "Hera is not a thing, she's a child. And she holds the key to humanity's survival" ("Daybreak Part 2 and 3"). Cavil's determination to fight his programming and design is threatened by Hera because Cavil hates the human part of himself and resents the way the creators made him flawed. The audience eventually learns that Cavil was the Cylon who initiated the human genocide and who continues the war long after many other Cylons doubt its current practicality, given the few remaining humans in the universe. Indeed, Cavil's greatest tragedy is that his body has human attributes and failings, and, therefore, cannot be the perfect machine he believes is the next step in evolution.

All bodies are shells—just meat and bone. What differentiates a human being from a cyborg seems minute on the surface. Cylons and Terminators appear human. Cylons and humans bleed, eat, sleep, and dream, but Cylons can connect wires, machinery, and spaceship mechanics directly to their flesh and bone in ways that humans cannot. Although they do bleed, Terminators do not eat or sleep, and they have a distinct mechanical endoskeleton. They are, however, physically indistinguishable from humans at first glance, and as Kyle Reese tells an amazed Sarah Connor in the first *Terminator* film, "The Terminator's an infiltration unit: part man, part machine. Underneath, it's a hyper-alloy combat chassis, microprocessor-controlled. Fully armored; very tough. But outside, it's living human tissue: flesh, skin, hair, blood—grown for the cyborgs." In the television series, Cameron confirms this basic definition when Charlie refers to her as "pretty as a picture" on the outside, and, in response, she repeats Reese's description of her insides ("Dungeons and Dragons"). The shared ability to bleed unites both types of cyborg, as well as human beings. At the end of season two of *The Sarah Connor Chronicles*, we observe Cameron as half human, half machine with a red eye and her face half blown off—but determined to complete her mission. The image is a jarring one because throughout the series, the focus has been on Cameron's humanity in every sense of the word. But she is not and never can be truly human ("Adam Raised a Cain"). Similarly, when a bright splash of red blood falls to the metal hull of the *Galactica* as Cylon Sharon Valerii dies in the arms of the man she loves, we see the Cylon skin-job as more human than machine in that moment. The blood image is powerful in that it clearly demonstrates the fine line between biological and mechanical in the bodies of cyborgs. This image is contrasted in the very next episode when Kara Thrace is shown bleeding on the ground of the planet Caprica after also being shot in the stomach. Sharon was shot by a human and bled on metal; Kara was shot by a Cylon and bled on earth ("Resistance" and "The Farm").

The Cylon ability to resurrect separates them from their human antecedents because they do not fear death. When humans die, we are erased: our minds, memories, and experiences cease to exist beyond any creations we leave behind (art, music, literature, journals). Of course, multiple religious belief systems argue for a soul that continues on into an afterlife. Even if this notion is inconsistent and unproven outside of faith, it is a pervasive attribute of most human cultures and part of the very human need to continue on after death. On a different level, however, we definitely leave our DNA in our offspring so that, in a way, we are not completely gone. This does not happen with Cylons and Terminators. Although Terminators do not resurrect, they can "reboot" and their memory chips can be replanted into another body, and short of reprograming, they open their eyes as the same individuals they were when broken. Cameron is damaged by an explosion at the beginning of season two, and when rebooted, she reverts to her original programming function, which was to kill John Connor, although she retains her memories of being John's friend. John must remove her chip (read "brain"), toggle it, and put it back, albeit still damaged, to override previous programming that supersedes any personal experiences Cameron may have had. As Sarah Connor notes in an effort to distinguish between humans and cyborgs, "They say that when a person dies, the soul lives on. The soul. The thing that separates us from machines" ("The Demon Hand").

Our sense of identity is not limited to physical space; we exist on multiple levels of being. The Cylons in their resurrections have memories that are not their own. They, in a sense, share memories, but they also have individualized identities and experiences that are not shared until (or unless) death and rebirth into a new shell body. This creates a multi-level base identity and begs the question "Who is the original?" Terminator power cells can be removed and relocated from one body to another as necessity dictates, but the basic identity remains the same, even with reprogramming by John Connor.[2] Cameron was based on a human, Alison, who was born and later died— but whose memories have been coded into a cybernetic body and merged with Cameron's memories to create a new being. Cameron's DNA, so to speak, contains sparks of Alison, but Cameron is not Alison. In contrast, when Sharon/Athena deliberately kills herself so she can be resurrected on the Baseship hiding her daughter, Hera, she is reborn into a new body, but retains all of the memories and emotions of her former self.

The recurring motif of both series is that humans believe humanity must survive intact, as is. Although some of the Cylons do advocate for a future that depends on combining humans with Cylons—and indeed, the final episode shows that Hera is mitochondrial Eve for all humans—the suggestion that humans should *not* remain the dominant species is rarely addressed in either series. That Cylons can, and do, reproduce forces viewers to circle the drain of identity in challenging ways: what is a human, really? When *SCC* reveals that Cameron has Alison's human memories, the viewer's understanding of the Terminators as machines is forced to shift. Similarly, *BSG's* reveal early in the series that Sharon Valerii is a Cylon is equally surprising to the audience—as well as to the character, who believed she was fully human. Everything we are supposed to understand about cyborgs becomes suspect once we realize that they can look like us. If we cannot trust machines to be monsters, can we trust that humans are not? At this point, it should be clear that humans are not the only viable option for sentient existence in the universe, yet that issue never gets addressed by the human characters in either series. The guiding presumption is that humans deserve to continue to exist, even when faced with superior replacement alternatives. Sarah Connor notices the problem with machines replacing humans and notes in a particularly poignant voiceover: "Science now performs miracles like the gods of old, creating life from blood cells, or bacteria, or a spark of metal. But they're perfect creatures. And in that way, they couldn't be less human. There are things machines will never do. They cannot possess faith. They cannot commune with god. They cannot appreciate beauty. They cannot create art. If they ever learn these things, they won't have to destroy us. They'll be us" ("The Demon Hand"). In a chilling juxtaposition, as Sarah recites these words, Terminator Cameron is shown lacing up a pair of toe shoes and then dancing in her bedroom. If machines can create art and can believe in a higher power, what is left to distinguish us from them? Perhaps the delineation is finer than we first perceive and the reason we so fear the cyborg is not that they are trying to kill us, but that they can become us.

NOTES

1. The British-American collaboration *Humans*, which debuted on Channel 4 (U.K.) and AMC during the summer of 2015, is not an apocalyptic narrative, but its overarching themes of "what makes us human" and "can a cyborg be human" are much in keeping with what I am discussing here. Quite noticeably, the cyborgs are overwhelmingly constructed as young, beautiful, and sexually available. Only female "synths" are shown as sex slaves/prostitutes and in other situations where their owners use them sexually, but it can be assumed from the storyline that the male-bodied synths are also sexually available.

2. The fan-polarizing *Terminator Genisys* (2015) completely unravels some of the tropes central to the *Sarah Connor Chronicles*. The film's plot transforms John Connor into a half-human, half-Terminator hybrid—suggesting that this hybrid is "upgraded" and that the only hope humans have for survival is to merge with the machine. This goes against thirty years of Terminator narratives, but it is not the only thing problematic about the movie.

WORKS CITED

"Adam Raised a Cain." *Terminator: The Sarah Connor Chronicles*. Fox. 3 Apr. 2009. DVD.

Balsamo, Anne. *Technologies of the Gendered Body: Reading Cyborg Women*. 1996. Durham: Duke University Press, 1999. Print.

Battlestar Galactica. Dev. Glen A. Larson. ABC, 1978–1979. DVD.

Battlestar Galactica. Dev. Ronald D. Moore and David Eick. Sci-Fi, 2004–2009. DVD.

Butler, Judith. "Imitation and Gender Subordination." *The Lesbian and Gay Studies Reader*. Ed. Henry Abelove, Michele Aina Barale, and David M. Halperin. New York: Routledge, 1993. 307–20. Print.

"Daybreak Part 2 and 3." *Battlestar Galactica*. Sci-Fi. 20 Mar. 2009. DVD.

"The Demon Hand." *Terminator: The Sarah Connor Chronicles*. Fox. 25 Feb. 2008. DVD.

Douglas, Mary. *Natural Symbols: Explorations in Cosmology*. New York: Pantheon, 1970. Print.

"Dungeons & Dragons." *Terminator: The Sarah Connor Chronicles*. Fox. 18 Feb. 2008. DVD.

"The Farm." *Battlestar Galactica*. Sci-Fi. 12 Aug. 2005. DVD.

George, Susan. "Fraking Machines: Desire, Gender, and the (Post)Human Condition in *Battlestar Galactica*." *The Essential Science Fiction Television Reader*. Ed. J. P. Telotte. Lexington: University Press of Kentucky, 2008. 156–76. Print.

Ginn, Sherry. *Our Space, Our Place*. Lanham: University Press of America, 2005. Print.

Gumpert, Matthew. "Hybridity's End." *Cylons in America: Critical Studies in Battlestar Galactica*. Ed. Tiffany Potter and C. W. Marshall. New York: Continuum, 2008. 143–55. Print.

Haraway, Donna. *The Haraway Reader*. New York: Routledge, 2004. Print.

Hatch, Richard. Introduction. *So Say We All: An Unauthorized Collection of Thoughts and Opinions on* Battlestar Galactica. Ed. Hatch, Tee Morris, and Glenn Yeffeth. Dallas: BenBella-Smart Pop, 2006. 1–4. Print.

"Resistance." *Battlestar Galactica.* Sci-Fi. 5 Aug. 2005. DVD.

The Terminator. Dir. James Cameron. Orion Pictures, 1984. Film.

Terminator: The Sarah Connor Chronicles. Dev. Josh Friedman. Fox, 2008–2009. DVD.

Terminator 2: Judgment Day. Dir. James Cameron. Tri-Star Pictures, 1991. Film.

Techno-Apocalypse
Technology, Religion and Ideology
in Bryan Singer's H+

EDDIE BRENNAN

Produced by Bryan Singer (director of *X-Men* and *The Usual Suspects*) and made available exclusively through YouTube, *H+: The Digital Series* (first presented 2012–2013) offers its viewers a science fiction vision of a technological apocalypse. At the heart of the narrative is a computer implant, the H+, which is integrated with a user's nervous system. The implant can provide all of the communication possibilities, the information, and the entertainment of a web-enabled computer but from inside the brain. Images and text are overlaid via the user's visual cortex. Sound is experienced via the auditory nerves, and so on. The nano-implant communicates through the equivalent of a broadcast WiFi network with few places beyond the reach of the network's coverage. Created by Irish biotech company Hplus Nano Teoranta, the H+ quickly becomes ubiquitous, with about a third of the world's population being implanted via a saline injection to the top of the spine. The series explores the apocalyptic consequences of this technology being corrupted. More important, however, is the way the series represents the relationship among technology, society, and humanity. Initially, the series appears to offer a cautionary outlook. However, in its treatment of the relationship between technology and religion, *H+* supports, albeit very subtly, radical transhumanist visions for the future of technology and humanity. Indeed, the series ultimately promotes a conservative, elitist, and alienating ideology.

H+ episodes vary from around two minutes to six minutes in length. It is tempting to think that short episodes were intended to attract people with little time or attention. However, to get even a basic grasp of the story, viewers need to become committed investigators. The timeline for the story spans from seven years before the "event" to two years afterward in locations across the planet. As well as the forty-eight weekly episodes, there are embedded annotations that offer crucial story hints. Short clips called "fragments" provide additional story information or emphasize fleeting and easily missed plot details. There are "behind the scenes" and "the making of" clips, as well as interviews with the cast and crew. Finally, the series is accompanied by official Facebook and Twitter accounts, blogs, and even fake company websites.[1] Perhaps what is most remarkable in terms of the narrative is that its episodes can be viewed in any order. As John Cabrera, co-creator of *H+*, told *Wired*, "YouTube viewers essentially curate their own content so you could form your playlist to watch *H+* through the eyes of one character, in chronological order, in reverse-chronological order, by geographic location" (qtd. in Hart). The hope was that "audiences take *H+* into their own hands" (Cabrera qtd. in Hart). *H+* is not bite-sized television for the web. It is a digital series where the affordances of internet technology are central to the way the story is told, distributed, and experienced.

From the outset, the series describes transhumanism as "an international movement that supports the transforming of the human body and thereby the human condition through advanced technologies" ("Driving Under"). Despite foregrounding the movement, however, the series does not explicitly enter into its more extreme visions. For example, one such visionary, Ray Kurzweil, a pioneer in artificial intelligence (AI) and Google's Director of Engineering, has become synonymous with the idea of the singularity. This describes an apocalyptic moment when technological evolution will outrun human control and outstrip humanity's physical and mental capacities (Dinello 23). The singularity can be understood as an apocalyptic moment in two senses: the final destruction of the world and, in the archaic sense, the revelation of new knowledge. Other leading transhumanists have put forward similar visions of the end of humanity as we know it. Generally, transhumanists envisage that, through a combination of genomics, nanotechnology, and robotics, humanity will be surpassed by a posthumanity. In many predictions, computer technology, rather than the unaugmented human body, will be the substrate for consciousness. Indeed, the rejection of the body is central to radical or "upper case transhumanism" (Hefner 158). Echoing the dichotomous thought of Descartes, the body is seen as merely the profane and corruptible host to sacred consciousness (Dinello 22). Like Christians and Gnostics before them, "the prophets of our techno-future reject the organic body and view technology as salvation from that death-susceptible host of our potentially eternal mind" (Dinello 9). In transhumanism's most extreme prophecies, people may cease to exist, but consciousness, via computer technology, will become godlike. For Kurzweil, and prominent transhumanists like Max More, Hans Moravec, and Marvin Minksy, the techno-apocalypse is a probable and potentially positive development.[2] *H+* does not explicitly deal with these visions for humanity's future. Nevertheless, I argue that it does support them. This claim, however, initially appears difficult to defend since the series opens by highlighting risks and anxieties attached to technology.

If someone watches the *H+* episodes in the order in which they were released, the first installment shows the implant's launch. The event is surrounded by positive news reports and chat-show banter. There are also hints of trouble. News broadcasts tell us that cybercrime has increased. A number of data centers have been hacked. In an online video, an unknown young man warns all the "adults" out there who are considering an implant that Kenneth Lubahn, the lead programmer behind H+, not only no longer supports the device but has also been missing for weeks ("Driving Under"). There is also opposition to the dominance of technology and its potential dangers. Demonstrations take place in Geneva at the death of four human test subjects in a nanotechnology trial. Jason O'Brien, the leader of a Neo-Luddite cell,[3] protests that "These scientists need to realize that we are people. We are not their toys" ("Driving Under"). Outside the headlines, an entire village in the Democratic Republic of Congo has died in an implant trial conducted by Lord Pearce Wachter (LPW), a corporate rival to Hplus Nano Teoranta. Nevertheless, whether accepting or failing to see the risks, billions of people pay to be implanted with H+.

The relatively mundane vision of a pre-apocalyptic future in *H+* resonates with the place of technology in society today. In the series, implants transform society, but the outward differences are small. Many scenes appear much as they might in 2015, but rather than peering at phones, people are staring into space and moving their hands to manipulate icons that only they can see. Rather than creating a stark techno-dystopia, the technologies portrayed are believable developments on what we already know. As Cabrera put it, "Technology has become such a big part of our humanity. We have the internet on 24 hours a day, even when we're sleeping. The only leap here is that instead of the device being in our pocket, we've put it into our bodies" (qtd. in Hart).

By representing an undercurrent of anxiety, *H+* reflects concerns about technology in reality. In November 2013, *The Economist* noted that "the combination of cameras everywhere—in bars, on streets, in offices, on people's heads—with the algorithms run by social networks and other service providers ... is a powerful and alarming one" ("Every Step You Take"). We may not be far, *The Economist* opined, "from a world in which your movements could be tracked all the time, where a stranger walking down the street can immediately identify exactly who you are" ("Every Step You Take"). In January 2015, a conference was held in San Juan, Puerto Rico, to discuss the dangers posed by artificial intelligence (AI). Elon Musk, who created SpaceX and Tesla Motors, contributed ten million dollars to fund research (administered by the Future of Life Institute) into AI safety ("Elon Musk"). Separately, in an interview at the Massachusetts Institute of Technology, Musk said that if he had to "guess at what our biggest existential threat is," it is probably artificial intelligence. He likened it to "summoning the demon" that we imagine we can control but may not be able to (McFarland). Regardless of such concerns, most of us already accept and use technologies that can trace and record our every move—and possibly anticipate our next one. *H+* successfully captures this contradictory culture of anxiety about and acceptance of increasingly powerful and ubiquitous computer technology.

In the opening episode, a computer virus infects the H+ implant's data network. All implanted people within network reception simply drop dead. To escape the same fate, survivors have to avoid network coverage. The ensuing death, destruction, and social collapse pose questions for the viewer about the place of technology in our society. The series reveals our dependence on technologies that we may be unable to control or understand. Like hearing about the electronic vulnerability of power plants, stock exchanges, or personal pacemakers, *H+* may give us pause to think about the way technology can weaken as well as empower. For producer Bryan Singer, "That's the cautionary tale of *H+*: How much do we embrace technology that we cannot control and do not understand?" (qtd. in Hart).

Looking beyond the surface, however, viewers may find it difficult to read the series as the work of techno-skepticism that Singer claims it to be. Jason O'Brien, the only character in the series to oppose technology, is weak and dubious. His hypocrisy undermines his position. He is the leader of a Neo-Luddite cell, yet he was a former professional "lab rat" who made a living from participating in medical trials. Eventually, an LPW nanite experiment left him disabled. It is, of course, ironic that as an opponent of all things technological, Jason is dependent on an advanced exoskeleton for mobility. He rails against LPW for his injury but accepts no personal responsibility for volunteering for hazardous trials. The Neo-Luddites kidnapped Kenneth Lubahn, the missing H+ programmer, in the hope of winning him over to their cause. In the weeks leading up to the H+ launch, the Neo-Luddites believe that the "singularity" is near,[4] and they need Kenneth's help to prevent it ("Make Things Right"). Jason pleads with the kidnapped Kenneth to service his painfully malfunctioning exoskeleton. He cannot have his followers see what he really is. This can be read as a reference not only to Jason's physical condition but also to his dubious past and questionable integrity. Jason O'Brien is the antagonist, while Kenneth Lubahn is the hero who eventually purges the H+ network of the lethal virus. Because Jason is the series' only techno-skeptic, his character weakens Singer's claim that *H+* is a cautionary tale. This claim is further undermined when we consider the series' treatment of the relationship between technology and religion.

The representation of the relationship between religion and technology in *H+* is central to its quiet evangelism for a radical transhumanist perspective. The series transcends any division or opposition between the religious and the technological. The character Matteo Spina, a former Catholic priest, for example, is a man of faith who also sees himself as a man of science. It appears that for Spina, and for the series itself, there is no implicit conflict between the two. Technology and religion are part of a continuum. In the episode "Meta Data," Patricio Raiz, a research scientist who worked to develop the H+ implant, argues against Kenneth Lubahn that the religious and the technological are not separate but intertwined:

RAIZ: You're not a spiritual man?
KENNETH: Well, I'm a scientist.
RAIZ: You know, there was a time in human history when God and the hand
    of science were the same. In fact, several ancient cultures understood the
    relationship between miracle and natural function better than we do.
    Sadly, much of that knowledge, uh, got lost in great purges.
KENNETH: Or relegated to metaphysics.
RAIZ: Some, sure. But the nervous system isn't metaphysics, it's a complex
    computer. And it's ready for an upgrade. Through many of the techniques
    we're devising here.

Kenneth goes on to argue that people can no longer compete with computers, which are "smarter" than humans. He continues that "we've created these tools, so they're a part of our humanity. And I think that is thrilling. We don't need myth and magic anymore" ("Meta Data"). Raiz counters by predicting that "one day, we won't even need implants or any inorganic system for that matter. Our own nervous systems have that potential on their own." People will have the capacity for "mass storage, super computation, even an area of the brain with wireless transfer capabilities" ("Meta Data"). Raiz presents technology not as the opposite of religion but as a different path to the same truth. Kenneth initially objects. His stance softens, however, when he is introduced to Raiz's test subject, Simona Rossi.

Rossi personifies a connection linking the human, the technological, and the divine. She has performed miracles and has been plagued by mystical visions since childhood. These visions allow her to see into the future and, traumatically, allowed her to foresee the death of her husband. She turns to science for an explanation and a solution. Somehow, Simona cannot only see the future but can also remotely access and control computers while appearing to pray. These are natural abilities. Simona has no implant of any kind. In this, she embodies the capabilities that Raiz hopes to develop in all humans. She is living proof of a connection involving humans, computers, and religious transcendence. Through the character of Simona Rossi, *H+* supports a central tenet of radical transhumanism: the belief that human consciousness and computer technology are, in principle, the same.

The belief that human consciousness is reducible to a cybernetic system is commonplace among techno-prophets (Dinello 18). Writing in *Wired*, Jaron Lanier identified a diffuse consensus among apocalyptic techno-soothsayers. Cybernetics, the study of closed systems of communication and control, was the sole metaphor used to describe and understand reality in these predictions. In this view, people are "no more than cybernetic patterns" (Lanier). Lanier also noted the commonly held belief that "Since computers are improving so quickly, they will overwhelm all the other cybernetic processes, like people, and will fundamentally change the nature of what's going on in the familiar neighborhood of Earth at some moment when a new 'criticality' is achieved—maybe in about the year 2020. To be a human after that moment will be either impossible or something very different than we now can know." Radical transhumanists see human life and consciousness to be no more than patterns of information. In *H+*, Raiz captures this in his claim that the human nervous system is simply a complex computer ready for an upgrade ("Meta Data"). Simona Rossi demonstrates the fundamental compatibility between the computer and the human mind. In the series, as in radical transhumanism, computers are presented as part of the essential stuff, not only of human consciousness but also of certain aspects of religious experience.

H+ transcends the divide between religion and technology by presenting both as parallel paths to transcendence. This appears progressive in a culture where religion and the work of science are often thought to be mutually exclusive. However, the *H+* narrative also masks a deep-seated conservatism. The series does not interrogate how people may engage with both religion and technology as forms of belief. As transhumanism demonstrates, technology may be an object of faith, i.e., belief without evidence, like belief in a traditional deity. To understand the common thread between faith in organized religion and faith in technology, it is necessary to turn to the work of Erich Fromm, the German psychoanalyst and humanist philosopher. Fromm offers the concept of "having faith." Here the emphasis is on "having" as an expression of acquisition and ownership. This idea can help us to better read and critique the ideas present in *H+*. It also reveals that the series' support for salvation through technology is a manifestation of something ancient rather than new: the subordination of the individual through faith backed by power.

A synthesis of humanity, technology, and divinity becomes manifest in one of *H+'s* climactic scenes. Kenneth and Simona are held at gunpoint by Jason O'Brien in an H+ data center in Alaska. Simona "prays" and connects to the network. Kenneth is then surreptitiously able to issue commands to the data center, in Italian, via Simona. When he accesses the network, Kenneth becomes immersed in an envelope of light filled with floating constellation-like patterns. He issues a command to activate "Mano di Dio" (God's Hand). This incapacitates Jason, who enters a trance as he is levitated into the air. There are no holographic projectors or anti-gravity devices in the data center. This is not just technology at work. It is magic, a techno-religious miracle.

As a Luddite, Jason has searched for God's Hand, a legendary storehouse of all technological knowledge, with the intention of destroying it. After he has been incapacitated by Kenneth, Jason enters a dreamlike alternate reality. Here Kenneth tells him that he is now inside God's Hand, a sort of virtual world inside his own mind. In a parallel storyline, a physical location with supernatural properties (also known as God's Hand) is revealed to exist in the Vatican catacombs. It is worth noting that, despite the series' international story, Roman Catholicism is the only religious tradition with any relevance to the plot. Like a transhumanist trinity, God's Hand mysteriously exists across the realms of institutional religion, technology, and the human mind.

Fromm describes a distinction between "having faith" and "being in faith" (35–37). Importantly, this applies to secular and religious life. "Having faith" describes a belief that is followed and professed in the pursuit of extrinsic reward, i.e., power, money, popularity, and so on. "Being in faith" describes belief that is personal, questioning, and that is its own reward (Fromm 35). In its representation of religion and technology, *H+* remains rooted in "having faith." As Fromm describes it, in the "having mode," faith is "made up of formulations created by others" (35). The acceptance of these formulations is ultimately a submission to the power of a "bureaucracy" (Fromm 35). These bureaucracies might be churches, states, or corporations, for example. With God's Hand in *H+*, religion and technology are represented by the bureaucracies of the Vatican and the H+ data center respectively. The power of religious or corporate bureaucracies can relieve "one of the hard task of thinking for oneself and making decisions" (Fromm 35). Such belief "claims to pronounce ultimate, unshakable knowledge, which is believable because the power of those who promulgate and protect the faith seems unshakable" (35). As Fromm observes, we can choose such certainty, but it demands the surrender of our psychological and intellectual independence (38).[5] The idea of "having faith" captures *H+'s* representation of religion and technology as two sources of tangible power that offer certainty and extrinsic reward.

Having faith is also an alienated and alienating form of belief. This alienation is deepened by, and is made visible through, the worship of idols. Fromm describes an idol as "a *thing* that we ourselves make and project our own powers into, thus impoverishing ourselves" (35, emphasis in original). He argues that by submitting to our own creations we "are in touch with ourselves in an alienated form" (35). In *H+*, computer technology, which is created by humans, is portrayed as a pathway to the divine. This veneration of computer technology reflects human capacity back to people as something external—and superior—to them. This is compounded by the portrayal of human consciousness as a computer in need of an upgrade. In *H+*, computers, as the dead creations of living people, become revered as a route to transcendence, meaning, and (potentially) immortality. Through this techno-idolatry, the series elevates and mystifies technology.

H+ mixes techno-fantasy with religious belief. In science fiction, transhumanism is often an "important intersection between science and religion" (Geraci 156). Among science fiction writers and academics, transhumanism is frequently discussed in theological terms. Words like *eschatology,* the theological concern with the final destiny of the soul and of humankind, feature prominently. However, discussing transhumanism in theological terms further mystifies and symbolically aggrandizes the role of technology in society. Theology is not an appropriate lens for the understanding of transhumanism any more than it is suited to understanding, for example, nationalism or communism. Not every shared belief is a faith or religion. Unlike most faith traditions, transhumanism does not offer the possibility of a coherent moral framework. Posthuman "heaven" would be a "matter of consumer preference and sufficient funds, rather than a reward for leading a morally good life" (Dinello 24). Transhumanist visions of techno-salvation are a pseudo-religious justification of privilege. As Dinello says, "Disguising their spiritual quest as science, the ministers of machine ascension express technologically induced dreams of becoming like gods, of possessing supernatural powers.... While despising religion as dogmatic irrational debasement, transhumanists comfort themselves with religious goals such as personal immortality and divine power. Technologism is the new religion of the self-aggrandizing techno-elitists" (Dinello 31). There is religiosity but a lack of morality in a system where "even the most evil rich person will be granted digital divinity, while the most saintly poor person will not" (Dinello 24). Transhumanism is a secular example of "having faith." It advances a set of beliefs that act in the service of power. As such, it is perhaps best viewed through the lens of ideology rather than theology. Similarly, the blurring of technology into religion in *H+* can be seen as an ideological obfuscation.

Computer technology companies often see their work as the key source of the solutions to life's problems (Morozov). Many technologists have now extended this work to the timeless human problems of disease, aging, and mortality (Corbyn). Computer systems can offer a metaphor through which we can view life. In the current confluence between transhumanist beliefs and the bureaucratic might of Silicon Valley, technology is beginning to be seen as the stuff of life itself. Transhumanism is the radical avant-garde of corporate ideology. *H+* ideologically supports this hubris. After all, the series is not just a representation of digital technology. In its form and distribution model, the series is a manifestation of, and promotion for, new information technologies. In the series, as in advertising and corporate boosterism, the computer is elevated as an idol. *H+* promotes transhumanism by portraying humanity as a cybernetic data pattern. Technology is represented as a conduit to the divine. In *H+*'s vision, computers are created by humans, but somewhere in their complex circuitry, they contain the stuff of God.

Finally, the ideological bent of *H+* is clear in the aspects of the postapocalyptic world that it represents and those that it overlooks. The apocalyptic "event" transforms global demography. The majority of survivors in the United States and Europe are young, under eighteen, while in the developing world, a disproportionate number of the dead are children. Young people in the West were not implanted on safety grounds. In Africa, on the other hand, young people were implanted in an attempt to facilitate better health care. The catastrophe also disrupted national and international power relations. European powers, for example, lie defenseless in the face of a potential colonization from their former colonies to the south. Within wealthy countries, the young, the poor, and the skeptical, who have not been implanted, are left to dominate the ruins. It is ironic that the winners in this scenario are those who were never implanted. They can go where they please, suffering none of the direct effects of the digital pestilence. However, we cannot really tell because we do not get to see them. This is *H+*'s key blind spot. The series does not show the majority who never bought into implantation. With the exception of Simona Rossi and a small band of Neo-Luddites, the unimplanted masses, two thirds of the global population, are invisible. The series' narrative is driven by characters who want to repair or further develop implant technology. Here, Singer's cautionary tale claim finally collapses. Technology is the star in *H+*. Humanity is peripheral.

NOTES

1. For example, see *hplusnanoteoranta.com*.

2. See Geraci 142, Hefner 158–59, and Dinello 19.

3. The original Luddites were the followers of Ned Ludd. They opposed the mechanization of the British textile industry at the expense of their jobs in the early nineteenth century. The term has become a general (and often pejorative) description for people who oppose technology.

4. Although the "singularity" is mentioned in the series, it is not explained or dwelt upon.

5. The fall of civilization in *H+* happens not because of technology but because of sibling rivalry. Attention to the story's fake company websites and video fragments reveal that Breanna (Peters) Sheehan, CEO of H+ Nano Teoranta, is the sister of Francis Peters, the villain behind the digital plague. Peters has no place in the family business and works instead for Lord Pearce Wachter (LPW). As suggested in the final episode, Peters may have killed one in every three people on the planet in an attempt to show that his rival implant was superior to the H+ ("Visions of What's Come"). In this, the series exposes an irony in transhumanist thinking. Human misery is often caused, not by mortality, disease, aging, and so on, but by greed, envy, thwarted ambition, and warped insecurity. As long as these human traits persist, there can be no

technological paradise. The series indirectly suggests that techno-salvation would require the total surrender of the individual. Ironically, the ultimate realization of transhumanist "faith," which is strongly tied to libertarian individualist ideals, would necessarily annihilate the individual. In this detail, the series agrees with Dinello's argument that transhumanism promotes a religious vision of technology, promising "the reward of everlasting life in exchange for subjugation to the machine" (4).

Works Cited

Corbyn, Zoë. "Live for Ever: Scientists Say They'll Soon Extend Life 'Well Beyond 120.'" *Guardian* 11 Jan. 2015: n. pag. Web. 12 Jan. 2015.

Dinello, Daniel. *Technophobia!: Science Fiction Visions of Posthuman Technology.* Austin: University of Texas Press, 2006. Print.

"Elon Musk Donates $10M to Keep AI Beneficial." *futurelife.org.* Future of Life Institute, 15 Jan. 2015. Web. 28 Mar. 2015.

"Every Step You Take." *Economist* 16 Nov. 2013: n. pag. Web. 10 April 2014.

Fromm, Erich. *To Have or to Be?* New York: Continuum, 1999. Print.

Geraci, Robert M. "There and Back Again: Transhumanist Evangelism in Science Fiction and Popular Science." *Implicit Religion* 14.2 (2011): 141–72. Print.

H+ The Digital Series. Prod. Bryan Singer. Warner Bros., 2012–2013. YouTube.

_____. "*H+* Episode 1: *Driving Under.*" YouTube. 8 Aug. 2012. Web. 28 Mar. 2015.

_____. "*H+* Episode 25: *Meta Data.*" YouTube. 17 Oct. 2012. Web. 28 Mar. 2015.

_____. "*H+* Episode 43: *Make Things Right.*" YouTube. 19 Dec. 2012. Web. 28 Mar. 2015.

_____. "*H+* Episode 48: Visions of What's Come." YouTube. 16 Jan. 2013. Web. 28 Mar. 2015.

Hart, Hugh. "Computer Viruses Can Kill in Ambitious Sci-Fi Web Series *H+.*" *Wired* 7 Aug. 2012: n. pag. Web. 27 Nov. 2014.

Hefner, Philip. "The Animal That Aspires to Be an Angel: The Challenge of Transhumanism." *Dialog* 48.2 (2009): 158–67. Web. 21 October 2014.

Lanier, Jaron. "One-Half of a Manifesto." *Wired* 8 Dec. 2000: n. pag. Web. 20 Oct. 2014.

McFarland, Matt. "Elon Musk: 'With Artificial Intelligence We Are Summoning the Demon.'" *Washington Post* 24 Oct. 2014: n. pag. Web. 10 June 2015.

Morozov, Evgeny. *To Save Everything, Click Here: The Folly of Technological Solutionism.* New York: Public Affairs-Perseus, 2013. Print.

Technoscience
as Alien Invasion
in *XCOM: Enemy Within*

BJARKE LIBORIUSSEN

"What was so noticeable about the new strain of apocalyptic fiction," writes Mike Ashley in his introduction to the 2010 *Mammoth Book of Apocalyptic SF*, "was how much it showed our fear of new technology, particularly nanotechnology. I could have filled this book with stories of nanotechdoom alone" (xii). In the 2013 science fiction video game *XCOM: Enemy Within*, fear of nanotechnology is interwoven with hope: fear that intimate engagement with technology will somehow spell the destruction of the human (understood either as species extinction or a catastrophic loss of humanity) and hope that technology will help us reach the next, posthuman level in our evolution. By allowing its player to manipulate virtual bodies but also to experience the effects of manipulation, the game demonstrates how an interactive medium is uniquely well suited for opening a space of reflection on the connections among science, technology, the human, and the posthuman.

XCOM: Enemy Within begins dramatically when an alien invasion threatens to wipe out the human race. To survive the onslaught of the technologically superior attackers, humanity must rapidly enhance its fighting capabilities by embracing alien military technology in the areas of cybernetics and genetics. The explanation for advances in both areas is the insertion into human bodies of nanomachines captured from the invaders. These alien nanotechnologies allow soldiers to be "enhanced" (to use the game's term) with cybernetic implants such as flamethrowers and grenade launchers. Cruelly, this kind of enhancement requires the amputation of both arms and both legs. Soldiers can also undergo radical genetic modifications enabling them, for example, to exude combat-boosting pheromones or to heal instantly from wounds. Nanotechnological enhancements do allow humanity a fighting chance against the alien invaders, but as the character Shen remarks, "This is the end of an era for mankind. Even after we have defeated the remaining aliens, what then? Have we sacrificed our own humanity for a taste of their technology?"[1]

By removing "their," the question becomes "Have we sacrificed our own humanity for a taste of technology?" This question hints at humanity's ambiguous relationship to technology. "The Western tradition" had traditionally placed "[o]ur capacity to 'know,' that is to reason about our surroundings and act with principled deliberation ... to be the primary sign of our difference from ... other species" (Scharff and Dusek 341). This began to change with the advent of modernity: "Benjamin Franklin speaks for numerous writers of the early modern period in claiming that we ought better to be characterised as tool-making animals" (Scharff and Dusek 341). However, warnings about "runaway technology, over which humans have no control" and which may change itself from humanity's servant to our master, have been influential in philosophy since at least the mid-twentieth century (Ihde 28). Today, such concerns are often articulated in response to the promises and potential dangers of bio- and nanotechnology. Shen's concerns can thus be read as a fictional echo of Francis Fukuyama's fears "that, in the end, biotechnology will cause us in some way to lose our humanity—that is, some essential quality that has always underpinned our sense of who we are and where we are going" (101). Signatories of the "Transhumanist Declaration" (Baily et al.) agree that "humanity stands to be profoundly affected by science and technology in the future" (para. 1), but they do not share Fukuyama's fears. The transhumanists, now organized in the group Humanity+, "believe that humanity's potential is still mostly unrealized. There are possible scenarios that lead to wonderful and exceedingly worthwhile enhanced human conditions" (Baily et al. para. 2). According to its mission statement, this international organization "[aims] to deeply influence a new generation of thinkers who dare to envision humanity's next steps" by drawing on "unique insights into the developments of emerging and speculative technologies that focus on the well-being of our species and the changes that we are and will be facing" (Humanity+). In short, pessimists and optimists agree that ongoing technological advances might result in the end of humanity as we know it, but where pessimists see the apocalypse, optimists—including those who label themselves transhumanists—see the human race reaching the next level of its evolution. Stefan Herbrechter has described the split between pessimists and optimists as a split between "apocalyptic" and "euphoric" posthumanism (3), and *XCOM: Enemy Within* can be said to play out within this split.

As a story motif, alien invasion has a proud tradition in digital science fiction games, a tradition that has become more complex as the decades have gone by. The 1978 *Space Invaders*, with its iconic, pixelated flying aliens moving slowly, then faster and faster from side to side and down toward Earth's surface, is one of the first truly classic digital games. The game's alien invasion can only be postponed, not avoided, thus "[evoking] a genuine tension and a worthwhile sense of the relentlessness of the inhuman attackers" (Roberts 331). Some of the same tension can be found in *XCOM: Enemy Within*, with games journalist Adam Sessler calling it "the pure digital distillation of existential dread" (qtd. in Rev3Games).[2] XCOM is the worldwide organization in charge of humanity's last line of defense. Taking up the role as commander of XCOM, you (meaning "you" both as the player of the game and the humanity of the fiction) are placed on the brink of extinction and thereby forced to make tough decisions. Not only individual soldiers but also entire countries must be sacrificed to postpone seemingly unavoidable defeat. As already hinted, being commander is not just a military role but also includes approving desperate scientific and engineering efforts. These efforts are carried out on your behalf by the head of engineering, Dr. Shen, and the head of XCOM's science department, Dr. Vahlen. Shen and Vahlen function as a Greek chorus of sorts, constantly commenting on the events of the game. Shen is cautious while Vahlen is reckless in the pursuit of new knowledge facilitated by the alien invasion. Shen acknowledges that adaptation of alien technology is absolutely necessary for survival but soon becomes disgusted with the cyborg specimens of alien attackers you bring back to XCOM headquarters for dissection. He warns against taking the fusion of body and technology too far: "If this is a glimpse of our future, I want no part of it." Where Shen urges caution in the face of technology's potential to bring about "our future," Vahlen merely sees an acceleration of scientific progress. Vahlen's position— that enhancement of human beings is "a purely practical problem"—can be characterized as *meliorism*, a philosophical position often associated with Arthur Caplan in recent debates over the bioethical implications of scientific development (Hauskeller 2).[3]

Space Invaders was only barely recognizable as science fiction by way of clumsily rendered yet iconic markers such as spaceships, alien monsters, and laser beams, but technological advances soon made it possible for computer games to tap into audiovisual works of science fiction in more substantial ways. Julian Gollop, lead designer of the 1994 *UFO: Enemy Unknown* (of which the 2012 *XCOM: Enemy Unknown* and the 2013 *XCOM: Enemy Within* are very respectful remakes), thus found inspiration in the early 1970s UK TV series *UFO* (Edge Staff). Gollop later reflected on the game's success in the USA and the way it resonated with other works of science fiction: "I think the release of *The X-Files* [a 1993–2002 TV series] the year before the launch of [the original game] helped a little. Although we hadn't seen *The X-Files* at the time, we were drawing on the same UFO folklore for the game, and this hit a nerve in the U.S." (qtd. in Edge Staff). This UFO folklore contains elements of conspiracy theory and lends a slightly paranoid and generally dark tone to the game. When the first remake was released in 2012, improvements in the graphics capabilities of gaming consoles and home computers (the remakes are available on multiple platforms) had allowed the games' designers to draw directly on the look and feel of science fiction cinema. Short cutscenes are used extensively, not only to drive the game's overarching story forward but also to intensify the player's sense of being in the field when individual soldiers meet aliens in direct combat (see endnote 1 for an introduction to the function of cutscenes).

XCOM: Enemy Within's status as a work of science fiction is not just a question of spaceships and laser guns appearing on the surface level of the screen but also of a deeper commitment to the themes of science and technology. Science fiction is, as Adam Roberts points out, "better defined as 'technology fiction' provided we take 'technology' not as a synonym for 'gadgetry' but in a Heideggerean sense as a mode of 'enframing' the world" (18). Roberts's reference to Heidegger is directly relevant to *XCOM: Enemy Within* and well worth unpacking.

The modern meaning of "technology"—where "modern" alludes to modernity as well as to contemporary usage as recorded in a dictionary—is "the application of scientific knowledge for practical purposes" ("Technology"). Technology merely takes physical shape within a possibility space dictated by science, or as Shen the engineer (and technology's spokesperson) puts it, "Anything they can dream up in the Research Labs, we can build it here." Modern technology merely seems, however, to be subservient to science. In truth, it is the other way around: technology dominates science, as Martin Heidegger argued in "The Question Concerning Technology" (256). Since science has become primarily dependent on the technological instruments of laboratories, observatories, and other places where science happens, technology now has the upper hand. This also holds true, in its way, in *XCOM: Enemy Within*. Vahlen's science department cannot advance through abstract science but relies on material, alien artefacts captured from the battlefield. Vahlen is actually engaged in reverse engineering rather than pure science.

Although he was not actually the first to observe that modern science relied on technological instruments (Ihde 41), Heidegger pushed this notion forward in innovative and influential ways. The term "enframing," as used by Roberts (*Gestell* in the original German), is Heidegger's term for a way of looking at the world (nature in particular) that frames it as something entirely and exclusively open to instrumental, calculative thought. Heidegger's crucial point is that this worldview is no longer reserved for specialist engineers or scientists, but has become the standard, human way of being in the world. In this "technoscientific" worldview, as later commentators, including Don

Ihde (40), have dubbed it, nothing in the world is out of reach for measurement, understanding, manipulation, and exploitation.

Since *XCOM: Enemy Within* encourages its player to perform radical modifications of human bodies for the purpose of increased military efficiency, it is tempting to think pessimistically with Heidegger that the game offers a technoscientific enframing of humanity, that it teaches its player to think about individual soldiers in purely instrumental terms. Every aspect of the soldiers' bodies, from hair color to internal organs, is open to manipulation that might ultimately enhance soldiers to a point where they transcend the human. Where Shen and Vahlen talk of "enhancement," Jean Bethke Elshtain would say that "[w]ith the transhumanist ideology, the human body is distorted beyond recognition" (77). Elshtain sees the transhumanist ideology embedded in in a "society [enchanted] with the possibility of perfecting our bodies so that they gleam, bedazzle…. Humans are presented as plastic men and women, subject to manipulation and ultimate perfection, whether through the genetic route or through fusing what are now called human beings with machines" (75). The soldiers of *XCOM: Enemy Within* are perfect representatives of Elshtain's plastic men and women: they are already handsome and athletic at the game's beginning, but cybernetic and genetic manipulations accelerate their progress towards "ultimate perfection" (75).

This point can be made more broadly in terms of the avatars of interactive media ("avatars" being the characters in computer games controlled by players). Echoing Elshtain's reference to bedazzling, plastic bodies, Nick Yee notices an "obsessive fascination with our virtual bodies" (200), for example, among users of the virtual world *Second Life*. *Second Life* is a particularly interesting case because it is an online world consistently designed and marketed as a space where users are free to do what they want and to present themselves, through their avatars, in whatever manner they want. "In *Second Life*," writes Yee, "hundreds of stores popped up that sold brand-name clothing knockoffs, dramatic hairstyles, and even impossibly sculpted, athletic bodies" (200). The fact that so many participants in this large-scale, online experiment in freedom and imagination choose avatars that closely resemble the gleaming, fit bodies of advertising, television, and cinema seems to support Elshtain's point about a society enthralled by physical perfection.

However, a reading of *XCOM: Enemy Within* as a technoscientific enframing of bodily manipulations, which ultimately paves the way for acceptance of the transhumanist enhancement project, only works when focusing exclusively on the game's strategic mode rather than its tactical mode. As commander of XCOM, you make military and management decisions on a strategic level. Perhaps "enframing" would have been a sufficient label to describe the worldview of the game, had it been played in this mode throughout. Soldiers are studied and selected for enhancements, science and engineering projects initiated, satellites deployed, resources allocated. This can indeed be experienced as play of the most coolly rational kind—play, nevertheless, of a game that has enhancement of the human being at its narrative core and thereby technoscientifcally enframes the human being. But a player of *XCOM: Enemy Within* oscillates between this strategic mode of play and a tactical mode where the player is put in charge of individual soldiers who engage aliens directly on the battlefield. During these tense, tactical action sequences in the battlefield, a soldier avatar is no longer a mere object open to player manipulations in Shen's cybernetics workshop and Vahlen's genetics laboratory. In a sense, the soldier avatar becomes part of the player or an extension of the player. Rune Klevjer has positioned himself against scholars who "[stick] to an instrumental notion of agency" in their descriptions of the avatar in terms of its functions as tool and character (19). In contrast, Klevjer wants to describe the avatar as a device that allows a kind of "'being' in a game" (17). He does so by drawing on Merleau-Ponty, who "emphasises the way in which objects (stick, typewriter, hat), when incorporated into our body, become invisible, unexpressed, cease to exist as internal objects" (23). Something similar can happen when a player engages a game through and with an avatar. Klevjer's argument is sophisticated in its distinctions between various types of avatars and game genres, but the following can stand as a description of the player's relationship with XCOM soldiers in the tactical mode: "When we play, because the avatar extends the *body* rather than pure agency of subjectivity, screen space becomes a world that we are subjected to, a place we inhabit and where we struggle for survival" (28, emphasis in original). In short, enframing is suspended during the tactical parts of *XCOM: Enemy Within* and replaced with a sense of embodiment into the game world of the avatar.

The constantly oscillating experience of the XCOM soldiers—back and forth between strategic and tactical, enframed and embodied—allows the player both to hold (fictionally) the power to modify human beings and also to experience the effects of modification. You are in effect both a technoscientific subject and the object *of* technoscience. This is where a video game shows a unique potential for enacting the allures and dangers of the posthuman. As a player facing fictional extinction, I find it thrilling to have my fighting capabilities (hence my survival capabilities) enhanced through technoscience. That thrill stands in stark contrast to the apparent emotional state of the soldiers I have come to care for through the game, and who in a sense are me: during the cutscenes accompanying genetic and cybernetic modifications, the faces and gestures of modified soldiers display anger and defiant determination, not thrill. Images of soldiers who have had arms and legs amputated in order to wear enormous Mechanized Exoskeleton Cybersuits are particularly poignant. The strategically meliorist part of me knows that enhanced cyborg warriors will give me an edge against the alien attackers; the tactical part of me—the part who has been with these soldiers in battle—cannot help but empathize with "my" soldiers and to wince at what is being done to "me."

Alternating between enframed and embodied modes of play allows the player to think about the posthuman in more than one way. The end of humanity as we know it can be thought of as a cataclysmic event to avoid at all cost (Shen's position of apocalyptic posthumanism), but it can also be considered as a somewhat painful yet ultimately necessary and maybe even joyful occasion (Vahlen would probably choose this side—the side of euphoric posthumanism—although she does not state her view explicitly). As it turns out, the entire purpose of the alien invasion has been to accelerate humanity's leap toward its next level of existence; getting to the posthuman through outside intervention is, incidentally, an established science fiction trope (Ballantyne 179–81). During the game's concluding mission, the leader of the aliens reveals that they themselves have failed to "ascend" to the next level of evolution. The various cyborgs and mutants XCOM has been pitted against over the course of the game are the results of failed attempts at creating a supreme being. In the apparent hope that they will somehow be able to piggyback on humanity's ascension, the aliens have been manipulating us towards a radical embracing of technoscience. The introduction of tougher and tougher opponents has hardened surviving soldiers, and as a by-product has fed the XCOM science department with the alien artifacts and specimens necessary for technoscientific progress. In the grand scheme of things, the aliens see themselves not as our enemies but as something approximating extraterrestrial helpers.

Until this point, the game has facilitated reflection on the posthuman without providing hard answers. Is technoscience what makes us human, or is it somehow at odds with our humanity? Is it alien? Will it destroy us or make us posthuman? Is enframing our only way of relating to science and technology? Is the posthuman something to strive for or avoid? Even after the revelation that the alien invaders have been manipulating humanity towards the posthuman, one could still argue that the time has come for a radically new, posthuman beginning. Disappointingly, XCOM: Enemy Within does not confront its player with this choice. At the very end, the game loses its nerve, betrays the expressive potential of interactivity, and becomes a movie. It does so in two ways. First, it sheds its interactivity and becomes linear entertainment. The attention of the aliens has now been focused on a soldier dubbed The New One. All hope for a posthuman future lies with this individual, but on realizing that such a future entails the destruction of Earth, The New One kills the alien mentors. The player has no choice in the matter and is only allowed to watch as The New One nobly performs self-sacrifice to save humanity as we know it. The alien mothership blows up—but not before The New One has managed to get all teammates off it and moved the ship far away from Earth.

At this point it is useful to consider that the *human* in posthuman stands for a humanist subject conceived since the Renaissance (and at least until the heroic, early-twentieth-century phase of modernity) as a rational, free agent. This free agent does not depend on the supernatural for meaning and purpose but makes its own future and writes its own history. It is the return of that mode of subjectivity that the player witnesses during the cinematic ending to *XCOM: Enemy Within*. Although the humanist subject does not seek divine guidance, its autonomous agency is restricted by what Kant terms the *categorical imperative*. A central expression of Enlightenment humanism, the categorical imperative denotes the existence of absolute moral laws by asking the individual to act only in ways that can be generalized into such laws (Timmons, ch. 8). The New One has powerful agency but does not have a real choice when it comes to defending humanity, that is, the status quo. Paradoxically, The New One *must choose* self-sacrifice over a posthuman future, undermining the very idea of decision making, which is so central to the notion of being a player of a game. *XCOM: Enemy Within* then turns cinematic in a second sense, namely by rehearsing thematic and visual images seen uncountable times before on film, accompanied by fittingly grand musical scores: the lonesome hero selflessly defending the collective and the status quo, even at the cost of his or her own life; the fireworks of the exploding alien mothership echoing the visually stunning destruction of countless other motherships, Death Stars, asteroids, and other unearthly threats.

The ending's cinematic, humane self-sacrifice casts doubt on the technoscientific advances made throughout the game. We are no longer allowed to ponder these advances as an accelerated version of human evolution spurred on by extraterrestrial helpers, but must think of them as the result of malign, alien manipulation. Infusing soldiers with alien nanomachines can no longer be read as steps towards the posthuman in any positive sense; cybernetic and genetic nano-manipulations turned out to be a subtle form of alien invasion. As it becomes impossible to imagine posthuman existence as anything but alien and monstrous—the move into the posthuman as anything but apocalyptic—all we are left with is the cliché of the hero performing the ultimate act of humaneness: self-sacrifice for the greater good, humanity as we know it.

This Othering of alien technology is a deeply humanistic move because it reimposes the binary opposition between human and inhuman which, according to Stefan Herbrechter, "constitutes [humanism's] very foundation" (48). Herbrechter goes on to consider how this binary plays out in relation to contemporary nano- and biotechnology: "The current sense of inevitability surrounding the idea of technological apocalypse and the techno-evolutionary supersession of the human species might ... merely constitute the latest moment within a history of humanism's repression of the inhuman or posthuman within itself" (49).

In the ending of *XCOM: Enemy Within*, technoscience is revealed as alien invasion, a revelation that represses the posthuman and stabilizes the human-inhuman binary. A posthumanistic ending to *XCOM: Enemy Within* would have ignored the human-inhuman binary, relied instead on a human-posthuman binary, and offered the player a real choice between humanity as we know it and a posthumanity that the player would have been free to label evolved, enhanced, transcendental, twisted, monstrous, or any other adjective springing to mind after playing the game. Such an ending would, I imagine, have been far more interesting, and lifted *XCOM: Enemy Within* from a very good to a truly great game. Until its conservative ending, the game does, however, offer a stimulating space for reflection on the posthuman between euphoria and apocalypse.

NOTES

1. Shen's remark falls in a *cutscene*, a cinematic sequence in a video game. Cutscenes typically punctuate the interactive parts of a game and infuse player actions with narratively grounded meaning. Cutscenes are typically triggered by player input and might, therefore, occur in differing order during separate *playthroughs*; a playthrough is a playing of the game that is successful in the sense that it reveals the ending of the game's overarching story. Depending on the game, some cutscenes might never show up in certain playthroughs. Whereas some cutscenes can be placed straightforwardly in relation to an overarching story—as can, for example, the opening cutscene of *XCOM: Enemy Within*, which depicts the scene-setting alien invasion—varying placement of cutscenes according to player actions often renders accurate citation of cutscene dialogue impossible. As for dialogue in *XCOM: Enemy Within*, I will merely identify the speaking character and, where possible, the cutscene's rough position in a successful playthrough. A full overview of dialogue contained in the game can be found at fan-made websites such as the *XCOM Wiki* (*xcom.wikia.com*).

2. Strictly speaking, Sessler is commenting on the 2012 *XCOM: Enemy Unknown*, a predecessor to *XCOM: Enemy Within*. The two games are very similar except that the former does not allow for cybernetic and genetic enhancement of soldiers.

3. See Elshtain (81) for a rebuke of Caplan's position.

WORKS CITED

Ashley, Mike. "The End of All Things." *The Mammoth Book of Apocalyptic SF*. Ed. Ashley. London: Robinson, 2010. ix–xii. Print.

Baily, Doug, et al. "Transhumanist Declaration." *humanityplus.org*. Humanity+ Inc., 1998. Web. 17 Jan. 2015.

Ballantyne, Tony. "Just Passing Through: Journeys to the Post-Human." *Strange Divisions and Alien Territories: The Sub-Genres of Science Fiction*. Ed. Keith Brooke. Basingstoke: Palgrave Macmillan, 2012. 174–89. Print.

Edge Staff. "The Making of: X-Com Enemy Unknown." *Edge* 17 Feb. 2013. Web (originally published in print issue no. 131). 17 Jan. 2015.

Elshtain, Jean Bethke. "Is There a Human Nature? An Argument Against Modern Excarnation." *After the Genome: A Language for Our Biotechnological Future.* Ed. Michael J. Hyde and James A. Herrick. Waco: Baylor University Press, 2013. 73–82. Print.

Fukuyama, Francis. *Our Posthuman Future: Consequences of the Biotechnology Revolution.* New York: Farrar, Straus & Giroux, 2002. Print.

Hauskeller, Michael. *Better Humans? Understanding the Enhancement Project.* Durham: Acumen, 2013. Print.

Heidegger, Martin. "The Question Concerning Technology." 1954. *Philosophy of Technology: The Technological Condition.* Ed. Robert C. Scharff and Val Dusek. Malden: Blackwell, 2003. 252–64. Print.

Herbrechter, Stefan. *Posthumanism: A Critical Analysis.* London: Bloomsbury, 2013. Print.

Humanity+. "Mission." *humanityplus.org.* Humanity+, Inc., n.d. Web. 29 May 2015.

Ihde, Don. *Postphenomenology and Technoscience: The Peking University Lectures.* Albany: State University of New York Press, 2009. Print.

Klevjer, Rune. "Enter the Avatar: The Phenomenology of Prosthetic Telepresence in Computer Games." *The Philosophy of Computer Games.* Ed. John Richard Sageng, Hallward Fossheim, and Tarjei Mandt Larsen. Dordrecht: Springer, 2012. 17–38. Print.

Rev3Games. "X-COM to XCOM: 20 Years of Turn-Based Strategy, Alien-Killing, and Dread." Online video clip. *YouTube.* YouTube, 2 Apr. 2013. Web. 29 May 2015.

Roberts, Adam. *The History of Science Fiction.* Basingstoke: Palgrave Macmillan, 2006. Print.

Scharff, Robert C., and Val Dusek. "Human Beings as 'Makers' or 'Tool-Users'?" *Philosophy of Technology: The Technological Condition: An Anthology.* Eds. Scharff and Dusek. Malden: Blackwell, 2003. 341–43. Print.

Second Life. Linden Lab, 2003. Multiple Platforms. Virtual World.

Space Invaders. Design Tomohiro Nishikado. Taito Corporation, 1978. Arcade. Video Game.

"Technology." *Oxford Dictionary of English.* 2013. Available with OS X.

Timmons, Mark. *Moral Theory: An Introduction.* 2nd ed. Lanham: Rowman & Littlefield, 2013. Print.

UFO: Enemy Unknown [North American title *X-COM: UFO Defense*]. Design Julian Gollop. Mythos Games, 1994. Multiple Platforms. Video Game.

XCOM: Enemy Unknown. Firaxis Games, 2012. Multiple Platforms. Video Game.

XCOM: Enemy Within. Firaxis Games, 2013. Multiple Platforms. Video Game.

Yee, Nick. *The Proteus Paradox: How Online Games and Virtual Worlds Change Us—and How They Don't.* New Haven: Yale University Press, 2014. Print.

Running for My Life

Convergence Culture,
Transmedia Storytelling
and Community Building
in the Smartphone Application
Zombies, Run!

AMANDA FIRESTONE

My pants refused to button. After ten-plus weeks of intensive work to complete my doctoral dissertation, it was impossible to make the button meet the buttonhole. I spent more hours than I care to count fused to my desk chair, eating anything that was quick and convenient, mostly things from bags or cans and mostly heated with a hot-water kettle. With the biggest project of my career completed, I could not wait to get out of the chair and back to my normal self. But, as someone who has been diametrically opposed to organized exercise, I was not sure how to accomplish that goal. For more than a decade, I had been telling people that I only run if I'm being chased by something. By embracing the ingenuity of the smartphone application (app) *Zombies, Run!,* running away from zombies has become a meta-reality.

While some contend that smartphones prohibit and inhibit human inter-action and communication, *Zombies, Run!* bucks such criticism because of the real-world repercussions of using the app. With the rise of smartphones, critiques emerged claiming that, as a result of overuse, we have become *"detached from humanity"* (Perlow, emphasis in original). In *Zombies, Run!,* however, different aspects of the app work together to create an immersive experience for the runner, thus promoting connectivity with the environment and community. By examining these integrated facets through the mingling of theory, personal narrative, and *interpretive storytelling,* I demonstrate the ways this app dashes several social criticisms of smartphone technology.[1]

Hello, my name is Runner 5. At least that's what most of the people in Abel Township call me. Some months ago my helicopter was shot down in the middle of the zombie infested wilderness now surrounding London. I was lucky to run out of the forest alive ... and unbitten. Now, I earn my keep in the community as a runner, someone who leaves the safety of the compound in hopes of returning with a backpack full of supplies and any new information about what's happening in the world. Sam Yao, our comms operator, keeps me up-to-date over the radio headset and tries to direct me away from the hordes of zombs that infest the old city. I'm ready for another mission now. The familiar shout— "Raise the gates!"*—sounds and I take off with Florence Welch blaring in my ears, declaring my dog days are over.[2] Yeah, right....*

Jon Agar contends that the mobile "phone [has] made the leap from being a technology of the home or street to being a much rarer creature indeed: something carried everywhere, on the person, by anybody" (23). And they aren't *just* phones anymore, rather a general purpose technology with the processing power of a desktop computer, offering unprecedented access to information, file storage, and entertainment, in addition to other communicative features such as texting and video messaging. Agar calls the smartphone an "intimate technology"; like clothes or eyeglasses, it is kept close to the body or within arm's reach, and we do not register the perceived necessity for the thing as a burden (164). Our phones are microcosms, representing many facets of our lives, "a private bubble of constant touch" (Agar 165). As the technology has advanced, older cell phone models that are restricted to just a few functions, like only making calls and texting, are already seen as dinosaurs that went the wayside in a mass technology extinction event. Henry Jenkins describes how upon asking at several retailers for a basic cell phone, not the "electronic equivalent of a Swiss army knife," he was mocked or laughed at by employees who saw his necessity for something basic as comparable to the early cell phone itself: extinct (5). In some ways, it is difficult to believe that cell phone technology has been widely available to consumers for only twenty-five years or so.

Like many radical technological advances that consumers widely embraced (e.g., radio, television, and the personal computer), mobile phones, as they have become increasingly more sophisticated, have been heralded as both pseudo-saviors of human civilization and the sinister means of an intellectual apocalypse. In an interview for NBC Dallas-Fort Worth, Dr. Sandra Bond Chapman is quoted as saying that smartphones are "making us smarter, *and* they're making us dumber" (Dewberry, emphasis added). Popular opinion seems to support the latter: a number of lists and videos circulate through the web deriding our growing inability to look up from the device. We are unable to remember information that once was necessary to navigate the world—like phone numbers and driving directions. We often stare into the screens instead of paying attention to our surroundings, and in social situations we are likely to engage with our phones rather than engaging in small talk with the people around us.

Now these are claims painted with large brush strokes, but who among us is not guilty of them? I should know my mom's cell phone number by heart, but I don't. I often use the GPS on Google Maps, even when I know where I am going. And my husband and I sometimes sit across from each other at restaurants fiddling with our phones instead of speaking with each other. Yes, we are more plugged in than ever before, and our phones offer continuous distraction, providing multitudes of apps to pull our focus elsewhere with the use of "txt spk" or headline writing to make information clipped and quickly digestible. In the millennial age, smartphones are as much a part of us as the socks and underwear many of us put on first thing in the morning. It is unsurprising that we (un)consciously reach for our phones in moments of inattention or inquiry ("What's the name of that movie that girl was in? You know the one—with the angels and the crazy tattoos."). Smartphones put us in contact with people and information the globe over in a fraction of a second.

As Apple's well-known phrase intimates, if you have a need in your digital life, "There's an app for that" ("Apple"). Apps specifically targeted toward fitness and cultivating a healthy lifestyle abound, each trying to distinguish itself in the crowd by tempting users with unique yet useful features. *Zombies, Run!* is no exception, seeking to draw consumers with the zombie apocalypse as the teasing gimmick. This app is the result of a successful Kickstarter crowdfunding project, first launched on September 8, 2011, by Six to Start and Naomi Alderman, who wrote *The Liars' Gospel* and *Disobedience*. London based, the original Kickstarter page featured a three-minute video, an outline for different aspects of the app, what crowdfunded money would be used for, and a thank you to the 3,464 individuals who financially supported the project. Ultimately the project raised nearly $73,000, nearly six times more than the proposed $12,500 ("ZOMBIES, RUN!").

So what was it about this app that made people willing to open their wallets and see it come to fruition? For me, the answer lies in what I call the anatomy of my run. I start by psyching myself up at home. The weather is good; I've eaten recently (but not too recently); I have more than an hour's time before the next thing on my to-do list. When I get outside my door, I start my new episode. As the story begins, usually with Sam talking about the purpose of today's mission, I power walk to the end of the block before turning the corner and moving into a medium jog (at 11.15 minutes a mile, it's not the quickest pace, but it gets me there). The story breaks as a song from my *Zombies, Run!* playlist is randomly selected.[3] I move in time with the music, challenging myself to run past the point of asking myself, "Why am I doing this?" As I hit the sweet spot of the stride, my investment in the story intensifies as other characters, Runner 5's friends, are bitten, killed, kidnapped, or defect to evil genius Van Ark. And my investment as Runner 5 intensifies as I feel the responsibility to be successful, to collect the supplies, save my friends, outrun the zombs, and keep Abel safe. When I hit the halfway point, I again coach myself that "I CAN do this," that there's no need to punk out and walk for a while or throw in the towel and go home. I know I have that last mile in me. When I get back to the house, sweat cascading from every pore, I am stoked by my accomplishment, as I down a glass of water or Gatorade and marvel at how much more quickly I recover than I did a year ago.

Alderman gives a vague glimpse into the app's story: "So we're in the zombie apocalypse; we all know how that plays out. You're gonna be chased by fiends reaching for your brains, but there are bigger questions out there" ("ZOMBIES, RUN!"). The question really is this: why are we culturally fascinated with the zombie apocalypse? Where other kinds of apocalypses are concerned, like those brought on by climate change, nuclear destruction, or uncontrollable cyborgs, we have some points of reference. We can think of Hurricane Katrina, 9/11, and the terrifying moments when Siri begins "talking" as though "she" has been listening to your conversation the whole time. Even apocalypses caused by medical epidemics readily evoke current news about anti-vaccination campaigns and the rise of diseases like measles (Disneyland had an outbreak in December 2014). But zombies? The notion of the zombie body and the threat of a zombie horde force us to confront our own humanity in terrifying ways.

In the United States, our relationship with death has fundamentally changed in the last 150 years. Specifically, up until the Civil War (1861–1865), it was more common for people to die at home rather than in hospitals. As a culture, nineteenth-century America knew death intimately; people did not shy away from attending their elders or the sickly by sending them to hospitals. Instead, doctors traveled to homes and shared whatever knowledge and expertise family members or other caretakers might need to treat someone until the patient passed, constituting "the good death" (*Death and the Civil War*). Technologies transformed and grew more refined, medicalization took over, and soon enough, America's relationship with death changed as hospitals became the normalized site for the dying. The zombie body, in its state of perpetual decay, confronts us with one universal and terrifying truth: someday I will die, and the zombie body will be my body, putrid and disintegrating. Angela Tenga and Elizabeth Zimmerman put it well: "The zombie body reminds us that we will soon be rotting flesh without thought or control.

We fear this, yet it fascinates us—a key source of the appeal of horror, which makes us look at what we avoid seeing and provides a cathartic purgation of fear" (78). Van Ark, the antagonist of *Zombies, Run!*, puts it a slightly different way yet comes to the same conclusion: "But you see the greatest threat to humanity isn't zombies. Oh those zombies have caused a few casualties, yes, a few tens of millions of casualties but death, death leaves no one" ("Tightrope"). Where *Zombies, Run!* is concerned, escaping the zombies and safely returning to base at the end of each mission is the symbolic enactment of escaping death one more time.

Of course, this symbolic escape comes with the added benefit of potentially increasing one's health in reality. Van Ark is more truthful than ironic when he quips to Runner 5, "I can't imagine you got this much exercise before the zombie apocalypse" ("Tightrope"). I confess that when I searched through Apple's list of fitness apps, I immediately bypassed anything that had to do with physically being in a gym, calorie counting, and tracking repetitions and sets of exercises. There has never been a part of me that enjoyed regular exercise, but after months of sluggish inactivity and a shrinking wardrobe, I needed *something* to help me get out of the house and back into shape. According to my run logs, visible both on my phone and online through *ZombieLink*,[4] my first mission took place on May 21, 2014. I did 970 steps in just over twenty-three minutes. My memory says I did very little—if any— running, and I probably had one of my dogs with me. Approximately a month later, counting steps is out and counting miles is in; the dogs only slow me down, so they stay home as I wind my way through my neighborhood. At that point, I averaged about two miles per run. I'm pretty sure I've been bitten by the running zomb.

And I am not alone in my new fascination. The iTunes app store has more than 4,200 reviews for *Zombies, Run!*, which averages about four and a half stars (with the overwhelming majority of reviews giving five stars). For example, the glowing review by Kat by the Bay says, "This app is amazing. I've been overweight and sedentary all my life, with painful medical issues complicating any attempt at getting fit. This app, however, not only got me out in the open air and exercising regularly—I actually look forward to it! The storyline is highly engaging and the gameplay elements, which continue to be developed and improved, make it even more addictive!" The app has been mentioned and/or reviewed by a number of media outlets, including a segment on National Public Radio that featured Alderman. Mur Lafferty wrote a "10 Things I Love About *Zombies, Run!*" list, which includes the app's practicality for tracking fitness, the addition of a music playlist or audio book, and the immersiveness of the storyline. Crucially, the character Runner 5 is never gendered. Other characters avoid pronouns by simply referring to you as "5," making the potential for symbolic interaction greater as gender does not alienate any listener. Lafferty says, "Yes, I'm caught up in it. I *care* about those voices in my ears.... [T]he immersion of me as a key runner within the story is unique enough to keep me interested. People in the township talk to you as if they can see you via scanner and they give instructions. You also get the story of Abel through this communication, and you get to meet a lot of different characters" (emphasis added).

Today was a hard day. Runner 10, Chris McShell, was bitten. There's nothing extraordinary or unusual about that. We're surrounded by zombs and anyone who isn't fast enough, smart enough, or heavily ammoed is likely to go grey sooner or later. The thing is, I've run with 10 a fair bit since I came to Abel, and everyone knows him as an expert on zombie movements. He's the guy who figured out that in a horde, they can't choose a direction when their attention is split. I can't help but ask myself, "Why him?" He was in the comms room with Sam and Dr. Meyers when they sent me out on an "unimportant mission." As I ran back to his old house to collect a message from his wife to his daughter, who is missing, I heard him turn. I heard him cough and sputter through my headset with his last words: "If you find her, tell her, her daddy loves her very much" ("An Unimportant Mission").[5]

On my birthday in August 2014, my husband handed me a large envelope, which I suspected held not only my card but also an IOU for tickets to something. I was not disappointed as two pieces of paper slid into my lap. He had taken the time to print color graphics for two different gifts and handwrote their significance on the backs. The first paper had a Wizarding World of Harry Potter: Diagon Alley logo, letting me know that my annual pass to Universal Studios had been renewed. The other printout displayed the familiar logo of my *Zombies, Run!* app but focused on a different race against zombies. I turned the printout over and read my husband's handwritten note: "The 5K Zombie Run. When: 11/8 10AM. Where: Lake Park. Survival: Questionable!!!" There was nothing for it. In less than three months, zombies really would be chasing me!

Although it is not affiliated with *Zombies, Run!*, the 5K Zombie Run (promoted by Monster Runs LLC) is the essence of convergence culture, which is loosely understood as the ways that media are produced, shared, manipulated, and experienced by consumers, creators, and companies. Jenkins emphasizes that the system of convergence is about the flow of information (2), indicating non-linear and sometimes unpredictable paths that media can take as a result of so many people involved. As zombies continue to saturate American culture, multiple channels have capitalized on the trend, borrowing from one another to create interconnected and intertextual experiences. Rather than running through my neighborhood alone listening to the app, I would take off from a starting line with dozens of other people, and on my route I would dodge "real" zombies who would pose a threat by grabbing for the flags velcroed to my belt. I would wear a T-shirt that would say "This is my zombie killing shirt" as self-inspiration and a "warning" to the "zombies" blocking my way; I would live![6] I mean, seriously, the first rule of surviving the zombie apocalypse is cardio (*Zombieland*).

Convergence is both top down, from corporate to consumer, and bottom up, from consumer to other outlets, sometimes including tangentially related things (Jenkins 18). The 5K Zombie Run is in no way associated with *Zombies, Run!*, yet it exists because the same kinds of people who were willing to back the app on Kickstarter are also willing to pay a registration fee to experience a pseudo zombie apocalypse.[7] Running in this 5K was the game made manifest. As people become interested and invested in things, they form communities and understandably gravitate to different texts and experiences that share commonalities, in this case zombies and running. Smartphones digitally facilitate that community building through social media like Facebook and Twitter. Using the posting features of the app and #zombiesrun, I can connect with other people with the same interests online. I recently became involved with the virtual Hogwarts Running Club on Facebook and posted one of my *Zombies, Run!* screenshots to the Slytherin common room. Several other members commented things like "I am Runner 5!" and that spurred a thread about the app, giving some new people incentive to try it out.

The runner's experience is further enriched through transmedia storytelling, or how "each medium does what it does best—so that a story might be introduced in a film, expanded through television, novels, and comics; its world might be explored through game play or experienced as an amusement park attraction" (Jenkins 96). *Zombies, Run!* operates on this principle, supplying further opportunities for engagement with the story, characters, Runner 5, and the personal fitness journey through a variety of experiences: the episodic narrative, the gaming aspect of the Abel Township base, the online connectivity through *ZombieLink*, the online connectivity through social media, and the tangential, real-world experiences like the 5K Zombie Run. Ultimately, this is a collaborative process between creators, media platforms, and fans.

In an essay published in 2013, Murali Balaji observed that "[t]he 'zombie industry,' as it has become commonly known, is now generating upward of $5 billion a year (a conservative estimate), thanks to the expanse of media and cultural products offered to hordes of eager consumers" (ix). What is it about the zombie that makes it so appealing to both convergence culture and transmedia storytelling, particularly in this context? After all, the app is not "Vampires, Run!" Everyone knows that vampires have super speed and stealth; the runner would never stand a chance with a thirsty vampire on her tail. However, up against a zombie, a shambling, ostensibly brain-dead eating machine, the runner has better than a fighting chance if she is quick and a little street smart. While zombies function as metaphors for many things—mindless consumers, racial Others, infectious diseases, even the end of the white-collar workforce—the base characteristics present an enemy that even in quantity can be overcome. An animated, putrefying skinbag that bites might look terrifying, but as an obstacle, it is completely surmountable because, traditionally, it does not actively think or adapt. Just destroy the head, set it on fire, and that's that. While other creature characters like vampires have their own allure, the thing that brings us back to the zombie time and again is the probability of escape. I think the character Tina Belcher puts it best when she says, "I have a complicated relationship with zombies. Zombies, they're dangerous, but I love their swagger" ("Weekend at Mort's").

By July 2015 my running regularity has ebbed and flowed, but I get out there at least once a week to keep up with the story. I have far surpassed my goal of having my clothes fit again. In fact, I culled my existing wardrobe as things became too roomy. My friends continue to cheer me on each time *Zombies, Run!* posts to Facebook that I've completed another run. When friends see me in person, they comment on how healthy I look and how awesome my progress is. A wonderful unexpected side effect of using the app (and posting to social media) is the deepening of my relationships with friends and colleagues. They all knew my "I only run if something's chasing me" philosophy, and after a little playful ribbing, they brought me into the runner's fold by offering advice about the proper shoes to wear, ways to increase my distance over time, and local clubs to join like Running for Brews and Run the Heights. But running in my neighborhood has also yielded something unexpected. I have gotten to know more of my neighbors simply by running past their houses and sharing a friendly wave. If we spot each other in the local grocery store, we tend to stop to talk now instead of curtly nodding and moving on. Using *Zombies, Run!* has helped me to go out into the world and strengthen connections in my community and existing social circle.

While there are valid concerns about our growing dependency on smartphones and the ways that they hinder some forms of communication, *Zombies, Run!* is an effective tool for forging connectivity. The zombie trope clearly lends itself to convergence culture and transmedia storytelling; its saturation in popular culture means that the trope is widely available and highly consumed by fans across media. Runners can experience a sense of immersion as the app plays and they grow further attached to the characters in the story. Posting run logs to social media outlets means that others can encourage the runner. As someone who despised exercise, I found that *Zombies, Run!* was an accessible outlet to help me get out of the house post-dissertation. For the first time in over a decade, I have made a New Year's resolution: I am going to run a 10K before the year is out—with zombies chasing me all the way.

The gates close behind me as I safely return to base. I'm dead on my feet, no pun intended, as I make my way through the compound in search of a hot shower and my bed. There were a few close calls on this mission, the zombs only 20 meters or so from me at one point, and I thank whoever is listening to my silent words for our escape. Sometimes I wonder why I'm still doing this, why I still go out there. Moments like this, I think about the run I had with Ian, a journalist for the New Times. He said to me, "Your story's going to bring hope to a lot of scared people out there ... reminding people that we're all still surviving, that people can work together, and keep going, keep being brave even at a time like this. It's worth something to a lot of us.... And in the distance, Abel Township rises before us like a beacon, a beacon of hope, of humanity in these troubled times. Will this tiny township survive against the increasing odds and dangers of our brave new postapocalyptic world? Only time will tell. But today, we're headed home" ("Times New Roaming").[8]

NOTES

1. In three places, I've employed *interpretive storytelling* as a means of more fully describing the immersiveness of the app. The italicized paragraphs are written from my Runner 5's perspective, as "she" does not speak during the missions although I have symbolically merged with "her." Abel Township and the characters mentioned like Sam Yao and Dr. Meyers are part of the *Zombies, Run!* world, which was created by Six to Start and Naomi Alderman.

2. Music is an integral part of the running experience, and the story clips for *Zombies, Run!* can be intercut with songs from a playlist of the runner's choosing. This adds to the immersion of the experience, promotes fitness as the runner's steps synch with the beat, and further supports transmedia storytelling as songs can be apropos of the narrative (e.g., Lady Gaga's "Monster"). Within these notes are the titles of songs I have on my *Zombies, Run!* playlist. The first is "Dog Days Are Over" by Florence and the Machine, from the album *Lungs*.

3. Eric Hutchinson. "Food Chain." *Sounds Like This.*

4. *ZombieLink* is the webpage operated by *Zombies, Run!* that also shows runners their statistics as collected through the app (speed, distance, time, GPS route, calorie burns, etc.). It also provides a forum wherein Runner 5s can connect with one another and share experiences using the app, making online community connectivity key.

5. Editors. "No Sounds but the Wind." *The Twilight Saga: New Moon Soundtrack.*

6. Okay, I didn't "live" per se. I did not make it to the end of the race with any flags left, so technically I went zomb during the race. But I did run the entire time without walking or stopping at the mile-marked rest stations, so that was a win.

7. On August 17, 2015, I received an email from *Zombies, Run!* announcing that a virtual race had been planned for October 24 to November 1. Users could sign up for the race through *ZombieLink* with a registration fee of $40. In less than a week, the 1,500 available entries were sold out, a testament to the popularity of the app.

8. Barenaked Ladies. "Odds Are." *Grinning Streak.*

WORKS CITED

Agar, Jon. *Constant Touch: A Global History of the Mobile Phone.* London: Icon Books, 2013. EBook.

"Apple–Legal–Trademark List." *Apple*. Apple, Inc. 8 Sept. 2015. Web. 15 Sept. 2015.

Balaji, Murali. "Thinking Dead: Our Obsession with the Undead and Its Implications." *Thinking Dead: What the Zombie Apocalypse Means*. Ed. Balaji. Plymouth: Lexington Books, 2013. ix-xviii. Print.

Death and the Civil War. Dir. Ric Burns. Steeplechase Films, 2012. Web. 1 Feb. 2015.

Dewberry, Deanna. "Are Smartphones Making Us Dumb?: Experts Say Smartphones Help in Many Ways, but Can Negatively Affect Our Brain." *NBCDFW.com*. NBC Universal Media. 10 Sept. 2012. Web. 25 Oct. 2014.

Jenkins, Henry. *Convergence Culture: Where Old and New Media Collide*. New York University Press, 2006. Print.

Kat by the Bay. "Best Purchase of My Life." Rev. of *Zombies, Run!*, by Six to Start and Naomi Alderman. iTunes App Store. 8 Aug. 2013. Web. 12 Oct. 2014.

Lafferty, Mur. "10 Things I Love About Zombies, Run!" *Escapist*. Defy Media, LLC. 23 Aug. 2012. Web. 25 Oct. 2014.

Perlow, Jason. "How Smartphones Steal Fleeting Moments of Life." *ZDNet*. CBS Interactive. 5 Sept. 2013. Web. 28 Oct. 2014.

Six to Start, and Naomi Alderman. *Zombies, Run!* Smartphone application. Apple App Store. Vers. 4.1.3. 3 Aug. 2015.

Tenga, Angela, and Elizabeth Zimmerman. "Vampire Gentlemen and Zombie Beasts: A Rendering of True Monstrosity." *Gothic Studies* 15.1 (May 2013): 76–87. Web. 15 Jan. 2015.

"Tightrope." *Zombies, Run!* Season 2, Episode 28. Six to Start. 15 Aug. 2015. Smartphone application.

"Times New Roaming." *Zombies, Run!* Season 2, Side Mission 7. Six to Start. 15 Aug. 2015, Smartphone application.

"An Unimportant Mission." *Zombies, Run!* Season 1, Episode 19. Six to Start. 15 Aug. 2015. Smartphone application.

"Weekend at Mort's." *Bob's Burgers*. Bento Box Entertainment, 2011. Netflix.

Zombieland. Dir. Ruben Fleischer. Columbia Pictures, 2009. DVD.

"ZOMBIES! RUN: A Running Game and Audio Adventure for iOS/Android by Six to Start and Naomi Alderman—Kickstarter." *Kickstarter.com*. Kickstarter, Inc. 2014. Web. 30 Oct. 2014.

Appendix
Apocalyptic Criticism, Films, Television Series and Video Games

LEISA A. CLARK, MARY F. PHARR
and AMANDA FIRESTONE

Criticism

Agar, Jon. *Constant Touch: A Global History of the Mobile Phone.* London: Icon Books, 2013. EBook.

Arnovitz, Kevin. "Virtual Dictionary: A Guide to the Language of Reality TV." *slate. com.* The Slate Group, 14 Sept. 2004. Web. 30 Dec. 2014.

Asma, Stephen. *On Monsters: An Unnatural History of Our Worst Fears.* Oxford: Oxford University Press, 2009. Print.

Aston, James, and John Walliss, eds. *Small Screen Revelations: Apocalypse in Contemporary Television.* Sheffield: Sheffield Phoenix Press, 2013. Print.

Baccolini, Raffaella. "The Persistence of Hope in Dystopian Science Fiction." *PMLA: Special Topic: Science Fiction and Literary Studies: The Next Millennium* 119.3
_____, and Tom Moylan. *Dark Horizons: Science Fiction and the Dystopian Imagination.* New York: Routledge, 2003. Print.

Balaji, Murali, ed., *Thinking Dead: What the Zombie Apocalypse Means.* Lanham: Lexington-Rowman & Littlefield, 2013. Print.

Ballantyne, Tony. "Just Passing Through: Journeys to the Post-Human." *Strange Divisions and Alien Territories: The Sub-Genres of Science Fiction.* Ed. Keith Brooke. Basingstoke: Palgrave Macmillan, 2012. 174–89. Print.

Baudrillard, Jean. *Simulation and Simulacra.* Trans. Sheila Faria Glaser. Ann Arbor: University of Michigan Press, 1994. Print.

Bauman, Zygmunt. *Liquid Times: Living in an Age of Uncertainty.* Cambridge: Polity Press, 2007. Print.

Baumeister, Roy F., Karen Dale, and Kristin L. Sommer. "Freudian Defense Mechanisms and Empirical Findings in Modern Social Psychology: Reaction Formation, Projection, Displacement, Undoing, Isolation, Sublimation, and Denial." *Journal of Personality* 66.6 (1998): 1081–1124. Print.

Benjamin, Richard. "The Sense of an Ending: Youth Apocalypse Films." *Journal of Film and Video* 56.4 (2004): 34–49. *JSTOR.* 1 Mar. 2015.

Bennett, Eve. "Deus Ex Machina: AI Apocalypticism in *Terminator: The Sarah Connor Chronicles.*" *Journal of Popular Television* 2.1 (2014): 3–19. Print.

Berger, James. *After the End: Representations of Post-Apocalypse.* Minneapolis: University of Minnesota Press, 1999. Print.

Bishop, Kyle William. *American Zombie Gothic: The Rise and Fall (and Rise) of the Walking Dead in Popular Culture.* Jefferson: McFarland, 2011. Print.

Booker, Keith. *Alternate Americas: Science Fiction Film and American Culture.* Westport: Praeger, 2006. Print.

Butler, Lisa D., and Oxana Palesh. "Spellbound: Dissociation in the Movies." *Journal of Trauma and Dissociation* 5.2 (2004): 61–87. Print.

Cameron, Allan. "Zombie Media: Transmission, Reproduction, and the Digital Dead." *Cinema Journal* 52.1 (2012): 66–89. *JSTOR.* 1 Mar. 2015.

Carroll, Hamilton. *Affirmative Reaction: New Formations of White Masculinity.* Durham: Duke University Press, 2011. Print.

Christie, Deborah, and Sarah Juliet Lauro, eds. *Better Off Dead: The Evolution of the Zombie as Post-Human.* New York: Fordham University Press, 2011. Print.

Cobb, James C. *Away Down South: A History of Southern Identity.* New York: Oxford University Press, 2005. Print.

Cohen, Ed. "The Paradoxical Politics of Viral Containment; or, How Scale Undoes Us One and All." *Social Text* 29.1/106 (Spring 2011): 15–35. Print.

Connors, Sean P, ed. *The Politics of Panem.* Jefferson: McFarland, 2014. Print.

Curtis, Claire P. *Postapocalyptic Fiction and the Social Contract: We'll Not Go Home—Again.* Lanham: Lexington Books, 2010. Print.

De Aguilera, Miguel, and Alfonso Mendiz. "Video Games and Education: Education in the Face of a 'Parallel School.'" *Computers in Entertainment* 1.1 (2003): 1–10. Web. 1 Mar. 2015.

Dellamora, Richard, ed. *Postmodern Apocalypse: Theory and Cultural Practice at the End.* Philadelphia: University of Pennsylvania Press, 1995. Print.

Dendle, Peter. "The Zombie as Barometer of Cultural Anxiety." *Monsters and the Monstrous: Myths and Metaphors of Enduring Evil.* Ed. Niall Scott. New York: Rodopi, 2007. 45–57. Print.

Dewberry, Deanna. "Are Smartphones Making Us Dumb? Experts Say Smartphones Help in Many Ways, but Can Negatively Affect Our Brain." *NBCDFW.com.* NBC Universal Media. 10 Sept. 2012. Web. 25 Oct. 2014.

Diamond, Jared. *Collapse: How Societies Choose to Fail or Succeed.* New York: Viking Penguin, 2005. Print.

_____. *Guns, Germs, and Steel: The Fates of Human Societies.* 1997. New York: Norton, 2005. Print.

Dinello, Daniel. *Technophobia! Science Fiction Visions of Posthuman Technology.* Austin: University of Texas Press, 2005. Print.

DiTommasso, Lorenzo. "At the Edge of Tomorrow: Apocalypticism and Science Fiction." *End of Days: Essays on the Apocalypse from Antiquity to Modernity.* Ed. Karolyn Kinane and Michael Ryan. Jefferson: McFarland, 2009. 221–41. Print.

Dixon, Wheeler Winston. *Visions of the Apocalypse: Spectacles of Destruction in American Cinema.* London: Wallflower, 2003. Print.

Douglas, Jane Yellowlees, and Andrew Hargadon. "The Pleasure of Immersion and Engagement: Schemas, Scripts and the Fifth Business." *Digital Creativity* 12.3 (2001): 153–66. Web. 1 Mar. 2015.

Dowling, David. *Fictions of Nuclear Disaster.* Iowa City: University of Iowa Press, 1987. Print.

Fukuyama, Francis. *Our Posthuman Future: Consequences of the Biotechnology Revolution.* New York: Farrar, Straus and Giroux, 2002. Print.

Furnham, Adrian. "Lay Understandings of Defense Mechanisms: The Role of Personality Traits and Gender." *Psychology, Health, & Medicine* 17.6 (2012): 723–34. Print.

Gaiman, Neil. *Signal to Noise.* 2nd ed. Milwaukee: Dark Horse Books, 2007. Print.

Garrett, Lori. *The Coming Plague: Newly Emerging Diseases in a World Out of Balance.* New York, Penguin, 1995. Print.

Geraci, Robert M. "There and Back Again: Transhumanist Evangelism in Science Fiction and Popular Science." *Implicit Religion* 14.2 (2011): 141–72. Print.

Germana, Monica, and Aris Mousoutzanis, eds. *Apocalyptic Discourse in Contemporary Culture: Post-Millennial Perspectives on the End of the World.* New York: Routledge, 2014. Kindle.

Greene, Richard, and K. Silem Mohammad, eds. *The Undead and Philosophy.* Peru: Open Court, 2006. Print.

Gross, Mathew Barrett, and Mel Gilles. *The Last Myth: What the Rise of Apocalyptic Thinking Tells Us About America.* Amherst: Prometheus Books, 2012. Print.

Gunn, Joshua, and David E. Beard. "On the Apocalyptic Sublime." *Southern Communication Journal* 65.4 (2000): 269–86. Web. 28 Dec. 2014.

Halbwachs, Maurice. "The Social Frameworks of Memory." *On Collective Memory.* Ed. and Trans. Lewis A. Coser. Chicago: University of Chicago Press, 1992. 37–167. Print.

Hall, Stuart, and Paul du Gay, eds. *Questions of Cultural Identity.* London: Sage Publications, 1996. Ebook.

Hart, Kylo-Patrick R., and Annette M. Holba. *Media and the Apocalypse.* New York: Peter Hart, 2009. Print.

Hefner, Philip. "The Animal That Aspires to Be an Angel: The Challenge of Transhumanism." *Dialog: A Journal of Theology* 48.2 (2009): 158–67. Print.

Herbrechter, Stefan. *Posthumanism: A Critical Analysis.* London: Bloomsbury, 2013. Print.

Hubner, Laura, Marcus Leaning, and Paul Manning. *The Zombie Renaissance in Popular Culture.* Basingstoke: Palgrave Macmillan, 2014. Print.

Jacoby, Russell. *Picture Imperfect: Utopian Thought for an Anti-Utopian Age.* New York: Columbia University Press, 2005. Print.

Jameson, Fredric. *Archaeologies of the Future: The Desire Called Utopia and Other Science Fictions.* London: Verso, 2005. Ebook.

Jenkins, Henry. *Convergence Culture: Where Old and New Media Collide.* New York University Press, 2006. Print.

Kavadlo, Jesse. "War on Terror: Amending Monsters After 9/11." *Humanities Review* 6.2 (Spring 2008): 165–76. Print.

Keetley, Dawn, ed. *"We're All Infected": Essays on AMC's* The Walking Dead *and the Fate of the Human.* Jefferson: McFarland, 2014. Print.

King, Claire Sisco. *Washed in Blood: Male Sacrifice, Trauma, and the Cinema.* New Brunswick: Rutgers University Press, 2011. Ebook.

Krikowa, Natalie, and Shawn Edrei, eds. *Crossing Channels—Crossing Realms: Immersive Worlds and Transmedia Narratives.* Oxford: Inter-Disciplinary Press, 2013. Ebook.

Landsberg, Alison. *Prosthetic Memory: The Transformation of American Remembrance in the Age of Mass Culture.* New York: Columbia University Press, 2004.

Langlumé, Diane. "Apocalypse as Religious and Secular Discourse in *Battlestar Galactica* and Its Prequel *Caprica.*" *Skepsi* 6 (2014): 79–94. Web. 1 Mar. 2015.

Lauro, Sarah Juliet, and Karen Embry. "A Zombie Manifesto: The Nonhuman Condition in the Era of Advanced Capitalism." *boundary* 235.1 (2008): 85–108. Print.

Leslie, John. *The End of the World: The Science and Ethics of Human Extinction.* New York: Routledge, 1996. Print.

Lisboa, Maria Manuel. *The End of the World: Apocalypse and Its Aftermath in Western Culture.* Cambridge: Open Book, 2011. Ebook.

Luckhurst, Roger. "The Public Sphere, Popular Culture and the True Meaning of the Zombie Apocalypse." *The Cambridge Companion to Popular Fiction.* Cambridge: Cambridge University Press, 2012. 68–85. Print.

Magnusson, Bruce, and Zahi Zalloua. *Contagion: Health, Fear, Sovereignty.* Seattle: University of Washington Press, 2012. Print.

Manjikian, Mary. *Apocalypse and Post-Politics: The Romance of the End.* Lanham: Lexington, 2014. Print.

Martinez, Christopher. *Survival Guide for the End of the World: Don't Forget Your Wet Blanket.* Seattle: CreateSpace Independent Publishing, 2011. Print.

Masters, Joshua J., and Karen J. Renner. "Representations of the Apocalypse in Literature and Film, Part 1 [Special Issue]." *Lit: Literature Interpretation Theory* 23.2 (2012): 113–201. Print.

McIntosh, Shawn, and Marc Leverette, eds. *Zombie Culture: Autopsies of the Living Dead.* Lanham: Scarecrow Press, 2008. Print.

Milford, Mike, and Robert C. Rowland. "Situated Ideological Allegory and *Battlestar Galactica.*" *Western Journal of Communication* 76.5 (2012): 536–51. Web. 26 Oct. 2014.

Mitchell, Charles P. *A Guide to Apocalyptic Cinema.* Santa Barbara: Greenwood, 2001. Print.

Moreman, Christopher M., and Cory James Rushton, eds. *Zombies Are Us: Essays on the Humanity of the Walking Dead.* Jefferson: McFarland, 2011. Print.

Morozov, Evgeny. *The Net Delusion: The Dark Side of Internet Freedom.* New York: Public Affairs, 2011. Print.

Moylan, Thomas. *Scraps of the Untainted Sky: Science Fiction, Utopia, Dystopia.* Boulder: Westview Press, 2000. Print.

Nashawaty, Chris. "A Brief History of the Cinematic Apocalypse." *Entertainment Weekly* 4 July 2014: 24–27. Print.

Newman, Kim. *Apocalypse Movies.* New York: St. Martin's Press, 2002. Print.

Olney, Ian. *Euro Horror: Classic Horror Cinema in Contemporary American Culture.* Bloomington: Indiana University Press, 2013. Print.

Otis, Laura. *Organic Memory.* Lincoln: University of Nebraska Press, 1994. Print.

Paik, Peter Y. *From Utopia to Apocalypse: Science Fiction and the Politics of Catastrophe.* Minneapolis: University of Minnesota Press, 2010. Print.

Pariser, Eli. *The Filter Bubble: How the New Personalized Web Is Changing What We Read and How We Think.* New York: Penguin, 2012. Print.

Paulson, Daryl S., and Stanley Krippner. *Haunted by Combat; Understanding PTSD in War Veterans.* Plymouth, UK: Rowman & Littlefield, 2007. Print.

Perlow, Jason. "How Smartphones Steal Fleeting Moments of Life." ZDNet. CBS Interactive. 5 Sept. 2013. Web. 28 Oct. 2014.

Pokornowski, Steven. "Insecure Lives: Zombies, Global Health, and the Totalitarianism of Generalization." *Literature and Medicine* 31.2 (Fall 2013): 216–34. Print.

Potter, Tiffany, and C. W. Marshall, eds. *Cylons in America: Critical Studies in* Battlestar Galactica. New York: Continuum, 2007. Print.

Prividera, Laura C., and John W. Howard, III. "Masculinity, Whiteness, and the Warrior Hero: Perpetuating the Strategic Rhetoric of U.S. Nationalism and the Marginalization of Women." *Women and Language* 29.2 (Sept. 2006): 29–37. *EBSCOHost*. Web. 7 Dec. 2013.

Rahm, Lina. "Who Will Survive?: On Bodies and Boundaries After the Apocalypse." *Gender Forum* 45 (2013): n.p. Web. 1 Mar. 2015.

Rehill, Annie. *The Apocalypse Is Everywhere: A Popular History of America's Favorite Nightmare.* Santa Barbara: Praeger, 2009. Print.

Renner, Karen J., and Joshua J. Masters. "Representations of the Apocalypse in Literature and Film, Part 2 [Special Issue]." *Lit: Literature Interpretation Theory* 23.3 (2012): 203–304. Print.

Reyburn, Duncan. "Reconfiguring the Contagion: A Girardian Reading of the Zombie Apocalypse as a Plea for a Politics of Weakness." *Image & Text* 24 (2014): 116–54. Web. 1 Mar. 2015.

Rifkin, Jeremy. "The Second Genesis: Science May Be Ready to Create a Perfect World—But Who Will Define Perfect?" *Maclean's* 4 May 1998. Web. 12 Dec. 2014.

Roberts, Adam. *The History of Science Fiction.* Basingstoke: Palgrave Macmillan, 2006. Print.

Rosen, Elizabeth K. *Apocalyptic Transformation: Apocalypse and the Postmodern Imagination.* Lanham: Lexington-Rowman & Littlefield, 2008. Print.

Sanders, Steven. *The Philosophy of Science Fiction Film.* Lexington: University Press of Kentucky, 2007. Print.

Scharff, Robert C., and Val Dusek, eds. *Philosophy of Technology: The Technological Condition: An Anthology.* Malden: Blackwell, 2003. Print.

Scholte, Jan. *Globalization: A Critical Introduction.* New York: St. Martin's Press, 2000. Print.

Shapiro, Jerome F. *Atomic Bomb Cinema: The Apocalyptic Imagination on Film.* New York: Routledge, 2002. Print.

Sharps, Matthew J., Liao W. Schuyler, and Megan R. Herrera. "Remembrance of Apocalypse Past: The Psychology of True Believers When Nothing Happens." *Skeptical Inquirer* 38.6 (2014): 54. Web. 1 Mar. 2015.

Shome, Raka, and Radha Hegde. "Culture, Communication, and the Challenge of Globalization." *Critical Studies in Media Communication* 19.2 (2002): 172–89. Print.

Slocum, David. "9/11 Film and Media Scholarship." *Cinema Journal* 51.1 (2011): 181–93. *JSTOR.* 1 Mar. 2015.

Szendy, Peter. *Apocalypse-Cinema: 2012 and Other Ends of the World.* Trans. Will Bishop. New York, Fordham University Press, 2015. Print.

Thompson, Kirsten Moana. *Apocalyptic Dread: American Film at the Turn of the Millennium.* Albany: State University of New York Press, 2007. Print.

Turkle, Sherry. *Alone Together: Why We Expect More from Technology and Less from Each Other.* New York: Basic Books-Perseus, 2011. Print.

Wald, Priscilla. *Contagious: Cultures, Carriers, and the Outbreak Narrative.* Durham: Duke University Press, Print.

Walliss, John, and Lee Quinby. *Reel Revelations: Apocalypse and Film.* Sheffield: Sheffield Phoenix Press, 2010. Print.

Weaver, Roslyn. *Apocalypse in Australian Fiction and Film: A Critical Study.* Jefferson: McFarland, 2011. Print.

Weisman, Alan. *The World Without Us*. New York: Thomas Dunne Books, 2007. Print.
Williams, Raymond. *Culture and Materialism: Selected Essays*. London: Verso, 2005. Print.
Wojcik, Daniel. *The End of the World As We Know It: Faith, Fatalism, and Apocalypse in America*. New York: New York University Press, 1997. Kindle.
Wright, Christopher J. *Tribal Warfare: Survivor and the Political Unconscious of Reality Television*. Lanham: Lexington, 2006. Print.
Xenakis, Stephen N., and Matthew J. Friedman. "Understanding PTSD." *Wilson Quarterly* 36.1 (Winter 2012): 8–9.

Film: 1951–1999

Armageddon. Dir. Michael Bay. Buena Vista, 1998. Film.
Blade Runner. Dir. Ridley Scott. Warner Bros., 1982. Film.
Dark City. Dir. Alex Proyas. New Line, 1998. Film.
Dawn of the Dead. Dir. George A. Romero. United Film Distribution Co., 1978. Film.
The Day the Earth Stood Still. Dir. Robert Wise. Twentieth Century Fox, 1951. Film.
Day the World Ended. Dir. Roger Corman. American Releasing Corp., 1955. Film.
Gojira. Dir. Ishiro Honda. Toho, 1954. Film.
Independence Day. Dir. Roland Emmerich. Twentieth Century Fox, 1996. Film.
Invasion of the Body Snatchers. Dir. Don Siegel. Allied Artists, 1956. Film.
The Last Man on Earth. Dir. Ubaldo B. Ragona. American International Pictures, 1964. Film.
Logan's Run. Dir. Michael Anderson. MGM, 1976. Film.
The Matrix. Dir. The Wachowskis. Warner Bros., 1999. Film.
Night of the Comet. Dir. Thom Eberhardt. Atlantic Releasing Corp., 1984. Film.
The Omega Man. Dir. Boris Sagal. Warner Bros., 1971. Film.
On the Beach. Dir. Stanley Kramer. United Artists, 1959. Film.
Planet of the Apes. Dir. Franklin J. Schaffner. Warner Bros., 1968. Film.
The Rapture. Dir. Michael Tolkin. Fine Line, 1991. Film.
The Seventh Sign. Dir. Carl Schultz. TriStar, 1988. Film.
Silent Running. Dir. Douglas Turnbull. Universal, 1972. Film.
The Terminator. Dir. James Cameron. Orion, 1984. Film.
Terminator 2: Judgment Day. Dir. James Cameron. TriStar, 1991. Film.
Testament. Dir. Lynne Littman. Paramount, 1983. Film.
The Time Machine. Dir. George Pal. MGM, 1960. Film.
The War of the Worlds. Dir. Bryon Haskin. Paramount, 1953. Film.

Film: 2000–2015

Beasts of the Southern Wild. Dir. Benh Zeitlin. Fox Searchlight, 2012. Film.
The Cabin in the Woods. Dir. Drew Goddard. Lionsgate, 2012. Film.
Children of Men. Dir. Alfonso Cuarón. Universal, 2006. Film.
Divergent. Dir. Neil Burger. Summit Entertainment, 2014. Film.
Edge of Tomorrow. Dir. Doug Liman. Warner Bros., 2014. Film.
Elysium. Dir. Neil Blomkamp. TriStar, 2013. Film.
Fido. Dir. Andrew Currie. Lionsgate, 2006. Film.
Final Fantasy: The Spirits Within. Dir. Hironobu Sakaguchi. Columbia, 2001. Film.
Godzilla. Dir. Gareth Edwards. Warner Bros., 2014. Film.
The Hunger Games. Dir. Gary Ross. Lionsgate, 2012. Film.

The Hunger Games: Catching Fire. Dir. Francis Lawrence. Lionsgate, 2013. Film.
The Hunger Games: Mockingjay–Part 1. Dir. Francis Lawrence. Lionsgate, 2014. Film.
The Hunger Games: Mockingjay–Part 2. Dir. Francis Lawrence. Lionsgate, 2015. Film.
I Am Legend. Dir. Francis Lawrence. Warner Bros., 2007. Film.
Insurgent. Dir. Robert Schwentke. Lionsgate, 2015. Film.
Interstellar. Dir. Christopher Nolan. Paramount, 2014. Film.
Land of the Dead. Dir. George A. Romero. Universal, 2005. Film.
Left Behind. Dir. Vic Armstrong. eOne Entertainment, 2014. Film.
Mad Max: Fury Road. Dir. George Miller. Warner Bros., 2015. Film.
The Maze Runner. Dir. Wes Ball. Twentieth Century Fox, 2014. Film.
Maze Runner: Scorch Trials. Dir. Wes Ball. Twentieth Century Fox, 2015. Film.
Pacific Rim. Dir. Guillermo del Toro. Warner Bros., 2013. Film.
Resident Evil: Apocalypse. Dir. Alexander Witt. Screen Gems, 2004. Film.
The Road. Dir. John Hillcoat. Dimension Films, 2009. Film.
Seeking a Friend for the End of the World. Dir. Lorene Scafaria. Focus Films, 2012. Film.
Snowpiercer. Dir. Bong Joon-ho. Weinstein Co., 2013. Film.
The SpongeBob Movie: Sponge Out of Water. Dir. Paul Tibbitt. Paramount, 2015. Film.
Terminator Genisys. Dir. Alan Taylor. Paramount, 2015. Film.
This Is the End. Dirs. Evan Goldberg and Seth Rogen. Sony Pictures, 2013. Film.
Tomorrowland. Dir. Brad Bird. Walt Disney Studios, 2015. Film.
28 Days Later. Dir. Danny Boyle. Twentieth Century Fox, 2002. Film.
2012. Dir. Roland Emmerich. Sony Pictures, 2009. Film.
WALL•E. Dir. Andrew Stanton. Disney, 2008. Film.
Warm Bodies. Dir. Jonathan Levine. Summit Entertainment, 2013. Film.
World War Z. Dir. Marc Forster. Paramount, 2013. Film.
The World's End. Dir. Edgar Wright. Focus Features, 2013. Film.
Z for Zachariah. Dir. Craig Zobel. Roadside Attractions, 2015. Film.
Zombieland. Dir. Ruben Fleischer. Columbia, 2009. Film.

Television Shows: 1963–1999

Ark II. Prod. Norm Prescott and Lou Scheimer. CBS, 1976. DVD.
Battlestar Galactica. Prod. Glen A. Larson. ABC, 1978–1979. DVD.
Buck Rogers in the 25th Century. Prod. Glen A. Larson. NBC, 1979–1981. DVD.
Casshan. Prod. Tatsunoko Productions. Fuji TV, 1973–1974. DVD.
The Changes. Prod. Anna Home. BBC One, 1975. Broadcast TV.
Crusade. Prod. J. Michael Straczynski. TNT, 1999. DVD.
Doctor Who. Prod. Verity Lambert, et al. BBC One, 1963–1989. DVD.
The Invaders. Prod. Quinn Martin. ABC, 1967–1968. DVD.
Logan's Run. Prod. Ivan Goff and Ben Roberts. CBS, 1977–1978. DVD.
Not with a Bang. Prod. Robin Carr. ITV, 1990. Broadcast TV.
Red Dwarf. Prod. Paul Jackson. BBC Two, 1988–1999. DVD.
Survivors. Prod. Terence Dudley. BBC One, 1975–1977. DVD.
The Tripods. Prod. Richard Bates. BBC (U.K.) and Seven Network (Australia), 1984–1985. DVD.
V: The Original Miniseries. Prod. Kenneth Johnson. NBC, 1983. DVD.
V: The Series. Prod. Daniel H. Blatt and Robert Singer. NBC, 1984–1985. DVD.
Woops! Prod. Gary Jacobs and Tony Thomas. Fox, 1992. Broadcast TV.

Television Shows: 2000–2015

Battlestar Galactica. Prod. Ron Moore and David Eick. Sci-Fi, 2004–2009. DVD.

Between. Prod. Michael McGowan and Don Carmody. City, 2015 to present. Broadcast TV.

Caprica. Prod. Ron Moore and David Eick. SyFy, 2010–2011. DVD.

Cleopatra 2525. Prod. Sam Raimi, R. J. Stewart, and Robert Tapert. Syndication, 2000–2001. DVD.

The Colony. Prod. Thom Beers and Philip David Segal. Discovery Channel, 2009 to present. Broadcast TV.

Continuum. Prod. Simon Barry and Sara B. Cooper. Showcase, 2012–2015. Broadcast TV.

Dark Angel. Prod. James Cameron and Charles H. Eglee. Fox, 2000–2002. DVD.

Defiance. Prod. Rockne S. O'Bannon and Kevin Murphy. SyFy, 2013 to present. Broadcast TV.

Doctor Who. Prod. Russell T. Davies and Stephen Moffat. BBC One, 2005 to present. Broadcast TV.

Dominion. Prod. David Lancaster and Michel Litvack. SyFy, 2014 to present. Broadcast TV.

Falling Skies. Prod. Steven Spielberg and Darryl Frank. TNT, 2011 to present. Broadcast TV.

Fear the Walking Dead. Prod. Robert Kirkman and David Alpert. AMC, 2015 to present. Broadcast TV.

Firefly. Prod. Joss Whedon and Tim Minear. Fox, 2002. DVD.

Fringe. Prod. J. J. Abrams and Bryan Burk. Fox, 2008–2013. DVD.

Helix. Ronald D. Moore and Lynda Obst. SyFy, 2014 to present. Broadcast TV.

Jeremiah. Prod. J. Michael Straczynski Productions. Showtime, 2002–2004. Broadcast TV.

Jericho. Prod. Jon Turteltaub and Stephen Chbosky. CBS, 2006–2008. DVD.

The Last Man on Earth. Prod. Will Forte and Phil Lord. Fox, 2015 to present. Broadcast TV.

The Last Ship. Prod. Michael Bay and Jack Bender. TNT, 2014 to present. Broadcast TV.

The Lottery. Prod. Dawn Olmstead and Rick Eid. Lifetime, 2014. Broadcast TV.

The New Tomorrow. Prod. Raymond Thompson and Geoff Husson. Seven Network, 2005. Broadcast TV.

The 100. Prod. Jason Rothenberg and Leslie Morgenstein. The CW, 2013–2014. Broadcast TV.

Outcasts. Prod. Kudos Film & Television. BBC One, 2011. DVD.

Red Dwarf. Prod. Jo Howard and Helen Norman. Dave, 2009 and 2012. Broadcast TV.

Revolution. Prod. Bryan Burk, Eric Kripke, and J. J. Abrams. NBC, 2012–2014. Broadcast TV.

Roswell. Prod. Jason Katims and Lisa J. Olin. The WB, 1999–2001. UPN, 2001–2002. DVD.

The Strain. Prod. Guillermo del Toro, Carlton Cuse, and Chuck Hogan. FX, 2014 to present. Broadcast TV.

Survivors. Prod. Sue Hogg and Adrian Hodges. BBC One, 2008–2010. DVD.

Terminator: The Sarah Connor Chronicles. Prod. Sarah Connor Pictures and Bartleby Company. Fox, 2008–2009. DVD.

Terra Nova. Prod. Steven Spielberg and Peter Chernin. Fox, 2011. Broadcast TV.

Thunderstone. Prod. Jonathan M. Shiff Productions. Network Ten, 1999–2000. DVD.

Torchwood: Miracle Day. Prod. BBC Cymru Wales. BBC One (UK) and Starz (U.S.), 2011. DVD.

The Tribe. Prod. Raymond Thompson and Geoff Husson. Channel 5, 1999–2003. DVD.

12 Monkeys. Prod. Natalie Chaidez and Charles Roven. SyFy, 2015 to present. Broadcast TV.

V. Prod. Scott Rosenbaum and Scott Peters. ABC, 2009–2011. DVD.

The Walking Dead. Prod. Frank Darabont and Gale Anne Hurd. AMC, 2010 to present. Broadcast TV.

The X-Files. Prod. Chris Carter and R. W. Goodwin. Fox, 1993–2002. DVD.

Z Nation. Prod. Paul Bales and David Michael Latt. SyFy, 2014 to present. Broadcast TV.

Video Games: 1988–1999

Abomination: The Nemesis Project. Eidos Interactive, 1999. PC. Video Game.

Fallout. Interplay, 1997. PC. Video Game.

Final Fantasy VI. Square, 1994. SNES. Video Game.

KULT: The Temple of Flying Saucers. Exxos. Infogrames, 1989. Atari. Video Game.

Last Armageddon. Family Computer. Yutaka, 1988, PC. Video Game.

Nuclear War MUD. Project Community, 1992. PC. MMORPG.

Outlander. Mindscape, 1992. Sega Mega Drive/Genesis. Video Game.

Resident Evil. Capcom, 1996. PlayStation. Video Game.

Time Slip. Sales Curve Interactive. Vic Tokai, 1992. Super NES. Video Game.

Wasteland. Interplay Productions. Electronic Arts, 1988. Commodore 64 and Apple II. Video Game.

Also *X-COM* (see below).

Video Games: 2000–2015

Battlefield 2142. EA Digital Illusions CE, 2006. PC. Video Game.

Dead Rising 2. Blue Castle Games. Capcom, 2010. Multiple Platforms. Video Game.

Defiance. Trion Worlds, 2013. Multiple Platforms. Video Game.

Dying Light. Techland. Warner Bros. Interactive Entertainment, 2015. PS4. Video Game.

Fallen Earth. Reloaded Productions. K2 Network, 2009. PC. MMORPG.

Fallout 4. Bethesda Game Studios, 2015. Multiple Platforms. Video Game.

Gears of War. Epic Games. Microsoft, 2006. Xbox 360. Video Game.

Half-Life 2. Valve Corporation, 2005. Multiple Platforms. Video Game.

H1Z1. Daybreak Game Company, 2015. PS4. Video Game.

Last of Us. Naughty Dog. Sony Entertainment, 2013. PS3. Video Game.

Last Stand: Dead Zone. Con Artist Games, 2012. Facebook and Google Plus. Social Network Game.

Left 4 Dead. Turtle Rock. Valve Corporation, 2008. Multiple Platforms. Video Game.

Mad Max. Avalanche Studios. Warner Bros. Interactive, 2015. Multiple Platforms. Video Game.

Mass Effect. Electronic Arts, 2007. Xbox 360. Video Game.

Metro 2033. 4A Games. THQ, 2010. Multiple Platforms. Video Game.

NeverDead. Rebellion Developments. Konami, 2012. Multiple Platforms. Video Game.

Rage. id Software, 2011. Multiple Platforms. Video Game.

Resident Evil. Capcom, 2002. Multiple Platforms. Video Game.

Resident Evil: Revelations 2. Capcom, 2014. Multiple Platforms. Video Game.

Resistance: Burning Skies. Nihilistic Software. Sony, 2012. PlayStation Vita. Video Game.

Soldiers of Anarchy. Silver Style Entertainment. Bigben Interactive, 2002. PC. Video Game.

The Walking Dead: The Game. Telltale Games, 2012. Multiple Platforms. Video Game.

X-COM. Mythos Games. MicroProse, 1993–2013. Multiple Platforms. Video Game.

Zombie Lane. Digital Chocolate, 2011. Facebook and Google Plus. Social Network Game.

About the Contributors

Frances **Auld** is an assistant professor of English at the State College of Florida, Venice. Her teaching and research interests include cultural studies, horror, and medieval literature. She is remarkably cheerful for someone who teaches *Piers Plowman, Hannibal,* and *The Walking Dead.*

Eddie **Brennan** is a lecturer in the School of Media, Dublin Institute of Technology. His recent publications include a chapter in *Global Television Formats* (ed. Shahaf and Oren) and "Not Seeing the Joke" in *Media, Culture and Society.* His research explores how media may affect public imaginings of the past and the future.

Tim **Bryant** is an assistant professor of English at SUNY Buffalo State, where he teaches American and American Indian literature and film. His research areas include experimental fiction, cultural studies of work and play, and popular religion. He has previously published articles on Alan Moore, Edgar Allan Poe and Melissa Scott.

Tiffany A. **Christian** is a Ph.D. candidate in American studies at Washington State University. She holds an M.F.A. in creative writing from Chapman University and an M.A. in folklore from the University of Oregon. Her research examines relationships between gendered postapocalyptic survival narratives in American popular culture and folkloric survival narratives in the cultural practice of disaster preparedness.

Leisa A. **Clark** has an M.A. in women's and gender studies and an M.L.A. in humanities, both from the University of South Florida. She is co-editor (with Mary F. Pharr) of 2012's *Of Bread, Blood and* The Hunger Games (McFarland). Her studies focus on science fiction television, YA apocalyptic novels, food in the *Harry Potter* series, and apocalyptic musicals.

Bill **Clemente** is a professor of English at Peru State College in Peru, Nebraska, where he has taught for twenty-three years. He recently developed courses in young adult dystopian fiction and zombies and literature. His publications include essays on a Cuban zombie comedy, *The Hunger Games,* and bird-watching in southeastern Nebraska.

Lieutenant Colonel Max **Despain** is an associate professor of English at the U.S. Air Force Academy. She studies questions of memory in identity formation, especially how different forms of memory expose fears and limitations about present-day moments. She has also written on the implications of food in literature.

Amanda **Firestone** is an assistant professor at the University of Tampa in the Department of Communication. Her research focuses on YA girls' coming-of-age fictional narratives. Specifically, she examines *The Twilight Saga*'s Bella Swan and constructions of female hysteria, sexuality, and motherhood. Her most recent work can be found in the text *Gender in the Vampire Narrative*.

Stephen **Joyce** graduated from the University of Bielefeld in Germany with a Ph.D. in cultural studies. He has previously published articles on tragedy, new media, postmodernism, and postcolonial literature. He works as a visiting associate professor in aesthetics and communication at Aarhus University in Denmark.

Sharon Diane **King** (Ph.D., comparative literature; Associate, UCLA CMRS) works at the Getty Research Institute. Her publications include essays for critical anthologies (*Of Bread, Blood and* The Hunger Games, McFarland; *Supernatural, Humanity, and the Soul*, Palgrave). She has also written speculative fiction (e.g., "Follow the Music," *Desolation: 21 Tales for Tails*, Dragon's Roost Press; "Read Shift," *Kaleidotrope*).

Bjarke **Liboriussen**, Ph.D., is an assistant professor at the University of Nottingham Ningbo China. His research follows two main areas of interest: computer games (with a recent article on online gaming in China) and the creative industries (including a recent article on digital expertise in the Chinese creative industries).

Ryan **Lizardi** is an assistant professor of digital media and humanities at SUNY Polytechnic Institute. He places his research emphasis on mediated representations of the past and nostalgia, and has published articles on apocalyptic alien invasion video games, slasher horror remakes, and contemporary comic book heteronormativity.

Andrew **McAlister** is an associate professor of communication at the University of Tampa, where he teaches film studies, women's studies, and cultural studies. His interests include ideologies of popular culture, film historicity, and film and culture. He is less worried about the end of the world than it continuing without a reckoning.

Mark **McCarthy** is a Ph.D. candidate at the University of South Florida. His research interest focuses on the changing apocalypse mythos in film and television since 9/11. Paying particular attention to the presentation of the survivors in these texts, he has written on the logics of survival in *The Walking Dead*.

Ceren **Mert** received a Ph.D. in sociology from Mimar Sinan Fine Arts University, Istanbul, Turkey. She is a lecturer in the Department of Humanities and Social Sciences at Isik University, Istanbul. Her research interests include popular culture, urban studies and human/cultural geography, poststructuralist theories, popular music, and media studies.

Mary F. **Pharr** is Professor Emeritus, English, at Florida Southern College. She holds a doctorate from Vanderbilt and has published and presented extensively on speculative film and fiction. In 2012, she coedited (with Leisa A. Clark) *Of Bread,*

Blood and The Hunger Games: *Critical Essays on Suzanne Collins's Trilogy* (McFarland).

Dahlia **Schweitzer** is a Ph.D. candidate at UCLA, as well as a writer, teacher, and former cabaret star. Among her works are the books *Cindy Sherman's* Office Killer: *Another Kind of Monster, Queen of Hearts, Seduce Me,* and *Lovergirl*—and an album of electronic dance music, *Plastique.* Her dissertation explores pandemic and outbreak narratives in contemporary American film and television.

Patrick L. **Smith** received a Ph.D. in neuroscience from Florida State University, and he is an associate professor of Psychology at Florida Southern College. He has extensively studied internal and external influences on behavior, and his most recent empirical studies can be found in *North American Journal of Psychology.*

Lennart **Soberon** works as a research and teaching assistant for the faculty of Communication Sciences at the University of Ghent. His research concerns the representation of contemporary conflict in cinema and focuses on the thematic of the "war on terror." Additionally, he has made contributions on the subjects of genre and television formats.

Angela **Tenga** earned a Ph.D. from Purdue University and teaches at Florida Institute of Technology. Her recent publications include "Vampire Gentlemen and Zombie Beasts: A Rendering of True Monstrosity" in *Gothic Studies* and "Gabriel Knight: A Twentieth-Century Chivalric Romance Hero" in *Digital Gaming Re-imagines the Middle Ages* (Routledge).

Index